VICTORIAN SAPPHO

Yopie Prins

PRINCETON UNIVERSITY PRESS

PRINCETON, NEW JERSEY

LIBRARY OF CONGRESS CATALOGING-IN-PUBLICATION

PRINS, YOPIE.

VICTORIAN SAPPHO / YOPIE PRINS.

P. CM.

INCLUDES BIBLIOGRAPHICAL REFERENCES (P.   ) AND INDEX.

ISBN 0-691-05918-7 (CLOTH : ALK. PAPER).—ISBN 0-691-05919-5

(PBK. : ALK. PAPER)

1. ENGLISH POETRY—GREEK INFLUENCES.   2. LOVE POETRY, GREEK—

TRANSLATIONS INTO ENGLISH—HISTORY AND CRITICISM.   3. HOMOSEXUALITY

AND LITERATURE—ENGLAND—HISTORY—19TH CENTURY.   4. SAPPHO—

CRITICISM AND INTERPRETATION—HISTORY—19TH CENTURY.   5. SAPPHO—

TRANSLATIONS INTO ENGLISH—HISTORY AND CRITICISM.   6. FEMINISM AND

LITERATURE—ENGLAND—HISTORY—19TH CENTURY.   7. LOVE POETRY, GREEK—

HISTORY AND CRITICISM—THEORY, ETC.   8. WOMEN AND LITERATURE—

ENGLAND—HISTORY—19TH CENTURY.   9. ENGLISH POETRY—19TH CENTURY—

HISTORY AND CRITICISM.   10. WOMEN AND LITERATURE—GREECE—HISTORY.

11. SAPPHO—APPRECIATION—ENGLAND.   12. SAPPHO—INFLUENCE.

13. POETICS.   I. TITLE.

PR129.G8P75   1999   821′.809—DC21   98-28067

To my loved ones

εἶς, μία, ἔν

CONTENTS

ILLUSTRATIONS

ACKNOWLEDGMENTS

I GRATEFULLY acknowledge a National Endowment for the Humanities Fellowship during the 1993–94 academic year, when I began working on *Victorian Sappho*. I am deeply grateful, as well, for recognition and support from the Institute for Research on Women and Gender at the University of Michigan, which funded an academic leave during the fall of 1996 for the completion of the book. The Office of the Vice President for Research and the Rackham School of Graduate Studies at the University of Michigan generously awarded research funds and travel grants, and in 1992 I was honored to receive an Incentive Award from the *Journal of Classical and Modern Literature*.

An early version of Chapter 1 appeared as "Sappho's Afterlife in Translation" in *Re-Reading Sappho: Reception and Transmission,* edited by Ellen Greene (Berkeley: University of California Press, 1997): 35–67; it is reprinted in expanded form by permission of the University of California Press. The first half of Chapter 2 was previously published as "Sappho Doubled: Michael Field" in *The Yale Journal of Criticism* 8 (Spring 1995): 165–86, and the second half of Chapter 2 was published as "A Metaphorical Field: Katherine Bradley and Edith Cooper," in *Victorian Poetry* 33.1 (Spring 1995): 129–48. I am grateful to the editors of both journals and The Johns Hopkins University Press for permission to reprint these materials in their present form. A portion of Chapter 4 first appeared as "Personifying the Poetess: Caroline Norton, 'The Picture of Sappho,'" in *Women's Poetry Late Romantic to Late Victorian: Gender and Genre,* edited by Isobel Armstrong and Virginia Blain (Hampshire: Macmillan Press Ltd., 1998), 50–67; it is reprinted with revisions by permission from St. Martin's Press and Macmillan.

I also wish to name here the colleagues, friends, and family who have seen me through the years of declining a name. *Victorian Sappho* would not have been written without you.

I am fortunate to count among my friends the teachers who have taught me how to read, in English and in Greek: David Bromwich, Robert Fagles, Anne Carson, Ulrich Knoepflmacher, Lucy McDiarmid, Richard Martin, Glenn Most, Martin Ostwald, Gil Rose, Froma Zeitlin. They have all been an inspiration and I thank them for their intellectual generosity and personal encouragement. From my former colleagues at Oberlin College I have learned how to teach, and I appreciated their warm support even when I was no longer in their midst: Lawrence Buell, Patrick Day, Phyllis Gorfain, Nicholas Jones, Katherine Linehan, Anuradha Dingwaney Needham, Carl Peterson, Gloria Watkins, Sandra Zagarell, and the rest of my friends in English, Classics, Women's Studies, and related departments. I found comraderie and creative stimulus in my writing group at Oberlin, otherwise known as the Flaming Bitches: Ann Cooper Albright, Sibelan Forrester, Wendy Hesford, Wendy Kozol.

At the University of Michigan, I have discovered another community that sustains my teaching and research. The English Department welcomed me as a Victorianist, and the Program in Comparative Literature has been an ideal environment for interdisciplinary work. I am grateful to Stuart McDougal and Robert Weisbuch for supporting me in the transition between academic institutions, to Martha Vicinus, Simon Gikandi, and Abby Stewart for their continued support, and to Linda Gregerson for interrupting her lyric vocation in order to be my advocate. I thank my friends and colleagues at the University of Michigan, and in particular those who read and responded to my work at crucial moments: Tim Bahti, Elizabeth Barnes, Ross Chambers, Alina Clej, Richard Cureton, Jonathan Freedman, Sandra Gunning, Andrea Henderson, Sally Humphreys, Ludwig Koenen, Marjorie Levinson, Anita Norich, Jim Porter, Suzanne Raitt, P. A. Skantze, Rei Terada, David Thomas, Valerie Traub. Patsy Yaeger has been a sympathetic confidante and an ever-flowing fountain of ideas, and Adela Pinch a keen reader as well as a kindred spirit. I am deeply grateful to the members of my writing group in Ann Arbor, the Fellow Flaming Bitches, for their loyal friendship and fierce intelligence: Catherine Brown, Kali Israel, Elizabeth Wingrove. I have been buoyed by conversation with graduate students at the University of Michigan, especially those pursuing exciting new research in Victorian poetry: Lee Behlman, Jean Borger, Monika Cassel, Frauke Lenckos, Eliza Richards, Laura Williams. Special thanks to Laura and Lee for proofreading. I also have great respect and admiration for the undergraduates at Oberlin and Michigan, who participated in my classes in Victorian poetry and on "Sappho and the Lyric Tradition" and shared their enthusiasm and ideas with me: thank you, to all.

I have learned much from numerous colleagues, on whom I depend for dialogue and exchange of ideas even from afar: April Alliston, Isobel Armstrong, Alison Booth, Joseph Bristow, Susan Brown, Richard Dellamora, Alice Falk, Helene Foley, Andrew Ford, Simon Goldhill, Ellen Greene, Judith Hawley, Diana Henderson, Margaret Higonnet, the late James S Holmes, Philip Horne, Gerhard Joseph, Danny Karlin, Joseph Koerner, George Levine, Jayne Lewis, Mary Loeffelholz, Jonathan Loesberg, Tricia Lootens, Tomoko Masuzawa, Andrew Miller, Cornelia Pearsall, Linda Peterson, Kathy Alexis Psomiades, Diane Rayor, Matthew Rowlinson, Linda Shires, Maeera Shreiber, Eva Stehle, Jane Stevenson, Herbert Tucker, Karen Van Dyck, and many others, more than I can possibly enumerate, but to whom I am also truly grateful. Michael Lucey has been my loyal friend and ally since graduate school, and Anne Carson a beacon to illumine a path between English and Greek. I owe a long-standing debt to Tom Cohen who made a difference, too. In completing *Victorian Sappho,* I thank Carolyn Williams for reading the manuscript so brilliantly and lending her eloquence to the introduction, Leslie Kurke for her invaluable comments on each chapter, Mary Murrell for her editorial encouragement, and Marta Steele for her cheerfully patient copy-editing.

Most of all, this book reflects a deep and ongoing collaboration with Virginia Jackson, who anticipated every word I wrote and spelled it back to me, letter by letter; the words I have to thank her she already knows. I have a special appreciation for the women friends who have given me strength over the years, as well: Martine Muller, Rachel Rue, Tanina Rostain, Wynette Yao, Photini Sinnis, Gelina Harlaftis, Sara Frankel, Linda Gaal, Abby Frucht, Anita Kruse, Rebecca Cross, Melissa Gross, Margery Adelson. I write in the memory of my father, Willem Prins, and with the lifelong support of my mother, Jonny Winterwerp Prins. My love and gratitude go to her (also for helping with the index), and to my extended family for all their support as well: Dietz Kessler, Jan Prins, Jane Marshall, Nienke Dosa, Joseph Dosa, Annabel Prins, Dave Williams, my relatives in the Netherlands, and the Daugherty clan, including Willis, Patrick, Tim, Matt, and Tom. Finally—first, last and always—I am indebted to Michael Daugherty who shares with me his music and a musical daughter, Evelyn Prins Daugherty. Michael has helped by harmonizing his musical compositions with my need to compose in words, and in my long absences Evelyn composed her own ode to Sappho, a daily inspiration:

> Sappho Sappho
> Say it sing it
> Sappho Sappho
> Read it write it

VICTORIAN SAPPHO

DECLINING A NAME

The Victorian Legacy of Sappho

Victorian Sappho combines a literary historical thesis, a theoretical argument about lyric, and a series of questions in the field of feminist criticism and gender studies. I trace the emergence of Sappho as an exemplary lyric figure in Victorian England, when the Sapphic fragments circulated in an increasing number of scholarly editions, poetic translations, and other literary imitations. Sappho of Lesbos became a name with multiple significations in the course of the nineteenth century, as the reconstruction of ancient Greek fragments attributed to Sappho contributed to the construction of Sappho herself as the first woman poet, singing at the origin of a Western lyric tradition. This idealized feminine figure emerged at a critical turning point in the long and various history of Sappho's reception; what we now call "Sappho" is, in many ways, an artifact of Victorian poetics. Reading the fragments in Greek alongside various English versions, I show how the Victorian reception of Sappho influenced the gendering of lyric as a feminine genre, and I consider why Victorian poets—male and female, canonical and noncanonical, famous and forgotten—often turned to Sappho to define their lyric vocation. In this book I reconfigure the study of Victorian poetry through the figure of Sappho, and I ask more generally how a history and theory of lyric might be declined in Sappho's name.

The Victorian period is an important moment in Sappho's reception because of its particular fascination with the fragmentation of the Sapphic corpus. While Greek fragments attributed to Sappho were collected and translated from the Renaissance onward, the recovery of "new fragments" of Sappho in the course of the nineteenth century coincided with a Romantic aesthetic of fragmentation and the rise of Classical philology, culminating in the idealization of Sappho herself as the perfect fragment. Out of scattered texts, an idea of the original woman poet and the body of her song could be hypothesized in retrospect: an imaginary totalization, imagined in the present and projected into the past. Of course Sappho has always been a figment of the literary imagination. Invoked as a lyric muse in antiquity and mythologized for posterity by Ovid, Sappho entered into the tradition of English verse through the Ovidian myth of her suicide, and until the early nineteenth century she was primarily known by English imitations of her two most famous poems, the "Ode to Aphrodite" and "Ode to Anactoria" (now identified by modern scholars as fragments 1 and 31).[1] The interest in Sappho as an increasingly fragmentary text of many parts is a distinctly Victorian phenomenon, however, as we see in an influential popular edition compiled by Henry Thornton Wharton in 1885, entitled *Sappho: Memoir, Text, Selected Renderings, and a Literal Translation.* Implicit in these "renderings" is the rending of Sappho as well. Wharton's book simultaneously composes a portrait of the woman poet and presents her as a decomposing text; Sappho is exhumed and deciphered from the crypt of ancient Greek. The close relationship between nineteenth-century philology and Victorian poetics produces this reading of Sappho, whose texts are made to exemplify the formal mechanism through which a body, person, subjectivity, and voice can be imagined as prior to, yet also produced by, a history of fragmentation.

The projected fantasy of a female body and a feminine voice through linguistic scattering, grammatical dismemberment, rhetorical contradiction—as well as other forms of disjunction, hiatus, and ellipsis—suggests why Sappho became exemplary of lyric in its irreducibly textual embodiment, and exemplary of lyric reading as well, in its desire to hypothesize a living whole from dead letters.[2] It is a Victorian legacy that continues well into the twentieth century, as is evident in the aestheticized fragmentation of Sappho in early Modernism. In *The Pound Era,* for example, Hugh Kenner notes that the young Ezra Pound read Wharton's *Sappho* carefully, and discovered in those pages a "muse in tatters."[3] Pound's 1916 poem "Papyrus," inspired by a newly discovered Sapphic fragment, is a meditation on lyric desire that makes Sappho synonymous with the desire for lyric:

> Spring . . . .
> Too long . . . . . .
> Gongula . . . . . .

While the fragment points to a moment beyond itself—some idea to make the poem complete—surely the point(s) of the ellipses would also be to make the fragment itself into an aesthetic ideal. It is a literary representation of a literally fragmented text, in which time is suspended and meaning deferred, prolonging ("too long") the desire for something lost. Thus Pound also introduced Hilda Doolittle to the literary world in 1913

---

[1] Here and throughout the book, I refer to the Lobel-Page numbering of the Sapphic fragments.

[2] I owe this formulation to Carolyn Williams.

[3] Kenner describes in further detail how Pound used Wharton's edition of Sappho to develop a "poiesis of loss" and an "aesthetic of glimpses" (1971: 56,71). On H. D.'s aesthetic of fragmentation, also inspired by Sappho, see Gregory 1998. On the Romantic fragment poem and the aesthetic of fragmentation in nineteenth-century England, see Levinson 1986.

as a Sapphic fragment, with her name abbreviated into the elliptical letters H.D., the embodiment of an "Imagist" aesthetic inspired by Sappho's Greek. "It all began with the Greek fragments," H.D. later wrote, reflecting on a career that began with her poetic imitations of a Sappho whose initial appeal was perhaps more Victorian than Modernist (1979: 41).

Not only does the nineteenth-century legacy of Sappho manifest itself in early-twentieth-century poetry, it also influences later generations of scholars, translators, and critics. Taking Wharton's earlier edition as a model, *The Songs of Sappho: Including the Recent Egyptian Discoveries* was published in 1925, annotated by David Moore Robinson and translated into English verse by Marion Mills Miller, as part of an ongoing reconstruction of the Sapphic fragments in England. This desire to reconstruct Sappho led to the definitive edition of *Poetarum Lesbiorum Fragmenta* in 1955 by Edgar Lobel and Denys Page, displacing German philology with the authority of British scholarship. Page also published a Sappho commentary including "The Contents and Character of Sappho's Poetry," a long essay written very much in the English tradition of Wharton: here too, the contents of Sappho's poetry depend on how the character of Sappho is construed (Page 1955).[4] The creation of Sappho in the character of the woman poet continued in Mary Barnard's popular translation, published a few years later and widely read for decades. In *Sappho: A New Translation* (1958) Barnard emphasizes the fragmentary image of Sappho, but by arranging her translations in sequence she also reimagines the life and times of Sappho in an implicitly chronological narrative, from youth to old age. Thus revived from fragments, Sappho seems to speak directly to modern readers; even today, Mary Barnard's Sappho is read as if it *is* the voice of Sappho, taught in the classroom either as representative of "women's voices" in antiquity or as representation of a timeless "feminine voice" in poetry.[5]

If the tendency to invoke Sappho as a female persona with an original lyric voice seems overdetermined to us now, it is because this reading of Sappho is inherited from the end of the previous century and repeated at the end of our own.[6] Indeed, with the publication of several recent books on Sappho, the proliferation of new translations, and the recla-

---

[4] DeJean (1989: 304–5) points out that Page promotes British Classical scholarship by referring to Victorian precursors such as John Addington Symonds. This Victorian scholarly tradition includes Wharton, who also draws extensively on Symonds in the introductory essay to his edition of Sappho.

[5] For further discussion of Barnard's Sappho translations, see Prins 1997: 63–66.

[6] Of course Sappho is not the only figure from archaic Greek lyric who is called upon to authorize a Western lyric tradition, as we see from a long tradition associated with Anacreon and the Anacreonta, or a Pindaric tradition associated with the epinician odes of Pindar. However, it is the privileging of Sappho as a point of "feminine" origin that makes twentieth-century readings of the Sapphic fragments a perpetuation of Victorian readings.

mation of a Sapphic tradition by contemporary women poets and feminist critics, it would seem that another Sappho revival is well underway.[7] In *Sappho's Immortal Daughters* (1995), for example, Margaret Williamson constructs a Sapphic voice from the poems she reads as Sappho's daughters, the creative offspring of a woman poet who lived and sang in a community of women on the island of Lesbos. Although Sappho is lost, her songs survive to create the idea "of a specifically female poetic inheritance" (16) according to Williamson. She identifies herself as "a feminist academic writing in the twentieth century" (x) but also aligns her work with the late-nineteenth-century "Sappho enthusiast, Henry Wharton," who pored over the same texts: both scholars contribute to the long history of Sappho scholarship, knowing that "the chain will continue; other generations will recreate Sappho in their own image" (ix-x). Yet in articulating the differences between herself and Wharton, Williamson demonstrates how closely linked they are in the chain. She seems to be making the very same Victorian link, in fact, as she writes, "I have had my own stake in straining to recover that earlier woman's voice" (x). Here again, the Sapphic fragments create a desire to identify with Sappho, to personify the woman poet and give voice to her.

The postmodern reading proposed by Page duBois in *Sappho Is Burning* (1995) can be understood as another version of this Victorian yearning. In her "Fragmentary Introduction," duBois insists on Sappho as fragment: "When I use the proper name 'Sappho' I mean only the voice in the fragments attributed to her, only the assembly of poems assigned to her name. She is not a person, not even a character in a drama or a fiction, but a set of texts gathered in her name" (3). Nevertheless the figure of voice continues to haunt this invocation of Sappho, as if the texts "gathered in her name" might be recollected as a disembodied voice if not a living body. Throughout her book, duBois celebrates the Sapphic corpus as a body-in-pieces, resisting the temptation to construct a whole, but still insisting on an idea of Sappho that persists as obscure object of desire, forever out of reach. "Sappho herself persists elusively always as an absent source . . . an origin we can never know. Her texts, as we receive them, insist on the impossibility of recapturing the lost body" (28–29). In turning to Sappho "herself" as the name for that absent origin, and metaphorizing "her texts" as part of the lost body, duBois returns us to the rhetoric of dismembering and remembering Sappho: as in Wharton's *Sappho*, textual mediation is sublimated into an organic figure.

---

[7] In addition to the books by duBois and Williamson, there has been a resurgence of interest in Sappho among Classical scholars; other recent books include Wilson 1996, Greene 1997a, 1997b. New translations of Sappho include Barnstone 1988, Balmer 1988, Roche 1991, Rayor 1991, Powell 1993. On the figure of Sappho in contemporary poetry, see Gubar 1984, Grahn 1985, Greer 1995, and Prins and Shreiber 1997: 187–259.

The seemingly inevitable personification of Sappho does not mean, however, that Williamson and duBois imagine the same Sapphic persona. What is most Victorian about the current Sappho revival is, in fact, the contradictory features of this feminine figure. The simultaneous publication of both books in 1995, each imagining Sappho differently, points to the contradictions that constitute the very idea of a Sapphic voice; whose desire does it articulate, and what kind of desire? In a book review comparing these contrary visions of Sappho as communal lyric poet and Sappho as postmodern lyric subject, Mary Loeffelholz poses the question most forcefully: "To judge from the Sapphos conjured up by Williamson's and duBois's readings, the value of Sappho for present-day feminism is her power to sponsor dramatically different accounts of female or feminist desire, its pasts and possible futures" (1996: 15). A vision of Sappho as lesbian also emerges in *Sappho and the Virgin Mary* by Ruth Vanita (1996) and *Lesbian Desire in the Lyrics of Sappho* (1997) by Jane Snyder. But in their conversion of Sappho of Lesbos into a lesbian Sappho, there are differences as well: while Vanita imagines Sappho as ancestor for a lesbian literary tradition in England, with the Victorian period as an important turning point for defining lesbian identity, Snyder imagines the more diffuse expression of homoerotic desire in the woman-centered world of Sappho.

Thus Sappho is variously invoked to authorize a female poetic tradition, or to embody postmodern fragmentation, or to affirm lesbian identity, but what these readings have in common is a (re)turn to Sappho as an exemplary, engendering figure for the reading of lyric. In *Victorian Sappho* I make a contribution to current Sappho studies as well as a critical intervention, as I seek to historicize and theorize in further detail the logic of lyric reading that has produced this idea of Sappho. My version of literary history relates Classical antiquity to the present time, while developing a focus on the late Victorian period as a crux or turning point; it is a literary history crucially inflected by gender as well, although in the course of my argument I will be calling into question some of the assumptions of feminist literary history. Questions about feminism, gender, and sexuality are central to my argument not only because Sappho has become synonymous with the woman poet—and throughout this book I emphasize the causes and effects of making that synonym seem self-evident—but also because such questions enable us to reread the canon of Victorian poetry from a new perspective. Rereading Victorian poetry, as Isobel Armstrong argues, means revising literary history as well: "The task of a history of Victorian poetry is to restore the questions of politics, not least sexual politics, and the epistemology and language which belong to it" (1993: 7). By demonstrating how sexual politics determine the production of Victorian poetry as well as its reception, *Victorian Sappho* offers a revisionary history of Victorian poetry and places contemporary lyric theory within that history. It is therefore not my interest to refute any particular reading of Sappho, but rather to spell out the implications of writing in the name of Sappho, in the last century and at the end of our own.

Who Wrongs Sappho?

What is Sappho except a name? "No day will ever dawn that does not speak the name of Sappho, the lyric poetess," proclaims one of the poets in the Palatine Anthology (Sappho Test. 28, Campbell 28–29).[8] Even if Sappho no longer speaks, her name will be spoken in the future, and indeed, in another epigram from the Anthology, Sappho herself is made to speak again by reclaiming her name from the past: "My name is Sappho, and I surpassed women in poetry as greatly as Homer surpassed men" (Sappho Test. 57, Campbell 46–47). Projected from the past into the future and from the future into the past, "Sappho" is presented to us now, in the present tense, as a name that lives on. Yet that name also raises questions, not unlike "The Homeric Question" that haunted nineteenth-century Classical philologists, obsessively disassembling and reassembling Greek texts in the name of a poet who never quite existed in the authorial form they imagined. Just as "Homer" names an epic tradition composed by many voices over time and recomposed in the long history of being written and read, "Sappho" is associated with a lyric tradition originating in oral performance and increasingly mediated by writing.[9] What we call Sappho was, perhaps, never a woman at all; not the poet we imagine on the island of Lesbos in the seventh century B.C., singing songs to her Sapphic circle, but a fictional persona circulating in archaic Greek lyric and reinvoked throughout antiquity as "the tenth muse." If Homer was the Poet, the Poetess was Sappho, a name repeated over the centuries as the proper name for lyric poetry itself, despite the scattering of the Sapphic fragments.

Sappho survives as exemplary lyric figure precisely because of that legacy of fragmentation; the more the fragments are dispersed, the more we recollect Sappho as their point of origin. "The passage of time has destroyed Sappho and her works, her lyre and songs," writes Tzetzes, a Byzantine scholar who laments the loss of Sapphic song (Sappho Test. 61, Campbell 50–51). By the twelfth century most of the Sapphic corpus had

---

[8] I refer to the Sappho Testimonia by number and by page, as they appear in Campbell 1982.

[9] For a survey of "Homeric Questions," see Nagy 1992; for further discussion of Sapphic songs in performance, see Calame 1977 (tr. 1997), Nagy 1996: 87–103, and Stehle 1997.

already disappeared, yet Sappho reappears twice in his sentence, in the reiteration of the name: "both Sappho and the works of Sappho," καὶ ἡ Σαπφὼ καὶ τὰ Σαπφοῦς. The declension from nominative to genitive, from *Sapphō* to *Sapphous*, measures the decline from Sappho to Tzetzes, who can only invoke her name in his own time by declining it. Nevertheless "nouns and verbs may be known by their declining," as the *Oxford English Dictionary* reminds us; the verb "to decline" comes (via Latin) from the Greek "to bend" (*klinein*) and the preposition "down" (*de*), meaning "to turn away," "bend aside," "fall down," "deviate," "digress," "descend," "decay." In the case of Sappho, we are declining a name in every sense. Nominative, genitive, dative, accusative, vocative: the name that is Sappho, the name of Sappho, the name given to Sappho, the Sappho that we name, or what we address as "O, Sappho." This lesson in grammar teaches us that even a proper name is only known by its variants, not a fixed identity but a series of inflections. Each grammatical inflection gives another meaning to the name, turning it into a wayward genealogy: always a repetition with a difference, a variation on the name and a deviation from it, a perpetual re-naming.

The name appears in four of the Greek fragments currently attributed to Sappho, as we see in the modern Loeb edition of the Sapphic fragments, recompiled and retranslated by D. A. Campbell in 1982.[10] In fragment 65, for example, six letters slip through the ellipses to spell out "Sappho," as follows:

. . . . .] . . . α[
. . . . .] ρομε
. . . . .] . ελασ[
. ροτήννεμε[
Ψάπφοι, σε φίλ[
Κύπρωι β[α]σίλ[
καίτοι μέλα δ . [
ὅ]σσοις φαέθων[
πάνται κλέος[
καί σ' ἐνν Ἀχέρ[οντ

The reconstruction of the ancient Greek in Campbell's edition is followed by his tentative translation in English:

. . . (Andromeda?) . . . Sappho (I love?) you . . . Cyprus . . . queen . . . yet great . . . all whom (the sun) shining . . . everywhere glory . . . and in the (house of) Acheron . . . you . . .

[10] Here and throughout, I follow the reconstruction of the Greek fragments as they appear in the Loeb edition of Sappho (Campbell 1982). English translations are my own, unless noted otherwise.

Campbell also offers an explanatory note after Sappho's name, to hypothesize a narrative context for this fragmentary text: "S[appho] is promised world-wide glory, probably by Aphrodite, the Cyprian." To make the Greek fragment readable, Campbell therefore reads it as Sappho's claim to fame, the great lyric poet radiating glory everywhere. The simple proclamation of the name, it would seem, is enough to reclaim Sappho as an unequivocal lyric subject. The name appears in the vocative, however, not in the voice of Sappho but as an address to Sappho: "Sappho, (I love?) you" (*Sapphoi, se phil* . . .). The fragment speaks the name of Sappho as that which is bespoken (perhaps, beloved) by another; "Sappho" is the citation of a name, divided from itself.

In another fragment the vocative is used again to name Sappho, this time in the form of a question. Fragment 133 is a line (Ψάπφοι, τί τὰν πολύολβον, Ἀφροδίταν . . . ;) partially reconstructed in Campbell's translation: "Why, Sappho (do you summon? neglect?) Aphrodite rich in blessings?" If in fragment 65 Aphrodite appears to confirm the name and fame of Sappho, in fragment 133 the relation between namer and named is more questionable. We do not know who speaks the name of Sappho, nor how Sappho speaks the name of Aphrodite; the verb is missing. Nevertheless the fragment is attributed to Sappho by Campbell, as if the name can be understood as an act of self-naming, as if Sappho can be identified with "Sappho." But even if we understand Sappho to be speaking (implicitly) in the first person in order to address herself (explicitly) in the second person in order to be named in the third person, how can the name confer identity without also deferring it? How do we refer the utterance back to Sappho? Only in the complex mediations between first, second, and third person can Sappho be named as a hypothetical lyric subject.

Likewise in fragment 94, "Sappho" is implicitly placed in quotation marks, disrupting the lyric utterance attributed to her. The name appears in a dialogue between parting lovers: "Sappho, truly, against my will do I leave you," says one, in a vocative that shows again how the name of Sappho is conferred from a position external to the first person lyric "I" (Ψάπφ', ἦ μάν σ' ἀέκοισ' ἀπυλιμπάνω). As the fragment continues, the "I" that responds exists only in relation to the one who has already addressed it: "And I answered: 'Go, be happy, and remember me'" (τὰν δ' ἔγω ταδ' ἀμειβόμαν· χαίροισ' ἔρχεο κἄμεθεν μέμναισ'). The very possibility of response is here predicated on the second-person address to "Sappho," producing a first-person "I" (ἔγω) who speaks in reply and then asks to be remembered by those who will repeat her name. Written into this scene of separation is the separation of naming from meaning, and the dispersal of the proper name. The memory of Sappho depends on the repetition of the name, no longer addressed to the second person but referring to it in the third person. The memory is more like a memorization, since to memorize a name—to make it repeatable—means that one must forget what it means: the "you" to whom it no longer refers, the one who has been left behind. Thus fragment 94 anticipates its own interruption: it predicts that Sappho must be forgotten, and already has been, in order to be called "Sappho."

While the question of the name may appear in these examples to be a function of their fragmentation, even the Ode to Aphrodite—the only complete poem in the Sapphic corpus—calls the name of Sappho into question. This famous ode begins with an invocation to Aphrodite and then stages a reversal of the invocation, when in turn the goddess invokes Sappho. In stanzas 3 and 4, the vocative "O Blessed One" (Sappho to Aphrodite) is reciprocated by the vocative "O Sappho" (Aphrodite to Sappho). Descending in her chariot drawn by sparrows, Aphrodite is recalled from the past to call Sappho by her proper name, in the present:

αἶψα δ' ἐξίκοντο· σὺ δ', ὦ μάκαιρα,
μειδιαίσαισ' ἀθανάτῳ προσώπῳ
ἦρε' ὅττι δηὖτε πέπονθα κὤττι
δηὖτε κάλημμι,

κὤττι μοι μάλιστα θέλω γένεσθαι
μαινόλᾳ θύμῳ· τίνα δηὖτε πείθω
ἄψ σ' ἄγην ἐς Ϝὰν φιλότατα; τίς σ', ὦ
Ψάπφ', ἀδικήει;

Quickly they came. And you O blessed one
smiling with your immortal face
asked what again did I suffer and what
again did I call for

and what did I most want to happen
in my maddened heart. Whom again shall I persuade
to lead to your love? Who, O
Sapph', wrongs you?

With the shift from third-person description to second-person address, past tense to present tense, narrative to dialogue, the ode also seems to shift voices from Sappho to Aphrodite, who now speaks on behalf of Sappho. "Who, O Sapph', wrongs you?" she asks, ready to set aright the injustice that has left Sappho abandoned by the girl she loves.

This would also seem to be the moment when the name of Sappho is justified, set aright by writing the wrong that she suffers: through the fiction of Aphrodite's voice, we read a Sapphic signature that apparently authorizes Sappho as the writer of the poem, and authenticates her narrative of suffering. The Greek adverb δηὖτε (a contraction of two words, "now" and "again") appears three times in the Ode to Aphrodite, to emphasize that again Sappho has suffered, and again Sappho has asked for divine intervention, and again Aphrodite has to lead some girl back into her arms. Sappho is identified in Aphrodite's address by the repeatability of that scenario: what is happening now has happened before, and what happened then had already happened before, and so on. As John Winkler points out, the poem multiplies different versions of Sappho by setting up multiple relations between past and present. "The doubling of Aphrodite (present and past) and the tripling of Sappho (present, past, and . . . pluperfect) leads like the mirrors in a fun house to receding vistas of endlessly repeated intercessions" (1990: 171). Where, in this infinite regress, is the original Sappho? Winkler tries to stop the mirror effect by suggesting that the poem can reflect Sappho back to us; he concludes that "the appearance of an infinite regress, however, is framed and bounded by another Sappho," by which he means "Sappho-the-poet," the one who appears to be in control of the poem (171).

But if the poem lets itself be signed in the name of "Sappho-the-poet," that signature is not of the author; another signs it, by repeating the name. Rather than authorizing Sappho, the Ode to Aphrodite reflects upon the rightful ownership of its signature. Is Sappho naming herself or being named, the origin of the name or its reiteration, the original or the copy? The narrative complexity of the Ode is not resolved ("framed and bounded," according to Winkler) by invoking Sappho-the-poet; to the contrary, it is produced by the invocation that leaves Sappho's name unresolved, in the form of a rhetorical question: "Who, O Sapph', wrongs you?" Here the question is not only "who" wrongs Sappho, but "who" is Sappho, other than the effect of a wrong that can never be written right in this poem? Even the name of Sappho is written wrong: a contraction makes the "o" at the end of "Sappho" disappear, while the vocative "O" makes it reappear at the beginning of the name. Thus Sappho becomes O Sapph' (ὦ Ψάπφ', in Greek), transposing the letters to spell the name out of order, and reversing the alphabet by placing the last letter first: the omega before the alpha, the end before the beginning, an alphabetical *hysteron proteron*. The disordering of the name destabilizes the authorial identity we might wish to ascribe to Sappho, for it shows that "Sappho" is subject to continual deformation and not a stable form: the Sapphic signature is made to appear by writing the name, in reverse, and in retrospect.

The Sapphic signature lends itself to infinite variations, not only in our interpretation of the Ode to Aphrodite but within the tradition of translating the Ode as well. In every version "Sappho" is transliterated, translated, transformed to produce yet another signature, in many languages over many centuries. Thus Wharton compiles various English translations in his late Victorian edition of the Sapphic fragments, an important book because it points to the proliferation of signatures in the name of Sappho. Each translator has placed the invocation to Sappho in a different context and then signed his own name to the text. What constitutes the Sapphic signature, in these examples, is the repetition of Sappho's wrong: "Tell me, my Sappho, tell me who?" (Ambrose Philips, 1711). "Alas, poor Sappho, who is this ingrate?" (Herbert, 1713). "Who, Sappho, who hath done thee wrong?" (John Herman Merivale, 1833). "Who hath wrought my Sappho wrong?" (F. T. Palgrave, 1854). "My Sappho, who is it wrongs thee?" (Edwin Arnold, 1869). "Who has harmed thee? O my poor Sappho" (T. W. Higginson, 1871). "Who thy love now is it that ill requiteth, Sappho?" (Moreton John Walhouse, 1877). "Who now, Sappho, hath wronged thee?" (J. Addington Symonds, 1893). "Who Sappho, wounds thy tender breast?" (Akenside, 1745). "Who doth thee wrong, Sappho?" (Swinburne 1866). Alongside these poetic versions a prose translation is also provided by Wharton himself, who signs his name below Sappho on the title page of his book: *Sappho: Memoir, Text, Selected Renderings, and a Literal Translation by Henry Thornton Wharton*. These various appropriations of the Sapphic signature demonstrate that the proper name of Sappho is no one's property, least of all the property of "Sappho." The name of Sappho is signed each time by someone other than Sappho, and each time it is written again by being written wrong.

Who Writes Sappho?

In the course of this book, I develop a theoretical argument about the Sapphic signature as well as a historical account of its significations in Victorian poetry. By the end of the century, Sappho had become a highly overdetermined and contradictory trope within nineteenth-century discourses of gender, sexuality, poetics, and politics. Each chapter of *Victorian Sappho* proposes a variation on the name, demonstrating how it is variously declined: the declension of a noun and its deviation from origins, the improper bending of a proper name, a line of descent that is also a falling into decadence, the perpetual return of a name that is also a turning away from nomination. By placing the texts of Sappho within a Victorian context—declining the name yet again—*Victorian Sappho* contributes to the study of Sappho's reception: the *Nachleben* or afterlife. Rather than reconstructing the life of Sappho within the historical context of archaic Greece, *Nachleben* studies trace the afterlife by considering constructions of Sappho within other historical contexts, demonstrating how Sappho is continually transformed in the process of transmission. Indeed, in the proliferation of many Sapphic versions, new visions and revisions, Sappho emerges as an imitation for which there is no original. Sapphic imitations are a product of their own historical moment and no longer measured against—except perhaps to measure their distance from—the time of Sappho.

The most comprehensive recent study of Sappho's reception is Joan DeJean's *Fictions of Sappho: 1546–1937,* surveying a Sapphic tradition in France over four centuries. Her book has given new impetus to such reception studies, by moving beyond thematic reading to a critical account of "Saphon, Sappho, Sapho, Sappho, Sapphô, Psappha" as "a figment of the modern imagination" (1); the name is variously spelled and, as De-Jean points out, "behind each spelling there is a story."[11] DeJean does not spell out the implications of Sappho's name for a critical understanding of *lyric,* however; as a "literary history à la Flaubert," her survey is broadly chronological in approach, narrative in emphasis, and focused primarily on French literature. Indeed, she tends to assume that English versions of Sappho merely recapitulate the French tradition, fifty years later: "The English discovery of Sappho reproduces so closely the structure of her entry into the French tradition a half-century earlier that an analysis of its unfolding would have been repetitive, without being essential to an understanding of the future of Sapphic fictions" (5).[12] Of course repetition always produces difference, and we can understand lyric as a historical form precisely because it depends on such repetition; I therefore argue that the fate of Sappho within English poetry is necessarily different from the French tradition, another way to predict "the future of Sapphic fictions" rather than a predictable repetition of the same.

In Victorian England, as we shall see, Sappho of Lesbos emerges as a proper name for the Poetess—and less properly, the Lesbian—according to a logic of lyric reading that distinguishes Victorian versions of Sappho from other Sapphic fictions. Sappho becomes an ideal lyric persona, a figure that provokes the desire to reclaim an original, perhaps even originary, feminine voice. Not only is Sappho personified by a reading that assumes a speaker and is predicated on the assumption of voice; as a personified abstraction, she comes to personify lyric at a time when it is increasingly read in terms of its personifying function. What I call "Victorian Sappho" is of course a double personification, identifying the lyric persona of Sappho with a historical period that is more commonly iden-

---

[11] In addition to earlier surveys of Sappho's reception in Robinson 1923 and Rudiger 1933, other recent reception studies include Saake 1972, Lipking 1988, Fornaro 1991, Greer 1995: 102–46, Jay and Lewis 1996, and Greene 1997b.

[12] Of course the wide scope of DeJean's book inevitably entails omissions, and she acknowledges that "concentration on the French Sapphic construct does not signify the exclusion of her presence in other national traditions" (4). Nevertheless she finds it "obvious that the French tradition has played throughout its development a privileged role as the nexus of [Sappho's] fictionalization" (5) and tends to assimilate other traditions into a French model.

tified with the person of Queen Victoria, another proper name. I invoke Victoria alongside Sappho, in order to name the second half of the nineteenth century as a time when feminine figures and figurations of femininity contribute in complex ways to the formation of aesthetic categories, and more generally to the feminization of Victorian culture. The question of Sappho thus converges with nineteenth-century debates around "The Woman Question." Throughout the reign of Queen Victoria, Sappho represents different ideas of Victorian womanhood, and like the Queen she becomes a "representative" woman who embodies the very possibility of such representations, allowing them to multiply in often contradictory forms.[13] Indeed it is the repeatability of the Sapphic figure that marks it feminine, as the variations on the name—its successive differences from the nominative—point to a principle of differentiation that also produces gender difference. The cultural formations that cluster around this poetic form—and in particular, the construction of nineteenth-century female authorship on a Sapphic model—will reveal what is uniquely Victorian about Victorian Sappho.

I do not present the Victorian reception of Sappho according to a chronology that often shapes reception studies, since one important objective of my book is to define an approach to literary history that does not assume an "original" prior to the moment of its "reception." Rather than organizing the chapters to imply a developing tradition or a linear progression, I emphasize the continual recirculation of Sappho within Victorian poetry. My argument proceeds in a series of differential repetitions; after demonstrating how Sappho is to be read as a non-originary figure in the first chapter, the other chapters show in further detail how its repetition takes different historical forms: the doubling of the Sapphic signature by Michael Field, the Sapphic rhythms performed by Algernon Swinburne, the reiteration of Sappho's leap by various Victorian poetesses. By returning to the question of the name in each context, *Victorian Sappho* offers a more fully contextualized analysis of the structures of repetition outlined by Jacques Derrida in "Signature, Event, Context" (1997). An insistence on the structural necessity of repetition—manifested in the iterability of the singular mark, the nonsingularity of the event, the overdetermination of context—is evident in the organization of my argument, even as I seek to mobilize a familiar deconstructive reading of lyric in a less familiar, more historical direction.

I begin Chapter 1 with a Sapphic riddle, a paradox serving as my paradigm for the conversion of a female body into written letters that be-

---

[13] On multiple representations of Queen Victoria in nineteenth-century England, see Munich 1996, Homans and Munich 1997, and Homans 1998; on the twentieth century as a "post-Victorian" age mourning various memories of the queen, see Dickson 1996; on the feminization of Victorian culture, see Psomiades 1997.

come vocal at the moment of their reception: when they are delivered to a reader, they seem to speak. But their arrival is unpredictable, as I show in a detailed analysis of fragment 31 of Sappho, first in Greek and then in a series of English translations. Every attempt to recuperate Sapphic voice repeats a break that is inscribed—indeed, prescribed—in this fragment: Sappho's tongue is broken, disarticulating a speaking subject even as it is also said to emerge. The repetition of the break nevertheless makes fragment 31 an exemplary lyric, I argue, and the most frequently translated text of Sappho; it is incorporated into an English lyric tradition from the seventeenth century onward, a tradition that is itself reincorporated into the Sapphic corpus by Wharton, who writes in the Preface to his third edition of *Sappho:* "As a name, as a figure pre-eminent in literary history, she has indeed never been overlooked" (xv). In Wharton's book the continual renaming of this figure allows Sappho to appear as a figure *for* translation: Sappho is simultaneously cause and effect of translation, and increasingly feminized in this process of transmission. Although Wharton introduces Sappho as the pure and unmediated voice of a woman poet who is the perfection of lyric song, his book demonstrates how Sapphic voice is mediated by text and marked feminine precisely because it does not speak. In this respect Wharton's *Sappho* is distinctively Victorian, as it reflects and influences a nineteenth-century ideology of lyric reading predicated on the figure of voice.

Wharton's first edition of *Sappho* in 1885 was the inspiration for a collection of Sapphic imitations entitled *Long Ago,* published in 1889 by "Michael Field," the pseudonym of Katherine Bradley and Edith Cooper. In Chapter 2, I argue that these two Victorian women—aunt and niece, who collaborated in writing poetry and considered themselves married— perform a self-doubling signature that unsettles conventional definitions of lyric as the solitary utterance of a single speaker. In Wharton's edition they discover not only the possibility for multiple signatures in the name of Sappho, but a space between Greek and English that allows for eroticized textual exchange. Fragment 2 of Sappho, an invitation to come to the island of Lesbos, becomes a lesbian topos in the Sapphic lyrics of Michael Field, allowing Bradley and Cooper to enter a metaphorical "field" of writing where the crossing out, over, and through of sexual identities can be performed. Bradley and Cooper writing as Michael Field, writing as Sappho, therefore appropriate a name that is simultaneously proper and improper, their own and not their own, and introduce the possibility of lesbian imitation not predicated on the assumption of voice. The reader is left to ponder the erotic appeal of Greek letters that spell out Sappho's name, without spelling it out completely. My chapter complicates the reclamation of Michael Field in the name of lesbian writing; such a reading depends on the rhetorical figure of antonomasia, taking a common noun for a proper name, and vice versa. Rather than identifying Lesbian Sappho with lesbian Sappho, the Sapphic lyrics in *Long Ago* enact the rhetorical conversion itself and remain suspended in that moment, both then and now.

The identification of, and with, Sappho as a "lesbian" figure is performed in yet another way by Algernon Charles Swinburne. The *succès de scandale* of his early Sapphic imitations encouraged readers to identify Swinburne with Sappho, and he is still read as the most important Victorian incarnation of Sappho. Swinburne invokes her as the greatest lyric poet who ever lived, his personal precursor and the proper name for all lyric song: "Name above all names." While this act of nomination creates a line of descent from Sappho to Swinburne, his repetition of the name also turns Sappho into a figure for decadence and decline: a descending cadence that is heard only as an echoing rhythm, memorized by Swinburne and recorded in the writing of his own Sapphic imitations. Swinburne's Sappho, I argue, is a rhythmicized body that disappears and reappears in the rhythms of its own scattering, according to a logic of disintegration and figurative reconstitution familiar from the Longinian treatise on the sublime. The subtext for this sublime reading of Sappho is not only fragment 31 (admired by Longinus), but also fragment 130: in both poems, the rhythmic force of eros, "the loosener of limbs," threatens to disarticulate the body of Sappho, while also articulating the Sapphic corpus into a perfect metrical body. Swinburne learns the fine art of suffering meter from Sappho, in a sublime scenario that I call "the Sapphic scene of instruction," played out in his Sapphic poems and in his flagellant verse as well. The beating of the body is internalized as the rhythm of poetry and transposed into the formal abstraction of meter: a written notation. The hyperbolic performance of this violent inscription can be understood as a perverse response to Victorian metrical theory, enabling Swinburne to constitute his own poetic corpus as a body of writing that materializes through and as meter. Initially abused by the critics for his Sapphic imitations, Swinburne presents himself as a body *for* abuse, rhythmically scattered and recollected like the fragments of Sappho. The reception of Swinburne at the turn of the century repeats the logic of Swinburne's Sapphic sublime and continues in current criticism on Swinburne.

Alongside the homoerotic Sapphism of Michael Field and the eroticized rhythms of Swinburne's Sapphic imitations, there also exists a tradition of Victorian women poets who turn to Sappho in order to perform the suffering of "woman" as an overdetermined heterosexual identification: doomed to die for love, Sappho becomes a proper name for the "Poetess." Prior to Wharton's edition of the Sapphic fragments in 1885, the popular reception of Sappho is primarily mediated by Ovid's "Sappho to Phaon," where Sappho laments her abandonment by the young ferryman

Phaon, before leaping to her death from the Leucadian Cliff. The Sapphic signature in Ovid's elegiac epistle is a postscript to a suicide that has already occurred, and sets a precedent for the "posthumous" writing of nineteenth-century poetesses. Their Sapphic imitations circulate as postscripts to the postscript, in a seemingly endless series of Sapphic signatures: P.S. Sappho, P.P.S. Sappho, P.P.P.S. Sappho, and so on. In Chapter 4 I offer another perspective on literary history, by tracing the repetition of Sappho's leap in women's verse from the early to the late nineteenth century. I refer back to Mary Robinson, L. E. L. and Felicia Hemans as important Romantic precursors for Victorian poetesses such as Christina Rossetti and Caroline Norton, all of whom turn to Sappho as the personification of an empty figure. Nevertheless, this Sapphic (non)persona is increasingly invoked in the cause of woman toward toward the century, as it circulates on both side of the Atlantic in the poetry of American and British feminists, such as Elizabeth Oakes Smith, Mary Catherine Hume and Catharine Amy Dawson Scott. While these names have been mostly forgotten in the twentieth century, they give us an insight into the rhetorical complexity of sentimental lyric; indeed, the forgetting of nineteenth-century poetesses is predicted in their verse as the very means of its literary transmission.

There are in fact more Victorian Sapphos than I can name, and I do not offer a comprehensive survey; each would deserve a detailed analysis, well beyond the scope of one book. The historical scope of my argument does expand from chapter to chapter, however. In the first chapter, I place a single text within the context of a single book: after reading fragment 31 in theoretical terms, I show how this logic of lyric reading is writ large in Wharton's 1885 edition of Sappho. The second chapter places this influential Victorian text within the context of its reception toward the end of the nineteenth century, by showing how its textual logic is reworked in the Sapphic lyrics of Michael Field. The third chapter ranges more freely over four decades to show how Swinburne is read as one famously scandalous Victorian incarnation of Sappho. The fourth chapter spans the entire reign of Queen Victoria, in order to present a long succession of women who write within the conventions of nineteenth-century sentimental lyric. The poets I consider in this book have been selected for their relevance to larger critical debates within the field of Victorian poetry: the relationship between gender and genre, the intersection between philology and poetry, the possibility of collaborative and cross-gendered writing, the question of lesbian poetics, the sexual politics of Victorian Hellenism, the implications of Victorian prosody, the historical reclamation of women poets, the rhetorical and cultural function of sentimental lyric, and the theoretical claims of formalist reading. This final question about form can only be addressed in the performance of reading itself, and it informs the attention to detail in my readings in each chapter. While I do not assume knowledge of ancient Greek from my readers, the juxtaposition of English and Greek might nevertheless serve as a reminder of the difficulty of reading all poetry, even in English.

As I define a Sapphic strain in Victorian poetry, I therefore want to insist more strenuously on the theoretical questions raised by reading lyric, or lyric reading. If "reading lyric" implies that lyric is already defined as an object to be read, "lyric reading" implies an act of lyrical reading, or reading lyrically, that poses the possibility of lyric without presuming its objective existence or assuming it to be a form of subjective expression. Traditional definitions of lyric depend on a generic model that assumes the continuity of a speaker, as Jonathan Culler points out: "To assume that interpreting a lyric means identifying the speaker is to forget that the speaker is inferred from a voice, which is itself a figure here; but once one begins to consider the figure of voice, the question arises of how far the intelligibility of lyric depends on this figure and whether the generic model or reading strategy of the lyric is not designed to maintain the notion of language as the product of and therefore sign of the subject" (1988: 298). Lyric reading predicated on the figure of voice creates the possibility of identification of and with a speaker, in order to defend against readings that could make lyric less intelligible, more resistant to the recuperation of a lyric subject. Culler therefore questions "the generic model or reading strategy" that allows lyric to be associated with subjectivity, as does Paul de Man in his essay on "Anthropomorphism and Trope in the Lyric." "What we call the lyric, the instance of represented voice, conveniently spells out the rhetorical and thematic characteristics that make it the paradigm of a complementary relationship between grammar, trope, and theme," de Man observes, leading him to conclude that "the lyric is not a genre but one name among several to designate the defensive motion of understanding, the possibility of a future hermeneutics" (1984: 261). Here lyric serves as proper name—"one name among several"—for anthropomorphic (mis)reading, in which anthropomorphism is "not just a trope but an identification" that freezes an endless series of propositions into a single assertion: "no longer a proposition but a proper name" (241). The essay performs a lyrical unreading that would refuse such identification, revoking what is invoked in its title, namely "the Lyric," and de Man concludes with a series of self-qualifying negations that place lyric in opposition to "non-anthropomorphic, non-elegiac, non-celebratory, non-lyrical, non-poetic, that is to say, prosaic, or, better: *historical* modes of language power" (262).[14]

[14] For further elaboration of de Man's theoretical account of lyric see Culler 1985; in Hosek and Parker 1985, see also de Man, "Lyrical Voice in Contemporary Theory" and Culler, "Changes in the Study of the Lyric." I owe my understanding of de Man's essay as a performance of "lyrical un-reading" to Virginia Jackson's brilliant reading of de Man, in chapter 2 of *Dickinson's Misery*.

Victorian Sappho works simultaneously within and against this critique of lyric anthropomorphism. According to de Man's logic, when Sappho is identified with lyric as a genre we project "the possibility of a future hermeneutics" into the past: we read the Sapphic fragments not only as "the instance of represented voice" but as the very origin of lyric voice itself. Such a reading does indeed designate a defensive motion of understanding, the conversion of trope into anthropomorphism. Within the context of my argument, however, the proper name of Sappho can also be read propositionally. If Sappho is an anthropomorphism—no longer a proposition but a proper name—nevertheless that name cannot be identified with a speaker, nor does it stop the chain of tropological transformations that de Man defines as reading. To the contrary, Sappho is an overdetermined trope within a history of continual transformation that never ends, enabling us to read lyric as structure for shifting identifications, rather than the fixing of an identification. To define another approach to lyric reading, it is not enough to question the complementary relationship between grammar, trope, and theme; we must question the historical relationship between gender and genre as well. While de Man opposes lyric to "*historical* modes of language power," what is at stake in *Victorian Sappho* is the undoing of this antithesis and an interest in reconstructing a history of lyric reading that de Man simultaneously assumes and erases. The effacement of gender in his theoretical account of lyric as a genre is, I argue, historically determined and itself a trace of the history that de Man claims does not fall properly within the domain of lyric.

To re-evaluate the genealogy of the genre assumed by contemporary lyric theory, and to demonstrate how *historical* modes of language power are always *gendered* as well, I propose a literary history that includes women poets, but also reflects further on the historical category of the "woman poet." As Denise Riley has argued in *"Am I That Name?" Feminism and the Category of "Women" in History,* the conversion of a proper name ("Woman") into a common name ("women") troubles the history of feminism, which instituted women as its founding category yet also found itself mediating "between the many temporalities of a designation." But if there is no originary woman, nevertheless "some characterisation or other is eternally in play," so that "the question then for a feminist history is to discover whose, and to what effects" (1988: 98). This is also the question for feminist literary history, and especially in feminist readings of women's poetry, where the characterisation of woman "in play" is already a personified rhetorical effect. Throughout my book a deconstructive critique of lyric is therefore coupled with feminist criticism: two approaches to critical reading that are not as incompatible as they might seem, insofar as both revolve around the problem of personification.

In an incisive analysis of the uncanny coupling of deconstruction and feminism, Barbara Johnson questions "whether there is a *simple* incompatability between the depersonalization of deconstruction and the repersonalization of feminism, or whether each is not in reality haunted by the ghost of the other" (1987: 44). The return of the personal in de Man's work takes the form of personification, according to Johnson, who describes how the transference of personal agency to rhetorical entities in his prose allows him to achieve "an elimination of sexual difference." "By making personhood the property of an 'it,' de Man is able to claim a form of universality which can be said to inhere in language itself, and which is not directly subject to ordinary feminist critique, however gender-inflected language can in fact be shown to be" (45). I argue that the transfer of personhood to rhetorical entities—especially as performed in lyric—is not the elimination of sexual difference but another way to articulate the historical effects of gender. If we extend Johnson's argument into nineteenth-century women's verse, we will find a precedent for this version of personification, making personhood the property of an "it" named Sappho that is explicitly marked feminine. A reading that insists on repersonalizing this "it" as a person might fall under the category of "ordinary feminist critique," but as Johnson points out, "what is interesting about this attempt at personalization is how quickly it slides into an assumption of generalizability" (46). Thus, "while de Man's writing is haunted by the return of personification, feminist writing is haunted by the return of abstraction," with each making the other "both possible and problematic" (46). To recognize and analyze the complex relation between the two would be the beginning of an extraordinary feminist critique.

My purpose in *Victorian Sappho* is to develop an approach to reading lyric that is both rhetorically and historically inflected by gender. Sappho spells out an alternative to "what we call the lyric," not only within de Man's rhetorical formulation but also within the historical account offered by Joel Fineman for the invention of poetic subjectivity. In *Shakespeare's Perjured Eye,* Fineman describes a lyric subject "willed" to literary history by William Shakespeare, in the sonnets that pun repeatedly on the name of "Will." The speaking of the proper name allows the poet to be spoken about, and thus to be read as author: "Naming himself, therefore, the poet to himself becomes a 'he,' someone to be spoken about, a third person elsewhere from and different from his first and second person" (1986: 291). Although this act of self-naming is also an act of self-division, nevertheless it authorizes a lyric subject who is gendered male: the poet "finds his 'Will' at odds with his 'I,'" (291) yet what he finds—a "Will" and an "I"—are still "his." Indeed, Fineman cannot imagine a lyric subject other than one defined by the will he owns, even if that will also disowns him by producing internal difference. "Whatever might be different from Shakespeare's poetry of verbal difference would therefore have to find, outside language, another name," Fineman concludes; such a "hypothetical successor" would have to be "outside history" (ibid.: 296).

But suppose this hypothetical successor is a predecessor that has already found, in Sappho, another name? If Shakespeare represents one possible origin for a highly speculative history of the lyric subject, I nominate Sappho to represent another possible point of departure for a lyric tradition—equally specular—that does not locate the signature within the subject. Declining the name of Sappho does not place it "outside language" or "outside history," however, but in a different relation to both. Rather than defining a poet who to himself becomes a "he" by self-naming, the relationship between the personal pronoun and the proper name might be articulated, differently, to pose the question of feminine difference. The effects of that difference would not be circumscribed by a proper name that signifies the "will" of an authorial intention. A gendered perspective on lyric would not have to depend on the invention of a "she" who speaks her own name—say, Sappho—but could be discovered unpredictably elsewhere, in the Sapphic signature that circulates at the specific moment of its reception. The Sapphic signature I trace in the following pages is also mine, of course. Who writes Sappho, now? Who wrongs Sappho? Who, O Sapph'? I am inclined to answer, there is no choice but to go on declining the name.

ONE

SAPPHO'S BROKEN TONGUE

The Sapphic Riddle

COLLECTED into nine books at the Alexandrian library, canonized as one of the nine Greek lyric poets, and ranked alongside the nine muses, Sappho was called "the tenth muse" in antiquity: a poet whose song resonates over the centuries, one of the first voices in a Western lyric tradition. Yet the afterlife of Sappho also presumes the death of a living voice. No longer bound to the time and place of oral performance, the songs attributed to Sappho live on in a literary tradition that memorializes lyric song. "The pages of Sappho's lovely song remain and will remain, white pages that speak out loud," writes the Hellenistic poet Posidippus, four hundred years after Sappho was said to have lived and died:

> Σαπφῷαι δὲ μένουσι φίλης ἔτι καὶ μενέουσιν
> ᾠδῆς αἱ λευκαὶ φθεγγόμεναι σελίδες
> (Sappho Test. 15, Campbell 16–17)

Paradoxically, Sapphic song "will remain" precisely because the songs do not remain. Even while reclaiming the voice of Sappho, the epigram marks its loss through a displacement of voice by writing.[1] The pages themselves seem to speak in place of Sappho: we must read past her name (*Sapphōiai*) at the beginning of the first line, and her song (*ōidēs*) at the beginning of the second line, in order to discover that the grammatical subject of the epigram is "pages that speak out loud" (*phtheggomenai selides*). Where then does Sapphic voice originate—from Sappho, or Sappho's song, or the pages of Sappho's song? After all, what remains is not the songs themselves but the pages of songs, twice removed from Sappho, their origin.

Furthermore, in the course of time even the pages of the songs of Sappho have been obliterated. Now the remains are fragmentary texts, excerpts quoted by ancient writers, papyrus scraps exhumed in Egypt at the turn of the century, torn into strips and recycled as wrappings for dead bodies. This is the scattered Sapphic corpus, no longer a living voice or even a body of writing, but an assortment of decomposing texts, dead let-

---

[1] On the mediation of voice by writing as a topos in Hellenistic poetry, see Bing 1988 and Goldhill 1991; on the memorialization of Greek lyric, see also Most 1982.

ters in a dead language. Still, even the most fragmentary of the Sapphic fragments provoke a desire for Sapphic voice. Fragment 185, "honey-voiced" (μελίφωνοι), survives because it is cited as "Sappho's delightful epithet," an epithet taken from the songs of Sappho and thus read as ep-ithet *for* the songs of Sappho (Philostratus, Campbell 178–79). Likewise, "soft-voiced" (μελλιχόφωνοι) is quoted out of context as "Sappho's most delightful word," as if that single word could convey, by synecdoche, the delight of all of Sappho's words (Aristaenetus, Campbell 180–81). De-spite the long and complex process of their textual transmission, the Sap-phic fragments are read as if they are themselves "soft-voiced" and "honey-voiced," the source of mellifluous song.

The transcriptions of tattered papyri point to a similar paradox, most obviously in the papyrus fragments discovered at Oxyrhynchus and labo-riously transcribed by scholars. The damage done to the Sapphic frag-ments is carefully marked with brackets, dots, ellipses, and parentheses, yet they are reconstructed as texts that we read as an invitation to song:

Fragment 21, lines 11–12:

]εα, λάβοισα
]ἄεισον ἄμμι

. . . taking (your lyre?)
. . . sing to us

Fragment 22, line 9:

.] . ε . [. . . .] . [. . . κ]έλομαι σ᾿ ἀ[είδην

. . . I call upon you to sing . . .

Fragment 27, line 5:

. . .]ικης μέλπεσθ᾿ ἄγι ταῦτα[

. . . come and sing this, all of you . . .

Fragment 70, lines 10–11:

πολυγ]άθην χόρον, ἄα[
]δε λίγηα . [

. . . delightful choir . . .
. . . clear-voiced . . .

Fragment 103, lines 9–10:

] . [. ὄ]ππετ᾿ ἀοιδαι φρέν[. . .] αν .[
]σαιοισα λιγύραν [ἀοί]δαν

. . . when . . . song(s) . . . the mind . . .
. . . hearing a clear song

How can any song be reclaimed from the tatters of such texts, torn out of context and riddled with gaps? How are these scattered letters "voiced"? The lacunae between and within words demonstrate how much scholarly speculation and conjecture are necessary to reconstruct a singing voice for Sappho. And yet the more disfigured her texts, it would seem, the more Sappho is read as a figure for voice.

Reading Sappho is a form of riddling, then. When we read the fragments, we ask a question about voice that we answer by projecting voice into the fragments: a circular conundrum, wonderfully exemplified in a riddle from a fourth-century Greek comedy entitled *Sappho*, by Antiphanes. Here Sappho appears as a character, who asks what female creature bears infants that do not speak yet are heard everywhere:

> There is a female being that hides in her womb (or, in the folds of her dress) unborn children, and although the children are voiceless (*aphōna*), they call out across the waves of the sea and over the whole earth to whomever they wish, and people who are not present can hear them and even deaf people are able to hear them too.

What kind of creature carries such offspring? What kind of infant is voiceless yet vocal? What kind of voice can be heard, even by the deaf? Sappho answers her own riddle, as follows:

> The female being is a letter (*epistolē*) that carries in itself the letters of the alphabet (*ta grammata*) as infants. Although the letters are voiceless (*aphōna*) they can speak to people far away, to whomever they wish, and if some other person happens to be standing near the one who is reading, he will not hear them.

The Sapphic riddle (Antiphanes fr. 196) revolves around the invention of silent reading in ancient Greece, when the letters of the Greek phonetic alphabet were no longer spoken aloud. These voiceless letters (*aphōna grammata*) seem to "speak" to a reader who can "hear" what is written, without the mediation of an external voice. An internalization of the speaking voice produces the metaphor of "letters that speak," an image of voice that appeals to the eye instead of the ear, as Jesper Svenbro points out: "For anyone reading in silence . . . the letters 'speak,' they 'cry out,' or even 'sing.' The eye *sees* the sound" (5).[2] Thus in the riddle the letters are figured as infants, calling out to a reader and delivered by a female body about to give birth: what bears, in all senses, the *aphōna grammata* is an *epistolē*, the feminine noun for "epistle." She is a letter that contains the letters, transporting them to anyone who is able to read; they will speak to this reader without being heard.

[2] Svenbro quotes the Sapphic riddle in Greek (1993: 158–59) and further explores the question of a voice that is seen rather than heard in his chapter "The Inner Voice: On the Invention of Silent Reading" (160–86).

The gendering of the riddle is significant, for it allows Sappho to be understood as its very embodiment. Sappho answers her own question, because she herself is the answer to the riddle: she too is a letter whose voiceless letters we are called upon to "hear," through reading. The *aphōna grammata* issuing forth from Sappho would then be her poems, as Svenbro suggests: "The letter is a woman; and the idea that the alphabetical signs are her squalling babies is probably a comic version of the basic idea that poems are the offspring of their author" (159). The Sapphic riddle becomes a paradigm for reading Sappho, no longer as oral poet but as a text whose "voice" depends on the transportation of written letters that become articulate at the moment of their reception, when they are delivered to the reader. The letters are put into motion through reading, so that they seem to become animated beings with a life of their own. Indeed, the animation of *aphōna grammata* requires this movement of transport, for the riddle emphasizes that they speak not to anyone standing nearby, but only to people far away, across the waves of the sea and the whole earth. Greater distance requires more motion and so increases the effect of animation: the texts of Sappho are increasingly animated as they are transported across great distances, both temporal and spatial. The *aphōna grammata* of Sappho are made to speak, but only at a distance.

Thus, in the course of Sappho's reception, readers discover an ever-amplifying voice in her poetry. In the Palatine Anthology, the songs of Sappho are figured as her undying daughters, no longer simply calling out like infants to the reader but singing now to all eternity: "Wherever you are, greetings to you, lady, as to the gods: for we still have your immortal daughters, your songs" (Sappho Test. 58, Campbell 48–49). While Sappho herself is gone, the songs survive because readers lend voice to them, animating the lifeless texts of Sappho by reading them *as if* they were alive, regenerating the songs *as if* they were her progeny. Sappho lives on through her future readers, who are themselves addressed by Sappho as if they were her children. In yet another turn on the Sapphic riddle, the Palatine Anthology includes a Hellenistic epigram written "as if it were by Sappho" to dedicate a statue: "Children, although I am voiceless I answer, if anyone ask, since I have had a tireless voice set at my feet" (Campbell 204–5). The "tireless voice set at my feet" refers to the dedication inscribed at the foot of the statue, which seems to speak to anyone who will stop to read the inscription; it is voiceless yet never tires in answering the reader, for at the moment of being read it is "voiced" again. The epigram answers the Sapphic riddle, not only by referring its utterance back to "Sappho," but by demonstrating how Sappho's answer depends on the reader's question, "if anyone ask."

But can the Sapphic riddle be solved in this way, or is it a trick question? While attributing the answer to Sappho—allowing her to name the answer, and her name to be the answer—the riddle raises other unanswerable questions. If the letter is a woman and the woman is Sappho, is Sappho "inside" or "outside" the letters contained in her letter? Do the letters issue from her, or she from them? And how is Sappho's letter delivered to us? While the riddle promises to deliver *aphōna grammata* to the reader, if we follow the loop of its logic, their delivery is also deferred. The reader (who may be absent, distant, or even deaf) cannot hear the original utterance conveyed by *aphōna grammata,* and so the writing is made to "speak" in its place; but once letters are put into circulation, who knows what detours they will take? What further displacements will take place? The letters are literally unpredictable, since they cannot speak before being read: we do not know in advance what they will be seen to have said. The unpredictability of *aphōna grammata* is written into the Sapphic riddle as the necessary condition for their seeming to speak at all. The very moment of their arrival also necessitates their deferral, for if they stop circulating they can no longer be read. In the transport, transfer, or metaphor of reading, the letter of Sappho is always postponed; although asking to be answered, it can never reach its final destination.

The Sapphic riddle is not only unpredictable, but contradictory as well. Unresolved is the simultaneous existence of two different conceptions of text: the text as figural body that contains voice, and the text as literal vehicle for the transport of written letters. Both are conceived by way of Sappho, bearing infants in her womb or folding *aphōna grammata* into the dress that is her envelope. What is literal and what is figurative here, the female body literalized as letter or the female letter figured as body, and why does the riddle choose Sappho as the embodiment of that contradiction? The engendering of voice by its deferral is also, I shall argue, its gendering. Giving birth to voiceless letters, Sappho is a body of writing marked as feminine because it seems to speak—it bespeaks—the contradiction of its own speaking. Sappho is associated with the question of voice in a way that binds together gender and genre inextricably: through Sappho we can trace the gendering of lyric as a feminine genre, not because we assume she was the first poet to speak as a woman, but because the assumption of voice in lyric reading produces Sappho as a feminine figure that does not speak.

No text of Sappho demonstrates this contradiction more dramatically than fragment 31 (*phainetai moi*), the famous love poem that seems to leave Sappho speechless: *glōssa eage,* we read in line 9, "tongue is broken." Here a conspicuous break points to a process of linguistic disarticulation that I shall analyze in further detail, in the next section of this chapter. I read fragment 31 according to the logic of the Sapphic riddle: its *aphōna grammata* cannot be read as voice but also cannot *not* be read as voice. The Greek text of fragment 31 is therefore a provocation to lyric reading that provokes, time and time again, an attempt to recuperate Sappho's broken tongue. One influential reader who makes the attempt is Longinus; in his treatise on the sublime, he admires Sappho as a sublime lyric subject who seems to speak beyond the moment of death. What is spoken, however, is the violence of Sappho's fragmentation. The rhetorical pathos of that sublime scenario, I argue, serves to feminize the figure of Sappho.

Sappho's reception is mediated by Longinus in important ways, not only because we owe the transmission of fragment 31 to his treatise, but because the Longinian reading of fragment 31 defines the terms of her afterlife. Sappho neither lives nor dies, but lives on in a movement of reading which Longinus calls sublime transport, or which the Sapphic riddle calls the transportation of letters, and which I explore in terms of translation, as yet another way to mobilize Sapphic voice. In the third section of this chapter, I demonstrate how Sappho is transported into an English lyric tradition through translations of fragment 31, the most frequently translated of the Sapphic fragments. A tradition of performing Sapphic song is therefore displaced by a tradition of translators, who contribute to the afterlife of Sappho through the performance of translation. But to make Sappho speak again in English, every translator repeats the break in fragment 31: what speaks, in translation, is Sappho's broken tongue. The repetition of that break increasingly produces the gendering of Sappho as a female lyric subject, as I shall suggest with reference to selected English versions of fragment 31 from the seventeenth century onward. The chapter concludes with a more detailed discussion of Victorian translators of Sappho, as compiled by Dr. Henry Wharton in his 1885 edition of the Sapphic fragments. I consider all the features of Wharton's book—the juxtaposition of Greek text and multiple English versions, the introductory "memoir," the prefaces and appendix—in order to demonstrate how Sappho is made to embody the contradictions of a Victorian lyric ideology that is predicated on voice yet mediated by text.

Tongue Is Broken

Sappho is often placed at the origins of Western lyric, a *naissance du moi lyrique* giving birth to a lyric "I" that also speaks as a generalized lyric subject.[3] Page duBois describes the historical emergence of lyric subjectivity

---

[3] The phrase *naissance du moi lyrique* comes from Gans 1981, drawing on a critical tradition of reading Sappho as individual lyric subject; see, e.g., Snell 1953 on this model of lyric subjectivity in Greek poetry and Johnson 1982 on "the idea of lyric" in general. Other critics emphasize the emergence of a communal "I" in Sappho's lyrics; see, e.g., Williamson 1995 on the construction of a collective voice in the lyrics of Sappho, and Miller 1994 more generally on the public function of lyric. Despite various constructions of a "self" for Sap-

in archaic Greece, during the seventh and sixth centuries B.C.: "Sappho and the poets who are her near contemporaries are among the first to inhabit fully the first person singular, to use the word 'I' to anchor their poetic speech, to hollow out for their listeners and readers the cultural space for individual subjectivity" (1995: 6). The interesting implication here is that subjectivity is a space hollowed out rather than occupied by Sappho. Indeed, in fragment 31 of Sappho the birth of a lyric subject seems to coincide with the moment of its death. Anne Carson's translation of the fragment shows how Sappho is suspended in the moment of dying:

> He seems to me equal to the gods that man
> whoever he is who opposite you
> sits and listens close
> to your sweet speaking
>
> and lovely laughing—oh it
> puts the heart in my chest on wings
> for when I look at you, a moment, then no speaking
> is left in me
>
> no: tongue breaks, and thin
> fire is racing under skin
> and in eyes no sight and drumming
> fills ears
>
> and cold sweat holds me and shaking
> grips me all, greener than grass
> I am and dead—or almost
> I seem to me.

Although the Greek text continues past the fourth stanza, Carson follows a long-established tradition of translating fragment 31 in four stanzas, framed by two verbs of seeming: "he seems to me" and "I seem to me." Carson therefore calls it "a strangely theatrical poem, as brightly lit as a stage set and much concerned with the problem of seeming."[4] Her translation sets the stage for us to read the poem, word by word, as a dramatic verbal event.

But where exactly does Sappho enter the scene? Is there an "I" to an-

---

pho—private or public, personal or general, individual or collective—all these readings refer the origin of lyric utterance back to the assumption of a "voice" speaking in the first person.

[4] Carson presents her translation in conjunction with a reading of fragment 31 in "Just for the Thrill" (1990: 149); an earlier version of the translation appears in *Eros the Bittersweet*, where she also uses a theatrical metaphor to describe the effect of fragment 31: "The poem floats toward us on a stage set. But we have no program. The actors go in and out of focus anonymously. The action has no location" (1986: 12–13).

chor poetic speech, to present Sappho as the central speaker, to dramatize the emergence of individual subjectivity? If we look at the first person pronouns in a reconstruction of the Greek fragment, it is difficult to
identify Sappho as the lyric subject, even grammatically:

> φαίνεταί μοι κῆνος ἴσος θέοισιν
> ἔμμεν᾽ ὤνηρ, ὄττις ἐνάντιός τοι
> ἰσδάνει καὶ πλάσιον ἆδυ φωνεί-
> σας ὑπακούει
>
> καὶ γελαίσας ἰμέροεν, τό μ᾽ ἦ μὰν
> καρδίαν ἐν στήθεσιν ἐπτόαισεν·
> ὡς γὰρ ἔς σ᾽ ἴδω βρόχε᾽, ὤς με φώναι-
> σ᾽ οὐδ᾽ ἒν ἔτ᾽ εἴκει,
>
> ἀλλὰ κὰμ μὲν γλῶσσά ⟨μ᾽⟩ ἔαγε, λέπτον
> δ᾽ αὔτικα χρῷ πῦρ ὑπαδεδρόμηκεν,
> ὀππάτεσσι δ᾽ οὐδ᾽ ἒν ὄρημμ᾽, ἐπιρρόμ-
> βεισι δ᾽ ἄκουαι,
>
> κὰδ δέ μ᾽ ἴδρως κακχέεται, τρόμος δὲ
> παῖσαν ἄγρει, χλωροτέρα δὲ ποίας
> ἔμμι, τεθνάκην δ᾽ ὀλίγω ᾽πιδεύης
> φαίνομ᾽ ἔμ᾽ αὔτ[α.[5]

The first-person "I" appears obliquely in fragment 31, first as indirect object (the dative *moi* in lines 1, 5, 13), and then as direct object (the accusative *me* in line 7) and finally as a reflexive (*em' autai* in line 16), but
never in the position of grammatical subject (the nominative *egō*). Not
until line 14 is the first person singular marked by gender (in the adjectives *paisan* and *chlōrotera*), followed by the verb "I am" in line 15 (*emmi*)
but immediately qualified by the verb "I seem" in line 16 (*phainomai*). The
only other verbs in the first person refer to seeing (*idō*, in stanza 2) and
not seeing (*oud'. . .orēmmi*, in stanza 3), creating a highly specularized
lyric subject that invites speculation about its own claim to subjectivity.

So we also enter the theater of fragment 31 as spectators, without knowing where to look or what to see. "The action of the poem is in a true

---

[5] I follow the reconstruction of the first four stanzas of fragment 31 in Campbell 78–81.
The first line of the fifth stanza is tentatively reconstructed as ἀλλὰ πὰν τόλματον, ἐπεὶ καὶ
πένητα and translated by Campbell, "But all can be endured, since . . . even a poor man. . . ."
This apparent reversal suggests a longer narrative from near death back into a life that must
be endured, and it is now generally accepted among scholars that the poem continues after
the fourth stanza. In the long history of its reception, however, scholars and translators have
most often read fragment 31 as a poem that leaves Sappho suspended in the moment of
dying, at the end of stanza four. For discussion of textual difficulties in fragment 31, see
Page 1955; for an assessment of variant readings, see Wills 1967 and Lidov 1993.

sense spectacular," Carson observes: "We see the modes of perception reduced to dysfunction one by one; we see the objects of outer senses disappear, and on the brightly lit stage at the center of her being we see Sappho recognize herself: *emmi*, "I am," she asserts at verse 15" (1990: 150). And yet what we "see" in Carson's translation, spectacular in its own way, is the *de*centering of Sappho "at the center of her being." In Greek, as in Carson's English, the syntax shows a lack of personal agency: "no speaking is left in me," "tongue breaks," "fire is racing under skin," "in eyes no sight," "drumming fills ears," "cold sweat holds me and shaking grips me." These oddly impersonal constructions present "Sappho" as object rather than subject of bodily sensation, and the grammatical split between subject and object persists in *phainom' em' autai*, doubling self-reflexively back on itself: "*I* seem to *me*." Although Carson's reading centers on "I am" in the preceding line, her translation demonstrates how the Greek text proceeds to decenter this self-assertion: *emmi* is immediately followed by *tethnakēn*, reversing being into its own negation. Carson translates this final sequence into her own series of reversals, rendering the status of "I" increasingly ambiguous: "I am" is juxtaposed with "and dead" and followed by "—or almost" and qualified by "I seem." What emerges as "I" is neither subject nor object, but somewhere in between, perhaps—alive and almost dead, dead and almost alive, neither dead nor alive, both dead and alive. Framed as it is by the verbs *phainetai* and *phainomai* (from the Greek verb "to seem"), the poem (as we have it here) points to a phenomenon that we call "Sappho" yet is difficult to personify.

The performance of subjectivity is less the central assertion of fragment 31 than its central problem, then. Instead of presenting Sappho as phenomenalized subject, the poem would seem to be, as it were, an inquiry into the phenomenology of its own seeming. What Carson calls the "mise-en-scène" of the poem is more like a mise-en-abyme, as this text is an infinitely regressive structure, an exercise in referential circularity that leaves its readers groping for a stabilizing referent. For example, the poem has often been referred back to "that man" in line 1 as one possible point of reference: he may be a real man at a wedding, or a rhetorical convention.[6] However, after the demonstrative (*kēnos*) the man rapidly fades out of sight (in the contraction of definite article and noun in *ōner*), and he loses definition altogether in the indefinite relative pronoun (*ottis*

---

[6] See, for example, Snell's "wedding hypothesis" to create a "real" dramatic context for fragment 31 (1931), or Winkler's suggestion that Sappho is reworking the Homeric "makarismos" convention (1990:178–80). Attempts to create a narrative context for, or a coherent narrative within, fragment 31 are too numerous to summarize here—indeed, such a summary would amount to a history of Sappho's scholarly reception. My point here is not that such interpretations are right or wrong, but that they are symptomatic of the desire for a stable referent in a poem where the problem of reference is foregrounded.

in line 2): "that man whoever he is who . . ." He is, in the words of Anne Burnett, "a faceless hypothesis" (1983: 234). He appears at the beginning of the poem only to disappear, much as the appearance of "I" at the end of the poem is predicated on its own disappearance. Despite an apparent contrast between seeming immortal and seeming mortal, the deeper question pertaining to both "he" and "I" is how to refer seeming to being at all—it is the illusion of reference itself, staged as the "spectacular action" of fragment 31.

This question about referentiality is enacted even more dramatically by the Greek relative pronoun τό in line 5, introducing a relative clause. The antecedent of τό has been the focus of much debate among scholars: what is it in stanza 1 that sets the heart in commotion in stanza 2 and thus sets the poem in motion? "Translators and commentators must all face the problem of the τό in line 5," Emmett Robbins remarks in a survey of various scholarly responses to this problem (1980: 256). He observes a tension between grammatical and rhetorical readings of fragment 31: while the "speaking" and "laughing" of the girl in lines 3–5 can be read grammatically as the immediate antecedent of τό, rhetorically this reading creates an abrupt transition from sound to sight in line 7. By repunctuating fragment 31, Robbins attempts to restore continuity but in doing so, he overlooks the implications of his own analysis, insofar as it points to an important anacoluthon that interrupts the referential function of language in fragment 31. What τό means is less significant that how it functions in the poem: it marks a decisive break that reduces "he" and "you" in stanza 1 to mere pretext, and produces the remaining text as a discontinuous utterance that cannot be referred back to "I" without interruption.[7]

Carson's translation conveys the interruption with a dash and a dramatic enjambment: "—oh it / puts the heart in my chest on wings." Suspended at the end of the line, "it" retains the ambiguity of τό, although the anacoluthon also eases into an apostrophe: the interjection of "oh" translates the break into a spoken utterance that implies the continuity of a speaker and allows the poem to be read as the representation of speech. One way to "face the problem of the *to*" (as Robbins puts it, perhaps punningly) is to give face to it, by projecting voice into the text and thus assuming a speaking persona as well. The creation of such a persona for Sappho has been the primary critical strategy in recent interpretations of fragment 31: as a monologue in which we may "refer to the *persona loquens* as Sappho" (Koniaris 1968: 173), or a dramatized dialogue that creates Sappho as dramatic speaker (Lidov 1993) or an internal dialogue in which Sappho speaks as "the face behind the mask" (McEvilley

---

[7] Privitera 1969 also argues against the attempt to find a clear antecedent for τό although his appeal to its "intentional ambiguity" transfers the problem of reference to the inference of authorial intention, thus supplying a cause where there is only an effect.

1978). But what, we might ask, is *behind* the face behind the mask? How can we personify the speaker of a poem in which face is a figure that depends on the fiction of a voice and voice is a fiction that arises from the figure of face? Indeed, if we follow speculation that Sappho was a stock persona in archaic poetry rather than a living person, to what degree is Sappho a "speaker" at all?[8]

Facing the problem of the τό means not only to notice the problem of reference, but to notice the complex relation between face and voice in fragment 31 as well. The act of seeing and hearing the girl in stanza 1 leads, by means of a chiastic reversal, to the loss of hearing and sight in the following stanzas. Likewise the assertion of voice leads to its negation: the "sweet speaking" of the girl leads to "no speaking is left in me," and the parallel placement of *phōneisas* and *phōnais'* (in lines 3–4 and 7–8) further emphasizes the mutual implication of speaking and not speaking in this poem. The anacoluthon thus opens a space for personification and depersonification, producing prosopopoeia as the figure that gives face by conferring speech upon a voiceless entity, yet in doing so also defaces it. Paul de Man defines *prosopopoeia* etymologically: "Voice assumes mouth, eye, and finally face, a chain that is manifest in the etymology of the trope's name, *prosopon poien* [*sic*], to confer a mask or face (*prosopon*) (1984a: 76). In translating the name of the trope, de Man both describes and enacts the relationship between defacement and the giving of face in prosopopoeia: he decomposes the word into component parts, thus simultaneously "giving face" to this figure and "defacing" it as a mask.[9] Likewise fragment 31 performs its own figuration as an act of disfiguration: the face is systematically disfigured, broken down into component parts—tongue, skin, eyes, and ears—that do not function together. Thus the prosopopoeia in fragment 31, rendering face faceless and voice voiceless, points to its own anthropomorphism as a deadly trope. What seems dead yet "speaks"—what speaks of death—is the language itself, simultaneously articulating and disarticulating a lyric subject.

The most striking instance of this linguistic disarticulation is the "lingual" break in line 9: *glōssa eage*, "tongue is broken." Instead of voice, we discover a broken organ of speech alienated from a speaker: *glōssa* displaces *phōnē*, the word that usually designates voice in the Sapphic frag-

---

[8] Lardinois pursues the proposition that some Greek archaic poets are in fact fictional characters in the tradition they were supposed to represent; he suggests that Sappho may have been "a poetic construct rather than a real life figure in sixth-century Lesbos" and notes that the existence of metrical variants on the name of Sappho is typical of stock characters in an oral poetic tradition. Nevertheless his interpretation of the Sapphic fragments still depends on constructing Sappho as "the speaker, although not necessarily the performer" (1994: 62–63).

[9] For further discussion of defacement and the giving of face in prosopopoeia, see Chase 1986: 82–112.

ments.[10] Furthermore, the hiatus between *glōssa* and *eage* creates a break in the meter that leaves the tongue literally and figuratively broken. How shall we interpret this metrical break? Some scholars avoid the metrical difficulty through textual emendation. Campbell's reconstruction of fragment 31, for example, follows Sitzler in interpolating ⟨*m'*⟩ as an elided first person pronoun: *glōssa m'eage,* "my tongue is broken." The interpolation of the dative *moi* prevents hiatus and restores apparent continuity to the utterance, but as hypothetical reinscription of a speaking subject it also raises questions about where to place this speaker, since the grammatical subject is the tongue and not "I." Another emendation proposed by West would change the verb *eage* from third to first person: *glōssan eaga,* to be translated as "I have broken my tongue," or more literally, "I am broken with regard to my tongue" (1970: 311). By turning the tongue into a grammatical object, West attempts to recuperate a speaking subject "without implying intent or contributory activity." But here again, the implied speaker lacks personal agency, since the action of the verb cannot be referred back to an intentional subject.

Yet another way to make the break pronounceable is to assume a digamma, a lost letter from the primitive Greek alphabet that often accounts for metrical hiatus in Homeric epic. Parry has argued that the digamma also left its trace in the Lesbian dialect of Sappho's time, although it was no longer pronounced. The presence of a digamma in *glōssa* ⟨*F*⟩*eage* would make the vowels *a* and *e,* otherwise elided, pronounceable. The hiatus would then mark the trace of a letter that existed within an oral tradition, allowing fragment 31 to be construed as a spoken utterance and Sappho to be inferred as its speaker. The appeal to a lost digamma for the restoration of voice is odd, however, since the hiatus functions equivocally to mark both the absence and presence of a letter that used to be voiced: the digamma is a non-sound, a voiceless consonant representing something written or read but *not* heard. Indeed, the digamma is displaced in the text by two gammas (in *Glōssa* and *eaGe*), enclosing the hiatus like two glottal stops around a gap in sound. How, then, can the digamma resolve the question about voice in fragment 31? Instead of reading the poem as representation of speech, we might look at the hiatus as the unsolvable crux in a text that points to the problem of its own voicing.

Gregory Nagy therefore reads the meter mimetically, as performance of the very break that *glossa eage* describes: "The expression γλῶσσα ἔαγε displays a hiatus otherwise intolerable in this Lesbian genre. The ἔαγε should not be deemed corrupt on that account. Rather, hiatus is the very

---

[10] See, for example, the compound adjectives "clear-voiced" (fr. 30: λιγύφωνος, "soft-voiced" (fr. 71: μελλιχόφων), "sweet-voiced" (fr. 153: ἀδύφωνον), and "honey-voiced" (fr. 185: μελίφωνοι).

factor that creates the special effect, namely, that the form is arranged in such a way that it symbolizes what it means" (1974: 45). One consequence of a mimetic interpretation of the meter, however, is that it reads voice into the break in order to reclaim the voice of Sappho prior to that moment in the text—a tautological solution that hypothesizes voice in order to confirm it, even (or especially) in the absence of a speaking subject. Thus the "special effect" described by Nagy is recuperated by Dolores O'Higgins in terms of authorial intention, to suggest that the metrical irregularity in the hiatus is "deliberate, intended audially to reproduce the 'catch' in the poet's voice; Sappho dramatically represents herself as being almost at the point she describes—losing her voice altogether" (1990: 159). While O'Higgins understands speech to be the central question in fragment 31, she does not call into question the status of Sappho as its speaker; to the contrary, her account of fragment 31 as representation of "the poet's own voicelessness" uses the silence of Sappho to reinstate her as speaking subject within an unequivocally oral tradition.

Jesper Svenbro proposes, instead, that we read Sappho as the subject of writing, or rather as a subject displaced by writing. He situates fragment 31 in the context of emerging literacy around the time of Sappho and suggests that the break in *glōssa eage* reflects on the conversion of her voice into writing: "Sappho understands that, as a consequence of writing, she will be absent, even dead. For although her poem takes the form of a transcription of a living voice, that voice "breaks" (line 9) even as she transcribes it. She loses her voice as she writes the poem" (1993: 152). In this reading of fragment 31, Sappho is still present in the written speech act of her poem, but soon to be separated from what she has written; hence she is "almost dead"—but not quite yet, or not for long, since the poem is triangulated in such a way that Sappho may be revived by the voice of a reader, who lives in a future when she will be dead. Thus Sappho's "death by writing" is also the birth of reading: Sappho speaks as "I" (in the first person) in order to predict how the reader ("that man" in the third person) will read her poem (addressed as "you" in the second person). What is unusual about this configuration, according to Svenbro, is the personification of the written utterance as "you," in contrast to archaic inscriptions in which the inscribed object refers to itself in the first person, names its writer in the third person, and addresses the reader (directly or indirectly) in the second person. However, fragment 31 is unique in allowing both writer and reader to address the poem as "you," with the effect of animating the writing itself, giving it face and voice.

This prosopopoeia becomes increasingly complex, however, in the rhetorical triangle described by Svenbro. In order to allegorize how Sappho "loses her voice" in writing, he assumes an originary voice that exists prior to writing and may be recuperated by the reader. Indeed, he confidently invokes what "Sappho understands . . . as a consequence of writ-ing" without acknowledging that personification as a consequence of his own reading. But did "Sappho" ever own the voice that she "loses"? Where, in the continual rotation of speakers, shall we locate a first-person utterance? The position of a first-person speaker keeps shifting (the girl speaking to the man, "Sappho" speaking to the girl, "the reader" speak-ing to the poem) and in each case what the address to "you" conceals is an objectified utterance that is already dead or rather was never alive to begin with: instead, it is personified by means of a second-person address. Indeed, what happens when the reader who "voices" the poem in the first-person singular encounters the break in line 9 and repeats its broken tongue? Isn't the reader, like Sappho, already an effect of that break? The prosopopoeia of fragment 31 produces a speaker whose utterance points to the impossibility of a speaker and so introduces another triangle where this logic repeats itself.

To stabilize this infinite regress, Svenbro's allegorical reading of frag-ment 31 conjures up the figure of a "Reader" to take the place of the writer. The disappearance of Sappho as the "mortal" writer guarantees the appearance of an "immortal" reader, each fixed in seemingly sym-metrical relation to the other through the personification of the poem as "you." But can such a "Reader" offer, or be, the final answer to a poem in which first, second, and third person positions are asymmetrical and self-dislocating? Does the lyric triangle stop here, or will reading fragment 31 exceed every attempt to achieve the position of the first person "I"? By virtue of its own prosopopoeia, fragment 31 does not lead to the discov-ery of the poem as "you," but rather, to the discovery that "you" is the per-sonification of an "it" that remains mute. What we discover, in other words, is neither the death of Sappho as speaker nor the death of speak-ing voice as such, but dead letters that leave us deaf and dumb: hence, tongue is broken. How is "Sappho" to be recuperated from that break— except, perhaps, as a name for it?

Thus fragment 31 proves to be another version of the Sapphic riddle: a riddling that makes lyric reading possible even while resisting it. Re-peatedly the fragment provokes an attempt to phenomenalize voice, by means of the prosopopoeia it sets into motion; we try to read the letters of the poem as if they are a letter from Sappho. Yet a rhetorical reading of Sappho as the speaking subject is complicated, as we have seen, by the dislocations of the grammatical subject in the poem. The disjunction be-tween rhetorical and grammatical reading returns us to reading on the level of the letter: the phenomenon that we call Sappho is literally "gram-matized" in the letters of the poem, the *aphōna grammata* that ask to, yet cannot, be voiced.

The repetition of this riddling logic determines the afterlife of Sappho, who is made to speak "posthumously" as a lyric subject precisely because she does not speak. In the treatise "On the Sublime" attributed to "Longinus," fragment 31 is singled out as an example of sublime poetry. The transportation of letters in the Sapphic riddle is here redefined as a movement of sublime transport: not only a horizontal movement (transporting Sappho to the reader, across the distance of space and time) but also a vertical movement (transporting the reader up to the "height" or *hypsos* of Sappho). In his commentary on fragment 31, Longinus poses the riddle in the form of a rhetorical question. "Are you not amazed," he asks, "how at one and the same moment she seeks out soul, body, hearing, tongue, sight, complexion as though they had all left her and were external, and how in contradiction she both freezes and burns, is irrational and sane, is afraid and nearly dead, so that we observe in her not one single emotion but a concourse of emotions? All this of course happens to people in love; but as I said, it is her selection of the most important details and her combination of them into a single whole that have produced the excellence of the poem" (Campbell 80–81). To answer his own question, Longinus makes Sappho speak "in contradiction" (*alogistei*) about her own predicament. Thus he repeats the logic of the Sapphic riddle: he cites the text of fragment 31 and then converts its *aphōna grammata* into a figural body, in order to discover its voice. He conflates poet and poem: in his reading, Sappho is simultaneously losing composure and composing herself, falling apart *in* the poem and coming together *as* a poem that seems to speak, with heightened eloquence, to the reader.

It is Longinus who makes Sappho eloquent, however, by paraphrasing the poem and making it speak thus, "as I said." While his first sentence enumerates the parts of Sappho "as though they had all left her," the second sentence begins with a unifying phrase ("all this") that reintegrates these parts "into a single whole." She is on the verge of death, torn apart by contradictory emotions, yet comes to life through the "selection" and "combination" of these details into a formal structure. The disintegrating body of Sappho is incorporated into the "body" of the poem, which Longinus reads as if it were alive: his paraphrase serves to animate her text and to revive Sappho as its speaker, even if—*especially* if—she seems to have died. This movement between literal disintegration and figurative reconstitution is the sublime turn that Neil Hertz, in "A Reading of Longinus," identifies throughout the treatise on the sublime: a transfer of power, reversing passive and active elements, is dramatized in "the shift from Sappho-as-victimized-body to Sappho-as-poetic-force" (1985: 7). Longinus therefore quotes Sappho to confirm the doctrine of organic unity, the belief that a poem must be organized like a living organism in order to speak.

Yet as Hertz points out, fragment 31 becomes sublime precisely when the figure of the body is most threatened: "It is clear that Longinus admires the poem because when it becomes 'like a living creature' and 'finds its voice,' it speaks of a moment of self-estrangement in language that captures the disorganized quality of the experience" (5). What fragment 31 speaks, in other words, is the violence of its own speaking; its speech is a catachresis, an "abuse" of language that makes us aware of the violent power inherent in the sublime. Throughout the treatise Longinus emphasizes the powerful impact of sublime language: "A well-timed flash of sublimity scatters everything before it like a bolt of lightning and reveals the full power of the speaker at a single stroke" (1.4, Fyfe 124–25).[11] In fragment 31, however, that scattering force is turned against the speaker, who appears sublime precisely because she is scattered. Sappho is subjected to an external force that demonstrates the persistence of an ecstatic moment in the sublime and cannot be recuperated in terms of a self.[12]

Not only does fragment 31 leave Sappho suspended in *ekstasis,* literally standing outside of a self, but the fragment leaves its reader in a suspended state as well. According to Longinus, sublime rhetoric may strike us down but it is also uplifting, "as if we had ourselves produced the very thing we heard" (7.2, Fyfe 138–39). In his reading of fragment 31, we see the shifting identifications that structure the Longinian sublime. The self-scattering in Sappho's fragment is transferred to the reader, who is also scattered in the process of reading it. Longinus himself enacts this transferential logic by repeating the movement of Sappho's poem in his own prose: the "concourse of emotions" that he discovers in his analysis of fragment 31 nearly causes his own sentence to fall apart, until he takes recourse to his synthesis of the poem as an organic unity. Rhetorical effect is thus transposed into readerly affect, the transport of a reader who is "mastered" by the power of sublime language and therefore identifies with the fate of Sappho. Longinus takes the place of Sappho in order to enact his own displacement or *ekstasis,* momentarily standing outside of himself. He too is ravished and shattered by submitting to the violence of a sublime scenario that threatens to leave him speechless, as well.

For this reason Sappho plays a crucial role in the treatise on the sublime. Indeed, "the 'broken tongue' of Sappho could be an emblem of the Longinian sublime," as Paul Fry suggests, because it "represents the lapse into incoherences, the disarticulation of syntax . . . that is caused by certain figures of speech"; what interests Longinus is "the moment of dis-

---

[11] I shall refer to Longinus by section numbers and page numbers, corresponding to the Greek text and Fyfe's English translation in the Loeb edition (Fyfe and Roberts, 1991).

[12] Guerlac cites fragment 31 within the context of the treatise on the sublime, to demonstrate "a more radical force at work in the Longinian sublime, one which threatens the very notion of the subjectivity, or the unified self-identity of the subject" (1985: 275).

memberment, and he expects that moment will be represented in language that risks inarticulateness" (1983: 56–57). The disfiguring of the body is a recurring theme in the sublime passages Longinus chooses to quote in his treatise, and determines his choice of rhetorical figures as well; he considers figures such as hyperbaton, asyndeton, and polyptoton to be sublime, precisely because they rupture syntax. Sappho's syntactic dismemberment is evident in the final stanzas of fragment 31, just barely held together by "and" (*de* in Greek). Repeated seven times, the conjunction emphasizes the increasing disjunction of the Sapphic body: "*and* under my skin runs fire *and* I do not see with my eyes *and* ears roar *and* sweat drips down *and* trembling takes hold of me *and* greener than grass I am *and* dead." In the Longinian paraphrase of the fragment, however, this polysyndeton becomes an asyndeton that emphasizes even more dramatically the scattering of Sappho. "She seeks out soul, body, hearing, tongue, sight, complexion as though they had all left her and were external," Longinus writes, leaving out the conjunctions in order to cut the "body" of the poem into even smaller pieces. Rather than reintegrating a unified lyric subject, Longinus therefore perpetuates the fragmentation of Sappho. He reads the fragment as a living body, only to mutilate that bodily figure; he incorporates part of the Sapphic corpus, only to present us with an already-dismembered corpse.

As Longinus performs his autopsy on Sappho, he produces a lyric subject that is not only dead but increasingly feminized. Here the figure of Sappho—or rather the violent disfiguring of that bodily figure—points to a gendered subtext throughout the Longinian treatise, which often describes the impact of sublime language on a reader in terms of masculine domination and feminine submission. Because Sappho is identified with the figurative feminization of the reader, she also becomes identifiable *as* a feminine figure through that very structure of transference. Gender is generally and perhaps inevitably implicated in any account of the sublime, as Hertz acknowledges: "Questions of gender enter here: when these dramas turn violent, women are frequently the victims of choice— are they bound to be?" (1985: 223). Yet Hertz does not articulate the implications of this question for his own reading of Longinus, where the description of Sappho as victimized body makes that choice seem inevitable.[13] Is it coincidence that Longinus quotes Sappho—the only poet presumed to be a woman in the treatise on the sublime—precisely when

---

[13] In a feminist critique of Hertz, Freeman questions why Sappho must be read as a "victimized body" and argues that "Sappho rather describes a kind of excess that cannot exist within Hertz's (or Longinus') conceptual framework" (21). Freeman uses fragment 31 as model for a feminine sublime that is defined in terms of radical flux, self-dispersal, and "a potentially unrecuperable excess" (22); the recuperation of Sappho as "woman poet" within Freeman's conceptual framework remains open to question, however.

he wishes to embody an argument for organic unity that is both deeply ironic and full of pathos? If Sappho is bound to be victimized by this argument, however, the reason is not that she exists as a female body prior to the Longinian reading of fragment 31, but that the Sapphic body is gendered in the very process of being read: it bears the mark of gender, posthumously, by bearing its own death. The reception of Sappho therefore produces an increasingly morbid repetition of the Sapphic riddle. Rather than bearing infants that come to life when they are delivered to the reader, Sappho gives birth to a tradition of lyric reading that kills the very thing it would bring to life.

Afterlife in Translation

The transmission of Sappho depends on multiple translations of fragment 31, transporting Sappho into a lyric tradition that reads her—in the wake of Longinus—not only as example of, but also the ideal medium for, sublime transport. Thus Sappho lives on beyond death, but only in translation. In his theoretical reflections on translation, Walter Benjamin defines *übersetzen* as a form of *überleben,* a survival or "living on" within an original text that is manifested in its translations. "A translation issues from the original—not so much from its life as from its afterlife," he writes in "The Task of the Translator" (1982: 71), emphasizing that this task is, by definition, to fail: to give up the original and allow it to survive in another form. Indeed, only through the failure (*Aufgabe*) of the translator can the original be renewed: "For in its afterlife—which could not be called that if it were not a transformation and a renewal of something living—the original undergoes a change" (73). The relationship between *übersetzen* and *überleben* is exemplified in the *Nachleben* of Sappho, whose afterlife is both cause and effect of translation: Sappho survives as something simultaneously translating itself and being translated, as both the active principle "in" translation and the product "of" translation.

This point about the double valence of prepositions like "in" and "of," which mark "a vacillation between two modes, active and passive, transitive and intransitive, on either side of the relation they splice" is made by Philip Lewis in his essay "The Measure of Translation Effects." Sappho, too, is a translation effect: her sublimity is a function of her translatability, to be measured not only in terms of a movement from "original" to "translated" text but also in terms of the reverse effect of translation on the original. Following Benjamin, Lewis argues that the task of the translator is to produce difference rather than identical meaning, to "abuse" a text in the etymological sense of *ab-use:* as the preposition *ab* indicates, translation swerves away from the uses of the original text, departing from this origin in order to expose its already self-differing structure. Insofar as this abusiveness also implies a violation of meaning, it is not a random act of textual violence but directed at a specific place in the text to be translated: "a decisive textual knot that will be recognized by dint of its own abusive features" (1985: 32). Thus, Lewis concludes, the translator will "rearticulate analogically the abuse that occurs in the original text," by actively reproducing that original abuse and reactively transforming it (42–43).

In fragment 31, which we have already recognized, "by dint of its own abusive features," as a self-defacing text, the breaking of the tongue is the "decisive textual knot" that forces translators into abuse or excess of the original. In attempting to make Sappho speak, every translator repeats the break in fragment 31; inevitably, Sappho must be translated again. The repetition of the break nevertheless renews the original, allowing it to live on by manifesting something that is both in and beyond the original: the hiatus between *glōssa* and *eage,* the very moment when "tongue" is "broken." Sappho's broken tongue therefore lends itself to perpetual translation, in many different tongues, and indeed in the long history of translating fragment 31, we discover the radical literalism of that broken tongue: a literal *lingua* that points to "pure language" (*reine Sprache*) as Benjamin defines it, demonstrating not only the differences between languages but the internal disjunction—the *glōssa eage*—within every language.[14]

The historical consequences of Sappho's broken tongue vary, of course, according to the specific context of each translation. Sappho enters into the tradition of English lyric through numerous versions of fragment 31, and as Lawrence Lipking has noted, "A history of lyric poetry could be written by following the ways that later poets have adapted her lines to their own purposes."[15] I want to consider several translations of fragment 31 that I take to be paradigmatic, in different ways, for the gendering of Sappho as a female lyric subject over the course of several centuries: a seventeenth-century version by John Hall who introduces Sappho to English readers by way of Longinus, an influential version by Ambrose Philips who suspends Sappho "in transport" according to the conventions of the eighteenth-century sublime, and a representative ver-

---

[14] For further discussion on the literalism of Benjamin's *reine Sprache,* demonstrated in particular by the "monstrosity" of interlinear translation, see Jacobs 1975.

[15] Lipking surveys Sappho "descending" and "ascending" in various translations and imitations of fragment 31 from Catullus onward (1988: 57–126). See also Warren, who describes the history of translating fragment 31 as "a small instance of lyric lineage, a type of model for poetry's perpetual re-engendering of itself" (1989: 200); Barnstone, who compares several English versions of the fragment to illustrate a poetics of translation (1993: 98–105); Greer, who traces "the erotic tradition founded by Sappho" by tracing versions of fragment 31 from the Renaissance to the nineteenth century (1995: 132ff.); and Prins 1997 (in an earlier version of the present argument).

sion by Mary Hewitt who associates Sappho with a nineteenth-century rhetoric of the sentimental suffering body. Each of these versions is mediated by the Longinian reading of Sappho, in order to rearticulate in English what is missing from the Greek text of fragment 31: the "voice" of Sappho, pronounced dead at the very moment of its recovery. The increasingly violent repetition of Sappho's broken tongue also determines the gender of Sappho in the very process of transmission, demonstrating the mutual implication of gender and genre in a tradition that turns to Sappho as exemplary lyric subject.

I begin with John Hall, who is not the first to imitate Sappho in English but does offer the first version of fragment 31 taken directly from Greek, as part of his translation of Longinus: *Peri Hypsous or Dionysius Longinus of the Height of Eloquence rendered out of the Original,* published in 1652. Translating Sappho within the context of the Longinian sublime, Hall introduces her into the tradition of English lyric as an apparently self-recuperating lyric subject:

> He that sits next to thee now and hears
> Thy charming voyce, to me appears
> Beauteous as any Deity
> >That rules the skie.
>
> How did his pleasing glances dart
> Sweet languors to my ravish'd heart
> At the first sight though so prevailed
> >That my voyce fail'd.
>
> I'me speechless, feavrish, fires assail
> My fainting flesh, my sight doth fail
> Whilst to my restless mind my ears
> >Still hum new fears.
>
> Cold sweats and tremblings so invade
> That like a wither'd flower I fade
> So that my life being almost lost,
> >I seem a Ghost.
> Yet since I'me wretched must I dare . . .

Hall preserves the first line of the fifth stanza and recuperates Sappho from the moment of near death, so that she may live on past the ellipses. Indeed, Hall's Sappho seems to "quicken" in every sense: although her life is "almost lost" and she might "seem a Ghost," in the rapid stanzas of this translation her mind is "restless," her ears "still hum" and she speaks emphatically "now" in the present tense.

Only momentarily does Hall's translation lapse into the past tense, in describing how "voyce fail'd" in stanza 2. The failure of voice is therefore projected into the past while stanza 3 immediately shifts back to the present: "I'me speechless." In this temporal transition it is difficult to locate the exact moment when the tongue breaks: the sequence of the Greek (where "no speaking is left in me" is followed by "tongue is broken") seems to be reversed in the English (where "my voyce fail'd" is followed by "I'm speechless"), so that voice seems to fail *before* rather than *after* the inability to speak. The implication here is that voice can still be recovered through speech, even if the speaker is temporarily speechless, and this recovery of voice is already implied at the beginning of Hall's poem, where the Greek phrase "sweet speaking" is translated, proleptically, into "charming voyce." If Hall's Sappho has lost her tongue in this poem, it is never quite as literally as the tongue breaking in fragment 31. Nowhere, in fact, does the word "tongue" appear in this English translation, which insists on the persistence of voice without leaving much room for the linguistic break in Greek—except perhaps in the break between stanzas 2 and 3. This stanzaic break creates an empty space, a silent interruption, in a poem that otherwise flows with effortless rhymes; here, in the breaking of Sappho's tongue between two stanzas and its disappearance into that break, we rediscover the hiatus of *glōssa eage*. The death of Sappho haunts the white spaces between stanzas, as the spectral emanation or afterlife of the Greek text: "I seem a Ghost."

What do we make of this ghostly manifestation of Sappho's broken tongue? If Hall seems to bring Sappho back to life, it is to inscribe her death into the margins of this English translation after all—not only in the stanzaic break but in the final line: "Yet since I'me wretched must I dare . . ." The ellipses here open the possibility for various interpretations, allowing the utterance to be recontextualized. When fragment 31 is placed within the larger context of Sappho's Renaissance reception, a reader might speculate about another, more familiar ending to Hall's translation: perhaps, like Ovid's Sappho, she is "wretched" in her unrequited love for Phaon and therefore "must dare" to perform her suicide— the infamous leap from the Leucadian cliff into the waters of posterity, as described by Ovid in "Sappho to Phaon." Throughout the Renaissance Sappho is primarily known by the Ovidian narrative, which transforms Sappho of Lesbos into a woman love-struck by a man and the translation by Catullus, who transforms the poem of Sappho into the expression of a man love-struck by a woman. This heterosexual reading of Sappho explains, as well, the change of pronouns in Hall's translation of fragment 31: no longer addressed to a girl, it describes "How did *his* pleasing glances dart / Sweet languors to my ravish'd heart." Hall exploits the ambiguous anacoluthon in Greek to suggest it is not the girl but the man (Phaon?) who leaves Sappho "ravish'd" in stanza 2, and erotically deflowered in stanza 4: "Cold sweats and tremblings so invade / That like a wither'd flower I fade." Pierced by his "pleasing glances," Sappho acquires lyric subjectivity through subjection to a man whose presence is more central in Hall's translation than he ever was in the Greek.

Indeed the presence of the man proves to be a rhetorical necessity in Hall's translation, which is mediated not only by Longinus and Ovid but also by the conventions of Renaissance love lyric. The ravishing of Sappho by a male gaze allows fragment 31 to be read as another version of Petrarchanism, described by Nancy Vickers in terms of the obsessive dismembering and re-membering of the female body by male poets. Vickers argues that the scattering of Laura's body in Petrarch's scattered rhymes allows his voice to emerge while her speech is silenced—or rather, reified as another one of the many body parts enumerated but never unified by Petrarch. Hall's Sappho therefore "speaks" from the position of Petrarch's Laura, through a Petrarchan legacy of fragmentation that, according to Vickers, leaves "bodies fetishized by a poetic voice" and poetic voice fetishized as one of the "exquisitely reified parts" of the body (107). Here the logic of Petrarchan lyric converges with the Longinian reading of fragment 31, to produce Sappho as a paradoxical lyric subject: she is made to speak as "woman poet," but only by dying.

The Sapphic body undergoes even more violent fragmentation in the following century, as Addison introduces Sappho to readers of the *Spectator* in 1711: she is one of the "famous Pieces of Antiquity," to be compared to "the Trunc of a Statue which has lost the Arms, Legs, and Head" (*Spectator* No. 229). Recalling how Michelangelo learned "his whole Art" from a "maimed Statue," Addison urges readers to find beauty in Sappho's "mutilated Figure." The fragmentary Sapphic corpus is therefore identified with the mutilation of the body, or rather the dismembered simulacrum of a body: a maimed and truncated statue, serving as the figure for a literal disintegration that can only be made whole by translation. Just as the artist is inspired to breathe new life into broken images, Addison claims, the translator revives the spirit of Sappho from scattered fragments: indeed, because he insists that Sappho is "extreamly [sic] difficult to render into another Tongue," it would seem that the inspiration for rendering Sappho in English derives directly from the rending of Sappho into many parts.

The translator Addison cites as example is Ambrose Philips, whose version of fragment 31 is "written in the very Spirit of Sappho." If this translation is indeed inspired, however, it is by figuring Sappho's broken tongue as loss of breath:

Bles't as th'Immortal Gods is he,
The Youth who fondly sits by thee,
And hears and sees thee all the while
Softly speak and sweetly smile.

'Twas this depriv'd my Soul of Rest,
And rais'd such Tumults in my Breast;
For while I gaz'd, in Transport tost,
My Breath was gone, my Voice was lost;

My Bosom glow'd; the subtle Flame
Ran quick thro' all my vital Frame;
O'er my dim Eyes a Darkness hung;
My Ears with hollow Murmurs rung:

In dewy Damps my Limbs were chill'd;
My Blood with gentle Horrours thrill'd;
My feeble Pulse forgot to play;
I fainted, sunk, and dy'd away.

The break in *glōssa eage* is conveyed in the comma between "My Breath was gone, my Voice was lost." The lack of a conjunction indicates a disjunction in Sapphic voice which can only be recovered as posthumous utterance; this translation leaves no doubt that Sappho is dead. Like Hall, Philips shifts from present to past tense in stanza 2, but unlike Hall he does not return to the present. The final line is a series of verbs in the past tense, "I fainted, sunk, and dy'd away," as if spoken by a dead speaker, now fallen into silence.

Nevertheless Sappho is reanimated by detailed description of the dying body, which quickens as "the subtle Flame / Ran quick thro' all my vital Frame." In a note to his translation, published in *Odes of Anacreon and Sappho* (1711:74–75), Philips writes that fragment 31 is "the most inimitable Example of the most artificial Union, or rather Combat, of all the Passions, and of all the moving Circumstances that can enliven a piece" (69–70). Although the fragment seems "inimitable," Philips imitates its "moving Circumstances" in the movement of his translation. The language becomes tumultuous, beginning with "such Tumults in my Breast" and leading into a series of verbs that appeal vividly to the senses: the bosom that "glow'd" and the fire that "ran quick," the darkness that "hung" and the ears that "rung," the limbs that were "chill'd" and the blood that "thrill'd." The "vital Frame" of Sappho is revitalized in the elaborate structure of his own verse, in the framing of its rhythm and rhyme: the division of stanzas into two rhyming couplets, the division of couplets into two lines, the division of lines into two balanced phrases, the division of phrases into four syllables each, the division of syllables into phonemes, the division of phonemes into letters. Thus Philips seems to "enliven" the piece (or pieces) of Sappho: she is divided into separate parts yet also held together in "the most artificial Union," in the formal mechanism of his versification. This artful recomposition of the Sapphic body produces rapture at the very moment of rupture and is explicitly named sublime in line 7: Sappho is "in Transport tost," transported by a translator who breathes life into her dying body and allows her poem to live on beyond death.

According to Addison, the translation by Philips is "as near the Greek as the Genius of our language will possibly suffer" (*Spectator* No. 229). The appeal of fragment 31 is not only that Sappho suffers death, but that the rendering of Sappho's tongue into another tongue does violence to "our language" as well: the English language must suffer in order to create new possibilities for expression. Indeed, it is only by repeating the death of Sappho so dramatically that the mechanical movement of the Philips translation can be infused with spirit and enthusiasm: the "feeble Pulse" of Sappho's dying body nevertheless pulsates in English, which seems increasingly animated ("with hollow Murmurs rung" and "with gentle Horrours thrill'd") as Sappho is de-animated. Thus Philips performs the Longinian sublime as a form of suffering that is directed against the "body" of his own language, bringing it to life in the very pathos of this rhetorical performance.

Such pathos—not to say bathos—increasingly determines the course of Sappho's reception in England, making Philips the most influential English translator of Sappho throughout the eighteenth century, and well into the nineteenth. Addison ignores all previous versions of Sappho when he introduces Philips as the first English translator of the Sapphic fragments, and in William Smith's popular edition of Longinus (first published in 1739 and reprinted numerous times to displace earlier editions of the treatise, including the translations by Boileau and Hall) the Philips version of fragment 31 is presented as if it is, without question, the best. The rhetoric of suffering that Philips associates with Sappho is amplified in Smith's note on fragment 31, where he considers her "tormenting Emotions" and "variety of Torture" to be the "Subject of the Ode" (Smith 1739: 134). By transferring the torments of Sapphic passion to the passionately tortured language of the Philips translation, Smith implies that Sappho is no longer the subject of the poem; the "Subject of the Ode" has become the moment of "Transport" itself.

The conversion of Sappho into an exemplary medium for sublime transport contributes to the gendering of eighteenth-century discourses on the sublime and defines a "Sapphic" strain in Romantic lyric as well.[16] Byron mocks the fashion for imitations of Sappho inspired by Longinus: "I don't think Sappho's Ode a good example / Although Longinus tells us there is no hymn / Where the sublime soars forth on wings more ample" (*Don Juan* I:42). Sappho's name has become synonymous with the sentimentalism of women's verse, where (in Byron's pun) "no hymn" is also "no him." Ambrose Philips therefore acquires the reputation of "Namby-Pamby," an effeminate poet who is emasculated by a translation that now seems too pathetic, too closely associated with a "feminized" literary market that thrives on pathos. His version of Sappho is widely read in nineteenth-century anthologies such as *The Household Book of Poetry* (Dana 1857: 257), and the broad appeal of fragment 31 to women poets in particular leads Byron to ask, "Is not Philips' translation of it in the mouths of all your women?" (Robinson 1963: 199–200). This tongue-in-cheek question has serious implications, however, for the women writers who align themselves with Sappho. How do all those women speak, with Sappho's broken tongue in their mouths? How do they revive a lyric voice that is predicated on its own death? If the translation of fragment 31 by Philips is reputed to be as close to Greek as the English language will "suffer," women poets perform that suffering in even more extravagant terms, making the body bear witness—ironically—to the disembodiment of Sapphic voice.

Mary Hewitt, for example, is an American "Poetess" not nearly so well known in the history of translating Sappho as Ambrose Philips, but nevertheless representative of the contribution made by nineteenth-century women poets to Sappho's afterlife in translation. Hewitt's "Translation of an Ode of Sappho" was published in *The Broadway Journal* (June 14, 1845: 379) and can be read in response to Philips, as *her* translation of *his* translation:

Translation of an Ode of Sappho

Blest as the immortal gods is he
  On whom each day thy glances shine;
Who hears thy voice of melody,
  And meets thy smile so all divine.

Oh, when I list thine accents low
  How thrills my breast with tender pain—

---

[16] In a chapter on "The Sapphic Sublime and Romantic Lyricism," Vanita further traces the Longinian influence on eighteenth-century translations of Sappho and suggests how these might serve as model for the Romantic ode; her emphasis on "the intensely personal voice" of Sappho (37) differs from my argument, however.

Fire seems through every vein to glow,
  And strange confusion whelms my brain.

My sight grows dim beneath the glance
  Whose ardent rays I may not meet,
While swift and wild my pulses dance,
  Then cease all suddenly to beat.

And o'er my cheek with rapid gush,
  I feel the burning life-tide dart;
Then backward like a torrent rush
  All icy cold upon my heart.

And I am motionless and pale,
  And silent as an unstrung lyre;
And feel, while thus each sense doth fail,
  Doomed in thy presence to expire.

The "vital Frame" of the Philips translation is refigured as "an unstrung lyre" of a body about "to expire," making his pun on inspiration and expiration even more explicit. However, while Philips translates Sappho's broken tongue in the past tense ("my Breath was gone"), Hewitt translates into the present tense and ends with an infinitive, to suspend Sappho in the very moment of dying.

By translating fragment 31 in the perpetual present, Hewitt makes the lyric subject embody even more dramatically the contradiction of its own speaking. In contrast to "thy voice of melody" in the first stanza, the body plays out the melody of its death in the following stanzas, until it finally falls "silent" and all senses "fail." The translation makes dying seem a desirable form of suffering, in the eroticized description of fire that "seems through every vein to glow," or the "burning life-tide" that rushes "o'er my cheek with rapid gush" and then turns "all icy cold upon my heart." What speaks, in other words, is a body made eloquent by "tender pain—." The dash functions here like the hiatus in *glōssa eage*, to mark a disjunction; it points to the separation of voice and body, a body that is anatomized in this poem to describe the symptoms of its suffering with pseudo-medical objectivity, as if the dying body were already a corpse. It speaks, in other words, in anticipation of a death that is both the condition and the consequence of speaking. Indeed the title reminds us that this translation "of" an ode "of" Sappho merely reiterates a death that has been spoken of before: it is the repetition of a death that has already happened, more than once.

Hewitt's translation was published by Edgar Allan Poe, then the editor of *The Broadway Journal,* in the same issue that also features his own lurid tale, "The Premature Burial." It is no coincidence that Poe's story appears in conjunction with Hewitt's translation, since both present the reader with the paradox of a speaking corpse. Poe's account of "living inhumation" replays the sublime scenario of fragment 31, as he describes a man "seemingly dead" who survived his own burial and "in broken sentences spoke of his agonies in the grave" (1845: 370). Poe also describes how another man "pronounced *dead* by his physicians" revived and "then— spoke," much to everyone's "rapturous astonishment" (370). Finally, he describes his own "authentic" experience of death: "I grew sick, and numb, and chilly, and dizzy, and so fell prostrate at once," and when buried, "I endeavored to shriek . . . but no voice issued" (372). As Poe turns his increasingly extravagant report of "authenticated instances" into a fiction that comically exposes its own assumption of authentic voice ("I read . . . no bugaboo tales—*such as this*," 373), his story raises a question about the authenticity of Hewitt's claim to Sapphic voice as well. Is fragment 31 another premature burial? Can Sappho, pronounced dead, be resuscitated to speak of her agonies in the grave? If Hewitt seems to exhume Sappho as a case of "living inhumation"—a dead speaker who keeps coming back to life—nevertheless her translation also demonstrates the impossibility of bringing Sappho back from the dead. The more Sappho is read as a figure for a living voice, the more that voice proclaims itself no longer alive: a fitting epilogue to Poe's story.

"The death of a beautiful woman is, unquestionably, the most poetical topic in the world," Poe writes in "The Philosophy of Composition," ironically transforming an organic model of poetry into a form of mechanical repetition (1965: 3.211). Indeed, insofar as a tradition of lyric poetry is predicated on the death of Sappho in particular, it would seem that Sappho is the very embodiment of Poe's proposition: her death has become a recurring topos among Poe's contemporaries and especially among the women poets of the day, who call upon Sappho to authorize a voice that proclaims itself dead, again and again. While Poe's response to that rhetorical predicament is parody, Mary Hewitt responds by translating Sappho into the sentimental rhetoric of the suffering body. Hewitt's Sappho embodies the contradictions of the nineteenth-century "Poetess," as a figure for spontaneous utterance that is nevertheless entirely and self-consciously conventional. To bear witness to the impossibility of speaking in an "original" voice, she therefore performs her own death in increasingly hyperbolic terms.

In a later version of fragment 31, entitled "Imitation of Sappho" (1854: 56), Hewitt reflects further on the ironies of declaring Sapphic voice:

Imitation of Sappho

> If to repeat thy name when none may hear me,
>> To find thy thought with all my thoughts inwove;

To languish where thou'rt not—to sigh when near thee—
    Oh! if this be to love thee, I do love!

If when thou utterest low words of greeting,
    To feel through every vein the torrent pour;
Then back again the hot tide swift retreating,
    Leave me all powerless, silent as before—

If to list breathless to thine accents falling,
    Almost to pain, upon my eager ear;
And fondly when alone to be recalling
    The words that I would die again to hear—

If at thy glance my heart all strength forsaking,
    Pant in my breast as pants the frighted dove;
If to think on thee ever, sleeping—waking—
    Oh! if this be to love thee, I do love!

Here again Hewitt uses fragment 31 to anatomize a body suffering "almost to pain," according to the conventions of sentimental love lyric. The seemingly spontaneous overflow of powerful feeling becomes "the torrent" pouring through every vein, "the hot tide" rising in the blood and then ebbing, to leave behind a speaker who is paradoxically speechless, "silent as before—" and "breathless." This breathlessness is conveyed throughout the poem in the abundant use of dashes, much as the dash appears in the earlier translation of fragment 31 to convey the break in Sappho's broken tongue. And again, by exchanging breath for the panting of the heart "in my breast," Hewitt finally locates the utterance not in a living voice but in a dying body, at the moment when inspiration and expiration coincide, in the sigh of "Oh!"

Hewitt's "Imitation of Sappho" replays the scenario of her "Translation of an Ode of Sappho" and furthermore insists on its repeatability, already in the first line: "If to repeat thy name when none may hear me." While "thy name" is not heard in the poem, Sappho's name appears in the title to suggest that Hewitt's poem is not only an imitation *of* Sappho but an address *to* Sappho who does not bring voice to life. By invoking Sappho, Hewitt thus reinvokes her own translation of fragment 31, finding "thy thought with all my thoughts inwove" in order to repeat the moment of Sappho's death. In the repetition of "thy name," Hewitt may be identified with Sappho, but without being named; she turns herself into a posthumous figure by incorporating the dying words of Sappho—"the words that I would die again to hear"—into her own dying body. For to hear those words and to repeat that name without being heard means falling into silence, to lose voice, to die again. The poem is therefore presented as a nonoriginal utterance, predicated on an "if" at the beginning of each stanza that renders what "thou utterest"—as well as what "I" cannot utter—entirely conditional. In this complex mediation of Sapphic voice, the identification of Hewitt with Sappho can only be discovered as an effect of repetition, as an imitation of a translation of an ode of Sappho that plays out an infinitely repeatable death.

Hewitt's translation of fragment 31 is, in fact, only one in an endless series of nineteenth-century Sapphic imitations that are written over the dead body of Sappho, according to a logic further elaborated by Elisabeth Bronfen in *Over Her Dead Body: Death, Femininity and the Aesthetic*. In response to "the most poetical topic" infamously proposed by Poe, Bronfen asks: "What is the reciprocity between femininity and aestheticisation, between beauty and death? And above all why the unconditional 'unquestionably,' why the superlative '*most* poetical'?" (1992: 60). Woman is both the medium for aesthetic articulation and mediated by that articulation, Bronfen argues, and the incorporation of that aesthetic turns her into a dead corpse. This aestheticizing logic creates manifold representations of dying women in the nineteenth century, both visual and verbal, and increasingly makes feminine death the formal condition of representation itself, as Bronfen concludes: "The 'death of a beautiful woman' marks the *mise en abyme* of a text, the moment of self-reflexivity, where the text seems to comment on itself and its own process of composition, and so decomposes itself" (71).

If this nineteenth-century philosophy of composition seems to repeat the Longinian reading of fragment 31, the reason is that the analogy between composing a poem and decomposing a female body has become overdetermined to the point that Poe can ironically reassert the analogy in the form of a tautology: an oxymoron that is also, as Bronfen points out, a pleonasm (63). What Poe proposes "unquestionably" may be understood not only as a parody of nineteenth-century poetics and a riposte to the women poets of his day, but as his answer to the Sapphic riddle, a question repeated so often in the course of Sappho's reception that it has become moribund. For as Sappho is made to speak repeatedly through the moment of dying, and seems to speak beyond death to a lyric tradition that remembers her dismembering, fragment 31 has indeed become "the most poetical topic." In the long history of being translated, this fragment produces more and more versions of the dying Sappho and therefore "the *most*" feminine death. Thus Sappho emerges as a superlative lyric figure, whose decomposition constitutes the very possibility of poetic form. By tracing Sappho's afterlife in translation, especially in later nineteenth-century versions of fragment 31, we can now begin to see why and how Sappho contributes to the Victorian gendering of lyric as a genre simultaneously feminine and dead.

Wharton's Rend(er)ings

In 1885 Dr. Henry Wharton, a medical doctor and amateur Classicist, published *Sappho: Memoir, Text, Selected Renderings, and a Literal Translation*. It proved to be the most popular English edition of the Sapphic fragments by the turn of the century, as it went into broad circulation, reprinted in 1887, 1895, 1898, and 1907.[17] Eager to reclaim Sappho for a tradition of English verse, Wharton announces at the start of his Preface to the first edition (xv–xvi):

> SAPPHO, the Greek poetess whom more than eighty generations have been obliged to hold without a peer, has never, in the entirety of her works, been brought within the reach of English readers. The key to her wondrous reputation—which would, perhaps, be still greater if it had ever been challenged—has hitherto lain hidden in other languages than ours. As a name, as a figure pre-eminent in literary history, she has indeed never been overlooked. But the English-reading world has come to think, and to be content with thinking, that no verse of hers survives save those two hymns which Addison, in the *Spectator,* has made famous—by his panegyric, not by Ambrose Philips' translation.
>
> My aim in the present work is to familiarise English readers, whether they understand Greek or not, with every word of Sappho, by translating all the one hundred and seventy fragments that her latest German editor thinks may be ascribed to her:
>
> > Love's priestess, mad with pain and joy of song,
> > Song's priestess, mad with joy and pain of love.
> >
> > SWINBURNE.

Wharton begins by naming "SAPPHO, the Greek poetess" in order to present her "as a name, as a figure pre-eminent in literary history," with the implication that she is also a figure produced *by* literary history. Her "wondrous reputation" is the result of translation into many languages, although regrettably "in other languages than ours." In England Sappho's reputation depends primarily on Addison, who introduced Sappho to English readers through the translations of Ambrose Philips, more than two centuries earlier. While Wharton is quick to proclaim Philips outdated, he implicitly aligns himself with Addison in order to make his own claim to fame: the present edition of Sappho will be as important to posterity as Addison's "panegyric."

---

[17] Wharton added new material to the second edition (1887) and the third edition (1895); a posthumous fourth edition (1898) further includes a memoir of Wharton. Since I refer to all four editions, page citations are taken from the fourth edition (reprinted 1907 and 1974, in facsimile).

Wharton's aim is to expand the Sapphic corpus beyond the two poems most famously attributed to Sappho, by collecting all the Greek fragments alongside various English translations. His edition is authorized by German classical scholarship, which Wharton appropriates for his own purposes: not only to canonize Sappho's poetry, but to create a "Sapphic" canon in English as well. He adopts a reconstruction of the Greek text by Theodor Bergk, but even while deferring to "the latest German editor" of Sappho, he also refers to the poetic authority of Swinburne. The citation of Swinburne's name here confirms the naming of Sappho at the beginning of the preface, as Wharton quotes from "On the Cliffs" (Swinburne's panegyric to Sappho, published in 1880) to demonstrate how Sappho survives as proper name for "the poetess" in English poetry. German scholars may excel in producing critical editions of Sappho, but (so Wharton implies) English poets will be the ones to make her immortal.

While the Greek text as reconstructed by Bergk lends a scholarly appearance to Wharton's edition of Sappho, the title of his book already announces it to be a more eclectic compendium of translations, in various forms: a "memoir" that translates the testimony of ancient and modern writers into a biography of Sappho, a "literal translation" of Sappho's fragments into prose by Wharton, and a selection of "renderings" by a wide range of English poets. The book also includes a compilation of explanatory notes, various appendices, and a bibliography that lists editions, translations, and imitations of Sappho over the centuries. Wharton therefore draws on a long history of translating Sappho, in order to present her as a figure *for* translation. "Sappho is, perhaps above all other other poets, untranslatable," Wharton declares in his preface (xvi), yet her untranslatability is precisely the reason for translating Sappho again and again. He articulates this contradiction in two consecutive sentences: according to Wharton "no Englishman has hitherto undertaken the task" of a literal translation, yet "many of the fragments have been more or less successfully rendered into English verse" (xvi). The task of the translator, once again, is to succeed by failing: the attempt to translate Sappho literally produces more and more "renderings" and thus repeats the rending of Sappho into fragments.

In Wharton's edition we can read the logic of Sappho's broken tongue writ large. He has collected the work of many different translators, in the hope that Sappho can be made to speak again in English:

> My sole desire is to present "the great poetess" to English readers in a form from which they can judge of her excellence for themselves, so far as that is possible for those to whom Aeolic Greek is unfamiliar. Her more important fragments have been translated into German, French, Italian, and Spanish, as well as English; but all previous complete editions of her works have been

written solely by scholars for scholars. Now that, through the appreciation of Sappho by modern poets and painters, her name is becoming day by day more familiar, it seems time to show her as we know her to have been, to those who have neither leisure nor power to read her in the tongue in which she wrote. (Preface to first edition, xxi)

Sappho is here introduced to readers who have neither "leisure nor power to read her in the tongue in which she wrote" but can imagine Sappho in another form: translated into English and transformed into the image of "the great poetess." Wharton is more interested in the construction of this image than reconstructions of the Greek text "solely by scholars for scholars," as he readily admits. "I have not concerned myself much with textual criticism," he continues in his preface, "for I do not arrogate any power of discernment greater than that possessed by a scholar like Bergk. . . . He wrote for the learned few, and I only strive to popularise the result of such researches as his" (xxi). Wharton's professed modesty as an amateur scholar, daunted by teutonic philology, nevertheless reveals his ambition to reach a wider audience by circulating his book beyond the small circles of classical scholars: to make Sappho more popular than ever before, and thus to stake an even greater claim to fame. He would reclaim the Sapphic fragments from "Aeolic Greek" as well as other foreign tongues—German, French, Italian, Spanish—in order "to show her as *we* know her to have been," in our own native English tongue.

To popularize Sappho (as "modern poets and painters" have already done), Wharton turns her into the figure of a person; he gives a face to the name of Sappho, whose "name is becoming day by day more familiar." This prosopopoeia has been implicit in readings of the Sapphic fragments all along but is now made explicit as the necessary condition for making Sappho readable to a larger public. Wharton helps his readers to form such an image of Sappho, by presenting a portrait in the frontispiece of his edition (figure 1). Underneath the letters that spell out Sappho's name in Greek is the profile of a pensive woman, hands folded under her chin. Gazing ahead into the distance, she also directs our gaze forward to the title page, where Sappho's name appears again in English, in capital letters corresponding in size to the Greek letters in the frontispiece. The face mediates between two versions of the name, between ΣΑΠΦΩ and SAPPHO, to make Sappho visible even to a reader who cannot decipher the Greek. This translation of Sappho is further mediated by another name on the title page, as the subtitle includes Wharton's name as well. Although his name appears in smaller typeface, subordinated to the name of Sappho, nevertheless she is presented as if authored by him: SAPPHO . . . BY HENRY THORNTON WHARTON. The subtitle identifies him as simultaneously author, scholar, editor, and translator

ΣΑΠΦΩ

FIGURE 1: Frontispiece from Wharton's *Sappho,* fourth edition (1898).

of Sappho, and indeed in constructing the most popular Victorian image of Sappho his name becomes increasingly interchangeable with hers: because of the success of his book, he was "known to book-lovers as 'Sappho Wharton'" (Wharton xxiii).

Wharton's image of Sappho is mediated by two other names, as well.

On the frontispiece, below Sappho's profile, we see the signatures of the artists L. Alma-Tadema and J. Cother Webb. Wharton explains in his preface that Webb's engraving is "after the head of Sappho in the picture by Mr. L. Alma-Tadema, R. A., exhibited at the Royal Academy in 1881" (xxii). Sappho is therefore identified as an image taken from another image, a copy of a copy of Sappho, translated from one medium to another to produce the idea of the original poet, yet only partially reproduced, and signed by names that are themselves only reproductions of original signatures. Nevertheless the image featured in the frontispiece conjures up the illusion of Sappho made whole again, as she appears in Alma-Tadema's painting: a beautiful body draped in Grecian robes and surrounded by her pupils on the island of Lesbos (figure 2).[18] It is a classic portrait of "the Poetess," yet she has given away the lyre to Alcaeus who sings while she listens pensively, detached from the lyric performance. No longer the singer, Sappho has become the centerpiece of a lapidary painting that presents itself as memorial to Sapphic song. There are Greek letters inscribed in the marble seats of Sappho's amphitheater, spelling out the names of girls that Sappho once sang about, and so also we are asked to "read" the image of Sappho presented to us by Alma-Tadema: we identify Sappho by reading the name that appears—as another inscription, or epitaph—in the title of his painting, "Sappho." Sappho hovers between visual and verbal representation, allowing for the conversion of a face into a name as well as the conversion of a name into a face. It is significant, then, that only the face is reproduced in Wharton's frontispiece: Webb's engraving "after the head of Sappho" is detached from Sappho's body and attached to the title of Wharton's edition, as if the book itself might be read as the body of Sappho.

Sappho is further embodied in Wharton's introductory "memoir," giving not only a name and a face, but also a life story to the figure of Sappho. The essay, entitled "The Life of Sappho," seems to bring Sappho back to life in the image of the Victorian poetess. As in the preface, Wharton begins with an act of nomination that sounds like an invocation: "SAPPHO, the one great woman poet of the world, who called herself Psappha . . . is said to have been at the zenith of her fame about the year 610 B.C."

[18] The painting of Sappho and Alcaeus (figure 2) by Sir Laurence Alma-Tadema (1836–1912) is described by Johnston, who notes that "the head of Sappho conforms to ancient portraits [of Sappho] such as the Valla Albani and the Oxford busts" (1982: 206). Indeed in this painting Sappho seems carved out of marble, as Alma-Tadema (characteristically) plays with various sculptural effects: the pallor of her skin matches the hues of the amphitheater, the folds of her robe repeat the lines sculpted in the circular seat, and her hair is gathered in the nape of her neck like the two busts in the background, facing out toward the sea. Just as these sculptures are literally an architectural extension of the amphitheater, Sappho is a figurative extension of the marble monument that frames and monumentalizes her as a lyric figure.

FIGURE 2: *Sappho and Alcaeus*, Sir Laurence Alma-Tadema (1881). The Walters Art Gallery, Baltimore.

He emphasizes what "is said" of Sappho, because she does not speak for herself; there are no "authentic records of the history of Sappho" and "little even of that internal evidence, upon which biography may rely, can be gathered from her extant poems, in such fragmentary form have they come down to us" (2–3). To write the life of Sappho as a woman who lived long ago, Wharton must first acknowledge that she is missing from history, and survives only "in fragmentary form." Indeed his account of Sappho begins, as most popular accounts still do, with the burning of the Sapphic fragments as a figure for the immolation of Sappho, as if she herself had to be burned in order to earn her epithet "burning Sappho."

It is precisely because of the loss of evidence, however, that Wharton is able to construct Sappho as a character in a "biography" authenticated—in the absence of "authentic records"—by the accumulation of various kinds of testimony from ancient and modern writers. Repeatedly Wharton emphasizes that nothing is known of Sappho's life, yet this lack of knowledge does not prevent him from creating a life story according to the conventions of biographical writing. "Of Sappho's parents nothing is definitely known," he writes and then proceeds to trace a detailed genealogy. He names her father and mother, her brothers and daughter, although he seems less certain of Sappho's claim to a husband ("the existence of such a husband has been warmly disputed," 7). Her dates of birth and death are also unclear: "how long she lived we cannot tell," Wharton admits, even while speculating about the exact dates of her "flourishing" (9). He dismisses Sappho's leap from the Leucadian Cliff as a legend, yet devotes a long discussion to the geographical location of the Cliff, and concludes finally that "it is strange that none of the many authors who relate the legend say what was the result of the leap—whether it was fatal to her life" (18). Indeed, it would seem in his essay on "The Life of Sappho" that Sappho has not died at all, as her life is entirely defined by her afterlife. If the essay begins by lamenting the lack of evidence about Sappho's life, it concludes by celebrating her fame "in the face of so much testimony to Sappho's genius" (48), for it is through such testimony that Sappho has been personified—given a face and a name—over the centuries.

In order to write the life of Sappho, Wharton therefore reads it into the poetry with which she is later identified. He draws on a long tradition of biographical reading that conflates the beauty of Sappho's poems with Sappho herself: "But though we know so little of Sappho's personal appearance, the whole testimony of the ancient writers describes the charm of her poetry with unbounded praise. Strabo, in his Geography, calls her 'something wonderful,' (θαύμαστόν τι χρῆμα) and says he knew 'no woman who in any, even the least degree, could be compared to her for poetry' (cf. p.10). Such was her unique renown that she was called 'The

Poetess' just as Homer was 'The Poet'" (27). Sappho is made to appear as a person through her poetry, not despite but *because* "we know so little of Sappho's personal appearance." In Strabo's description we see how she is progressively personified: "the charm of her poetry" makes Sappho into "something wonderful," a neuter thing (a *thaumaston ti chrēma*, literally "a thing that is a marvel") that is then gendered feminine, a woman who is comparable to "no woman," less a female person than an idealized feminine persona, "The Poetess." Twice Wharton quotes Strabo to make this point, as he refers us back to a previous page ("cf. p.10") where Sappho is singled out as a person among "the celebrated men" from the Island of Lesbos and then made into a woman whose celebrity has outlived them all: "Strabo in his *Geography* says: 'Mitylene (Μιτυλήνη or Μυτιλήνη) is well provided with everything. It formerly produced celebrated men, such as Pittacus, one of the Seven Wise Men; Alcaeus the poet, and others. Contemporary with these persons flourished Sappho, who was something wonderful; at no period within memory has any woman been known who in any, even the least degree, could be compared to her for poetry.' Indeed, the glory of Lesbos was that Sappho was its citizen, and its chief fame centres in the fact of her celebrity" (10–11). The complete quotation from Strabo is introduced here—to be repeated later—in order to authorize the personification of Sappho as an explicitly gendered lyric figure, a woman whose posthumous claim to fame now depends on Wharton's own reclamation of Sappho as exemplary "Poetess."

Wharton envisions Sappho according to the Victorian cult of ideal womanhood, and in accordance with nineteenth-century Classical scholars who sought to purify Sappho's reputation by construing her as a schoolmistress for young women.[19] Wharton's essay describes Sappho's circle, in fact, as if it were an English girls' school or London ladies' club: "Sappho seems to have been the centre of a society in Mitylene, a kind of

[19] Wharton aligns himself with Welcker's 1816 essay, "Sappho von einem herrschenden Vorurtheil befreyt," to defend Sappho's reputation as a poet who loved women "purely"; for further discussion of nineteenth-century theories about Sappho, see Parker 1993. DeJean 1989 points out that Wharton, in adopting Bergk's text, retains the female pronouns in the Sapphic fragments and therefore presents Sappho addressing herself to other women; according to DeJean his edition "opens with the first translation into any modern language of the 'Ode to Aphrodite' with a female object of desire" (248). It is inaccurate to conclude, however, that Wharton therefore translates Sappho into a lesbian figure, nor indeed does Symonds offer a "homosexual translation" (1873: 248), unless we understand Symonds to be cross-voicing male-male desire by translating Sappho. Symonds retains the male pronouns in his "Ode to Aphrodite" and indeed in his correspondence he quotes fragment 31 of Sappho in the context of his desire for another man, but his translations of Sappho do not define lesbian desire. It remains for Renée Vivien and (as I argue in Chapter 2) Michael Field to read a more lesbian Sappho into and out of Wharton's edition. For a discussion of eighteenth-century translations in which Sappho is already understood to be addressing a woman beloved, see Vanita 1996: 41ff.

aesthetic club, devoted to the service of the Muses. Around her gathered maidens from even comparatively distant places, attracted by her fame, to study under her guidance all that related to poetry and music; much as at a later age students resorted to the philosophers of Athens" (24). Sappho is simultaneously devoted to the service of the Muses and herself a Muse, reminiscent of Tennyson's Princess who forms her own society to inspire poetry and music in the maidens around her. Wharton insists that these maidens were attracted only by Sappho's fame, and that Sappho "blamelessly loved" her pupils by teaching them a "love for beauty and honour." Through the "beauty" of Sappho's poetry Wharton therefore claims to discover "testimony to the purity of her love for her girl-friends: πάντα καθαρὰ τοῖς καθαροῖς, 'unto the pure all things are pure'"(26).

Nevertheless, having made Sappho into a woman of flesh and blood, Wharton must work hard to clear her name. The Greek phrase πάντα καθαρὰ τοῖς καθαροῖς appears as epigraph to Wharton's book, printed in small Greek letters on the back of the title page, as an injunction to all readers of Sappho. In the preface to the first edition, in 1885, Wharton glosses the fragment as his personal motto; "whether the pure think her emotion pure or impure; whether the impure appreciate it rightly, or misinterpret it; whether, finally, it was platonic or not; seems to me to matter nothing," he concludes, "Sappho's poetic eminence is independent of such considerations" (xx). Here the purification of Sappho is connected, at least in part, to the desire to purify British Classical scholarship into the "pure" science of German classical philology. Wharton admires the work of nineteenth-century Sappho scholars like Welcker and Neue, whose "purification of the text was due to more accurate study of the ancient manuscripts" (xix). With each new edition, however, Wharton becomes more emphatic in defending Sappho's purity as a person. Toward the end of the century, his reconstruction of her "character" is increasingly open to question, as Sappho of Lesbos turns into a proper name within increasingly improper significations. In the preface to the second edition, in 1887, Wharton is pleased to discover another scholar whose "acceptance of her character greatly resembles mine," (xii) but when he writes the preface to the third edition in 1895, he seems more troubled about Sappho's reputation. He alludes to ongoing debates about Sappho but reaffirms that "my appreciation of Sappho's character cannot easily be shaken" (vii).

Wharton attributes the corruption of Sappho's image to a corrupt age not her own. In his essay he writes that "the unenviable reputation of the Lesbians was earned long after the date of Sappho," by which he means the Greek comedy performed for "the Athenians in the period of their corruption" (22). Displacing his own age onto that of the Athenians, he admits that Sappho's character has been—and might again be—misunderstood: "In a later and debased age she became a sort of stock character of the licentious drama. The fervour of her love and the purity of her life, and the very fact of a woman having been the leader of a school of poetry and music, could not have failed to have been misunderstood" (22). Sappho has degenerated into a "stock character," he complains, no longer a woman and certainly not a proper woman. Wharton's response is not only to reconstruct Sappho's character—making her, as we have seen, into a proper woman and an ideal feminine persona—but to reclaim her from debased drama (and other literary forms of a "later and debased age" in Victorian England, where Sappho circulated in sensational fiction and popular pornography) by making her into the very personification of lyric poetry itself. He therefore ends his essay on "The Life of Sappho" by reviving the music of her poems, as an idealized melody "best comprehended in the light of Plato's definition of *melos*" (45) and therefore not to be misunderstood as anything but the perfection of song. Wharton attributes to Sappho the invention of the "Mixo-Lydian mode" later known in the Church as "the angelic mode"(45), and he offers a musical notation of the scale (46) as well as a metrical notation for the Sapphic strophe perfected by Sappho (47); he also describes in detail the "many-stringed Lesbian lyres" that Sappho used to perform her lyrics (46). Through her music, Sappho becomes a muse "singing" through the centuries: a feminine figure who has become the very embodiment of lyric song, echoed by Swinburne who is quoted (once again, at the end of the essay) to confirm the survival of Sapphic melodies in English poetry. "With such lines as these ringing in the reader's ears," Wharton concludes, "he can almost hear Sappho herself singing."

To convert Sappho into an exemplary lyric figure, Wharton depends less on the professional expertise of German scholars and more directly on the instruction of his Victorian contemporaries, such as Algernon Swinburne and John Addington Symonds, who turned Classical learning to more poetic purposes. Wharton's essay quotes at length from *Studies of the Greek Poets* (1873) by Symonds; indeed, at times it is difficult to distinguish passages quoted from Symonds from Wharton's own prose, as he seems to discover "the clue to Sappho's individuality" (Wharton 11) in Symonds's account of Lesbos. The Aeolians, according to Symonds, "blazed out with a brilliance of lyrical splendour that has never been surpassed" because of "something passionate and intense in their temperament," and Symonds places Lesbos, "the island of overmastering passions," at the center of Aeolian culture because "the personality of the Greek race burned there with a fierce and steady flame of concentrated feeling" (Symonds 307, Wharton 12).

The Greek "personality" that Symonds describes is increasingly individuated over the course of several paragraphs, so that Sappho herself may personify it. At first "the sphere of individual emotions, ready to burst forth" is associated with the Aeolians in general, but then this "consuming fervour of personal feeling" finds expression on Lesbos in particular, and especially among "the Lesbian poets . . . who made a literature of Love," and most especially among the "Lesbian ladies," as Symonds rhapsodizes: "They were highly educated, and accustomed to express their sentiments to an extent unknown elsewhere in history— until, indeed, the present time. The Lesbian ladies applied themselves successfully to literature. They formed clubs for the cultivation of poetry and music. They studied the art of beauty, and sought to refine metrical forms and diction. Nor did they confine themselves to the scientific side of Art. Unrestrained by public opinion, and passionate for the beautiful, they cultivated their senses and emotions, and developed their wildest passions" (Symonds 308, Wharton 13–14). While the description of an "aesthetic club" for women is repeated by Wharton, he leaves it to Symonds to present a vision of Lesbos that appeals more explicitly to the senses. It might appeal more directly, as well, to women in the present (those who "express their sentiments to an extent unknown elsewhere in history"), although Symonds fends off any improprieties by warning that "Lesbos became a byword for corruption" and "mere decadence to sensuality ensued" (Symonds 307–08, Wharton 12–13). At its apex, however, "this passion blossomed into the most exquisite lyrical poetry that the world has known," and according to Symonds, Sappho is the very embodiment of that passion. The final perfection of the Greek personality, and its greatest expression, is to be found in the singularity of her person. "Sappho is the one," he proclaims, "whose every word has a peculiar and unmistakable perfume, a seal of absolute perfection and illimitable grace . . . embodying the profounder yearnings of an intense soul after beauty which has never on earth existed" (Symonds 310, Wharton 33).

Thus Sappho comes to embody the nineteenth-century definition of lyric as a genre, via a series of personifications (the Greeks, the Aeolians, the Lesbians, Sappho) that allows the Sapphic fragments to be read, finally, as "the ultimate and finished forms of passionate utterance" (Symonds 310, Wharton 33). They are "finished" utterances in many respects: completed long ago, no longer complete, and yet unto themselves complete. "So perfect are the smallest fragments preserved . . . that we muse in a sad rapture of astonishment to think what the complete poems must have been," Symonds writes, finding rapture in the moment of rupture itself (Symonds 309, Wharton 33). Although he laments the loss of Sappho's poems, the very fact of their fragmentation inspires the idea of Sapphic song, the yearning for a beauty which may never exist again or has never on earth existed, but is nevertheless expressed through, if no longer by, Sappho. Symonds concludes that her "dazzling fragments" will "ne'er expire" because they have already inspired poets for centuries; Wharton concurs, not only by quoting Symonds as the primary poetic authority throughout his own introductory essay, but by commissioning several new translations from Symonds for inclusion in the main text of his edition.[20]

To give expression to the Sapphic passion he so admires, Symonds translates the fragments of Sappho into the rhythm of the Sapphic stanza. "All is so rhythmically and sublimely ordered in the poems of Sappho that supreme art lends solemnity and grandeur to the expression of unmitigated passion," Symonds writes in his *Studies of The Greek Poets* (Symonds 309, Wharton 15), and in his own translation of fragment 31 he tries to recreate the sublime effect of a rhythmically ordered poem (Wharton 69):

> Peer of gods he seemeth to me, the blissful
> Man who sits and gazes at thee before him,
> Close beside thee sits, and in silence hears thee
>> Silverly speaking,
>
> Laughing Love's low laughter. Oh this, this only
> Stirs the troubled heart in my breast to tremble.
> For should I but see thee a little moment,
>> Straight is my voice hushed;
>
> Yea, my tongue is broken, and through and through me
> 'Neath the flesh, impalpable fire runs tingling;
> Nothing see mine eyes, and a noise of roaring
>> Waves in my ear sounds;
>
> Sweat runs down in rivers, a tremor seizes
> All my limbs and paler than grass in autumn
> Caught by pains of menacing death I falter,
>> Lost in the love trance.

The mellifluence of this translation, with its elaborate alliterations and assonance, creates a seemingly uninterrupted voice, "hushed" but not lost: the apostrophe in line 5 ("Oh this, this only") smoothes out the anacoluthon in the Greek fragment, the interjection "Yea" bridges the metrical break, and the gradual amplification of sound and acceleration of rhythm work together to create an incantatory effect. The fourth line of each stanza (corresponding to the final adonic in the Sapphic stanza) creates an echoing crescendo, culminating in the trance-like effect of the

---

[20] Wharton acknowledges his debt to Symonds, in his Preface to the first edition: "The translations by Mr. John Addington Symonds, dated 1883, were all made especially for this work in the early part of that year, and have not been elsewhere published. My thanks are also due to Mr. Symonds for much valuable criticism" (xxii).

final line: "lost in the love trance." Rather than falling into silence, this version of fragment 31 creates a surfeit of sound by imitating the cadence of the Sapphic stanza.

In translating Sappho's broken tongue, Symonds therefore creates a "finished form of passionate utterance" but without reclaiming Sapphic voice as the origin of that utterance. The figure of voice dissolves into rhythmic waves of sound, much as "a noise of roaring / Waves in my ear sounds." Not only are these waves a figure for echoing sound, but they also echo Sappho's legendary leap from the Leucadian cliff: she too was said to dissolve into the resounding echoes of waves, forever breaking. Symonds thus suspends fragment 31 in the moment of the breaking itself, between rapture and rupture. "Yea, my tongue is broken," he writes, actively invoking—indeed, provoking—the break in order to affirm the moment when language is no longer located in a speaker, but begins to resonate "through and through me." His translation of *glōssa eage* seems more literal than most, precisely because it is most metaphorical; Symonds makes Sappho's broken tongue into a metaphor for language, articulating Sappho into sounds and rhythms greater than herself. Insofar as Sappho becomes the very embodiment of pure sound, fragment 31 serves as a gloss on all the Sapphic fragments as Symonds envisions them, "embodying the profounder yearnings of an intense soul" and burning on through time, never to expire. Sappho may "falter" in his translation, "caught by pains of menacing death," but she lives on at the moment of dying, in the perpetual repetition of a break that produces a resounding echo.

Wharton follows this logic in presenting multiple translations of fragment 31, allowing Sapphic voice to resonate in the repetition of her broken tongue. Indeed, he devotes eight pages of his edition to different versions of the fragment (Wharton 64–71). First he gives the Greek text according to Bergk, who does not fill in the hiatus between *glōssa* and *eage* in line 9: there is no attempt at interpolation or textual emendation in order to smooth over the metrical break. Next, Wharton translates the fragment into his own "literal" prose, to emphasize the breaking of the tongue, without euphemizing: "I have no utterance left, my tongue is broken down." Then he cites the famous imitation of the fragment by Catullus, whose *lingua sed torpet* is translated from Latin into English as "my tongue is palsied" (by W. E. Gladstone) and "my tongue is dulled" (by R. F. Burton); these rather feeble imitations (English versions of a Latin version of the Greek) are followed by the 1711 translation of Ambrose Philips ("my breath was gone, my voice was lost") and a 1748 verion by Smollett which prolongs the breaking of the tongue for an entire stanza, to mock (in both senses) Sappho's famous ode:

> My faltering tongue attempts in vain
> In soothing murmurs to complain;
> My tongue some secret magic ties,
> My murmurs sink in broken sighs.

The tongue-tied speaker in this eighteenth-century parody manages "to complain" after all, simply by repeating how the tongue falters; twice "my faltering tongue" fails to speak, twice "my murmurs" sink, making the proclamation of silence ridiculously redundant.

The effect of these earlier versions of fragment 31—which Wharton presents chronologically, as if to demonstrate the development of the English tongue from obsolete parody to more inspired imitation—is that Sappho continues to speak precisely because her tongue is broken. Wharton includes a more solemn attempt to lyricize Sapphic voice at the moment of its failure, in a translation by John Herman Merivale from 1833:

> Blest as the immortal gods is he,
> The youth whose eyes may look on thee,
> Whose ears thy tongue's sweet melody
>   May still devour.
>
> Thou smilest too?—sweet smile, whose charm
> Has struck my soul with wild alarm,
> And, when I see thee, bids disarm
>   Each vital power.
>
> Speechless I gaze: the flame within
> Runs swift o'er all my quivering skin;
> My eyeballs swim; with dizzy din
>   My brain reels round;
>
> And cold drops fall; and tremblings frail
> Seize every limb; and grassy pale
> I grow; and then—together fail
>   Both sight and sound.

While this may look to a twentieth-century reader like another parody, an overblown version of the Romantic sublime, it registers all the special effects that would appeal to a nineteenth-century reader. Throughout his translation, Merivale emphasizes sight over speech in order to dramatize—only too melodramatically—the loss of voice as a visionary experience. Nowhere does he mention a broken tongue, in fact; the closest Merivale comes to translating *glōssa eage* is "speechless I gaze." He rather translates the fragment into language reminiscent of Wordsworth, as he describes the dizzying, reeling instant when an excess of sensation makes the light of sense go out: "and then—together fail / Both sight and sound."

It is left to Symonds, presented next in Wharton's edition, to reclaim the failure of sound in Merivale's translation as the triumph of pure sound in his own translation.

By assembling fragment 31 in different forms, Wharton thus reassembles Sappho in a form that seems to "speak" with new eloquence, especially to a Victorian reader whose ear is attuned to poets like Symonds and Swinburne. The great "Lord Tennyson" himself is also invoked as an authority on Sappho, simultaneously authorizing Sapphic voice and himself authorized by it. Wharton quotes a version of fragment 31 in "Eleanore" ("my tremulous tongue faltereth") to demonstrate Sappho's influence on Tennyson's early poetry, and in the preface to his second edition, Wharton is pleased to note that "our own Poet Laureate has again recurred, in his latest volume of poems, to a phrase from Sappho which he had first used nearly sixty years ago; and that he calls her 'the poet,' implying her supremacy by the absence of any added epithet" (xii).[21] By appealing to the authority of "our own Poet Laureate," Wharton also confers that title upon Sappho, whose supremacy as "the poet" is confirmed by Tennyson as "our Poet," and vice versa: through him, the voice of Sappho lives on.

Wharton concludes the section on fragment 31 with a scholarly note that refers to several ancient critics, as another way to confer and confirm a Sapphic voice that has survived for centuries: "Longinus, about 250 A.D., uses this, *The Ode to Anactoria*, or *To a beloved Woman*, or *To a Maiden*, as tradition variously names it, to illustrate the perfection of the Sublime in poetry, calling it 'not one passion, but a congress of passions,' and showing how Sappho had here seized upon the signs of love-frenzy and harmonised them into faultless phrase. Plutarch had, about 60 A.D., spoken of this ode as 'mixed with fire,' and quoted Philoxenus as referring to Sappho's 'sweet-voiced songs healing love'" (71). Wharton follows Longinus in recollecting Sappho through various translations of fragment 31, and placing them within a tradition that "variously names it." Indeed, it is within the context of many versions by many translators that we can understand the fragment to be "not one passion, but a congress of passions," carrying Sappho beyond the treatise on the sublime and into the long tradition of decomposing and recomposing the Sapphic corpus, according to the logic of the Longinian sublime: so often translated, Sappho becomes sublime through the multiplication of one passion into many passions, making her suffer translation again and again. The "signs of love-frenzy," repeated and amplified in each translation of fragment 31, thus

---

[21] The phrase to which Wharton refers is Sappho's description of evening (fragment 104), imitated by Tennyson in "Leonine Elegiacs" ("The ancient poetess singeth, that Hesperus all things bringeth") and again in "Locksley Hall Sixty Years After" ("Hesper, whom the poet call'd the Bringer home of all good things"). On other Sapphic fragments imitated by Tennyson, see Peterson 1994.

prove over time to be the very signs of that suffering and are gathered here by Wharton as a "congress of passions" in order to put the long-suffering Sapphic body on display. His edition makes the rending of Sappho the necessary condition for "selected renderings," in order to transfigure Sappho's broken tongue into "the perfection" of poetry, not unlike the Longinian reading of fragment 31. It seems, in fact, that Wharton himself rather than Sappho has "seized upon the signs of love-frenzy and harmonised them into faultless phrase," by transforming them (in yet another faultless phrase, from Philoxenus) into "sweet-voiced songs healing love." This sublimation of fragments into songs allows Sappho to be healed and made whole again by Wharton (a physician, we recall). The perfection and harmonisation of Sapphic song assumes this idea of voice, an ideal that is nevertheless predicated on an internal rupture.

I have dwelled in some detail on Wharton's presentation of fragment 31, because his entire edition of the Sapphic fragments is structured according to its logic. While Wharton invokes Sappho as an exemplary figure for lyric voice and creates a composite portrait of "the Poetess," in the course of his book she is also decomposed into a text of many parts. The juxtaposition of English and Greek already suggests the doubling and division of Sapphic voice, and the accumulation of proper names—poets, translators, modern scholars, ancient critics, all writing in the name of Sappho—further undermines the reclamation of a single voice for Sappho: the "original" or "authentic" Sappho is mediated by many signatures and is reconstructed only through mediations between many different kinds of texts. It is important, then, to notice the elaborate textual apparatus of Wharton's book: not only the opening pages (frontispiece, title page, prefaces, introductory essay) but the final pages (appendixes, bibliography) and the layout of the pages themselves. The fragments are set apart and numbered separately, interrupting the continuity of the book and disrupting the sense of a continuous utterance in one voice. Wharton emphasizes the textual mediation of the Sapphic fragments, as well, in his use of various fonts: Greek letters for the Sapphic fragments, italicized prose for the "literal" translations, capital letters for proper names of translators, large letters for titles and section headings, small print for notes and bibliography.

Wharton thus foregrounds a process of textual transmission that is further historicized in the bibliography, which "comprises most of the books and articles in Sapphic literature" consulted by Wharton. Here Wharton finalizes his conversion of Sappho into text: the final word belongs to the last bibliographical entry, on Johann Christian Wolf's 1733 edition of Sappho with scholarly notes and including a life of Sappho (*cum virorum doctorum notis integris, cura et studio Jo. Christiani Wolfii . . . qui vitam Sapphonis . . . adjecit,* 217), not unlike the edition that Wharton has himself just produced. As Anthony Grafton points out, the systematic elaboration of textual scholarship beyond Wolf led to the new philology of mid-nineteenth-century Germany, where there was an increasing tendency to "cut up preserved texts into their underlying, fragmentary sources with all the glee of an anatomy student set loose on his first corpse" (1983: 181).[22] Likewise, instead of "healing" Sappho, Wharton is more like an anatomist who dissects the Sapphic corpus by following the methodology of German scholars; he does not turn Sappho into a unitary text but collates fragmentary sources, variously excerpted, paraphrased, quoted, cited, or simply enumerated to refer us to yet more texts.

In this respect Wharton's edition also reflects the emergence of a decadent style, as defined by Paul Bourget and reformulated in English by Havelock Ellis in 1889: "A style of decadence is one in which the unity of the book is decomposed to give place to the independence of the page, in which the page is decomposed to give place to the independence of the phrase, and the phrase to give place to the independence of the word." The disintegration of the textual whole is a feature of literary decadence, illustrated in the very composition of this famous sentence, as it gradually separates itself from its subject, each phrase displacing the previous phrase and leaving the final phrase dangling with an infinitive. Such a style refuses to subordinate the parts to the whole, accumulating more and more details without unifying them, decomposing before our very eyes. So also, Wharton's edition decomposes the fragments of Sappho into increasingly smaller units: longer fragments displaced by shorter fragments displaced by single words, quoted from Sappho in various ancient texts, themselves also quoted out of context, in a final section entitled "Miscellaneous." The decomposition of the Sapphic fragments is also a decomposition of the unity of Wharton's book, which begins by anatomizing Sappho but increasingly presents only constellations of words atomized on the page.

Indeed, as Linda Dowling has argued, literary Decadence is a style developed for the printed page rather than the speaking voice, in response to a crisis in Victorian ideas about language: the new comparative philology introduced to England in the middle of the nineteenth century had declared written language to be "nothing more than an artificial dialect, a petrifaction, a dead tongue" (1986: 5). Max Müller, for example, based his linguistic science on the phonetic premise that all language is based

---

[22] Grafton further argues that German philology had become a "self-consuming artifact" by the end of the century because of its increasingly specialized professionalization, while "England, with its cheerfully amateur classicists" was more successful in making Greek texts available to a broader public of educated readers (184); Wharton's edition of Sappho exemplifies the difference between German and British philology as well as the different claims of "professional" and "popular" scholarship.

in sound, and in the "post-philological moment" described by Dowling, Victorian writers were confronted with the problem of reclaiming a literary language that had been pronounced dead.[23] Symonds responds to Müller by defining the music of language as pure sound, not voiced but "appealing to the mental ear and also to that 'inward eye'" (182), while Swinburne's poetry figures pure song as the material substance of language (177–78). Pater, on the other hand, responds by "embracing the relentless insistence of the new philology that literary English is quite literally a dead or moribund language, and attempting to establish a new mode of writing on its very morbidity" (111). In Wharton's edition we see contrary impulses: although Wharton drawns on Symonds and Swinburne as model for the recuperation of Sappho's broken tongue as pure sound or sweet-voiced song, the graphic arrangement of the book itself anticipates the mode of writing associated with Pater. The fragments are presented discretely on the page in a deliberately written form, divorced from speech and obtrusive in their juxtaposition of different textual elements, etymologies, archaisms, quotations: a display of dead letters, and not the reconstruction of a living voice.

The face of Sappho delineated in the frontispiece, mediating between the Greek letters ΣΑΠΦΩ and the English title SAPPHO, is therefore increasingly identified with the typeface of the letters themselves as they are printed in Wharton's edition. The Greek characters in particular are associated with the "character" of Sappho. In Wharton's introductory memoir, Sappho is personified by the identification of her personal beauty with the beauty of what she wrote: "The epithet 'beautiful' is repeated by so many writers that it may everywhere refer only to the beauty of her writings," Wharton observes (26–27). In the preface to his second edition, however, the epithet "beautiful" is further displaced from the poetry that Sappho wrote, to the letters that we read, a special type of Greek font that Wharton is proud to announce: "The cordial reception which the first edition of my little book met with has encouraged me to make many improvements in this re-issue. . . . Among other changes, I have been able to obtain a new fount of Greek type, which has to me a peculiar beauty. Unfamiliar though some of the letters may appear at first sight, they reproduce the calligraphy of the manuscripts of the most artistic period of the Middle Ages. This type has been specially cast in Berlin by favour of the Imperial Government. In a larger size it is not unknown

---

[23] See, e.g., the 1865 *Lectures on the Science of Language* of F. Max Müller. Professor Max Müller was an influential presence at Oxford University throughout the eighteen sixties, the same decade when Swinburne, Symonds, and Pater were students there. Wharton also studied at Oxford from 1867 to 1871, graduating with honors in natural science, but familiar to some degree with debates surrounding the "new philology," as well as being fairly well versed in Classical philology.

to English scholars, but such as I am now enabled to present has never been used before" (ix). Sappho's writing is reinscribed in the very etymology of "calligraphy," the beautiful writing reproduced in Greek letters that have "a peculiar beauty" and thus stand in for the beautiful Sappho herself. And again, in the preface to the third edition, when Wharton writes, "I would fain have enriched this edition of my *Sappho* with some new words of the poetess," he consoles himself that he can at least present "to the lovers of Sappho a good deal more than was heretofore in my power; in a new form, it is true, but with the same beautiful Greek type" (v). In lieu of "some new words of the poetess," he presents "the same beautiful Greek type" as his substitute for Sappho, who is now the very type of the "type": not only the prototype of "the poetess" but a "beautiful Greek type" to be admired in its visual form on the page. The conversion of Sappho into a Greek letter would seem to be the most "literal" translation that Wharton is able to offer "the lovers of Sappho," literally turning philology into a love of letters that are at once beautiful and dead.

Gradually then, Sappho is displaced and replaced by the text of Wharton. In the first line of his first preface, Wharton proclaims her name "SAPPHO, the Greek poetess" (xv) but at the beginning of his second preface she is transformed into "my little book" (ix), and in the third preface she has become "my *Sappho*" (v). The proper name is increasingly conflated with the title of Wharton's edition, as if the book is the very embodiment of Sappho, her textual body. But if Sappho is given a name, a face, a life story, and a body by Wharton in the opening pages of his book, the figure of Sappho is also curiously disfigured in the appendix. Here Wharton describes in detail a fragment in the Egyptian Museum at Berlin: "a tiny scrap of parchment" with Greek letters on it, deciphered by scholars and tentatively attributed to Sappho (181). Wharton includes a photograph "exactly the size of the original" and "reproduced in facsimile by the Autotype Company" (figure 3), with an apology for the illegibility of the image: "Some of the minutiae of the manuscript are lost in the copy, but it gives a fair general idea of the precious relic, and exhibits the manner in which it has been torn and perforated and defaced. It also shows some of the difficulties with which those who decipher ancient manuscript have to contend. Few, at first glance, would guess how much could be made out of so little" (181–82). The fragmentary text, "torn and perforated and defaced," serves as an ironic counterimage to the face of Sappho in the frontispiece. At the beginning of the book, Sappho appears to be intact, but by the end she has disintegrated into a tattered piece of writing: no longer a "pure" woman with an inviolable voice (as she is declared to be in the epigraph and the introductory memoir) but a corrupt text, violated by the ravages of time. "A restoration of such imperfect fragments must needs be guess-work," Wharton admits (183), and his appen-

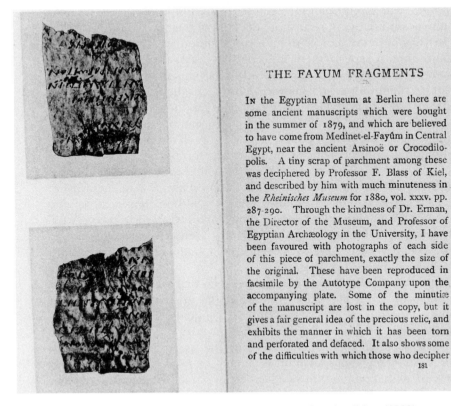

THE FAYUM FRAGMENTS

IN the Egyptian Museum at Berlin there are
some ancient manuscripts which were bought
in the summer of 1879, and which are believed
to have come from Medinet-el-Fayûm in Central
Egypt, near the ancient Arsinoë or Crocodilo-
polis. A tiny scrap of parchment among these
was deciphered by Professor F. Blass of Kiel,
and described by him with much minuteness in
the *Rheinisches Museum* for 1880, vol. xxxv. pp.
287-290. Through the kindness of Dr. Erman,
the Director of the Museum, and Professor of
Egyptian Archæology in the University, I have
been favoured with photographs of each side
of this piece of parchment, exactly the size of
the original. These have been reproduced in
facsimile by the Autotype Company upon the
accompanying plate. Some of the minutiæ
of the manuscript are lost in the copy, but it
gives a fair general idea of the precious relic, and
exhibits the manner in which it has been torn
and perforated and defaced. It also shows some
of the difficulties with which those who decipher
181

FIGURE 3: Appendix from Wharton's *Sappho,* fourth edition (1898).

dix goes on to describe in detail how Bergk's edition of Sappho has
guessed at some words that are "extant in full" while "others are only plau-
sible guesses, though some of them are indicated by the existence of accents and portions of letters" (184).

Who, indeed, would guess how much has been made out of so little by
Wharton, and how little he now makes of so much? Even while giving a
face to a name, Wharton's edition also defaces Sappho, as the Sapphic
fragments are systematically decomposed from the book to the page,
from the page to the phrase, from the phrase to the word, from the word
to the letter, and now from the letter to miniscule marks—mere "portions
of letters"—that are difficult to decipher and seem to disappear before
our very eyes. The "beautiful Greek type" of Sappho is here reduced to a
photograph of disintegrating calligraphy, a facsimile that is mechanically
reproduced by "the Autotype Company." What is this autotype but the
copy of a copy of a copy, in which the prototype, the "original" Sappho,

is lost? "The minutiae of the manuscript are lost in the copy," Wharton admits, yet he tries to recuperate the aura of this "precious relic" by advertising it, in the preface to his second edition, as "an exact reproduction of photographs of the actual scraps of parchment on which they were written a thousand years ago." He insists that "the Autotype Company has copied them with its well-known fidelity" (x), much as in the preface to the first edition he praises the engraving of Sappho for "fidelity" to Alma-Tadema's painting. But if the beautiful face featured in the beginning of the book is faithful in reproducing the figure of a woman, that figure is disfigured, with equal fidelity, by the "exact reproduction" of a torn piece of parchment at the end of the book. Insofar as the pictures in the frontispiece and the appendixes are both a copy of a copy—an engraving of a painting, a facsimile of a photograph—the idea of an original Sappho emerges in the interplay between these copies. Framed by two very different images that appear in contradictory relation to each other, Wharton's edition makes Sappho into the very embodiment of that contradiction, a self-disfiguring figure.

It is through the disfiguration of her texts that Sappho emerges most graphically in the appendix. Wharton claims to recognize Sappho even in the most fragmentary of the Sapphic fragments: "Every word of them makes one feel that no poet or poetess save Sappho could have so exquisitely combined simplicity and beauty," he asserts, and although Bergk prints these fragments "as of uncertain origin, *fragmenta adespota,*" Wharton insists they originate in Sappho: "To my mind there is little doubt that we have herein none but her very words" (183). Sappho is their origin because these "very words" allow Sappho to materialize in written form. Wharton's appendix demonstrates how the *fragmenta adespota* of Sappho have been transcribed and translated by Bergk: discrete words are enumerated in lists, interrupted by ellipses, and constellated in various patterns on the page, disconnected from meaning yet somehow in their "combined simplicity and beauty" they become the words of Sappho. No longer does it matter what they mean: "In the absence of any context the very meaning of the separate words is uncertain" (186), Wharton concedes, but he is certain about attributing them to Sappho because these words are to be read *as* Sappho: the text is Sappho and Sappho is the text. Rather than reading the texts of Sappho to produce the figure of a woman, in other words, the figure of Sappho is now read to produce a disfigured textual fragment.

In his attempt to reconstruct Sappho, Wharton therefore decomposes the Sapphic corpus into a body of dead letters. His edition vacillates between an idealist reading that recovers Sapphic voice and a materialist reading that discovers an increasingly fragmentary text. Contradictory as this Victorian version of Sappho might seem, it is consistent with the prosopopoeia that structures our reading of fragment 31, as well as a long tradition of translating that fragment. If such a tradition increasingly produces the pathos of Sappho as the long-suffering subject of and for translation, Wharton's Sappho is its culmination. Wharton presents her as a necessarily posthumous figure, not only by collecting various translations of the Sapphic fragments but by translating Sappho herself into a book that performs both the giving and the taking away of face: the very composition of his edition rearticulates Sappho's broken tongue. Thus Wharton creates an exemplary lyric subject that contributes to the Victorian revival of Sappho in significant ways, as we read in a tribute to Wharton after his death in 1895: "The result is one of the rare books that give fresh life to an ancient author, and beget other good books, such, in this case, as Michael Field's *Long Ago*. It appeals alike to the scholar, the bibliophile, and the general public; and by it the author's name will be preserved, along with that of the immortal poetess" (xxv). The "fresh life" given to Sappho is her afterlife in translation: not the reclamation of Sappho's voice but the breaking of that tongue in other tongues, recorded in a book that will therefore "beget other good books." What is preserved, along with "the author's name" and "that of the immortal poetess," is the possibility for the begetting of other names as well, such as "Michael Field," to whom I now turn.

TWO

SAPPHO DOUBLED: MICHAEL FIELD

Sly Scholars

IN 1889 a volume of Sapphic lyrics called *Long Ago* was published in London by Katherine Bradley (1846–1914) and Edith Cooper (1862–1913), aunt and niece, who lived as a married couple and wrote together as "Michael Field." Preferring to keep their authorial identities and the duality of their authorship unknown, they had published several lyrical dramas in the previous decade under this pseudonym. *Long Ago* was Michael Field's first collection of poetry—seven more were to follow, along with numerous plays—and it raises important questions about Bradley and Cooper's claim to authorship, and about the relationship between lyric subjectivity and sexual identity in Victorian poetry. How shall we read these poems written by two women writing as a man writing as Sappho? Hailed by *The Academy* as "one of the most exquisite lyrical productions of the latter half of the nineteenth century" (Gray 1889: 389), *Long Ago* seems to reproduce Victorian ideas about the lyric as a genre, but the collaboration of Bradley and Cooper also complicates generic assumptions about the lyric as the solitary utterance of a single speaker. Their volume of Sapphic imitations proves to be a complex performance of the Sapphic signature: simultaneously single and double, masculine and feminine, Michael Field's Sappho is a name that opens itself to multiple readings.

In writing *Long Ago,* Bradley and Cooper were inspired by Wharton's Sappho in particular. The Greek epigraphs to the Sapphic lyrics of Michael Field are drawn from his edition, which is acknowledged in the endnote as "a work which will be found of the highest value by those who desire to obtain a vivid impression of the personality, the influence, and the environment of the poet." Yet as we have seen, what emerges from Wharton's edition of Sappho is less "the personality of the poet" than a composite image made up of many Sapphos, in a multiauthored text that allows signatures to multiply under her name. This multiplication of different versions inspires Michael Field to publish their own Sapphic poems, which are, in turn, eagerly reincorporated as "felicitous paraphrases" by Wharton in subsequent editions of his book, as yet another contribution to the name of Sappho (Preface to third edition, vi). The poetic doubling of Sappho by Michael Field differs from Wharton's scholarly project, however, in redefining lyric authorship by means of a collaboration that destabilizes the Sapphic signature more radically than do the "selected renderings" collected by Wharton. Bradley and Cooper, writing as Michael Field, writing as Sappho, allow the signature to be read as plural and, possibly, lesbian.

Of course there is nothing new about two writers collaborating, as Walter Besant observes in 1892 in *The New Review*. His article "On Literary Collaboration" nevertheless reflects a renewed interest in and an increasing trend toward dual authorship in the last decade of the nineteenth century, particularly (according to Besant) in the writing of drama and fiction. He compares such collaborations to "the partnership of marriage" (207), uniting two in one, and insists that "true literary partnerships" achieve a unified voice: "We must hear—or think we hear—one voice" (205). Collaborative writing reaches its limit, however, on occasions "when there is need of profound meditation, of solemn self-interrogation, or of lofty imagination" (203)—the conventional occasion of lyric, that is, in an allusion to John Stuart Mill's famous definition of poetry as "the natural fruit of solitude and meditation," or "feeling confessing itself to itself, in moments of solitude" (Mill 1976:13,12). The genre of lyric is commonly understood, at least in its late nineteenth-century definition, as the written representation of an utterance not addressed to another person but spoken in private, a voice not heard but "overheard" by the reader. Besant therefore excludes lyric poetry from experiments in collaboration, because lyrics depend on the fiction of "one voice" more fundamentally than do other genres. "To touch the deeper things one must be alone," Besant writes, and again, "One must, alone, speak to the alone" (203).

What then of Sappho, the "original" lyric poet, doubled by dual authorship? If lyric as a genre assumes a single speaker, then Michael-Field-as-Sappho simultaneously exploits and explodes that generic assumption. On one hand, Katherine Bradley and Edith Cooper seem to unify their voices into one as Michael Field; the first product of their collaboration under this name, the drama *Callirrhoë*, was hailed by critics in 1884 as "the ring of a new voice which is likely to be heard far and wide" (Sturgeon 1922: 27). Michael Field's readers heard—or thought they heard—one voice, according to Besant's ideal, and Bradley and Cooper themselves also idealized their literary partnership by analogy to marriage. In a letter of introduction to Robert Browning, who was to become their friend, Cooper writes: "This happy union of two in work and aspiration is sheltered and expressed by 'Michael Field.' Please regard him as the author."[1] What emerges between Katherine and Edith—between their

---

[1] Quoted from the journals of Michael Field, excerpted in *Works and Days* (Sturge Moore 1933: 3). Quotations from the published journal will be cited as *WD* by page number. Quotations from passages in the unpublished journal of Michael at the British Library ("Works

respective nicknames "Michael" and "Field"—is a "him" authorized by the existing institutions of authorship, a voice that may be read in the masculine singular as "the author."

On the other hand, they describe their happy union of two not as wedlock in any conventional sense, but surpassing what Victorians considered to be the ideal marriage of the Brownings. After a visit with Robert Browning, Bradley reflects in her journal: "Those two poets, man and wife, wrote alone; each wrote, but did not bless or quicken one another at their work; *we are closer married*" (*WD:* 16). In the contrast between two poets who "wrote alone" and two who write together, heterosexual marriage is dismissed as an inadequate metaphor for literary partnership; the "*closer*" marriage of Bradley and Cooper makes writing for, with, and through "one another" the central metaphor for a relationship they never quite call lesbian. Nevertheless they turn to Sappho, whom they certainly understand to be Lesbian in more than the proper sense of the name, in order to develop a model of lyric authorship in which voice is the effect of an eroticized textual mediation between the two of them rather than the representation of an unmediated solitary utterance.

Bradley and Cooper therefore manipulate the conventions of authorship in ways that cross-couple gender and genre, and it is significant that this cross-coupling happens through Greek. Recognizing the erotic subtext of their poetry, Robert Browning called them his "two dear Greek women," and particularly admired the "Sapphics" in *Long Ago*. He received copy no. 2 in a limited edition of one hundred copies, bound in vellum and printed in two colors: the English poems in black letters, Greek epigraphs in orange-gold, and a personal inscription to Robert Browning followed by a phrase in Greek: ἐκ θεοῦ δ᾽ ἀνὴρ σοφαῖς ἀνθεῖ ἐσαεὶ πραπίδεσσιν (46777. May 23, 1889). This compliment to "a man forever eminent in wise understanding from god" declares an alliance between Michael Field and Robert Browning (whom they fondly called "the reverend elder") based on the command of ancient Greek, the cultural property of a privileged masculine elite. Like Browning, who had been publishing translations from Greek in the previous decade, Bradley and Cooper make a claim to classical scholarship in *Long Ago*. The bilingualism of their volume places Michael Field within an elite circle of poets who turn to Greek literature to redefine the language of English poetry, and Michael Field's assumption of poetic authority draws on the cultural prestige of Victorian Hellenism. Bradley and Cooper were pleased to hear, then, that Browning had lent *Long Ago* to a young man "to teach him

---

and Days, Journals 1868–1914," Add. Ms. 46776–46804) will be cited by manuscript number and date. I am grateful to the British Library for permission to quote from the journal of Michael Field.

the uses of Greek learning!" (*WD*:30–31). What Greek learning signifies, in this context, is more than linguistic: it marks a distinct though unspoken set of assumptions about sexuality as well as class and gender.

By imitating Sappho's Greek fragments, Michael Field enters into a domain often coded as masculine, and, by the end of the nineteenth century, increasingly homosexual. Recent criticism on Victorian Hellenism has explored, from various perspectives, the formation of British culture, politics, and aesthetics by analogy to ancient Greece. Richard Jenkyns (1980) and Frank Turner (1981) survey both radical and conservative tendencies in classical scholarship of the period, influencing a wide range of cultural practices, and this line of argument is developed by Linda Dowling (1994), who demonstrates how an aestheticized reading of classical Greek culture in Victorian Oxford opens a space for the discourse of homosexuality to emerge. Richard Dellamora also describes "the hermeneutic space known as 'thinking Greek'" with reference to the practice of pederasty in the history of the Dorians (1994: 54); he notes that Sappho was invoked as model for the Greek genius, defined by *male* pederasty (50). The philhellenism of Michael Field is derived, at least in part, from this discourse of homosexual desire and reflects, as Martha Vicinus points out, "Michael Field's fascination with the tropes of male homosexuality" (1994a: 103).

Bradley and Cooper tended to affiliate with homosexual couples, such as the artists Charles Ricketts and Robert Shannon, who also considered themselves married. After meeting Ricketts, Cooper observes in her journal that "he is an ardent lover of Shannon . . . loving him as my Love loves me" (46781.1893). A subsequent journal entry describes Ricketts's interest in the art and poetry of the Romanians because they are "a people with Sapphic passion" who celebrate same-sex marriages (46787.1898). Here Bradley and Cooper simultaneously adopt and adapt the homosexual discourse surrounding them: the "Romanians" are lesbianized in terms of "Sapphic passion." While drawing on the established associations between Hellenism and homosexuality, Bradley and Cooper therefore imply a lesbian eroticism distinct from the troping of homosexual desire. They imagine an ancient Greek world inhabited not only by the pupils of Socrates, but also by young women. Cooper describes a Greek ceramic figure she saw at an art exhibit: "Two young women sit in gossiping ease on a wayside sarcophagus—their knees are crossed under the chitons— one of the talkers has her hand on her hips, the breath of conversation hurries through their mouths—Every gesture tells of intercourse & emotion. . . . These bits of domestic art give me a sense of the grace of intimate Greek life" (46777. June 13, 1889). The intimacy of this vision resonates with Browning's description of Bradley and Cooper as "two dear Greek women," a couple whose every gesture tells of "intercourse & emotion" but without telling exactly how much. In this way Bradley and Cooper open Victorian Hellenism to the possibility of a lesbian reading that allows for the circulation of Greek eros among women as well as men.

Yet the lesbian implications of "Greek learning"—or "thinking Greek"— remain largely unexplored in current work on Victorian Hellenism. Critics have described the role of classical scholarship in the cultural construction of masculine identities and homoerotic desire, but without acknowledging the emergence of a Hellenizing discourse of lesbianism. Often denied access to formal education in Greek and Latin, Victorian women had a different relationship to classical discourses than their male counterparts. By the end of the century, however, the women's colleges at Oxford and Cambridge had created a place for students to pursue classical languages, and scholars like Jane Ellen Harrison at Newnham College were revolutionizing classical studies. Katherine Bradley herself had learned classical languages as a student at Newnham College, and later she initiated her niece Edith Cooper into the study of Latin and Greek as well. Together they read the *Greek Anthology,* and Wharton's 1885 edition of Sappho appealed in particular to Bradley and Cooper, who depended on the English translations of the primary texts, along with the secondary notes offered by Wharton, in order to assimilate Sappho's Greek.

While Bradley and Cooper create a scholarly context for their reading of the Sapphic fragments, they also remain aware of themselves as women who must resort to the popularized pseudo-scholarship of "Dr." Wharton, another amateur classicist. Excluded from the masculine domain of classical scholarship, Bradley comments balefully on "one sentence of Mr. Pater's which I would not say I could never forgive, because I recognised its justice; but from which I suffered, and which was hard to bear—that in which he speaks of the scholarly conscience as male" (*WD*:137). And later, again, she expresses a sense of inadequacy in her Greek learning: "I demonstrate that women cannot have the scholarly conscience" (*WD*:192). As Michael Field, however, Bradley and Cooper are able to claim the masculine authority of classical scholarship and use it transgressively, for their own purposes. This is the implication of a private journal entry, eagerly anticipating the publication of *Long Ago* to announce their public entry into the literary establishment: "Every day we are expecting the first copy of *Long Ago* (a specimen copy). Tiny marsh violets have been sent to Edith——they are like Violets that have put aside their loving, & made sly little scholars of themselves, mystic & 'beguiling'— tricky & fanciful—rather than luring and recluse" (46777. May 9, 1889). As they await a specimen copy of their book, Bradley and Cooper receive flowers—another kind of specimen—that prompt an association between their poems and the violets that have made "sly little scholars" of themselves: their Sapphic lyrics are also beguiling, tricky, and fanciful in their assimilation of Sappho's fragments, seeming to "put aside their loving" yet still making good use of the Greek tongue. Indeed, in writing *Long Ago,* Bradley and Cooper themselves seem to have become "sly little scholars," who might teach the uses of Greek learning not only to young men, but to young women as well. Their version of Victorian Hellenism, while mediated by a set of homosexual conventions, nevertheless implies the entry of Michael Field into lesbian writing as another "field" yet to be defined.

Bradley and Cooper therefore prove to be important figures for the historical recovery of lesbian writing, as is now evident in the resurgence of critical interest in Michael Field; increasingly, their Sapphic signature is read as a lesbian signature.[2] When Browning first read the Sapphic lyrics of *Long Ago* in draft, he "prophesied they would make their mark" but added that Michael Field might have to "wait fifty years" (*WD:* 20). The implication here is not only that *Long Ago* is long ahead of its time but also that the very structure of the Sapphic signature—"their mark"—requires the mediation of reading: it will be left to the reader of the future to decipher this sign. This is what I propose to do in the following pages: to read Michael Field's Sappho as an exploration of lesbian writing that is not predicated on the assumption of sexual identity or lyric voice but nevertheless puts those terms into play.

Elizabeth Meese describes such an approach—and performs it rhetorically—in her essay "Theorizing Lesbian: Writing—A Love Letter." The colon in this title marks a break between sexuality and textuality yet anticipates the implication of each in the other and points to the space in between as "a metaphorical field" or "a scene of transposition" (1990: 75). I use the colon in the title of this chapter to similar effect, allowing Sappho and Michael Field to be read in relation to each other but without being identified with each other; what happens in the break between the two names is transposition rather than identification. In reading "Sappho: Michael Field," with the implicit assumption of a colon that makes these terms simultaneously continuous and discontinuous, we enter a textual space where the crossing (out, over, through) of sexual identities can be performed. I will consider briefly why Bradley and Cooper turn to Greek to create that textual space, and then trace in more detail how the figure of voice in their imitations of Sappho is displaced by a process of eroticized intertextual exchange, or—to use their term—"interlacing." Thus the tracery of *Long Ago* is less the proclamation of a proper name— Katherine Bradley, Edith Cooper, Michael Field, Sappho, or Lesbian—

---

[2] Recent work on Michael Field includes Locard 1979, Moriarty 1986, Koestenbaum 1989, Leighton 1992, White 1992 and 1996, Vicinus 1994a, Prins 1995, Laird 1995, Vanita 1996, Reynolds 1996, Blain 1996.

than it is the circumscription of a metaphorical field of writing in which
the Sapphic signature is already in play as its own suggestive and seductive figure.

The Double Signature

Like the frontispiece of Wharton's Sappho, *Long Ago* features the image
of an archaic Greek woman on its cover: embossed in gold, it is a smiling
profile with hair looped in intricate involutions around the ear, and her
neck twined with a budding garland, or perhaps it is a string of beads
wrapped twice around the throat (figure 4).[3] The five buds, or beads, on
the necklace combine into an ornamental pattern that is repeated in five
Greek letters below the profile: Φ Σ Α Θ Ο (sic).[4] That graphic repetition
of five tiny circles on a string and five curlicued letters in a row, spelling
out the name of Sappho, connects the face and the name and indeed
gives face *to* the name, as if the letters outside the figure were already prefigured within it, internalized to make that figure legible, and allowing it
to be read, emblematically, as signature. But whose signature? Suspended
in midair, the letters maintain an ambiguous relation to the face: are they
issuing from the mouth or traveling to the ear? Is the figure of "Sappho"
speaking or listening, naming herself or being named? While the mouth
is closed, the ear is an open receptacle marked by a pattern of concentric
circles, emphasizing the ear's receptivity to a name that is the written representation of a spoken utterance no longer her own, though it might
once have been, "long ago."

To identify the figure as Sappho, we therefore read her as destination
rather than origin of the name, following the long and involuted trajectory of its reception, the prolongation of which is already announced in
the title, LONG AGO (printed over the figure), and further prolonged
by another signature (printed below): MICHAEL FIELD. How shall we
interpret this name in relation to Φ Σ Α Θ Ο? Has the Greek been translated into English by Michael Field, or is Michael Field a translation of
Sappho? The gold letters in English typeface are another attempt to give

---

[3] Inspired by a Greek black-figured calpis from about 500 B.C. (the earliest inscribed representation of Sappho), the profile on the cover of *Long Ago* is identified in Michael Field's
endnote as follows: "The archaic head of Sappho reproduced on the cover of this volume
is taken from a nearly contemporary vase, inscribed with her name, which is now in Paris,
the property of Prince Czartorysky (De Witte, *Antiquitées conservées a l'Hôtel Lambert*, pl. 3)."

[4] The archaic spelling of Sappho's name is erratic. Here, the name begins with a *phi* and
a *sigma* (these two letters are equivalent to the digraph *psi*), followed by *alpha, theta* (probably substituting for *phi*), and *omikron* (the old Attic version of *omega*). For speculation on the
etymology of the name Sappho and its various spellings, see Zuntz 1951.

FIGURE 4: Front cover of *Long Ago*, Michael Field (1889). Courtesy of The Rare
Books Room, The Pennsylvania State University Libraries.

face to Sappho, ascribing a name to the figure by inscribing it within that
figure, making it readable by the same logic that produces Sappho's signature—that is to say, readable only as the effect of a repetition or doubling. Here again, the name designates not a point of origin but the structure of naming itself, of deriving a name, of the name as derivation. Who

is the "original" author of the lyrics in this volume? The double signature beneath its title leaves us wondering—perhaps Sappho, perhaps Michael Field, perhaps both—and this ambiguous doubling is duplicated in the pseudonym of Katherine Bradley and Edith Cooper, who sign their nicknames "Michael" and "Field" together as one: Michael Field, a doubled signature that doubles Sappho, one double signature inside another.

Michael Field's self-doubling through the figure of Sappho is also evident in a miniature portrait of Edith Cooper, designed by their friend Charles Ricketts (figure 5).[5] Like Sappho on the front cover of *Long Ago*, Cooper is depicted in profile with her hair loosely gathered in a knot and a ribbon tied around her neck. The visual repetition is further emphasized by the placement of the initials MF below the chin (with M joined to F), exactly where the name of Sappho appears in relation to the Greek profile. As English letters take the place of the Sapphic signature in Greek, this figure opens itself to yet another double reading: Edith Cooper is named by two letters simultaneously divided and joined in a single line, "M" and "F" both masculine and feminine, both singular and plural, two letters that do not quite spell out "ME" yet allow the figure to be identified as the "I" of Michael Field. Ingeniously, the portrait reiterates the complex structure of the signature on the cover of *Long Ago*, simultaneously giving face to a name and name to a face, but only through the inscription of a self-doubling.

We might read the Sapphic signature of Bradley and Cooper as examples of the female autograph, inscribing a split subject rather than asserting the identity of the proper name; this logic has been elaborated in debates within feminist criticism around the status and signature of the signature in women's writing (Stanton 1984). At the same time, Michael Field's signature as Sappho also points to the subversion of linguistic propriety that Lee Edelman associates with homographesis, where "homo" serves as signifier of self-contradictory sameness and "graphesis" points to the inscription of inscription itself as difference (Edelman 1994: xix). The ambiguous ownership of the Sapphic signature—belonging to Bradley and Cooper, or to Michael Field?—suggests a continual exchange between autograph and homograph, both produced by an act of writing that defers identity and signifying (albeit in different ways) the impossibility of a single, self-authorizing, self-present feminine subject. Thus, when Bradley writes that she and her niece "make up a single individual, doubly stronger than each alone, i.e. Edith and I make a *veritable Michael*" (*WD:* 6), her insistence on the singularity of their authorship

---

[5] The initials of Michael Field (joined together as MF and finely etched to the right of the profile) are visible in the original portrait of Edith Cooper. The portrait is part of a jeweled pendant designed by Charles Ricketts and reproduced here by courtesy of the Fitzwilliam Museum, Cambridge.

FIGURE 5: Pegasus pendant containing miniature portrait of Edith Cooper
by Charles Ricketts (1901). Fitzwilliam Museum, University of Cambridge.

coincides with the moment of its doubling and thus allows Michael to
emerge as a third term that produces the interplay between identities, an
"I" that can shift to "we" and "you" and "he" and "she" and "they" (or "the
Michaels," as Ricketts called them). The name is "*veritable*" not because it
verifies authorial identity but because it enables the structure of their
writing together.

The ambiguous authorship of Michael Field was, in fact, an open secret. Bradley writes to Browning: "It is said that the *Athenaeum* was taught
by you to use the feminine pronoun. Again, someone named André Raffalovich, whose earnest young praise gave me genuine pleasure, now
writes in ruffled distress; he 'thought he was writing to a boy—a young
man . . . he has learnt on the best authority it is not so.' I am writing to
him to assure him that the best authority is my work" (*WD:* 6). What au-

thorizes Michael Field is the work itself, and that proves to be "the best authority," especially when the question about authorship, be it masculine or feminine, singular or plural, implicitly opposes and subordinates the second term to the first, to the detriment of writers like Bradley and Cooper. "It cannot be too frequently repeated," Bradley and Cooper warn in a letter to Vernon Lee, "that belief in the unity of M.F. is absolutely necessary, alike for the advance of his glory & his attaining of his favor. He is in literature *one.* Where the secret of his chance dualism is not known, the wise & kind preserve it & even public reference to him should be masculine. But need scarcely [*sic*] warn Vernon Lee on this point?"[6] Violet Paget, who wrote under the name Vernon Lee and also lived with a woman companion, might understand the need to preserve a secret, even when it is already known.

Nevertheless, by the time *Long Ago* appeared, its reviewers referred knowingly to Michael Field as "she," and in a letter praising the Sapphic lyrics as "a voice of one heart," George Meredith also knows "it is an addressing-of-two when one writes to Michael Field" (*WD:* 67). Bradley's concern is not simply the devaluation of "lady authorship" or "dual authorship," however. By appealing to "the unity of M.F.," she holds open the possibility of reading Michael Field within the context of homosexual writing—two women playing the part of "a young man" in circles where Sappho would be recognized as a trope for homoerotic desire. For contemporaries like Raffalovich and Vernon Lee, "the unity of M.F." is a signature that also signifies the merging of masculine and feminine in the third sex, exemplifying the theory that homosexuality unites a female soul in a male body or vice versa.

"Michael Field" is therefore more than a mere pseudonym to disguise the "true" identities of Bradley and Cooper, as Chris White points out: "The name contains a compelling contradiction: they both deploy the authority of male authorship and yet react against such camouflage. Michael Field is not a disguise. Nor is it a pretence at being a man" (1992: 40). By looking at various constructions of sexual identity embedded in their poetry, White concludes that the development of a "joint poetic persona" allows Bradley and Cooper to play out different ways of understanding a lesbian relationship. But the hypothesis of a persona, because it still assumes a speaker with an implicitly identifiable sexual identity, does not fully address the complexity of the Sapphic lyrics in *Long Ago.* Rather than personifying a speaker, even a "contradictory" one, these lyrics repeatedly call into question the figure of voice upon which lyric reading is predicated. The Preface to *Long Ago* invokes Sappho as

[6] Letter from Michael Field to Vernon Lee, dated January 29, 1890, quoted with permission from Special Collections, Colby College, Waterville, Maine. I am grateful to Christa Zorn-Belde for bringing this letter to my attention.

"the one woman who has dared to speak unfalteringly of the fearful mastery of love," and although White interprets this invocation as Michael Field's claim to Sapphic voice, it significantly ends in repetition with a Greek quotation: "again and again the dumb prayer has risen from my heart—σὺδ' αὖτα σύμμαχος ἔσσο." The Greek phrase "you be my ally" comes from the famous "Ode to Aphrodite," and allows Michael Field to conflate Sappho's appeal to the goddess with their own appeal to Sappho. This re-enactment of Sappho's prayer may suggest an alliance or merging of voices, but only in an ancient language that is no longer spoken.

Indeed, the presentation of Greek script alongside English typeface throughout the volume leaves us hovering between languages, in a textual bilingualism to be read rather than voiced; each poem begins with a fragmentary Sapphic epigraph, to emphasize the loss of a speaking voice and its fragmentation into text. Even the epigraph that introduces the entire volume is disconnected from a speaking "I": Ἠράμαν μὲν ἔγω σέθεν, Ἄτθι, πάλαι πότα is only partially translated on the back of the title page, as "A great while since, a long, long time ago." The translation leaves out "I loved you, Atthis," a first-person address to a second person, thus distancing the utterance from its source and marking the absence of a speaker for, and in, this text. Throughout *Long Ago,* the relation between epigraph and poem is structured by a similar gap, disarticulating a single "I" who desires "you" and tracing a more erratic trajectory of desire: not a movement from one fixed point to another, from origin to destination, but a reversible relation that is textually mediated.

What emerges from this performative space between Sappho's Greek and Michael Field's English is a poetic practice that does not assume identity with the original Sappho nor assume her voice; instead, it emphasizes a belated and secondary relationship to Sappho in order to perform the intertextuality of its own writing. The lyrics in *Long Ago* are self-consciously nonoriginal, the textual copy of a voice not their own, the doubling of Sappho's signature rather than the reclamation of her song. Bradley and Cooper in fact associate their Sapphic imitations with the cuckoo, as a model for themselves as Sapphic imitators. When *Long Ago* first appears in print, their journal gives thanks to God "for this accomplishing" and records a verse dedicated "To a cuckoo, heard early in the morning." Here the cuckoo's "iterating Voice" is the copy of "other song" heard only as echo:

> I hear thine iterating Voice in flight,
> While in the hedgerow other song is furled:
> To rise like thee! To take my range of light,
> And spread unravished echoes through the world!
>
> (46777: May 23, 1889)

A similar echoic figure structures the opening invocation in *Long Ago*, where a "maiden choir" of muses is recalled from the past to come "hither now," leaving "sweet haunts of summer sound"—the echoing realm of long ago—in order to enter the present moment of reading. The next poem in the volume returns us to the past, however, to establish a contrast between women who sang "in their time" and the loss of Sapphic song in the present. The Greek epigraph is translated into the first line of each stanza:

> Αὐτὰρ ὀραῖαι στεφανηπλόκευν
> They plaited garlands in their time;
> They knew the joy of youth's sweet prime,
>> Quick breath and rapture;
> Theirs was the violet-weaving bliss,
> And theirs the white, wreathed brow to kiss,
>> Kiss, and recapture.
>
> They plaited garlands, even these;
> They learnt Love's golden mysteries
>> Of young Apollo;
> The lyre unloosed their souls; they lay
> Under the trembling leaves at play,
>> Bright dreams to follow.
>
> They plaited garlands—heavenly twine!
> They crowned the cup, they drank the wine
>> Of youth's deep pleasure.
> Now, lingering for the lyreless god—
> Oh yet, once in their time, they trod
>> A choric measure.

The first word in the Greek epigraph (*Autar*, "but") emphasizes the gap between "their time" and "now," so that "Oh yet" in the final stanza also implies "but no more." In the passing of time, whatever "they" knew is lost, and whoever "they" were is unknown. How is the inspiration of those women, their "quick breath and rapture," to survive in the "lyreless" present? Transposing the measure "they trod" to the rhythm of its own metrical feet, this poem suggests that their song and dance might continue in the choreography of writing.

Thus Michael Field creates a textual space for the doubling and division of voices, in order to "kiss, kiss, and recapture" another kind of choral song. Preferring a chorus of voices to a single "I," this poem pluralizes and textualizes lyric voice by analogy to how "they plaited garlands," a phrase repeated at the beginning of each stanza and translated from the Greek *oraiai stephanēplokeun*. Here the verb *stephanēplokeun*

serves as figure for the plaiting, weaving, wreathing, and "heavenly twine"
of words themselves, allowing the garlands to accumulate reference, especially in stanza 2: "even these" refers back to the women garlanded by
the songs of their time, while also presenting the words on this page garlanded into a poem, and anticipating the garlanding of all the poems
within the pages (or "under the trembling leaves") of this book. The
poem is therefore structured by a textual figure that is, itself, derived
from the text of a Greek epigraph and interwoven with English. Sappho's
fragment generates the rhetorical structure of this poem and introduces
recurrent figures for such interweaving and intertwining of texts throughout *Long Ago.*

Poem 6, for example, translates the "sweet-voiced girl" of its epigraph
(Πάρθενον ἀδύφωνον) into Erinna, a poet included among "we who have
laurel in our hair" and given "immortal bloom" by one of the muses:

> Soon as my girl's sweet voice she caught
> Thither Euterpe sped,
> And, singing too, a garland wrought,
> To crown Erinna's head.

In this simultaneous reciprocation and transformation of her song,
Erinna's voice is "caught" and "wrought" into a garland. Gorgo with "the
strings of tender garlands twine / About her tender neck" receives similar praise in poem 8, and poem 13 urges Dica to put garlands in her hair
to please the immortals and be immortalized herself:

> They love the crowned and fragrant head
> But turn their face away
> From those who come ungarlanded,
> For none delight as they
> In piercing, languorous, spicy scent,
> And thousand hues in lustre blent:
> Such sacrifice, O Dica, bring!
> Thy garland is a beauteous thing.

Just as the plaiting of garlands was transferred from the verb *stephanēplokeun* to the intricate texture of poem 1, the Greek epigraph to poem
13 is woven into the English text, as it elaborates a contrast between *su de
stephanois* and *astephanōtoisi,* between "thy garland" and "those who come
ungarlanded." Dica's garland, with its "thousand hues in lustre blent,"
likewise suggests the blending of Greek and English into the garland of
this poem; ungarlanded, her voice could not live on as text.

The garlanding of Erinna, Gorgo, and Dica enables their names to live
on in the garland of Sappho's poetry and refers back to Sappho as she
appears on the cover of *Long Ago.* Here, with her poems refigured as a

garland around the head, and the letters of her name prefigured in the
garland around the neck, Sappho becomes a figure for the textuality of
her writing. Even Sappho's hair, gathered in a knot, is a textual figure. In
"A Knot of Hair," written by Michael Field around the time of *Long Ago*
(though not in response to any particular Sapphic fragment), a woman
who wears her hair always in "the same deep coil about the neck" seems
both infinitely readable and ultimately unreadable, because of the many
threads twisting and turning, maze-like, into a knot: "But there it twined
/ When first I knew her, / And learned with passion to pursue her." In
the Ricketts portrait, Cooper's hair is also gathered into a knot at the nape
of her neck; perhaps Bradley addressed this poem to Cooper as one of
many love lyrics written for her.

But the similarities in Cooper's portrait, Sappho's profile, and this
poem also suggest a deeper logic at work. The unnamed woman, invoked
as "O first of women who hast laid / Magnetic glory on a braid," inspires
a kind of musing that is like reading:

> The happy lot
> Be mine to follow
> These threads through lovely curve and hollow,
> And muse a life-time how they got
> Into that wild, mysterious knot.

The poem, with its weaving lineation, leads us into a process of following
"these threads" in the text and discovering them to be inextricably inter-
twined, like the texture of the hair. The woman is in fact a text to be read,
brought to life by a reading that seems to originate within her (as "the
first of women") yet also implicates the reader—a reader who will not dis-
entangle but rather "follow" the tangle of "that wild, mysterious knot."
What emerges from this textual entanglement is the structure of a double
signature, the woman as repetition and doubling of the reader's own
"musing," producing—as one possible reading—the name of Sappho.

We Cross and Interlace

Bradley and Cooper's entanglement in the figure of Sappho's signature,
like the plaiting of garlands in Michael Field's Sapphic lyrics, demonstrates the textual mediation necessary for the construction of voice—if
we may still call it that—in their own writing. "We cross and interlace,"
they avow in a letter to Havelock Ellis, who might understand their collaboration in terms of an eroticized textual exchange between each
other: "As to our work, let no man think he can put asunder what God
has joined. . . . The work is perfect mosaic: we cross and interlace like a

company of dancing summer flies; if one begins a character, his companion seizes and possesses it; if one conceives a scene or situation, the other corrects, completes, or murderously cuts away." (Sturgeon 1922: 47) Crossing from one to the other, simultaneously completing and cutting away, Bradley and Cooper prefer to think of their work as a "perfect mosaic" of textual fragments rather than a living voice: it is the product of writing and reading and rewriting, taking possession of each other's words yet also losing track of who owns what. The writing is "like mosaic-work—the mingled, various product of our two brains" and not to be "disentangled," according to Cooper (*WD:* 3). Sturgeon's biography of Michael Field adds, "The collaboration was so close, so completely were the poets at one in the imaginative effort, that frequently they could not themselves decide (except by reference to the handwriting on the original sheet of manuscript) who had composed a given passage" (63). Their plays and poems are therefore "composed" not by analogy to song but in the literal sense of being pieced together, placing bits of text next to each other and allowing them to interlace. The composition of Sapphic poems is particularly suited to this process, since Sappho's lyrics are themselves fragments for piecing together in English—and of course Wharton's edition of Sappho contributes even more pieces to the mosaic. Composing poems for *Long Ago,* Bradley and Cooper enact the very premise of their collaboration, the mutual implication of each in the writing of the other and the eroticizing of that textual entanglement by turning it into an infinitely desirable feminine figure.

I would not conclude as Sturgeon does, however, that they are "at one" in a "union so complete, that one may search diligently, and search in vain, for any sign in the work both wrought that this is the creation of two minds and not one" (62), nor do I wish to pursue the biographical reading of nineteenth-century romantic friendships proposed by Faderman, who argues that Bradley and Cooper achieved "perfect, absolute equality" in their relationship (1981: 213). To the contrary, the intertextuality of their relationship, the very possibility of crossing and interlacing, depends on difference between the two, and it is this asymmetrical doubleness produced by writing together that allows their work to be "joined" and them to be "*closer married.*" My reading of their relationship, in other words, emerges from the rhetorical structures operating within their poetry, particularly the figure of chiasmus or cross-coupling. Here I depart from Angela Leighton, who discovers "a new language of desire" in the Sapphic poems of Michael Field (1992: 209) and concludes that "Sappho has finally been recuperated for women as a model of poetry and of love together" (237). Indeed, the language of desire developed by Michael Field works against the recuperation of Sappho as unified lyric subject or lesbian identity, insofar as it depends on rhetorical doubling.

The poems in *Long Ago* that are inspired by Sappho's epithalamia demonstrate how various kinds of sexuality may be constituted through such textual doubling. These wedding poems, dedicated to Hymen, simultaneously repeat and exceed the binary opposition on which heterosexual marriage depends. For instance, Poem 42, introduced by the epigraph Χαίροισα νύμφα, χαιρέτω δ' ὁ γάμβρος (the bride rejoicing, let the bridegroom rejoice), expands this self-doubling fragment into eight stanzas that focus primarily on the bride. In the first stanza, she predominates:

> She comes, and youthful voices
> On Hymen praise confer;
> She comes, and she rejoices,
> Rejoice with her,
> O bridegroom! Let her see
> Thy brave felicity.

The groom's appearance is deferred until line 5; meanwhile, "She comes" is doubled in lines 1 and 3, and within line 3 "she" is doubled again in "she comes, and she rejoices," and even the pairing of verbs in "she rejoices / rejoice with her" places her before and after a "him" who is never quite present. In fact, although the poem is written in the form of a second-person address to the groom, he exists only to be invoked, and the very structure of invocation renders him absent. The apostrophe "O bridegroom" affirms this absence, and when the apostrophe is repeated in the final stanza, it renders him silent as well:

> She comes, thy hope fulfilling;
> O happy bridegroom, see,
> How gracious and how willing
> She comes to thee.
> Rejoice! Oh be not dumb!
> Rejoice, for she is come!

The bride comes "thy hope fulfilling," yet when she arrives at the end of the poem it is the groom who must respond to her. Here the Victorian ideology of marriage—as a complementary relationship between husband and wife, with her defined only in relation to him—is reversed: he is defined only in relation to her, while she is a self-doubled pair that exists both within and beyond their pairing.

The figure of Hymen is therefore deployed by Michael Field as a rhetorical chiasmus, or cross-coupling that reverses the subordination of feminine to masculine in the union of marriage and inverts heterosexual difference between two by articulating an already self-differing structure within one. This rhetorical doubling is emphasized in the invocation to the god of marriage in poem 55, where the Greek epigraph Ὑμεν᾽ Ὑμή-ναον (altered from Ἔσπετ᾽ Ὑμήναον, "Sing Hymenaeus," as the fragment appears in Wharton, 144) is translated into "O Hymen Hymenaeus"—the name generates its own repetition, but with a difference, allowing simultaneous union and division. When poem 55 concludes, "Thou linkest in a living joy / This virgin and this noble boy," the Hymen linking "virgin" and "boy" is also the hymen that separates the virgin from the boy. The contradictory logic of Hymen—a link that joins and separates—works throughout this volume of Sapphic lyrics, in which celebrations of marriage coincide with the celebration of maidenhood.

Thus in poem 47, another wedding song, the bride about to be joined with the groom is also kept separate, "undescried" and "inviolate":

> She has been kept for thee, I know not how;
> As, undescried,
> A blushing apple on the topmost bough,
> Heaven kept thy bride
> A fragrant, rare, inviolate thing
> For season of thy cherishing.

The girl is like an apple to be picked by the groom, an image that recalls Sappho's fragment about the apple beyond the reach of applepickers, forever "on the topmost bough." That famous fragment is translated into prose in Wharton's edition: "As the sweet-apple blushes on the end of the bough, the very end of the bough, which the gatherers overlooked, nay overlooked not but could not reach. . . ." (132). The very syntax of the protracted subordinate clause makes the apple more and more distant ("on the end . . . the very end . . . overlooked, nay . . . could not reach"), and likewise the comparison between apple and bride is never completed; as Anne Carson concludes from her reading of this Greek fragment, "If there is a bride, she stays inaccessible. It is her inaccessibility that is present" (27).

Michael Field's poem likewise suspends the girl in the moment of Hymen, in a state of in-between-ness that is neither the presence nor the absence of the hymen and cannot be described in either/or terms: "I know not how." The girl eludes description, as the Greek epigraph to this poem emphasizes: Οὐ γὰρ ἦν ἐτέρα πᾶϊς, ὦ γάμβρε, τοιαῦτα, "For there was no other girl, O bridegroom, like her," in Wharton's translation (144). The Greek fragment is translated into the present tense, however, in the final stanza of poem 47, keeping the girl perpetually suspended in the present moment of being about to be married:

> There is none like her, like thy girl, thine own,
> And, bridegroom, see!
> Honouring Hera of the silver throne,
> She turns to thee.
> Sappho, with solitary eyes, afar
> Will watch the rising of eve's fairest star.

Here again, instead of fixing the bride's identity in relation to the groom, marriage produces rhetorical doubling. Even as she "turns to thee" to become "thy girl, thine own," the poem also turns her into "eve's fairest star," not only far from "solitary" Sappho but separated from the groom as well, and still beyond reach.

By presenting Hymen as a rhetorical figure that simultaneously joins and separates, *Long Ago* opens a space for mediation, a way to cross binary oppositions and articulate what is both between and beyond. This crossing is most strikingly performed in poem 52, in which the Greek prophet Tiresias crosses from the male sex into the female, to learn "the mystic rapture of the bride." What he discovers, in comparing masculine and feminine experience of marriage, is greater "receptivity of soul":

> When womanhood was round him thrown
> He trembled at the quickening change,
> He trembled at his vision's range,
> His finer sense for bliss and dole,
> His receptivity of soul;
> But when love came, and, loving back,
> He learnt the pleasure men must lack.

Here Tiresias becomes an interchangeably doubled self: both masculine and feminine, self-divided yet coupled together. His "quickening change"—the ability to cross between sexual identities and be receptive to the split—also suggests the possibility of being *"closer married,"* as Bradley and Cooper describe themselves. They were fascinated with the figure of Tiresias, not only in this poem but in a journal entry that describes an idyllic portrait of a girl "yielding" to a shepherd. Quoting from the Tiresias poem, Cooper writes, "It is one of those works of art that 'reveal / What woman in herself must feel.' The diverse sexual frankness of enjoyment in giving (or rather taking) & receiving is clear as in Michael's *Tiresias*" (46780. April 25, 1892). This vision of Tiresias, simultaneously active and passive, defines the erotic interchangeability within Michael Field's Sapphic lyrics, as well as the textual exchange that makes the writing of these lyrics possible.

Read this way, Tiresias embodies the contradictions of a poem written by two women (Bradley and Cooper) writing as a man (Michael Field) writing as a woman (Sappho) who writes about a man (Tiresias) who was once a woman. It is significant that the Greek epigraph to the Tiresias poem is also quoted in the preface to *Long Ago,* as introduction to the contradictory authorship of the entire volume. The preface is written in the first person singular of Michael Field:

When, more than a year ago, I wrote to a literary friend of my attempt to express in English the passionate pleasure Dr. Wharton's book had brought to me, he replied: "That is a delightfully audacious thought—the extension of Sappho's fragments into lyrics. I can scarcely conceive anything more audacious." In simple truth all worship that is not idolatry must be audacious; for it involves the blissful apprehension of an ideal; it means in the very phrase of Sappho—Ἔγων δ' ἐμαύτᾳ τοῦτο σύνοιδα.

"And this I feel in myself" is Wharton's translation of the Greek phrase *Egōn d'emautai touto sunoida* from Sappho (80), asserting the language of personal experience yet also pointing to self-division: the doubling of "I" (the masculine or feminine pronoun *egō*) and "myself" (the feminine pronoun *emautai*), to produce "this" (the neuter demonstrative *touto*), as a knowledge that is neither masculine nor feminine but both simultaneously. Such cross-gendering anticipates the scenario of the Tiresias poem but also describes the multiple identifications and transgressions of gender involved throughout Michael Field's reading of Sappho—a "passionate pleasure" that is "delightfully audacious" because of its transgressive possibilities. The imitation of Sappho's fragments—or what is here called "the blissful apprehension of an ideal"—depends on this proliferation of selves: whatever Sappho knew "herself" Michael Field must assume "himself," and this assumption of a woman's *egō* by a man is implicitly doubled by the assumption of a man's *egō* by two women. So whose *egō* is it?

Not surprisingly, contemporary reviewers of *Long Ago* singled out Tiresias to pose questions about the authorship of the volume as a whole. In *The Academy* Tiresias is praised as "a myth in this poet's hands, serving to illustrate, in singularly penetrative fashion, the bi-sexual make of the poet" (18 June 1889, 388). This review substitutes bisexuality for dual authorship in order to avoid speaking of Michael Field in the plural, but the unspoken question is nearly audible: is Michael Field one sex, two sexes, or, perhaps, the third sex? A more censorious review in *The Spectator* considered the penetration of Tiresias by Michael Field "rude and coarse," however, if not altogether unspeakable: "It remains among the : and we wish that it had not found expression by a writer whose power we entertain, as we have more than once avowed, a profound respect" (July 27, 1889.119). Through Tiresias, whose story is to be spoken only in Greek, Michael Field has introduced "the ἄρρητα" (literally, "unspeakable things") into the English language.

Insofar as *Long Ago* finds expression for such things, it is precisely because of the ambiguity that surrounds Michael Field as the "speaker" of these Sapphic lyrics. Through the Greek fragments of Sappho, Bradley and Cooper enter a space for the interplay between sexuality and textuality, allowing various sexualities to emerge and finding new ways to engender the lyric as a genre. Their doubling of Sappho, I have suggested, takes many different forms: lyric voice is doubled by means of an eroti-cized textual exchange that is figured within their poems as interweav-ing; the self-doubling figure of Hymen enacts the rhetorical reversal and inversion of gender differences; and Tiresias embodies an interchange-ably doubled self. This continual interchange defines the closer marriage of Bradley and Cooper, who invoke a traditional Victorian ideology of marriage even while they rework its fixed opposition of masculine and feminine. Indeed their skepticism about "the modern sacrament of Mat-rimony" is expressed in a letter that recounts the wedding of Havelock Ellis: "It is revolting. 'Free love, free field,' is sacreder," they proclaim (*WD:* 193). What would it mean to celebrate, instead, "Free love, free field"? By imitating Sappho, Bradley and Cooper allow Michael Field to enter into a metaphorical field, where other sexualities come into play.

A Metaphorical Field

"To write lesbianism is to enter a rhetorical, that is a metaphorical, field— a scene of 'transposition ... [involving] the *figure as such*,'" Elizabeth Meese proposes, in her essay, "Theorizing Lesbian: Writing—A Love Let-ter." She cites Paul Ricoeur's reflections on metaphor in order to trans-pose his words into her own scene of "lesbian: writing," an essay that si-multaneously names and enacts "the problem of speaking metaphorically about metaphor" (1990: 75). This problem arises whenever "lesbian" en-ters any discourse, as an (im)proper name that calls into question the possibility of naming itself. While "lesbian" operates within a system of nomenclature that assumes and produces various kinds of sexual identity, what it also names is a figure for the lesbian—Sappho of Lesbos, a name and a place with multiple significations, a metaphor. By means of a rhetor-ical transposition, the place substitutes for the name, allowing Sappho to be read as original "lesbian," the precursor of lesbianism as it seems to be understood in the twentieth century: Sappho of Lesbos becomes lesbian Sappho. Although questions about Sappho have persisted for many cen-turies, her association with lesbian identity is a particularly Victorian phe-nomenon, and a legacy that persists in modern lesbian studies.

The emergence of a distinctive "lesbian" identity has been one impor-tant focus of such studies, with increasing emphasis on the historical specificity of this category as well as its historical variability. Meanwhile, the viability of such a category has been interrogated within the context of queer theory, as in the work of Judith Butler who explores the insta-bility of "the lesbian signifier" and argues for "working sexuality *against* identity, even against gender" (1991:15, 29). If this double movement— simultaneously toward and away from defining lesbian identity—replays an apparent opposition between literal and figurative reading, it does so only to demonstrate the implication of each in the other, as Martha Vicinus points out in "Lesbian History: All Theory and No Facts or All Facts and No Theory?" Because "lesbian history has always been characterized by a 'not knowing' what could be its defining core," Vicinus argues that an identity model of lesbian history is inadequate to the historian's task; on the other hand, she concludes that the definitional uncertainty embraced by queer theory "denies the historicity of all lesbian roles" insofar as it privileges the free play of metaphoric performance independent of social context (1994b: 59).

Recent work on Michael Field has begun to reconstruct such a context. Lillian Faderman offers a biographical account of Bradley and Cooper, as example of a nineteenth-century "romantic friendship" (1981), while Angela Leighton's reading of their poetry emphasizes a more erotic subtext (1992). Chris White focuses more specifically on Michael Field's Sapphic lyrics, in conjunction with the largely unpublished journals of Bradley and Cooper, in order to reclaim a nineteenth-century discourse of lesbianism that manifests sexual desire between women. It is important to trace the public articulation of lesbian as a social category in Victorian England, particularly by the end of the century when the figure of Sappho is increasingly lesbianized: she is invoked by decadent writers, sexologists, and classical scholars as "historical" evidence for the practice of lesbian sexuality at the moment of, and in reponse to, the regulatory heterosexual construction of male homosexuality. Bradley and Cooper therefore turn to Sappho as a highly overdetermined trope. To read Michael Field's Sappho as the self-reflexive performance of this trope is not to privilege performative free play independent of social context, but to situate *Long Ago* within a social context that produces such performativity: these Sapphic lyrics are the product of a particular historical moment in late-nineteenth-century England, when Sappho's fragments were in wide circulation. Many Victorian poets, male and female, imitated Sappho at this time, and it is precisely this proliferation of imitations that creates the possibility of lesbian imitation as well. Thus Bradley and Cooper appropriate Sappho as a name simultaneously proper and improper, their own and not their own.

"Michael Field frees the love lyric, long a genre of possession, into an ownerless, borderless 'field,'" Wayne Koestenbaum suggests in *Double Talk*, his study of male homoerotic collaborative writing (1989: 174). I want to pursue that suggestive pun on the name of Michael Field in the context of *Long Ago*, if not to the point of reading these lyrics as altogether "ownerless" then at least to put the terms of ownership into play: who owns the Sapphic signature, and how does it double as Michael Field's "own" lesbian signature? However, not unlike Judith Butler, "I am skeptical about how the 'I' is determined as it operates under the title of the lesbian sign" (14), and this skepticism pertains not only to the determination of lesbian identity but also to the determination of a lyric "I"—especially if both determinations occur in the name of "Sappho the Lesbian." Is it possible, then, to read the love lyrics in *Long Ago* under the title of the lesbian sign—or its signature—without assuming or producing a lesbian identity that is as much a phantasm for Sappho as it is for Katherine Bradley and Edith Cooper? How, in other words, might we read Michael Field in order to enter the metaphorical field of lesbian writing, and how do the Sapphic fragments introduce such transpositional logic? I propose a closer look at several lyrics in *Long Ago*, demonstrating how Sappho's Lesbos is translated into a lesbian topos: a textual space for the performance of lesbian *as* metaphor.

Fragment 2 of Sappho leads us into that scene of transposition. Reconstructed from a potsherd, it is a fragmentary text that invokes the goddess Aphrodite, also known as Cypris, to come to Lesbos from Crete. My translation of fragment 2 follows, as closely as possible, the word order in Campbell's reconstruction of the Greek text:

δεῦρύ μ' ἐκ Κρήτας ἐπ[ὶ τόνδ]ε ναῦον
ἄγνον, ὅππ[ᾳ τοι] χάριεν μὲν ἄλσος
μαλί[αν], βῶμοι δὲ τεθυμιάμε-
νοι [λι]βανώτῳ·

ἐν δ' ὕδωρ ψῦχρον κελάδει δ' ὕσδων
μαλίνων, βρόδοισι δὲ παῖς ὁ χῶρος
ἐσκίαστ᾽, αἰθυσσομένων δὲ φύλλων
κῶμα κατέρρει·

ἐν δὲ λείμων ἱππόβοτος τέθαλεν
ἠρίνοισιν ἄνθεσιν, αἰ δ᾽ ἄηται
μέλλιχα πυέοισιν[
[   ]

ἔνθα δὴ σὺ . . . . ἔλοισα Κύπρι
χρυσίαισιν ἐν κυλίκεσσιν ἄβρως
ομμεμείχμενον θαλίαισι νέκταρ
οἰνοχόαισον

Here to me from Crete, to this temple
A holy place where your lovely grove
Of apple trees is, and altars smoking
    With incense

And here cold water murmurs through the branches
Of apples, and with roses all the place

Is shadowed, and from the rustling leaves
     Deep sleep descends

And here the meadow where horses graze blooms
With spring flowers, and breezes
Breathe sweetly [
          [   ]

This is where . . . O Cypris, taking . . .
In golden cups luxuriously
Mingled with celebration the nectar
Pour

What place is this? A geographical location, a traditional *topos*? Some scholars insist that the holy temple and lovely grove of fragment 2 must be "real, not imaginary" (Page 1955:40). Perhaps it is a religious sanctuary, a nature scene, a landscape in Lesbos, a meeting-place for Sappho's circle of women. Other scholars read this fragment allegorically, in accordance with ancient Greek descriptions of paradise (Turyn 1942: 308–18). Perhaps it is the river Lethe in the underworld, the deep sleep of the afterlife, the ambrosial realm of the gods. Or perhaps the fragment can be placed in the context of a ritual, to create symbolic space for the worship of Aphrodite (Snyder 1991). The deictics at the beginning of each stanza lead the goddess into the moment of this ritual with increasing immediacy: "Come here" (*deuru*) followed by "And here . . . And here . . ." (*en d' . . . en d' . . .*), and culminating in "This is where" (*entha de*) in the epiphany of the fourth stanza. When Cypris is named, she enters the very ritual that makes her present: in the final verb (probably an imperative), she is about to pour nectar already mingled (in the previous line) with the celebration of her presence.

Or perhaps, as John Winkler suggests, fragment 2 is the locus of feminine desire: "But this place is, among other things, a personal place, an extended and multi-perspectival metaphor for women's sexuality. Virtually every word suggests a sensuous ecstasy in the service of Kyprian Aphrodite (apples, roses, quivering followed by repose, meadow for grazing, spring flowers, honey, nectar flowing). Inasmuch as the language is both religious and erotic, I would say that Sappho is describing a public ceremony for its own sake but is providing a way to experience such ceremonies, to infuse the celebrants' participation with memories of lesbian sexuality" (1990: 186). Although we might question the continuum from "women's sexuality" to "lesbian sexuality" in Winkler's account, he demonstrates how the invocation to Aphrodite serves as an invitation to erotic as well as religious experience. In the process of "describing a public ceremony," Sappho also circumscribes a highly eroticized space that blurs the boundaries between public and private, communal and personal, outside and inside. Merging external appearance and internal sensation, Sappho's sensuous description appeals to all the senses simultaneously: seeing and scenting the altars that smoke among the apple trees, feeling the cold water and hearing its murmur through the branches, seeing the roses and feeling their shade, hearing the leaves rustle and seeing them flicker, hypnotically, until a "deep sleep" or *kōma* descends. This *kōma* is a kind of trance induced by the synaesthesia of the poem, a commingling of sensations in the first three stanzas that anticipates the commingling of the nectar in the fourth, where the participle *ommemeichmenon* also has sexual connotations, as in the intermingling of bodies. The language of place shades into the language of the body, and in particular the female body, figured as holy temple, lovely grove, blooming meadow: the erotic topography of fragment 2 turns "all the place" (*pais o choros*) into metaphor. Thus Winkler reads the Lesbian topos as a lesbian topos, celebrating the multiple pleasures of woman's *jouissance* in "a multi-perspectived metaphor."

Yet this metaphorization of feminine sexuality depends on metonymy. Sappho's fragment is structured by syntactic contiguity: a series of places, presented in a paratactic sequence (the reiteration of "and"), increasingly associated with the female body, and leading to the epiphany of Aphrodite, who appears as the divine embodiment of a feminized space. We might think here of Luce Irigaray's attempt to put into play a "feminine" syntax that involves nearness and proximity, a syntax that enables the articulation of a female imaginary where it might be possible to speak (as) woman. In *This Sex Which Is Not One*, Irigaray assumes a metonymic relation between language and the female body, and her metaphor for this metonymy is two lips speaking together, neither one nor two, each touching the other without distinguishing what touches from what is touched. It is important to recognize that Irigaray theorizes this way of speaking (*parler femme*) on the level of its impossibility—as a utopian topos within a masculine economy of (in)difference—even while imagining its possibility among women: "In these places of women-among-themselves, something of a speaking (as) woman is heard" (1985:135). Perhaps fragment 2 points to this utopian lesbian topos, a place where "I" can address "you" as a figure of feminine self-doubling.[7] Its erotic intermingling functions like the metaphor of two lips, not to naturalize a female body that speaks but to inscribe that body within a different rhetorical structure

---

[7] See, e.g., Skinner 1993, who proposes Sappho as historical parallel for *parler femme*, while rejecting the theoretical implications of Irigaray's argument; in this respect Skinner exemplifies a tendency within Anglo-American feminist criticism to literalize the feminine metaphor in Irigaray's texts. For a critique of this tendency, see Fuss 1989 and Whitford 1989.

that addresses "you" as feminine. Irigaray's logic of touch, refusing the distinction between subject and object, is therefore evident not only in the confusion of boundaries and diffusion of senses in fragment 2, but in its very structure of invocation. The "you" comes into being in relation to an "I" who, in turn, comes into being at the moment of asking that "you" to come "here to me."

The question to ask about fragment 2, then, is not so much what it describes as what it performs—not what place this is, but what space it opens. The place in question, in other words, is the present performance of the song, a performative utterance that creates the space it describes. The holy place is here and now, opening the Lesbian topos in the moment of singing and inviting "you" to enter. The invocation to Aphrodite is also an invitation to the listener, to be seduced into the eroticism of Sappho's song. When the performative utterance of that song is transferred to the moment of reading, the invocation to Aphrodite becomes an invitation to the reader as well. Here "you" enter the lesbian metaphor of fragment 2, through the words on the page, pointing to the poem itself as the place for the erotic intermingling of reader and text: "This is where. . . ." At least, this is where Bradley and Cooper seem to enter the texts of Sappho, and how we are invited into the Sapphic lyrics of Michael Field: as a space performing not only the transposition of Lesbian place and lesbian body, but also transposing Sapphic song into written text. Rather than identifying with the "voice" of Sappho and assuming a "lesbian" identity, Bradley and Cooper use Sappho's fragmentary text to turn writing into a homoerotic topography: a graphic field rather than a sublimated figure.

Bradley and Cooper discovered their Lesbian topos in Wharton's edition of the Sapphic fragments. In his introductory essay, as I have noted, Wharton quotes at length from John Addington Symonds, who envisions the island of Lesbos as a place where "passion blossomed into the most exquisite lyrical poetry that the world has known: this was the flower-time of the Aeolians, their brief and brilliant spring" (Wharton 12). According to Symonds, the women of Lesbos lived in vividly sensuous landscape that taught them to speak, as if by nature, the language of the senses. Here Symonds (14) luxuriates in a detailed description that blends "perfumes, colours, sounds," to imagine a scene that appeals to all the senses simultaneously:

> All the luxuries and elegance of life which that climate and the rich valleys
> of Lesbos could afford, were at their disposal: exquisite gardens, in which
> the rose and hyacinth spread perfume; river-beds ablaze with the oleander
> and wild pomegranate; olive-groves and fountains, where the cyclamen and
> violet flowered with feathery maidenhair; pine-shadowed coves, where they

might bathe in the calm of a tideless sea; fruits such as only the southern sea and sea-wind can mature; marble cliffs, starred with jonquil and anemone in spring, aromatic with myrtle and lentisk and samphire and wild rosemary through all the months; nightingales that sang in May; temples dim with dusky gold and bright with ivory; statues and frescoes of heroic forms. In such scenes as these the Lesbian poets lived, and thought of Love. When we read their poems, we seem to have the perfumes, colours, sounds, and lights of that luxurious land distilled in verse.

Like fragment 2 of Sappho, the synaesthaesia of the passage allows the reader to enter "such scenes as these," and increasingly the landscape of Lesbos, with its valleys and rivers, spreading perfumes and feathery maidenhair, assumes the contours of a female body. What is "distilled in verse," in other words, is a highly eroticized scenario: seemingly natural, but increasingly metaphorical, inviting the reader to think of love just as "the Lesbian poets lived, and thought of Love."

Wharton follows Symonds in amplifying the feminine eroticism of the Lesbian landscape, especially in his commentary on fragment 2 of Sappho. His edition (following other nineteenth-century reconstructions of the text) prints the second and fourth stanzas of the fragment as separate poems, giving the Greek first, then several versions in English, and then offers a gloss on the parts of the poem that seem most closely associated with love.[8] He glosses the "nectar" in stanza 4: "Sappho seems to be here figuratively referring to the nectar of love" (76). So also, he locates stanza 2 in "the gardens of the nymphs" and cites a parallel passage from Theocritus about "the sacred water from the Nymph's own cave." These comments influence a poem in *Long Ago,* where Bradley and Cooper recreate fragment 2 in their own Sapphic language. The Greek epigraph is translated in the first three lines and further elaborated in the stanzas that follow:

XLIII.

Ἀμφὶ δὲ [ὕδωρ] ψῦχρον κελάδει δι᾿ ὕσδων
μαλίνων, αἰθυσσομένων δὲ φύλλων
κῶμα καυαρρεῖ·

Cool water gurgles through
The apple-boughs, and sleep
Falls from the flickering leaves,
Where hoary shadows keep

---

[8] Wharton adopts Theodor Bergk's reconstruction of the Sapphic fragment (Bergk 1882). The longer version of fragment 2 as we now have it was not published until half a century later (Norsa 1937).

Secluded from man's view
A little cave that cleaves
The rock with fissure deep.

Worshipped with milk and oil,
There dwell the Nymphs, and there
They listen to the breeze,
About their dewy hair
The clustered garlands coil,
Or, moving round the trees,
Cherish the roots with care.

There reign delight and health;
There freshness yields the palm
To musical refrain;
For never was such calm,
Such sound of murmuring stealth,
Such solace to the brain,
To weariness such balm.

Even a lover's pains,
Though fiercely they have raged,
Here find at last relief:
The heart by sorrow aged
Divinely youth regains;
Tears steal through parched grief:
All passion is assuaged.

Like fragment 2, this poem by Michael Field uses a progression of deictics (from "where" to "there" to "here") to create a space that is made present in the moment of reading. But in elaborating Sappho's Greek in English, the landscape is even more explicitly associated with the female
body: it is "a little cave that cleaves / The rock with fissure deep," inhabited by nymphs who take sensuous pleasure in their surroundings and
embody these pleasures in themselves. The κῶμα or "deep sleep" that descends in Sappho's fragment is refigured in terms of the autoeroticism of
these nymphs, as the fulfillment of desire, a balm for "lover's pains"
through which "all passion is assuaged." Bradley and Cooper thus assimilate the nymphs mentioned by Wharton into a lesbian space that is "secluded from man's view."

The idea of such a space is created not only by a thematic expansion
of fragment 2, but by locating the poem somewhere between two languages, allowing Greek to blur into English and English into Greek. The
poem lingers here, in this intermediate place. Does the quotation from
Sappho serve as title, epigraph, opening lines? Bradley and Cooper are

influenced, again, by Wharton's edition of the Sapphic fragments. Even more than his commentary, his graphic arrangement of the fragments is important in structuring their own Sapphic lyrics. What they discover in Wharton's juxtaposition of English and Greek is a place for poetic transposition: the brackets and ellipses within each fragment, the empty blanks around the fragments, the discontinuities from one fragment to the next, are all openings for Bradley and Cooper to write poetry that is implicitly if not explicitly lesbian. For this reason they prefer to imitate the short fragments, while avoiding the narrative context of Sappho's longer texts: for example, the famous poems known as the "Prayer to Aphrodite" and "Ode to Anactoria" (number 1 and 2 in Wharton's edition) are left untouched. But the more fragmentary texts, riddled with gaps, enable Bradley and Cooper to locate their own lyrics in a figurative gap, an open space out of which the possibility of lesbian writing emerges. Literally and figuratively, their Sapphic lyrics are located in the spaces between the Sapphic fragments—the lacunae in Wharton's text—in order to open a textual field that Bradley and Cooper may enter together as Michael Field.

Both fields are, of course, graphically circumscribed by the Greek fragments of Sappho, and perhaps this is why Bradley and Cooper keep returning to fragment 2 as their favorite topos in *Long Ago*. In another version of the fragment, the Lesbian landscape is not only the metaphorical space for the performance of Sapphic song, but metaphorized as the song itself. "This will I now sing deftly to please my girlfriends," is Wharton's translation of the Greek epigraph (78):

LIV.

. . . Τάδε νῦν ἑταίραις
ταῖς ἔμαισι τέρπνα κάλως ἀείσω.

Adown the Lesbian vales,
When spring first flashes out,
I watch the lovely rout
Of maidens flitting 'mid the honey-bees
For thyme and heath,
Cistus, and trails
Of myrtle-wreath:
They bring me these
My passionate, unsated sense to please.

In turn, to please my maids,
Most deftly will I sing
Of their soft cherishing

In apple-orchards with cool waters by,
Where slumber streams
From quivering shades,
And Cypris seems
To bend and sigh,
Her golden calyx offering amorously.

What praises would be best
Wherewith to crown my girls?
The rose when she unfurls
Her balmy, lighted buds is not so good,
So fresh as they
When on my breast
They lean, and say
All that they would,
Opening their glorious, candid maidenhood.

To that pure band alone
I sing of marriage-loves;
As Aphrodite's doves
Glance in the sun their colour comes and goes:
No girls let fall
Their maiden zone
At Hymen's call,
Serene as those
Taught by a poet why sweet Hesper glows.

The Lesbian vales in the first stanza are a rhetorical expansion of fragment 2, and also set the scene for the performance of that fragment as Sapphic song in the second stanza. Thus one song is contained within another, and figured as a landscape within a landscape: "the apple-orchards with cool waters" are yet another translation of Sappho's Lesbian topos, and the appearance of Cypris emphasizes its lesbian eroticism, especially because the Greek adverb *abrōs* is translated as "amorously." The third and fourth stanzas describe the girls who respond to this seductive song by "opening their glorious, candid maidenhood" and refusing "Hymen's call"—in the Sapphic circle they remain "my maids," not to be married. Like the nymphs "secluded from man's view" (in XLIII), the erotic response of these maidens is projected onto nature, and metaphorized as a lesbian landscape. Within this utopian setting, everyone exists in reciprocal relation to each other: the goddess's offering in stanza 2 corresponds to the poet's offering of a song "to please my maids," who in turn bring offerings "to please" as well.

The erotic reciprocity of Sapphic song makes this lyric interestingly interchangeable, so that the Greek epigraph refers to several performances
at once: not only the song within the song and the song about the song,
but also the poem that represents the song and even the epigraph that introduces the poem. The Greek demonstrative *tade* (in the plural, meaning "This" or "These things") at the beginning of the epigraph multiplies
in reference. In Wharton's translation of the Greek ("This will I now sing
deftly . . ."), what does "this" refer to? While implying various kinds of song,
"this" also points to the printed text of this poem. Bradley and Cooper
therefore use the Greek epigraph to mark the place of the page itself, as
another locus for the Lesbian vales: the place of writing, a literal space for
the inscription of a lesbian figure. Is it the name of Michael Field, perhaps,
metaphorically displaced onto the Lesbian vales as well as all the other
meadows, groves, and fields that we read about throughout this volume of
Sapphic lyrics? Through fragment 2, transposed by Bradley and Cooper
into a lesbian topos, it becomes possible for Michael Field to inhabit the
Lesbian topography of *Long Ago*. This name is produced by the metaphorical field of lesbian writing; it emerges from a textual field that opens between Sappho's fragments in Wharton's edition of Sappho and the Sapphic lyrics in *Long Ago*. It would seem, then, that in their first volume of
lyric poetry Bradley and Cooper are developing a metaphor that explores
the unspoken implications of their pseudonym as a lesbian signature.

In this theoretical context, we might rethink the reading of Michael
Field proposed by Angela Leighton. In her introduction to *Victorian
Women Poets,* she acknowledges that "the problem of the author, of the
'signature,' remains central to any feminist criticism," but her approach
to "the authorial name, and all the historical and biographical information that goes with it" (1992: 4) limits an exploration of this central problem in the poetry of Bradley and Cooper to a form of biographical reading that does not fully register the multiple textual mediations at work,
particularly in the Sapphic imitations. While Leighton's chapter on
Michael Field is an important contribution to the recovery of Victorian
women poets, introducing readers to the range of lyric poems written by
Bradley and Cooper, she assumes that their authorship is defined by lesbian identity rather than complicating the claim to such an identity—as
if the lesbian signature exists prior to writing rather than being produced
by it. As evidence of lesbian authorship, Leighton makes an appeal to an
"original homosexual context" (231) and authenticity of expression; in
contrast to the "unnatural invention" of Swinburne's Sappho, Michael
Field seems "authentically" Sapphic to Leighton (229). But it is only
through textuality—the transposition of the Sapphic fragments as another, though undeniably different, "unnatural invention"—that lesbian
writing can be named as such in the lyrics of Michael Field.

For example, Leighton admires "the naturalness of Michael Field" (230) in a lyric from *Long Ago* that seems anything but natural in its reconfiguration of the lesbian topos:

XXXIII.

Ταῖς κάλαις ὔμμιν [τὸ] νόημα τὦμον
οὐ διάμειπτον

Maids, not to you my mind doth change;
Men I defy, allure, estrange,
Prostrate, make bond or free:
Soft as the stream beneath the plane
To you I sing my love's refrain;
Between us is no thought of pain,
    Peril, satiety.

Soon doth a lover's patience tire,
But ye to manifold desire
Can yield response, ye know
When for long, museful days I pine,
The presage at my heart divine;
To you I never breathe a sign
    Of inward want or woe.

When injuries my spirit bruise,
Allaying virtue ye infuse
With unobtrusive skill:
And if care frets ye come to me
As fresh as nymph from stream or tree,
And with your soft vitality
    My weary bosom fill.

"To you, fair maids, my minds changes not" is the translation of the epigraph offered by Wharton, who quotes the Greek text "to show the Aeolic use ὔμμιν for ὑμίν, 'to you'" (80). But for Michael Field this use of ὔμμιν in Aeolic shows more than the difference of a Lesbian dialect; it introduces the possibility of lesbian language that addresses women differently. Unlike Wharton, Michael Field's poem places "Maids" first in its translation of the Greek epigraph, and the parallel placement of "Maids" and "Men" in lines 1 and 2 generates a grammatical distinction between second-person address (placing woman in the subject position) and third-person description (placing man in the object position). While men are merely acted upon, women are actively desiring subjects in this poem, able to reciprocate desire: "But ye to manifold desire / Can yield response." Indeed, in Michael Field's elaboration of Sappho's fragment, the very possibility of an address to "you" depends on this capacity for response, which takes the form of "presaging" or "divining" what the "I" has to say—as if the articulation of one cannot exist without anticipation by the other. Thus "you" and "I" are interfused in the reciprocal exchange of "love's refrain," returning us to the Lesbian topos of fragment 2 one more time: what I sing "soft as the stream beneath the plane" in the first stanza is echoed by you "as fresh as nymph from stream to tree" in the third stanza.

Leighton considers the parallel flow of stream and song "a description of an unhampered woman-to-woman's language as suggestively labial as any Irigarayan writing of the body" (230), and although it is misleading to think that such a language can be "described" thematically rather than performed rhetorically, Irigaray does pose a question relevant to the performance of this particular poem. "How can I speak to you? You are in flux," she writes in "When Our Lips Speak Together." This essay can be read as a sustained lyric apostrophe, the elaboration of a rhetorical structure that allows "I" and "you" to come together in a "we" that is neither one nor two; it is a relation of "unceasing mobility" like "streams without fixed banks, this body without fixed boundaries" (215). Michael Field's poem enacts a similar movement, as it moves from "To you" and "I sing" to "Between us," in a relation eroticized beyond heterosexual opposition into more fluid desire. Yet in comparing the mobility of this language to "the stream beneath the plane," Leighton literalizes Irigaray's metaphor in a way that tends to naturalize Michael Field as well. Her insistence on the "naturalness" of this lyric extends to reading "the natural imagery of Michael Field's love poetry" (233) in general, which in her view "seems to belong out in the open air of nature" (204). The effect of such a reading is the literalization and naturalization of a lesbian figure that is derived from the poetry of Michael Field yet attributed to the life of Bradley and Cooper.

Even the journals of Bradley and Cooper, where we might expect glimpses of life, are self-consciously mediated by the many texts they read and write together. During the composition of lyrics for *Long Ago*, Bradley and Cooper often construct their daily experience with reference to and indeed *through* Sappho's Greek fragments. In the spring of 1888, Bradley writes, for example: "Nature becomes dumb from the moment she grows green. We shall have no more communion till she summons me to her death bed. They have hurt + trampled the hyacinths; but one day last week in a field of vetches I saw them growing safe. . . ." (46777. April 18, 1888). This journal entry betrays a profoundly antinatural impulse: the natural world comes to life only at the moment of dying, and in the personification of a Nature who summons the poet "to her death bed"—a highly self-conscious literary artifice. Since the natural world is dumb,

Bradley takes up communion with a Sapphic text that speaks to her as if it were nature. "They have hurt + trampled the hyacinths" is a direct allusion to fragment 94 in Wharton's edition: "As on the hills the shepherds trample the hyacinth under foot, and the flower darkens on the ground" (134). This fragment is assimilated into one of the opening lyrics in *Long Ago:*

V.

Οἴαν τάν ὑακίνθον ἐν οὔρεσι ποίμενες ἄνδρες
πόσσι καταστείβοισι, χάμαι δέ τε πόρφυρον ἄνθος

As on the hills the shepherds tread
A hyacinth down, and withered
    The purple flower
Is pressed to earth, and broken lies,
Its virgin stem no more to rise
    In summer hour;
And death comes stealing with the dew
That yester evening brought anew
A fresher growth and fragrant grace,
Ere footsteps crushed the grassy place:

So underneath thy scorn and pride
My heart is bowed, and cannot hide
    How it despairs.
O Phaon, weary is my pain;
The tears that from my eyelids rain
    Ease not my cares;
My beauty droops and fades away,
Just as a trampled blossom's may.
Why must thou tread me into earth—
So dim in death, so bright at birth?

It is an extended simile, associating the trampled hyacinth with the loss of virginity and the pain inflicted by Phaon—Sappho's mythical lover who haunts the margins of *Long Ago* as a figure for the ravages of heterosexual desire. Early in the volume Phaon is a prominent figure, but gradually he is banished from the other lyrics expressing desire of, for, and between women in a different idiom. Phaon, like the shepherds in the fragment and "They" in the journal entry, represents a transgression or interruption of the feminine space circumscribed by Michael Field, and the reclamation of this field as a lesbian topos in *Long Ago* corresponds to the Bradley's discovery of hyacinths: "But one day last week in a field of vetches I saw them growing safe." What Bradley "saw" is mediated by

her reading of Sappho—not only the natural world but the Greek hyacinth fragment, not only a field of vetches but the name of Michael Field,
who revives the figure of the hyacinths and makes them speak through
Sappho's text when nature falls dumb.

And again in May, Bradley discovers hyacinths growing in a metaphorical field associated with Sappho: "In Edith's Valley the other evening we
found a bank of hyacinths. Above them, overlooking low oaks, was a full,
pale moon, not shining, not yet an influence—a steady dominating presence. . . ." (46777. May 25, 1888). Edith's Valley is like the Lesbian vales
of *Long Ago,* a space for the recreation of Sapphic song. The hyacinths are
left untouched here, and Sappho's influence is felt in the presence of the
moon. A similar scenario is recreated in XVII, a longer narrative lyric in
Long Ago:

> The moon rose full: the women stood
> As though within a sacred wood
> Around an altar—thus with awe
> The perfect, virgin orb they saw
> Supreme above them. . . .

The opening lines are based on Sappho's description of a full moon, and
indeed in this lyric Sappho herself is figured as the moon, shining down
on a circle of women who are awaiting "Sappho's word" and "responsive
to her music's sound." Bradley's journal entry anticipates the writing of
that lyric, as if she and Edith are about to enter the Sapphic circle in the
light of Sappho's moon—"not yet an influence" but soon to be "a steady
dominating presence." The journal demonstrates how Sappho's fragments permeate the "natural" details of Bradley and Cooper's writing at
this time, to the point that they perceive the Greek text as a second nature to be inhabited by Michael Field. Notwithstanding Leighton's attempt to naturalize Michael Field, what emerges here is a textual field
mediated by Sappho. Indeed, the translation of Lesbian into lesbian requires the mediation of Greek, allowing the space of writing itself to be
"lesbianized."

Instead of assuming Sapphic voice, Michael Field's Sappho therefore
emerges as a function of reading Greek text. A poem from *Underneath the
Bough* (1893), published four years after *Long Ago,* reflects further on this
transfer of Sapphic song to the scene of reading. It is an invitation to the
reader, addressed as a "Lady," to enter a place where "thou" and "I" can
read books together. To create this metaphorical space, the first four stanzas use the same rhetorical devices as the invocation to Aphrodite in fragment 2 of Sappho. In a second-person address, repeating the imperative
"come" and the demonstrative "there," the poem literally and figuratively
opens itself as a room for erotic interplay:

AN INVITATION

Come and sing, my room is south,
Come with thy sun-governed mouth,
Thou wilt never suffer drouth,
    Long as dwelling
In my chamber of the south.

On the wall there is woodbine,
With its yellow-scarlet shine;
When my lady's hopes decline,
    Honey-smelling
Trumpets will her mood divine.

There are myrtles in a row;
Lady, when the flower's in blow,
Kisses passing to and fro,
    From our smelling,
Think, what lovely dreams will grow!

There's a lavender settee,
Cushioned for my sweet and me;
Ah, what secrets there will be
    For love-telling
When her head leans on my knee!

Assimilating fragment 2 of Sappho as well as various imitations of that fragment in *Long Ago,* this poem tropes on Michael Field's own lesbian topos: the room turns into a tropical "chamber of the south" where nature grows unnaturally lush and vivid to all the senses. Here the "yellow-scarlet," "honey-smelling trumpets" of woodbine, and the scent of myrtle "when the flower's in blow" recreate both the scenario and the synaesthesia of Sappho's poem, situated not in nature but within an imaginary interior where "lovely dreams will grow." These dreams, like the κῶμα produced by fragment 2, anticipate the sensuous intermingling of "my sweet and me" in the act of reading.

The reader is thus invited into the space of the poem, to be initiated into the erotics of reading. In stanza 5, the poem continues:

Books I have of long ago
And to-day; I shall not know
Some, unless thou read them, so
    Their excelling
Music needs thy voice's flow. . . .

Of course, one of those books "of long ago" is *Long Ago,* referring back to Bradley and Cooper's reconfiguration of lyric voice through the figure of

Sappho. Their reading of the Sapphic fragments, and our reading of their Sapphic lyrics, assumes a complementary relation of two rather than the solitary utterance of one; this music "needs thy voice's flow," within an erotic context that allows "thou" and "I" to come together. What follows is a list of other books as well, allowing the lover's tongue to play in various languages, such as the music of Campion, the French of Flaubert and Verlaine, the Latin of Catullus, and—in the final stanza—the Greek of Sappho:

> And for Greek! Too sluggishly
> Thou dost toil; but Sappho, see!
> And the dear Anthology
> For thy spelling.
> Come, it shall be well with thee.

Although "The Invitation" begins with an invitation to sing, it ends here as an invitation to read a language that is deliberately difficult to pronounce: ancient Greek is written, not spoken, a text for spelling rather than singing. But if Sappho's fragmentary texts can't be voiced by one person, they can be spelled out between two lovers reading to each other: the "Lady" and "I." In this way the poem re-enacts a Sapphic eros that also created the Sapphic imitations in *Long Ago*. It reinscribes the encounter with Sappho's Greek text as a lesbian seduction, spelling out the name of Sappho, while leaving the implications of that name unspoken.

The frontispiece to *Long Ago* illustrates how Bradley and Cooper present Sappho to the reader "for thy spelling"—as a name half-spelled, to be completed in the moment of reading. In this illustration (figure 6), a woman is in the pose of a reader, drawn from a fifth-century hydria at the Athens National Museum.[9] Is this Sappho? The first three letters of Sappho's name are given—sigma, alpha, pi, the beginning of a signature. But if the figure is Sappho, she is curiously suspended between reading and speaking, estranged from the writing on a bookroll which may or may not be her own. According to the endnote in *Long Ago*, she is reading a prayer to the gods to become the messenger of new songs. Will she sing or read them? Perhaps she is not the original Sappho but a figure for the Sapphic imitator, someone who writes in Sappho's name. The Greek letters hovering between the woman and the text open a textual field, out of which Michael Field emerges to sign the name of Sappho. But if this is a lesbian signature, does it belong to Sappho, Michael Field, Bradley and Cooper,

---

[9] The end note to *Long Ago* identifies the frontispiece as follows: "The frontispiece is reproduced from a figure of Sappho, seated and reading, on a vase in the museum at Athens. [Dumont et Chaplain, Ceramiques, pl. 6.] Part of her name Σ Α Π is given. The manuscript in her hands has been read as follows: θεοι, ηεριων επεων αρχομαι αγγ[ελος] ν[εων] υ[μ]ν[ων. The date of this vase is about 420 B.C."

FIGURE 6: Frontispiece from *Long Ago,* Michael Field (1889). Courtesy
of The Rare Books Room, The Pennsylvania State University Libraries.

or is it an effect of our own multiple readings? The Sapphic signature of
Long Ago belongs, finally, to the reader as she is figured in the frontispiece.
Here she sits, already beginning to spell out the name of Sappho as she
begins to read the Sapphic lyrics in the book. Thus we too are invited to
read between two languages, to mediate between reading Σ Α Π Φ Ω literally and reading Michael Field metaphorically, to read a signature from
long ago doubled in *Long Ago.*

THREE

SWINBURNE'S SAPPHIC SUBLIME

Loose Limbs, Mutilated Fragments

WHY is Algernon Charles Swinburne remembered as the most Sapphic of Victorian poets, if not indeed the very reincarnation of Sappho? "No bard of the present age has a genius more akin to hers, more passionate and fiery, than Mr. Swinburne," proclaims an anonymous reviewer in the *Athenaeum:* a conventional opinion, but curious because it appears in the context of a review of Michael Field (Athenaeum 1889: 56). While offering praise for the Sapphic lyrics in *Long Ago,* the reviewer believes that Michael Field "has not, indeed, the impulsive spring of uncontrollable passion which is characteristic of the true lyric poet," nor "the infinite command of musical metres" of a poet like Swinburne (57). What is "impulsive," "uncontrollable," and infinitely "musical" in Swinburne is his unsurpassed metrical virtuosity, the passionate rhythms that rule his verse, and especially his imitations of Sappho. In "Anactoria," his most famous and most scandalous poem, Swinburne turns Sappho's lyricism into a lurid meditation on the pleasures of rhythm: the beating of Sappho the Lesbian into a lesbian body. In contrast to the playful troping on the name of Sappho by Michael Field, Swinburne therefore makes a lesbian reading of Sappho sexually explicit.

The differential use of Sappho within male and female homoeroticism is an important issue, as Thaïs Morgan points out: through his identification with Sappho, Swinburne constructs a male lesbian body, a transgressive female figure for "homoerotically inclined masculinity, but a masculinity that continues to define itself in difference from femininity, including a lesbian femininity" (1992: 52). This subtle formulation allows us to distinguish between various "lesbian" versions of Sappho and may explain in part why Michael Field is so easily eclipsed by Swinburne: the Victorian Sappho we remember is his dominatrix, a dominant poetic figure throughout the late Victorian period. But to read his masculine version of lesbian desire in terms of homosexual practice, as Morgan suggests in concurrence with Richard Dellamora and other recent critics, is not to read one important part of the Sapphic body as it is figured by Swinburne. While Morgan concludes that "in 'Anactoria,' Swinburne imagines homosexual practice between men through the analogy of lesbian coupling" (49), I suggest that the Sapphic body emerges in Swinburne's

poetry as a rhythmicized, eroticized form: less a "male lesbian body" than
an embodiment of the rhythm of eros itself, a scattering movement too
diffuse to be contained within any single body, and increasingly formalized by Swinburne into a metrical pattern.

For Swinburne, Sapphic eros is a structure of repetition that allows the
body to emerge in the reiteration of its own undoing. His reading of Sappho derives from fragment 130, which dramatizes the effects of eros on
a body that trembles in violent contradiction, at the moment of coming
apart:

> Ἔρος δ' ηὖτέ μ' ὁ λυσιμέλης δόνει,
> γλυκύπικρον ἀμάχανον ὄρπετον
> And eros again the loosener of limbs makes me tremble
> A sweet-bitter unmanagable creature.[1]

Eros is often called "the loosener of limbs" in archaic Greek lyric: Ἔρος
λυσιμέλης . The epithet *lusimelēs* (associated with the verb *luo,* "to
loosen," and the noun *melē,* "limbs,") describes a force so powerful it dissolves the joints and disjoins the body, disarticulating the parts from the
whole. The grammatical subject of fragment 130 is *eros lusimelēs,* turning
"me" into its tremulous object, subjected to contrary sensations both
sweet and bitter (*glukupikron*). This painful pleasure is enacted in the present tense, yet also repeated over time, as is evident in the adverbial
phrase "and . . . again." While in Greek *d'ēute* follows the word *eros,* the
elided postpositive particle "and" (*de*) is properly read as preceding *eros,*
implying that this erotic subjection has happened before and will happen again: Sapphic eros is always already happening, a continual movement, a kinetic event.

The epithet for eros, "the loosener of limbs," is more than merely for-
mulaic in this context, as it names a rhythmic effect that is also performed in the pseudo-dactylic rhythm of the fragment, making eros
move insidiously like an *amakhanon orpeton,* a creature creeping up, impossible to fight off, relentlessly advancing in the meter itself. Indeed,
fragment 130 has been preserved precisely because of its metrical appeal. We owe the transmission of this Sapphic fragment to the *Handbook of Metres* of Hephaestion, who quotes the two short lines as example of "the Aeolic dactylic tetrameter acatalectic" (Campbell 147).
Metrical analysis (the verb "to analyze" is also derived from the Greek
verb *luō,* "to loosen") is another way to measure the rhythms of *eros
lusimelēs,* since the Greek word for limbs (*melē*) can refer both to the parts
of the body and to the parts of song. The *melē* or "limbs" of Sappho decomposed by *eros lusimelēs,* may thus be recomposed in the *melē* or

---

[1] Fragment 130 (Campbell 146); the English translation is my own.

"melody" of Sapphic song. This is how Sappho, famous for the invention of new rhythms in her Aeolic dialect, came to be known in antiquity: Alexandrian scholars collected Sappho's songs into volumes entitled *Sapphous melē,* a Sapphic corpus celebrated for its metrical perfection, and anatomized by ancient colometrists such as Hephaestion. By analyzing the meter of Sappho's fragment—figuratively "loosening" its "limbs," again—Hephaestion repeats the rhythmic disarticulation and rearticulation of the Sapphic body, and turns Sappho herself into a metrical body that is manifested *through* and *as* meter.

There exists, then, a long tradition of reading Sappho as if she were a metrical body. Greek colometry described different kinds of meter by measuring poetry into body parts such as *kōla* (legs), *podes* (feet), *daktyloi* (fingers), and the Longinian treatise on the sublime also draws on this established homology between poem and body. Meter, according to Longinus, is an important source of sublimity when it organizes language by analogy to the composition of various members of the human body: "None of the members (*melē*) has any value by itself apart from the others," he writes, "but if they are united into a single system and embraced moreover by the bonds of rhythm, then by being merely rounded into a period they gain a living voice" (Longinus 40.1, tr. Fyfe). His reading of fragment 31, as we saw in Chapter 1, makes Sappho speak as if "with a living voice" by turning the poem into a body, a formal composition that is held together by the bonds of rhythm. The rhetorical recuperation of fragment 31 therefore assumes a tradition of metrical reading that takes fragment 130 as one of its subtexts, enabling Longinus to exchange the *melē* of Sappho's body for the *melē* of her song: the body scattered by *eros lusimelēs* is metrically reconstituted—bound together and "rounded" into a period—within the perfect cadence of the Sapphic stanza.

However, as I further argued in my first chapter, the Longinian reading of Sappho also calls into question the doctrine of organic unity. What we discover in the treatise on the sublime is not the rounded body of Sappho's poem, but a fragmentary text, quoted out of context: when Longinus cites fragment 31, he breaks it off from the Sapphic corpus, and when he further paraphrases the fragment, he enumerates the parts of Sappho that have "wandered apart from herself" in a sentence that also pulls apart the body of the poem. While arguing for Sappho's recuperation as a unified poetic subject, Longinus therefore perpetuates the fragmentation of Sappho; her poem is a mutilated text rather than a living organism, ironically anatomized as if it were a body, yet resisting integration into an organic whole. Thus Longinus performs not only a movement from literal fragmentation to figurative reconstitution—the sublime turn described by Neil Hertz—but a reversal of that sublime turn, from figurative reconstitution back to a literal fragmentation.[2] Such a reversal points to a counter-reading implicit within the Longinian sublime, a systematic disarticulation of the body that manifests the materiality of language rather than producing a sublimated figure.

It is within this rhetorical tradition that I wish to locate Swinburne's Sapphic sublime. Swinburne judged Sappho to be "the very greatest poet that ever lived," as he wrote in a letter of 1880: "Such, I must confess, judging even from the mutilated fragments fallen within our reach from the broken altar of her sacrifice of song, I for one have always agreed with all Grecian tradition in regarding Sappho, beyond all question and comparison to be . . . Sappho is simply nothing less—as she is certainly nothing more—than the greatest poet who ever was at all.—There, at all events, you have the simple and sincere profession of my lifelong faith." (*Letters* IV:124) According to Swinburne's sacrificial logic, Sappho is "nothing less" and "nothing more" than the greatest poet precisely because nothing survives, other than "mutilated fragments." The long clause ("judging even from . . . ") that seems to qualify his judgment is hardly concessive here, for it defines the necessary condition of Sappho's afterlife. What makes Sappho sublime is the mutilation of the Sapphic fragments, allowing her to be simultaneously dismembered and remem-

---

[2] We might recall once more that Longinus paraphrases fragment 31 in the form of a rhetorical question: "Is it not wonderful how she summons at the same time, soul, body, hearing, tongue, sight, colour, all as though they had wandered off apart from herself?" (10.2, Fyfe 156–57). Here the doctrine of organic unity—which the fragment is meant to confirm—is also the question most urgently posed by Longinus in his reading of Sappho, and elsewhere in the treatise. Hertz certainly recognizes the ironic implications of the question, as he traces "the persistent play throughout the treatise of the paired terms 'body'/'fragment'" (214). By turning this irony into the pathos of self-loss, however, Hertz repeats a rhetorical reading that depends on the doctrine of organic unity, which he seems to take unironically within the context of the Longinian argument. "It is certain that Longinus takes the doctrine seriously," Hertz insists (4), and in a note on the rejection of inorganic discourse he adds, "It would be a mistake to see in this either inadvertence or irony." (241) As Jonathan Lamb points out, this "oddly unironic recuperation" (Lamb 1993: 548) provokes a critique of Hertz by Paul de Man, who claims that the post-Longinian sublime is a tradition "finally ironized, though not necessarily exorcised" in Hertz's essay (de Man 1996: 110). In several late essays, de Man pursues an account of a material sublime, disarticulating the figure of the human body (as in "Phenomenality and Materiality in Kant," de Man 1996: 70–90), and developing a nonmimetic model that "reduces to nought . . . the pathos of rhetorical analysis" (as in "Hegel on the Sublime," de Man 1996: 105–118, 116). Frances Ferguson observes that de Man's deconstructive materialism "provides the basis for imagining the text in hyperformalist terms that both exceed and repeat the doctrine of organic unity that de Man has repeatedly attacked" (Ferguson 1992: 13). We might try to imagine the poetry of Swinburne in such "hyperformalist terms" even if (as Ferguson says of de Man) such a reading "makes . . . masochists of us all" (15). Indeed, that would be the point (and *pace* de Man, pathos) of Swinburne's Sapphic sublime.

bered, in a complex mediation between corpse and corpus: the body of the poet is sacrificed to the body of her song, and this body of song is sacrificed to posterity, which recollects the scattered fragments in order to recall Sappho herself as the long-lost origin of lyric poetry. What is "fallen within our reach" is thus uplifted—sublimated—by Swinburne into a sublime persona, the immortal Sappho; her afterlife is the profession of his "lifelong faith," and he defines his vocation as lyric poet by worshiping at the broken altar of her sacrifice.

Swinburne's own poetic corpus, I argue, is also constituted on a Sapphic model, as Swinburne is increasingly cast—by himself as well as by his readers—in the role of Sappho. But just as the Longinian reading of Sappho is predicated on catachresis—the figure of abuse, disfiguring the body—Swinburne's Sapphic imitations also perform the undoing of the Sapphic body. Swinburne turns Sappho into a *figure for* the figure of abuse, a double catachresis that makes her both cause and effect of a rhetorical violence that forcefully scatters the body. In "Anactoria," the notorious Sapphic monologue that provoked the succès de scandale of *Poems and Ballads* in 1866, Swinburne presents Sappho as a body simultaneously abusing and abused:

> My life is bitter with thy love; thine eyes
> Blind me, thy tresses burn me, thy sharp sighs
> Divide my flesh and spirit with soft sound,
> And my blood strengthens, and my veins abound.
> I pray thee sigh not, speak not, draw not breath;
> Let life burn down, and dream it is not death.
> I would the sea had hidden us, the fire
> (Wilt thou fear that, and fear not my desire?)
> Severed the bones that bleach, the flesh that cleaves
> And let our sifted ashes drop like leaves.
> I feel thy blood against my blood: my pain
> Pains thee, and lips bruise lips, and vein stings vein.
>
> (1–12)

The opening lines of this dramatic monologue are a repetition of fragment 31: eyes are blinded, ears are suffused with sound, fire burns under the skin, and the entire body trembles on the verge of death. But whose body? Sappho's or Anactoria's? "I" and "thou" suffer equally in a mutual subjection that divides subject from object, rending them apart yet also rendering them interestingly interchangeable. The enjambments in this passage suspend the body in a perpetual state of self-division: "thine eyes / Blind me," "thy sharp sighs / Divide my flesh," and culminating in "my pain / Pains thee." This enjambed chiasmus doubles the pain and directs it both ways, like the verbal doubling in "lips bruise lips" and "vein stings vein," leaving us unable to distinguish any longer between "thy blood" and "my blood." Divided into many parts, separate but also together, different but also the same, Sappho and Anactoria embody the paradox of "flesh that cleaves;" here, as so often in Swinburne's verse, the verb "to cleave" is used antithetically—meaning both "to join" and "to separate"—in order to describe a body held together only by falling apart. Thus Swinburne's Sappho is undone as she is made by the force of her own sublime rhetoric.

Not only is the fragmentation of the Sapphic body enacted rhetorically in the address to Anactoria, it is also manifested graphically in the manuscript of Swinburne's poem itself. In a draft of Anactoria, we see how Swinburne decomposes his Sapphic imitation in the very act of composing it. The draft is an extraordinary visual spectacle: it puts the text on display like a *corps morcelé* with its disjointed limbs scattered across the page, severed and splayed in every direction (figure 7).[3] The lines are written at several different angles, with interpolations and revisions in tortured writing along the margins. Line 9, for example, disintegrates under the pressure of Swinburne's revisions: "⟨Severed the⟩ ⟨Divided⟩ *Severed the* bones that bleach, the flesh that cleaves." What is severed, divided, and severed again is the "body" of language itself, disarticulated in the assertion of its own severing. A similar linguistic disintegration occurs in Swinburne's revision of lines 11–12, as they are scribbled in the margins of his draft: "I feel thy blood against my blood; ⟨thy veins⟩ ⟨*my pain*⟩ **my pain** ⟨Fill my⟩ ⟨Filling⟩ ⟨Pains thee,⟩ ⟨Pains thee *all through,* and vein throbs hard on vein.⟩ Pains thee, ⟨and mouth⟩ and lip hurts lip, ⟨and⟩ **and** vein ⟨aches on⟩ **stings** vein."[4] While these fragmentary lines are reintegrated in the final version of Swinburne's poem—harmonized into the lyricism of his couplet—they nevertheless reveal how the composition of Sappho into a lyric figure depends on the recomposition of many decomposing parts.

Swinburne's Sapphic sublime therefore vacillates between an ironic organicism and a linguistic materialism; Swinburne remembers Sappho by dismembering the Sapphic corpus, and like Longinus, he uses the figure of her mutilated body to materialize a fragmentary text. Of course the sublime sadomasochism of "Anactoria," a poem vehemently attacked by the critics, was a deliberate attempt to scandalize Swinburne's readers; but it further serves to demonstrate what Isobel Armstrong has aptly called "Swinburne's fevered sense of the brute materiality of language" (1993: 403). I agree with Armstrong that his poetry tends toward "a ma-

---

[3] I am referring in particular to the draft of "Anactoria" dated 1863, in the special collection at the Harry Ransom Humanities Research Center at the University of Texas, Austin. For a discussion of the draft, see Gosse 1919 and T. Burnett 1993.

[4] Here I follow the system of transcribing variants, and specifically the transcription of lines 11–12 of Swinburne's poem, as described by T. Burnett 1993: 149–50, 156.

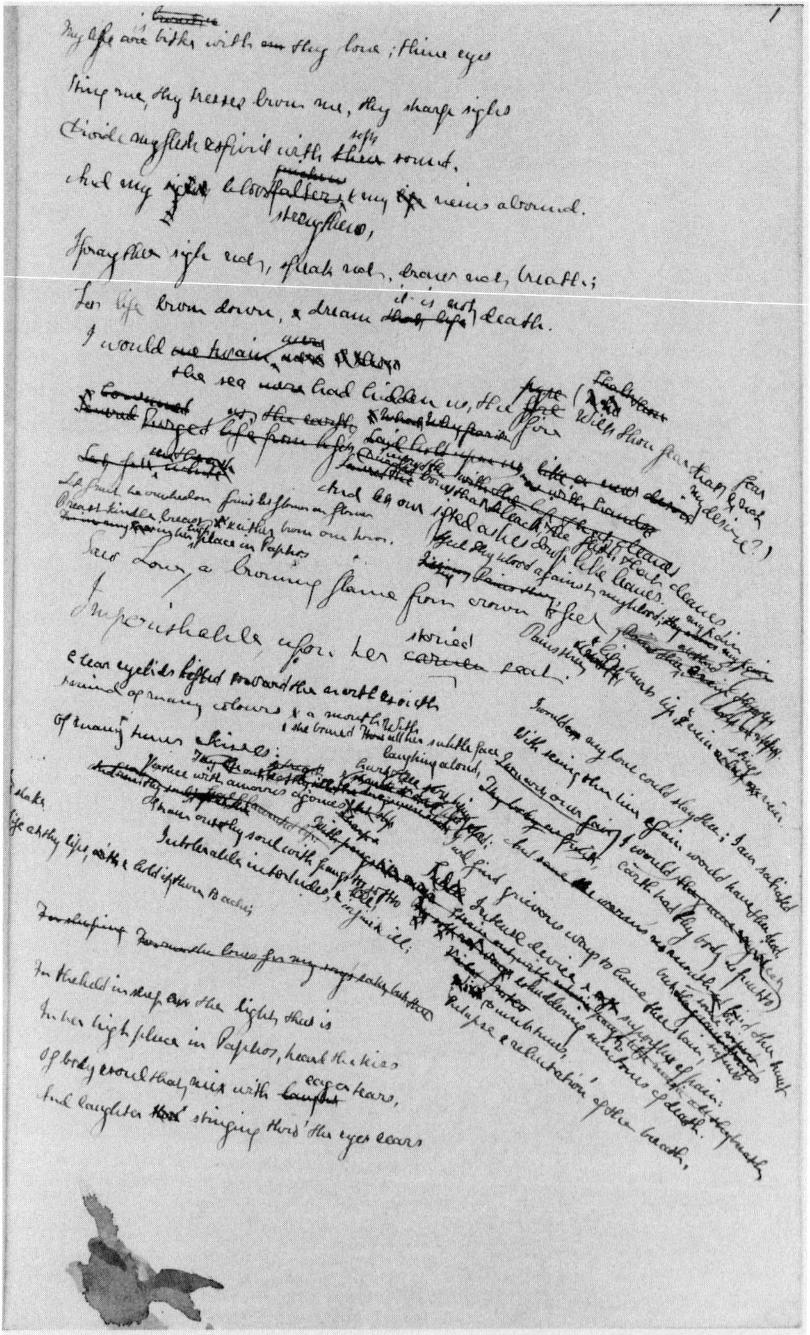

FIGURE 7: Draft of "Anactoria," Algernon Swinburne (1863). Courtesy of Harry Ransom Humanities Research Center, University of Texas at Austin, and by permission of Random House UK Ltd.

terialism which leaves us with the literal sign and that only" (404), and in the pages that follow, I will suggest why and how Swinburne discovers this radical literalism through Sappho in particular. Swinburne considered fragment 31 "a poem that could not be reproduced in the body" and in "Notes on Poems and Reviews," he defends "Anactoria" as a free imitation of the fragment because "I felt myelf incompetent to give adequate expression in English to the literal and absolute words of Sappho; and would not debase and degrade them into a viler form" (Hyder 1966: 21). When he incorporates the Sapphic fragments into the body of his own writing, Swinburne therefore performs the undoing of an organic figure for poetry; the impact of the missing "body" of Sappho is felt precisely in the pathos of Swinburne's literalism, in his attention to the "literal and absolute words" that are never adequate to or always "viler" (more fevered, more brute) than Sappho's.

To illustrate different versions of Swinburne's Sapphic sublime, I shall consider in further detail "Anactoria" and "Sapphics," both published in the first series of *Poems and Ballads* (1866), and "On the Cliffs," published in *Songs of the Spring-Tides* (1880). This long and complex later lyric reflects on Swinburne's earlier identification with Sappho, by reinvoking "the singing soul that makes his soul sublime / Who hears the far fall of its fire-fledged rhyme." Swinburne makes his claim to the sublime by measuring a long line of descent from Sappho to himself, as he echoes the cadence or "far fall" of Sappho's poetry in his own. This echo is heard in the repetition of her "singing soul" in his "soul," even while we also hear the word that is not repeated: the "singing" itself. Swinburne's Sappho emerges in this way as a decadent figure, a descending cadence, a song fallen into decline. Without repeating Sappho verbatim, Swinburne recalls her in his poetry by means of a rhythmic reiteration that takes the place of Sapphic song. What survives is a Sapphic rhythm, never fully remembered but also never forgotten.

In "Satia te Sanguine," another early lyric from *Poems and Ballads,* Swinburne describes Sappho dissolving into a sea that is his recurring figure for pure rhythm:

> As the lost white feverish limbs
>   Of the Lesbian Sappho, adrift
> In foam where the sea-weed swims,
>   Swam loose for the streams to lift.
>
> (9–12)

Sappho's suicidal leap from the Leucadian Cliff into the waters below is her immersion in a larger rhythmic body: forever dissolving in the streams that set her adrift, the body of Sappho is now absorbed in the sea's undulations. Her limbs are lost, loosened, and lifted by the waves in a perpetual motion that repeats the movement of the Longinian sublime: rising and falling, falling and rising, Sappho is suspended between literal disintegration and figurative reconstitution, a sublimated body no longer defined as an organic unity. She is, rather, a rhythmicized body that disappears and reappears in the rhythms of its own scattering: in the dissolution of her limbs is the melody of Sapphic song.

Swinburne therefore incorporates the fragments of Sappho into his own poetry by undoing the Sapphic body: his stanza recalls the "feverish" body of fragment 31, pale and trembling on the verge of death, and points to the rhythmic repetition of *eros lusimelēs* in fragment 130 as well. In his Sapphic imitations, Sappho is the embodiment of a rhythm that Swinburne increasingly turns into an abstract metrical principle. In the following section of this chapter, I read "Anactoria" as an allegory of sublime rhythm: in this dramatic monologue, Sapphic eros is allegorized as a rhythmic effect that recollects the scattered body of Anactoria into Sapphic song and scatters the body of Sappho into the world. This Sapphic vision is projected into the future, when Sappho will be remembered in all the rhythms of nature, and live on in the memories of men. "On the Cliffs"—written more than two decades later—is the memory of one such man, namely Swinburne himself, who creates a lyric autobiography by projecting his own future vision of Sappho back into the past. He recalls a nightingale heard in youth and calls it Sappho, yet as I shall argue, the song he remembers proves to be a memory of memorization. In the long apostrophe of this poem, Sapphic song is necessarily mediated by writing, a structure of citation and reiteration that repeats the words of Sappho in written form and performs the conversion of Sapphic rhythm into meter as a form of material inscription.

In the third section of the chapter, I demonstrate how meter itself materializes in graphic form, in Swinburne's poem "Sapphics." It is a display of metrical virtuosity, written in Sapphic stanzas, and published along with "Anactoria" as a less scandalous yet equally spectacular exploration of Swinburne's Sapphic sublime. Here the sublime affect of "Anactoria" is transposed into a metrical effect; rather than personifying Sappho in a dramatic monologue, Swinburne embodies her in the form of the Sapphic stanza. This body of Sapphic song—the "Lesbian music" that Sappho is said to have inspired—is visualized graphically, in a metrical pattern presented to the eye: the "visible song" of Sappho is a music we no longer hear but see. I place my reading of "Sapphics" within the context of Victorian metrical theory, and in particular the 1857 "Essay on English Metrical Law" by Coventry Patmore, who defines meter as the corporeal element in language. Swinburne's experiments in meter can be read as a perverse response to Patmore. He displays the corporeality of language in his early Sapphic imitations, and, even more hyperbolically, in his flagellant verse from the same decade. But this imposition of a metrical pattern on a rhythmicized body also refuses an organic reading of meter. By surrendering to compulsory form, or "suffering meter," Swinburne offers himself up to another account of meter that makes the body legible only through the counting of marks and the measuring of intervals between: a formal abstraction.

My chapter concludes with a brief recounting of Swinburne's reception, insofar as it repeats the logic of his Sapphic sublime. Abused by critics, Swinburne becomes a body *for* abuse, mutilated and sacrificed to posterity so that he may emerge, not unlike Sappho, as an exemplary lyric figure. Toward the turn of the century Swinburne is increasingly admired for his metrical virtuosity, and after his death he too is read as the perfect incarnation of meter: his poetic corpus is remembered as a metrical body, inspiring the next generation of poets to renewed experimentation in quantitative verse, and reflecting the emergence of the new prosody in mid-century England. Thus, although Robert Buchanan in "The Fleshly School of Poetry" famously attacked "the Swinburnean female" as "the large-limbed sterile creature who never conceives," Swinburne's conception of Sappho generates a rebirth with Victorian poetry. In his famous elegy for Swinburne, Thomas Hardy echoes the melody that issues from the limbs of Swinburne's Sappho: "His singing-mistress verily was no other / Than she the Lesbian," Hardy writes in "A Singer Asleep." He imagines Swinburne repeating the rhythms of Sappho, fallen into a sea "where none sees," dissolving into the waves like Sappho, and sighing as a phantom to her "spectral form." Having memorized the Sapphic cadence of Swinburne, however, Hardy never fully remembers him; the elegy is also a way of forgetting Swinburne, a repetition that leaves behind an empty form. This melancholy emptying out of form is a keen response to the formalism of Swinburne's poetry and initiates a tradition of reading that recollects Swinburne, like Sappho, in scattered parts.

The Sapphic Scene of Instruction

"We in England are taught, are compelled under penalties to learn, to construe, and to repeat, as schoolboys, the imperishable and incomparable verses of that supreme poet; and I at least, am grateful for the training" ("Notes on Poems and Reviews," Swinburne 1966: 20). In Swinburne's reminiscence "that supreme poet" is of course Sappho, and the compulsory—indeed, for Swinburne, compulsive—repetition of her verses introduces what I would like to call the Sapphic scene of instruction. It is a primal scene, surcharged with libidinal investments that make his initiation into Classical learning the origin of both pain and pleasure:

not merely a translation from Greek into English, but a stern discipline enforced by corporal punishment. In Victorian England schoolboys were whipped for not knowing the rules of Greek grammar and prosody, or, in the case of Swinburne, knowing them only too well. He attributes his metrical virtuosity to the time in his youth when Classical meters were literally beaten into his body. Thus in a personal letter, Swinburne recalls a tutor whose "pet subject was *metre*," and although "my ear for verses made me rather a favourite," he is pleased to confess that this rigid disciplinarian "never wanted reasons for making rhymes between his birch and my body" (*Letters* I: 78). The tutor, playing on the boy like an instrument, has taught him a masochistic relation to language: through rhythmic beating Swinburne learns to internalize the beat of poetry. Memorization becomes a form of incorporation for him, the figurative repetition of a literal violence as well as the literal repetition of a figurative violence. This is how Swinburne has memorized the verses of Sappho, by incorporating their rhythm into his own punished body, "compelled under penalties" yet "grateful for the training."

Sappho serves, then, as part of Swinburne's education in the disciplinary measures of meter. "More than any other's, her verses strike and sting the memory," he writes in "Notes on Poems and Reviews" (1966: 21), transferring the painful punishment of English schoolboys to the aesthetic pleasures of learning Sapphic rhythm. Indeed, he casts Sappho in a role not unlike his fantasmatic tutor: a singing mistress, verily, who teaches Swinburne the striking power of her poetry by forcing him to submit to its rhythm. In this respect the Sapphic scene of instruction replays a scenario of domination and submission familiar to us from the Longinian treatise on the sublime. According to Longinus, sublime language has the power to thrill and enthrall the reader, who is variously struck, pierced, stung, burned, scourged, beaten, and enslaved when the sublime strikes, like a bolt of lightning. "Such passages exercise an irresistible power of mastery (*dunasteian kai bian amachon*) and get the upper hand with every member of the audience," Longinus asserts (1.4; tr. Fyfe). This overwhelming force (*amachon*, Longinus calls it) resonates with the description of Sapphic eros as an irresistible (*amachanon*) creature, impossible to fight off, thus associating Sappho herself with an irresistible power of mastery that seduces Swinburne. Dominated by the sublime Sappho, Swinburne is only too eager to give her the upper hand; she is the mistress, he the slave. Thus he worships Sappho's "divine words which even as a boy I could not but recognise as divine" ("Notes" 20) and he "would not debase and degrade them into a viler form" (21). As a Sapphic imitator he would rather abase himself, degrading his own poetry in a self-reviling pose: "No one can feel more deeply than I do the inadequacy of my work. 'That is not Sappho,' a friend said once to me. I could only reply, 'It is as near as I can come; and no man can come close to her.' Her remaining verses are the supreme success, the final achievement, of the poetic art" (21). By placing Sappho on a high pedestal, Swinburne measure his descent from her, in both senses: no man can come close to her, but also, no man has come closer than he.

With his ear attuned to the sadomasochistic subtext of the sublime, Swinburne performs a perverse turn on Longinus—yet another example of the "poetic perversities" described by Richard Dellamora and other recent critics who find a transgressive eroticism in Swinburne's writing.[5] Mixing aesthetic and pornographic discourses, Swinburne produces ironic inversions of both semantic and sexual categories, reversing the hierarchy of masculine over feminine, making the female principle dominant, and implicitly feminizing the male subject. It is not surprising, then, to find a chapter devoted to Swinburne in Camille Paglia's *Sexual Personae,* imagining Sappho as his dominatrix: "Swinburne's Sappho, like the lesbian marquise of Balzac's *The Girl with the Golden Eyes,* is a female hierarch," Paglia writes (474), with emphasis on Swinburne's relish for suffering under such a despotic figure: "He revives Sappho *in propria persona* in order to be crushed yet again beneath female superiority" (477). While Paglia's wishful projection of a sexual persona for Sappho assumes a critical strategy of personification that my own argument calls into question, it is true that Swinburne's Sapphic sublime is a violence he rather *suffers* than asserts. Thus he defends "Anactoria" not as an attempt to identify with Sappho by imitating her words, but "to work into words of my own some expression of their effect: to bear witness how, more than any other's, her verses strike and sting the memory in lonely places, or at sea, among all loftier sights and sounds" ("Notes" 21). Here Swinburne strikes a characteristically masochistic pose, as he bears witness to verses that strike and sting by willingly bearing their pain; he expresses the effect of Sappho's words as a traumatic inscription, leaving their mark on his memory.

We encounter variations on the Sapphic scene of instruction in *Lesbia Brandon,* a novel that was indeed inspired by Balzac but left unfinished by Swinburne and unpublished during his lifetime.[6] Drafted when Swin-

---

[5] In his chapter on "Poetic Perversities of A. C. Swinburne," Dellamora describes Swinburne as a subversive poet "basing critique in perverse somatic processes" (1990:83); see also Sieburth 1984 and Psomiades 1997: 76-79. Over the past decade, critics have increasingly emphasized strategies of subversion and perversion in the poetry of Swinburne, and particularly in his use of Sappho. For relevant readings of "Anactoria," see, e.g., Cook 1971, Riede 1978, Brisman 1984, Morgan 1984, Paglia 1990, Anderson 1993, Wagner-Lawlor 1996.

[6] Swinburne's unfinished novel, which he called "an étude à la Balzac plus the poetry" (*Letters* I: 224) is an experiment in several genres including personal memoir, narrative fiction, prose poetry, and lyrical ballads. The title *Lesbia Brandon* was assigned by Thomas Wise

burne was also composing his early imitations of Sappho, this mock autobiography narrates the education of young Herbert Seyton, preparing for Eton. Like Swinburne, Herbert has a tutor whose "chief diversion was to play upon the boy's mind as on an instrument" (21): a euphemism for his rigorous and regular application of the birch to the boy's body, especially after Herbert's lessons in Latin and Greek. If he does not learn his Classical meters, Herbert is forewarned he will be "swished" even harder at Eton. Meanwhile, Lesbia Brandon is held up to Herbert as an instructive example for achieving perfect meter: a girl who "can do Sapphics fit for a sixth-form" (53) and writes English verses as if she were "the real modern Sappho" (54). When Herbert reads a volume of Lesbia's published poems, he discovers "a certain fire and music in the verse at its best which had stung and soothed him alternately with gentle and violent delight" (87). Struck by the power of her poetry, Herbert later confesses his passion to Lesbia; but she, "ignorant of man's love," is like an unapproachable goddess whose cold reply leaves him "wrung and stung meantime by strange small tortures" (100–101).

The sentimental, if not to say sensational, education of Herbert Seyton thus conflates subjection to a schoolmaster who whips with the birch, and eroticized submission to a Lesbian mistress who whips with words, making him particularly susceptible to poetic rhythm as a source of painful pleasure. Herbert's sister explains this peculiar susceptibility by describing poetry as another form of flagellation: "Things in verse hurt one, don't they? hit and sting like a cut. They wouldn't hurt us if we had no blood, and no nerves. Verse hurts horribly. . . . You have the nerve of poetry—the soft place it hits on, and stings" (148). The effect of verse is painful, not only by means of the simile "hit and sting like a cut," but in the very cadence of that phrase, as well as its repetition later on: "the soft place it hits on, and stings." It is through rhythmic beating that "verse hurts horribly," transferring the effect of "things in verse" to the action of the "verse" itself: it is like flagellation and it flagellates, it is both the whipping and the being whipped. Herbert's vulnerability to that painful reversal gives him "the nerve of poetry," in both the active and the passive sense, as the rhythms inscribed on his body by whipping are repeated in his experience of poetic rhythm.

Herbert feels this rhythmic effect on the body while swimming, as well. In the sea he hears "suppressed semitones of light music struck out of shingle or sand by the extended fingers of foam" and the waves are like "hard heavy hands that beat out their bruised life from sinking bodies of

---

to the manuscript, which was not completely collated and published until 1952 by Hughes. For a brief discussion of Swinburne as novelist, see Riede 1986; for a more recent discussion of *Lesbia Brandon* in particular, see Vincent 1997.

men"; thus he imagines the sea as a "visible goddess," who seems to "stroke and sting him all over as with soft hands and sharp lips" (9–10). Herbert submits to this goddess, just as he submits to the beatings of his heavy-handed tutor. In one particularly painful episode, Herbert returns from his swim, whipped by the sea, only to be whipped again by the tutor who makes him sing out sharply in pain: the half-suppressed sobs and gasps struck out of his body repeat the suppressed semitones of light music heard at sea (32–33). The tendency to associate the rhythms of the sea with flagellation and poetic rhythm—especially the sting of Lesbia's verse—recalls Swinburne's description of Sappho, whose verses also seem to "strike and sting the memory in lonely places, or at sea." Whipped and scourged like Herbert Seyton by the waves of that visible goddess— the sea as figure for Sappho, and Sappho as figure for the sea—Swinburne wants to feel her rhythms on his body.[7] Thus in a letter he confesses a desire "to satiate my craving (ultra Sapphic and plusquam-Sadic) lust after the sea" (*Letters* I. 305). This is more than a passion for swimming. The juxtaposition of Sappho and de Sade in parentheses suggests to what degree Sapphic imitation is already a sadomasochistic fantasy for Swinburne: to repeat Sappho's leap into the sea, to yield to its cold and cruel torture, to submerge himself in a Sapphic rhythm.

Such is the poetic fate that Lesbia, "the modern Sappho" of *Lesbia Brandon,* aspires to as well in the final chapter entitled "Leucadia." Here the suicidal Lesbia longs to dissolve like Sappho into a sea that will repeat the disarticulation and rhythmic rearticulation of the Sapphic body. "I dreamt once I saw her fall over a cliff. I wish I were dying out of doors, and by day. I should like my body to be burnt and the ashes thrown into the sea. It is I who have taken the leap now, not she," murmurs Lesbia in her dying words to Herbert (164–65). He visits "the living corpse of Lesbia" after she has swallowed poison; she looks "like one whom death was as visibly devouring limb-meal (158) and dies a sublime death, relaxing "her lifted limbs" (161) until finally "her limbs shuddered now and then with a slow general spasm" (165) and her Sapphic apotheosis is complete: "And that was the last of Lesbia Brandon, poetess and pagan" (166). The limbs of Lesbia's dying body repeat the rhythms of *eros lusimelēs,* so that she may become the reincarnation of Sappho, dissolving into the sea. This is the lesson learned—by Herbert, Lesbia, or Swinburne himself— through the Sapphic scene of instruction: a painful subjection to rhythm, rendering the body an aesthetic object by rhythmicizing it.

The sketchy plot and allegorical characters of *Lesbia Brandon* follow in narrative form—more or less, since Swinburne's draft reads less like a novel than an extended prose poem—the lyric logic that structures "An-

---

[7] On Swinburne's passion for swimming, see Sprawson 1993: 89–99.

actoria." In Swinburne's dramatic monologue, the exquisitely excruciating torture of Anactoria by Sappho also serves to rhythmicize the body. Although Anactoria is mute throughout the poem, she is lifted into language and articulated by the rhythms of Sapphic verse into "dumb tunes and shuddering semitones of death"—echoing the suppressed semitones struck out of Herbert and the shuddering death of Lesbia, in order to demonstrate, once again, how much "things in verse hurt." Addressing Anactoria, Sappho subjects her to a verbal violence that turns pain into poetry:

> I would find grievous ways to have thee slain,
> Intense device, and superflux of pain;
> Vex thee with amorous agonies, and shake
> Life at thy lips, and leave it there to ache;
> Strain out thy soul with pangs too soft to kill,
> Intolerable interludes, and infinite ill;
> Relapse and reluctation of the breath,
> Dumb tunes and shuddering semitones of death.
>
> (28–34)

The "intense device" found by Sappho is an intensification of her own poetic language. To "vex thee" the words of Sappho are themselves vexed and tortured into a curiously self-reflexive literalism, as if the rhyme and rhythm are both cause and effect of Anactoria's pain. Thus "shake" rhymes with "ache," "kill" with "ill," and "breath" with "death," and in the attenuation of phrases like "relapse and reluctation of the breath," the verse also corresponds rhythmically to the very rhythm it wishes to induce. The entire passage is a superflux of doubled meanings, turning Anactoria into the musical instrument or "device" for Sappho's melody, as Cecil Lang points out: "'intense' means 'keen,' but also has its Latin sense of 'strained or 'stretched,'" much as "'strain,' another pun, suggests 'stretch' or 'make taut' (as on the rack, in torture) and also the musical sense of tightening strings for raising pitch" (Lang 1968: 523–24). Anactoria's cries of pain will be the music played on the instrument of her tortured body: her tunes and tones are, literally, "interludes."

If initially Anactoria is made to feel the violent impact of Sappho's words on her body, increasingly that body becomes the very embodiment of Sapphic song, its lyre:

> Would I not hurt thee perfectly? not touch
> Thy pores of sense with torture, and make bright
> Thine eyes with bloodlike tears and grievous light?
> Strike pang from pang as note is struck from note,
> Catch the sob's middle music in thy throat,
> Take thy limbs living, and new-mould with these

A lyre of many faultless agonies?
Feed thee with fever and famine and fine drouth,
With perfect pangs convulse thy perfect mouth,
Make thy life shudder in thee and burn afresh,
And wring thy very spirit through the flesh?

(134–44)

The reiteration of "pangs" produces a rhythmic shuddering, in the verse as well as on the body of Anactoria: by hurting her "perfectly" with "perfect pangs"—striking "pang from pang as note is struck from note"—Sappho creates a "perfect mouth," expressing each painful pang as melodious note or rhythmic tone. In this way she can "catch the sob's middle music," making the voice "catch" or stop before words, in order to catch a melody that is beyond words and purely musical. Here Swinburne performs in poetry what he elsewhere declares in prose: "There is a value beyond price and beyond thought in the Lesbian music which spends itself upon the record of fleshly fever and amorous malady" (Hyder 1972: 147). He defines Lesbian music in terms of fleshly fever, in an implicit slip from "malady" to "melody," suggesting that Sappho's poetry records—literally, incorporates into the heart—a song of the body that is the only real body of song. Anactoria is the reincarnation of this Lesbian music, but only at the moment of dying, as the body disintegrates. Thus she is tortured into lyrical form: her living limbs are dismembered so that Sappho may remember and "new-mould with these / A lyre of many faultless agonies."

The eroticized torture of Anactoria is, of course, another repetition of *eros lusimelēs*. Her transfiguration into a lyre reconfigures the parts of the body—her limbs or *melē*—into the *melē* of Sapphic song. We can read Swinburne's dramatic monologue not only as an imitation of Sapphic fragment 31, where the body is undone by eros, but also as a rhetorical expansion of fragment 130, allowing the body to reappear rhythmically. That fragment is paraphrased by Swinburne to suggest the conversion of Anactoria's limbs into metrical feet:

Ah, ah, thy beauty! like a beast it bites,
Stings like an adder, like an arrow smites.
Ah sweet, and sweet again, and seven times sweet
The paces and the pauses of thy feet!

(115–18)

Eros strikes again, as in fragment 130: "like a beast it bites," an *amachanon orpeton* impossible to fight off, stinging like an adder, smiting like an arrow, to produce the rhythmic repetition of "ah, ah" and the measured cadence of "Ah sweet, and sweet again, and seven times sweet." In the very act of apostrophizing Anactoria, Sappho is subjected to the striking rhythm of her own language, traversed by "the paces and the pauses of thy feet." As a perfectly lyricized body, Anactoria is also the perfection of Sapphic meter, and indeed her very name lends itself to a metrical reading; we can scan the five syllables of "Anactoria" in English to correspond to the number of syllables in the final line of the Sapphic stanza. These five syllables serve as equivalent (more or less, since English does not follow the rules for quantity in Greek) to the metrical unit called adonic, a short fourth line left dangling at the end of the *kōlon*—another metrical "limb"—that concludes the stanzas composed by Sappho in the meter most directly associated with Lesbian song.

Anactoria is therefore invoked by Sappho as a musical body greater than her own: "but thou—thy body is the song, / Thy mouth the music; thou art more than I" (74–75). Contrary to what we might expect, the dramatic monologue is not named after Sappho herself; it is called "Anactoria," to identify Anactoria as the proper name for a Sapphic rhythm that is allegorized in Swinburne's poem. Although this name is nowhere to be found within the poem itself, and despite her silence throughout the poem, the title names "Anactoria" as the rhythmicized body produced *by* the poem; a silent, absent body made present through Sappho's verse, much as (on another level of representation) Sappho is also presented by Swinburne in the rhythmic form of his own verse. His poem, in other words, is an example of the poetic paradox that Aviram calls "telling rhythm"; he refers simultaneously to "an allegory that attempts to tell rhythm and a rhythm that tellingly cannot be allegorized" (1994: 24).[8] The violent force of Sapphic rhythm, played out on the body of Anactoria, can be understood, in Aviram's terms, as "an interpretation or representation—an *allegory*—of the bodily rhythmic energy of poetic form," even while this rhythm remains "uninterpretable and sublime" (19). Thus Anactoria appears in the title, as if in quotation marks, as a proper name for the Sapphic rhythm that she embodies: a figure fleshed out by the rhythms of Sappho and bodied forth as rhythm itself.

If we pursue an allegorical reading of rhythm along these lines, we see how Anactoria is made to appear through rhythm in fragment 16 of Sap-

---

[8] In *Telling Rhythm*, Aviram points to a new interest in rhythm and meter (as an object of critical inquiry within lyric theory, at least, since poetic practice is never far from such questions). Since in recent decades lyric reading has been primarily rhetorical in emphasis, Aviram calls for a theory of poetry that can account for the appeal of rhythm to the body, although in the course of his argument it becomes difficult to tell how literal he wants this bodily figure to be. Another approach to the reincorporation of rhythm is offered by Susan Stewart, who discovers in "rhythmic forms" the "possibility of a recovered somatic meaning." While acknowledging that the term *somatic* is "not coterminous with the *body*" (1995: 38–79). Stewart uses a psychoanalytic model that also tends toward an organic and expressivist reading of meter.

pho as well.[9] The fragment begins with a priamel, a rhetorical device that depends on repetition, in order to describe the movement of desire. What moves the heart, it tells us, is not a host of horsemen, nor an army of footsoldiers, nor a fleet of ships, but "whatsoever one loves" (ὅττω τις ἔραται): less the particular object of desire than desire itself, stronger than any other force on earth.[10] Helen of Troy is adduced as example, set into motion not only as desired object but as desiring subject, simultaneously passive and active in following the desire that led her away from home. Helen "went away" (eba) and thus introduces the memory of Anactoria, who has also gone away. At this point (after a lacuna in the text), fragment 16 leaves the epic past for the present moment of its own lyric performance, describing the loss of Anactoria and the desire to see her again:

> . . . νῦν Ἀνακτορί[ας ὀ]νέμαι-
> σ᾽ οὐ] παρεοίσας·
>
> τᾶ]ς κε βολλοίμαν ἔρατον τε βᾶμα
> κἀμάρυχμα λάμπρον ἴδην προσώπω
> ἢ τὰ Λύδων ἄρματα κἀν ὄπλοισι
> πεσδομ]άχεντας .

> . . .[something] now reminds me of Anactoria
> who is not here
>
> I would rather see her lovely walk
> and the bright lamp of her face
> than Lydian war chariots and full-armed
> footsoldiers

Despite her absence, Anactoria is represented—made present again—in the vivid language of fragment 16; it describes her appearance, her lovely

---

[9] The papyrus on which fragment 16 is written was found in Egypt in 1906 and first published in 1914 (Grenfell and Hunt 1914). I do not argue that Swinburne was influenced by this fragment, but rather that "Anactoria" sets a precedent for reading the appearance of Anactoria in fragment 16 as a rhythmic allegory.

[10] For further discussion of the priamel in fragment 16, see, e.g., Snell 1953: 47–50, A. Burnett 1983: 281ff., Winkler 1990: 176–77, all of whom argue that the poem is less concerned with a specific object of desire than a meditation on desire itself. According to this argument, the rhetorical structure of the priamel ("some say . . . and others say . . . and others say . . . but I say . . . ") allows for the emergence of a lyric subject, a first-person ego capable of reflecting on itself. Feminist readings of Sappho develop this reading into a discussion of Sappho as female lyric subject, whose use of the priamel asserts a specifically female desire; see duBois 1995: 120–24; Williamson 1995: 166–71. To insist on the *ego* in fragment 16 as placeholder for the female "voice" of Sappho is, in my view, not the only way to trace a gendered difference in the Sapphic fragments.

way of walking, her radiant face, in order to make her reappear before our very eyes.

This vision of Anactoria is conveyed not only visually but rhythmically as well. There is a recurring emphasis on movement in fragment 16, as Page duBois points out, linking the figures of Helen and Anactoria. In the description of Helen, according to duBois, "the line expresses motion," not only in the verb *eba* ("went") but in participles that "catch her endlessly moving, taking steps" (102). Likewise Anactoria enters the poem by taking steps, in the description of "her lovely walk" (*eraton bama*), duBois observes: "The *eraton*, 'lovely,' echoes *eratai*, 'one loves,' of line 4, makes whatever is lovely about Anactoria, her step, her way of walking, partake of the general statement at the poem's beginning. The *bama*, 'step,' 'stride,' is linked etymologically with the verb *eba*, 'went,' of line 9, and stresses the connection of Helen with the poet's desire, with the woman Anactoria" (103–4). Both Helen and Anactoria are set into motion as figures of desire, and in their movement—the taking of steps—they also seem to embody "the poet's desire," registered rhythmically in the poem itself, in the movement of its own "feet." Fragment 16 implies how desire might be mobilized to different ends than Homeric narrative; as a lyric composed in the Sapphic stanza, it moves according to another rhythm and with other consequences. The "lovely walk" of Anactoria manifests a rhythm that distinguishes the melodies of archaic love lyric from the military measures of heroic epic: in contrast to the relentless approach of Lydian armies, Anactoria moves gracefully into view, and the motion of her feet is more desirable than the noise of many footsoldiers (*pezomachentas*). Thus fragment 16 turns away from a familiar epic theme, the story of Helen's departure that is remembered by all, and toward a more intimate memory of Anactoria. While duBois does not read fragment 16 as a rhythmic allegory, she writes suggestively that "much of the intensity of the poem derives from the force of [Sappho's] personal preference, her ability to make Anaktoria walk before us" (106), as if the very cadence of her walk might be conveyed in the Sapphic stanza.

Rather than referring the "force" of the poem back to Sappho's "personal preference," however, we might consider it in terms of the force of its own rhythmic articulation. Since desire is set into motion through (and as) rhythm, it is only by subjection to such forces of rhythm that "Sappho" or "Anactoria" can be constituted, interchangeably, as either subject or object of desire: both are produced by the rhythm of the Sapphic stanza, rather than preceding it.[11] If indeed "Anaktoria exists briefly

[11] DuBois seems to endorse a reading of fragment 16 as "personal testimony" from Sappho (1995: 107), who emerges as a gendered lyric subject through the expression of desire for Anactoria. Rather than insisting on fragment 16 as the personal expression of a self,

for us, recalled to presence through poetry" (duBois 106), she is therefore recalled through poetic rhythm in particular. The recollection of Anactoria depends on the rhythmic recalling of her name, as the very mention of Anactoria brings her into the present tense, propelling the poem
out of the past into the lively description that animates her memory. "The
moment of presence," according to duBois, "arrives with the name of
Anaktoria. We are made aware of her absence with *ou pareoisas,* "not being
present"; the participle allows us to imagine her presence as well" (103).
To this subtle rhetorical reading, which discovers Anactoria's presence to
be already implicit in the proclamation of her abence, I would add that
the participle also makes Anactoria present again as a rhythmic repetition, in the five syllables that repeat the syllables of her name: *Anaktorias
. . . ou pareoisas,* "Anactoria . . . who is not here."

The name of Anactoria also echoes in Swinburne's poem, allowing us
to hear what is here, namely "Anactoria." While the Greek participle *ou
pareoisas* is not visible in the title of his poem in English, it is still audible
as a silent echo of the name of Anactoria, a spectral repetition that reminds us how she is simultaneously absent and present. It is only a step
further (so to speak) from this allegorical reading of rhythm to reading
"Anactoria" itself as an allegory of rhythm, transposing the feet of Anactoria who seems to "walk before us" into metrical feet. Throughout his
Sapphic monologue Swinburne sustains a pun on feet, beginning in line
18 with Sappho's invocation to the "cruel faultless feet" of Anactoria and
again "in the paces and pauses of thy feet" in line 118; as we have seen,
this line announces the embodiment of Sapphic meter in Anactoria, as
she reincarnates the metrical limbs of Sappho's song. In the second section of the dramatic monologue, modulating from address to Anactoria
to defiance of God, Sappho further imagines herself as the embodiment
of a larger rhythmic principle, with reference to her own "feet":

> If my feet trod upon the stars and sun,
> And souls of men as his have alway trod,
> God knows I might be crueller than God.
>
> (150–52)

Increasingly the treading of Sappho's feet is a rhythmic force opposed to
the "iron feet" of God (172) or the "slow feet" of Death (256), and the
poem culminates in the assertion of a sublime Sapphic rhythm that
strikes like lightning "with feet of awful gold."

---

however, we might consider lyric subjectivity in archaic lyric in terms of a subjection to the
forces of rhythm (cf. Archilochus fragment 67a: γίγνωσκε δ' οἶος ρυσμὸς ἀνθρώπους ἔχει,
"Know what rhythm holds human beings").

But me—
Men shall not see bright fire nor hear the sea,
Nor mix their hearts with music, nor behold
Cast forth of heaven, with feet of awful gold,
And plumeless wings that make the bright air blind,
Lightning, with thunder for a hound behind
Hunting through fields unfurrowed and unsown,
But in the light and laughter, in the moan
And music, and in grasp of lip and hand
And shudder of water that makes felt on land
The immeasurable tremor of all the sea,
Memories shall mix and metaphors of me.

(203–14)

The passage—an elaborate hyperbaton that exemplifies the rhetorical heightening of the Longinian sublime—is a grand refiguration and amplification of Sapphic fragment 31. Here, in the ten lines inserted between two assertions of "me," Sappho reveals herself to be a power that structures the entire world: the lightning that blinds, the thunder that deafens, the water that shudders, and "the immeasurable tremor of all the sea" all repeat the rhythms of the tortured and torturing Sapphic body.

Thus Sappho is scattered around the world and recollected by "men" (like Swinburne himself, perhaps: a self-fulfilling prophecy) who "shall not see" without seeing a Sapphic trace in everything they behold; everywhere "memories shall mix and metaphors of me." This complex line opens up multiple readings. If we take "memories . . . and metaphors" as the double subject of "shall mix"—a zeugma—then are metaphors turning into memories, or memories into metaphors? Where do these memories originate, in Sappho or in those who remember her? Are "metaphors of me" to be read as Sappho's metaphors or the metaphors made of Sappho? Whose memories and metaphors are they, anyway? The conflation of subjective and objective genitive in "of me" makes Sappho both cause and effect of a metaphorical logic that makes it difficult if not impossible to read her as the "speaker" of this dramatic monologue. She is less a persona than the name for a catachresis that generates a seemingly endless series of similes. Indeed, the phrase "metaphors of me" introduces a long repetition of "like me . . . like me . . . like me" over many lines, enacting the syntactic dispersal of "I" throughout the poem while also describing how Sappho is dispersed all over the world: "Like me shall be the shuddering calm of night" (215), "Like me the one star swooning with desire" (220), "like me the waste white noon" (222), "like me / The land-stream and the tide-stream in the sea" (224–25). As Sappho is revealed in the forces of nature, she becomes a force of nature herself; Swinburne's similes, as Edward Thomas observes of Swinburne's poetry in general, "are carried so far that the matter of the simile is more important in the total than what it appeared to intensify" (90). The confusion of tenor and vehicle in this metaphorical logic turns Sappho into the vehicle for the tenor, so that increasingly all the world is but a manifestation of Sapphic rhythm: "And the earth," Sappho proclaims, "Has pain like mine in her divided breath" (236).

Out of these many versions of "me," forever multiplying, emerges "I Sappho," in a moment of ecstatic self-naming:

> Violently singing till the whole world sings—
> I Sappho shall be one with all these things,
> With all high things for ever; and my face
> Seen once, my songs once heard in a strange place,
> Cleave to men's lives. . . .
>
> (275–79)

Rather than asserting a coherent identity, Sappho is identified here only as the effect of a self-displacing, self-disrupting sublime violence; "violently singing," she exists in the form of a violent disjunction to which the dash after "sings—" already points. "I Sappho" disappears and reappears through this dash, as a declaration purely in the nominative: a proper name that cannot be referred back to any unified self or organic unity. Often Swinburne's Sappho has been read by critics as a transcendent lyric subject, proclaiming her sublime transcendence of the material world.[12] However, if we follow the Longinian model that I have proposed, we can read Sappho as the medium for the disintegration of "the whole world" and its rematerialization in many parts. Swinburne's Sapphic sublime would then be the revelation of a material trace left by Sappho in "all these things." Each thing is part of "all high things forever," not by sublimation into a unified whole but by manifesting a power that divides and separates everything. Such perpetual self-division is the legacy of Sapphic song, and it will "cleave to men's lives" when they, too, are cleaved by it.

---

[12] The tendency to read Swinburne as a poet aspiring to transcendent song is evident in several generations of Swinburne criticism, surveyed by Rooksby and Shrimpton in *The Whole Music of Passion* (1993: 1–21); Rooksby himself also tries to recover a "core theme of transcendence" in Swinburne's work (1995: 27). An antitranscendent strain is articulated in "Anactoria," however, as several critics have argued: Cook emphasizes that "Sappho wills a death that is absolutely untranscendent" in Swinburne's poem (1971: 92); Brisman discerns a double impulse in Swinburne, simultaneously negating and reasserting the corporeality of things (1984: 210); Zonana argues that Swinburne's Sappho is not a source of transcendent revelation but a means of reincorporation (1990: 39). This "corporeality" or "incorporation" can be understood as even more radically "untranscendent" if we read Swinburne's poem on a nonorganic model, however.

To articulate more fully the implications of this Sapphic vision, Swinburne returns to the heights of the Longinian sublime in "On the Cliffs," virtually translating *Peri Hypsous* into the title of his poem as well as its location. Beginning with the preposition *between,* this later Sapphic lyric is precariously perched on a high point looking down, mediating between night and day, past and future, the Leucadian Cliff of Sappho and the North Sea landscape of Swinburne's own verse.[13] "On the Cliffs" is Swinburne's version of a crisis poem: a long and complex ode that confronts spatial and temporal disjunction through the figure of Sappho. As Swinburne exchanges the form of his earlier dramatic monologue for second-person address, the central act of nomination in his later poem is no longer "I Sappho," but a sustained effort to recall "a name above all names" (xii) until finally Sappho can be properly named and addressed. This prolonged apostrophe creates a rhetorical elevation, a visionary revelation "on the cliffs" that allows Swinburne to make his own claim to the sublime by reinvoking Sappho:

> The singing soul that makes his soul sublime
> Who hears the far fall of its fire-fledged rhyme
> Till darkness as with bright and burning rain
> Till all the live gloom inly glows, and light
> Seems with the sound to cleave the core of night.
>
> (XVI)

Here "the singing soul that makes his soul sublime" also makes each soul interchangeable with the other. As Jerome McGann points out, "All the terms have convertible referents" in this passage: "We may ask, for example, to what (or to whom) 'The singing soul' refers, or 'his soul . . . who hears,' or 'its fire-fledged rhyme.' In each case the answer waits upon the completion of grammar. 'The singing soul' is that which 'makes his soul sublime.' But this answer is only partially useful since we don't know to whom 'his' refers until we read still further: 'Who hears the far fall of its fire-fledged rhyme.' The referent of 'its' now becomes questionable, though one grasps soon enough that it goes back (for once) to 'singing soul'" (1972: 160–61). Where indeed does Sapphic song originate, in "the singing soul" or "his soul sublime"? And in "the far fall of its fire-fledged rhyme" does "its" refer to the song of burning Sappho, fledged in fire, or the fledgling rhyme that repeats it? Not only does the circularity of reference make "his," "who," and "its" questionable, it also raises questions about the status of song defined by a "far fall": a repetition of Sappho's cadence or a song fallen far from Sappho, a distant echo or a measure of distance from that origin? If, as McGann suggests, "the answer

---

[13] For a discussion of the sublime landscape in "On the Cliffs," see Fletcher 1986.

waits upon the completion of grammar" (and if indeed, as he also argues, the whole poem "turns upon Swinburne's own desire for an 'answer' from Sappho," 76), then the answering voice that Swinburne awaits is already emerging in the course of his own apostrophe to her.

Swinburne therefore writes from the perspective of one of those men who (as prophesied in "Anactoria") cleaves to, and is cleaved by, the song of Sappho. But in "On the Cliffs" he envisions Sapphic rhythm on an even larger scale, surpassing his earlier vision of Sappho in "Anactoria." Not only will Sapphic song "cleave" anyone who listens, but it will "cleave the core of night" as well, subsuming all the forces of nature and history in order to penetrate the rhythms of time itself. The "cleaving" of Sapphic song (again, to be understood both transitively and intransitively, to describe the scattering effect of words that are themselves already scattered) anticipates the final stanza of "On the Cliffs," where Swinburne meditates on a metaphysical power that produces the physical universe; in this visionary moment, it seems that even "the sundering of the two-edged spear of time" cannot stop the eternal rhythm of Sappho's scattering. The last line of the poem proclaims that Sappho's song is "fire everlasting of eternal life," repeating a line from stanza V where the song she will "bear till time's wing tire" is "life everlasting of eternal fire." The line is repeated with a subtle variation that makes both "life" and "fire" everlasting, not because the repetition of her song transcends time but because it is a measure of temporality itself; measured in time, the cadence (or "far fall") of Sapphic song therefore lasts forever.

"On the Cliffs" can be read as a metalepsis of "Anactoria," a temporal inversion casting a vision of the future into the past and a vision of the past into the future. Swinburne moves from the scandalous rhetoric of "Anactoria" to the metaphysical rhapsodies of "On the Cliffs," in a strategy of revision and self-reversal that is characteristic of Swinburne's later poetry.[14] In a letter Swinburne describes the new "rhapsody" he is composing, which abandons the pathos of his earlier dramatic monologue in order to meditate on his Sapphic sublime in more abstract terms. The inspiration for "On the Cliffs," he writes to Watts, is a nightingale he heard in youth and identified as Sappho:

> You will regret to hear that in subject-matter and treatment ["On the Cliffs"] is not akin to ["Anactoria"]. . . . I fear there is not overmuch hope of a fresh scandal and consequent "succès de scandale" from a mere rhapsody just four lines short of four hundred (oddly enough) on the song of a nightingale

---

[14] "The contradiction between the aberrant and the transcendent produce[s] the thematics of Swinburne's later verse," Armstrong observes (1993: 417); Greenberg (1976, 1991) considers more specifically how Swinburne revisits and revises his earlier Sapphic imitation in the later work.

by the sea-side. I don't think I ever told you, did I? my anti-Ovidian theory as to the real personality of that much misrepresented bird—the truth concerning whom dawned upon me one day in my midsummer school holidays, when it flashed on me listening quite suddenly 1) that this was not Philomela—2) in the same instant, who this was. It is no theory, but a fact, as I can prove by the science of notation. (*Letters* IV: 78)

Here the Sapphic scene of instruction is no longer a discipline imposed on boys at school, but discovered "one day in my midsummer school holidays," in a seemingly natural setting, "by the seaside." The nightingale, "the truth concerning whom . . . flashed on me listening," is a strange bird, however, not to be found in nature: the poetic genealogy of "that much misrepresented bird" includes not only the Ovidian Philomela but the nightingales of Milton and Keats (as well as Shelley's skylark, another important Romantic precursor). By tracing the lineage of the nightingale back to its "real personality," namely Sappho, Swinburne discovers an earlier point of origin for a song that is echoed by all other poets but is itself also defined as echo or repetition. What this bird teaches Swinburne is a song that reveals, "quite suddenly," in a flash of recognition, the sublime power of rhythm.

Swinburne's insistence that his "anti-Ovidian" theory can be proved "by the science of notation" is more than an afterthought in this account, for it defines the way in which Sappho's song is remembered, or more accurately, *memorized*. "Notation" here refers to the act of transcribing the nightingale's song into Sapphic rhythm as well as inscribing it in graphic form: Sappho's tones survive as *notes,* a metrical notation or written record that Swinburne memorized in youth but remembers as pure song by forgetting its origin in writing. The Sapphic scene of instruction is therefore inserted in "On the Cliffs" as a memory of memorization. Swinburne calls upon Sappho by recalling the nightingale he describes in his letter, a bird whose cry of spring—in the spring of his youth—was an early revelation of Sapphic rhythm:

> I have known thee always who thou art,
> Nor ever have given light ear to storied song
> That did thy sweet name sweet unwitting wrong,
> Nor ever have called thee nor would call for shame,
> Thou knowest, but inly by thine only name,
> Sappho—because I have known thee and loved, hast thou
> None other answer now?
> As brother and sister were we, child and bird,
> Since thy first Lesbian word
> Flamed on me, and I knew not whence I knew
> This was the song that struck my whole soul through,

Pierced my keen spirit of sense with edge more keen,
Even when I knew not,—even ere sooth was seen,—
When thou was but the tawny sweet winged thing
Whose cry was but of spring.

(XIII)

Swinburne represents his encounter with "thy first Lesbian word" as a memory of something already known ("I have known thee always") but without knowing its origin ("I knew not whence I knew") and without knowing what it means ("even when I knew not,—even ere sooth was seen—"); it is a memory of something memorized but forgotten as such, displaced onto a memory from childhood and projected onto nature.[15]

Despite the appearance of a natural setting, this passage self-consciously replays the sublime scenario by now familiar to us. Swinburne is "struck" and "pierced" by the song of the nightingale, even before learning to identify it "inly by thine only name," the name of Sappho; he knows the meaning of her cry because he has already incorporated its rhythm into his own body. Thus Swinburne distinguishes his lyric persona as a sublime Sapphic poet from imitators of Sappho who have merely "given light ear to storied song" about Sappho, without recognizing her as the embodiment of a larger rhythmic principle. Swinburne's inner ear, by contrast, is already attuned to the painful pleasures of such rhythm; like a bolt of lightning straight out of Longinus, Sappho's primal word "flamed on me" and with sublime violence she penetrates his "keen spirit of sense with edge more keen." The phrase "spirit of sense" recalls Sappho's desire "to wring thy very spirit through the flesh" in "Anactoria," and indeed, not unlike Anactoria, the body of Swinburne is rhythmicized by Sappho; she wrings the spirit through the flesh, making body and soul inseparable from each other, interpenetrated by her rhythm. Throughout "On the Cliffs" Swinburne therefore emphasizes the power Sappho exerts over him, in terms that recall the pattern of domination and submission implicit in the Longinian sublime: in stanza XVI he worships her "sovereign Lesbian song," and in stanza XXVII he is ruled by "thy ruling song" and transported "in thy strong rapture of imperious joy."

The sublimity of Sappho's rapturous, ruling song inheres, paradoxically, in the written word. For it is only through reinscription of that song "by the science of notation"—meaning notes or marks or any other material trace produced by memorizing Sappho's words—that the idea of Sappho can emerge. Swinburne writes "On the Cliffs" in the vocative as a sublime ode to Sappho, but even while his long invocation creates the

---

[15] In identifying "brother and sister . . . child and bird," and remembering a bird "whose cry was but of spring," Swinburne also revisits "Itylus," another early lyric from *Poems and Ballads.*

illusion of address, the echoing response he seeks from Sappho is achieved by textual repetition rather than vocal doubling; indeed, his poem emphasizes various forms of quotation, citation, allusion, and translation that mediate the claim to voice through writing. Such mediation is already announced in the epigraph to "On the Cliffs," where two words from Sappho are quoted (ἱμερόφωνος ἀηδών) to introduce the "lovely-voiced nightingale," or more literally, the nightingale with a voice that is both "desiring" and "desired." This nightingale celebrated by Sappho serves as Swinburne's figure *for* Sappho: simultaneously voicing desire and desiring voice, yet eternally unfulfilled in both. But as it is written in Greek, the epigraph also reminds us that the ἱμερόφωνος ἀηδών no longer sings in a pure unmediated voice; the song of the Sapphic nightingale is lost in translation, yet survives by being translated. The revelation of Sappho's "first Lesbian word" depends on multiple acts of translation from Greek to English, voice to text, past to present, bird to poet, all performed in Swinburne's poem.

Instead of smoothly paraphrasing Sappho in English, as he did in "Anactoria," Swinburne therefore presents the Sapphic fragments more explicitly as translated texts in "On the Cliffs." The words of Sappho appear in italicized passages, drawing attention to their own textuality even when they appear in the vocative. The first two lines of Sappho's famous "Ode to Aphrodite," for example, are repeated several times in italics:

> *O thou of divers-coloured mind, O thou*
> *Deathless, God's daughter subtle-souled*—lo, now
> Now to the song above all songs, in flight
> Higher than the day-star's height,
> And sweet as sound the moving wings of night!
> *Thou of the divers-coloured seat*—behold,
> Her very song of old!—
> *O deathless, O God's daughter subtle-souled!*
> That same cry through this boskage overhead
> Rings round reiterated.
>
> (XVII)

The Greek epithet for Aphrodite (reconstructed by scholars as *poikilophrōn*, "possessing a crafty mind" or *poikilothron*, "sitting on a crafted throne") is translated here several times, to correspond to variant readings of the text: she is "God's daughter subtle-souled," a goddess "of divers-coloured mind" on her "divers-coloured seat." The multiple translations of this single phrase disrupt the continuity of Sappho's invocation, which is further interrupted by Swinburne's interpolated comments; he interrupts the vocative "*O thou*" by writing "lo now / Now to the song above all songs," and again between the vocatives "*Thou*" and "*O deathless*" he inserts the comment, "Behold, / Her very song of old!" These demonstrative exclamations ("lo" and "behold") direct us to read the italics as the representation of pure voice, while also demonstrating that the reiteration of "that same cry" in Swinburne's poem inevitably takes the form of writing and *not* singing. At the very moment when Swinburne celebrates Sapphic voice, attempting to bring "her very song of old" into the present tense, he also marks the distance between that song and this poem; we see the repetition of her words made visible on the page, rather than hearing an audible echo.

Insofar as Sappho reappears through textual citation rather than vocal recitation, Swinburne performs the sublime as a citational structure. He apostrophizes Sappho's apostrophe, taking the words of Sappho out of context and placing them in the context of his own writing. Her words are repeated to refer back to Sappho, self-reflexively, so that she herself becomes as "deathless" and "subtle-souled" as the goddess she once invoked; the meanings of Sappho multiply, like the multiple translations of Aphrodite's epithet, into a "divers-coloured mind" that takes on the diverse colors of whatever context in which she is reinvoked. Sappho lives on forever through endless permutations and variations, in an infinite series of ever more subtle repetitions: her Sapphic song is an effect of writing, a reiteration and not an original utterance. Swinburne's Sappho is a catacoustic figure, whose song "heard once on heights Leucadian" is "heard not here / Not here" (XVII). What we cannot hear—ironically echoed in "not here"—is the voice of Sappho, absent from Swinburne's poem yet nevertheless presented as a series of reflected sounds. The inaudibility of this voice is made visible by Swinburne's writing, in the very italics he uses to quote Sappho's words.

To convey the absence of voice, Swinburne translates another Sapphic fragment with interpolated commentary as follows:

> *I loved thee,*—hark, one tenderer note than all—
> *Atthis, of old time, once*—one low long fall,
> Sighing—one long low lovely loveless call,
> Dying—one pause in song so flamelike fast—
> *Atthis, long since in old time overpast*—
> One soft first pause and last.
>
> (XVIII)

Again we are asked to listen to Sappho—"hark, one tenderer note"—and again this "note" is seen rather than heard; it is marked in italics and presented for us to *read*. The song, thus written down, is defined by its decline into silence, the "low long fall" of a voice "sighing" and "dying" so that we hear only its cessation, the pauses before and after sound rather than the sound itself: "one soft first pause and last." Sappho's song, previously invoked as "her very song of old," is now revealed to be a song of the past, in all senses: it is written in the past tense, about the past, and in the past it will remain. Swinburne therefore uses Sappho's own words ("*of old time, once*" and "*long since in old time overpast*") to refer to the impossibility of their recuperation as a song in the present. These words can only be read as a pause in Sapphic song, measuring the distance between then and now, in silent intervals.

These passages, excerpted from a poem that is a tour de force of poetic echoes,[16] suggest how Swinburne aligns himself with a Sapphic tradition, not by recalling the voice of Sappho or remembering the body of her song, but by re-citing the Sapphic fragments he has memorized. His writing is structured like memorization, as it repeats by rote the words of which the meaning is forgotten, and indeed the transmission or "memory" of Sappho depends on this act of forgetting: no longer (if ever she was) a woman, poet, persona, or bird, but purely a recurring rhythm. "On the Cliffs" therefore leads into a more abstract, nonrepresentational concept of rhythm than does "Anactoria." While the earlier poem produces an ironically organic figure—the simultaneous composition and decomposition of the Sapphic body—through an allegory of sublime rhythm, the later poem moves beyond an organic reading of rhythm into another kind of formalism: the revelation of Sapphic song, "by the science of notation," as a form of material inscription. The poem that mediates between these two visions of Sappho is Swinburne's "Sapphics": a metrical imitation of the Sapphic stanza that presents itself as the reincarnation of Sappho's song but materializes, graphically, in writing. The conversion of "embodied" song into a written pattern, a conversion of rhythm into meter, will demonstrate yet again what Swinburne has learned from the Sapphic scene of instruction: the impact of Sappho's "literal and absolute words" on the body of his own writing.

Suffering Meter

Swinburne's Sapphic sublime, I have been arguing, is a revelation of rhythm: in "Anactoria" the Sapphic body is manifested rhythmically throughout the world, and in "On the Cliffs" all time proves to be a manifestation of Sapphic rhythm as well. In "Sapphics" this vision of rhythm

---

[16] "On the Cliffs" deserves longer analysis than I can give here. By focusing on Sapphic citations I have bypassed numerous allusions to other poets such as Aeschylus, Wordsworth, Shelley, and Keats; the poem is a chamber of many echoes. As is the case with most of Swinburne's later poetry, there are few sustained readings of this complex poem; but see Raymond 1971, McGann 1972, Ridenour 1978, Riede 1978, Buckler 1980, Morgan 1992, Foss 1996.

takes a metrical form. If Anactoria emerges as the proper name for an allegory of rhythm in "Anactoria," "Sapphics" goes one step further in formalizing this allegory by naming the meter for which Sappho herself has become the proper name. In his poem Swinburne describes a long tradition of poets who come after Sappho (these poets are "Sapphics") and they repeat the rhythm of her song (in the meter known as "Sapphics"); furthermore, the title of his poem refers to his own repetition of Sappho's meter (in stanzas that are "Sapphics," again). Thus Swinburne aligns himself with a Sapphic tradition, and its line of descent is presented in a visionary sequence: first the appearance of Aphrodite, then a vision of Sappho turning away from the goddess, followed by a vision of her Lesbian song, echoing long after Sappho herself has disappeared. These descending visions do not seem to originate within Swinburne himself but descend upon him in the movement of the verse itself, a cadence that takes the form of the Sapphic stanza. Swinburne's poem, a dazzling experiment in English "quantitative" meter on a Classical model, therefore appeals simultaneously to the eye and to the ear, attempting to mediate between what is seen and what is heard, and indeed representing one in terms of the other, as if the legible could be made audible and the audible, legible.

At the beginning of "Sapphics," a Sapphic persona emerges in the dreamlike description of an external force that "beheld me," taking hold until "a vision came" and "I too was full of the vision." The agency of this "I" is curiously suspended as Aphrodite, invoked by Sappho in her famous ode, reappears without ever being actively reinvoked. The goddess is mobilized, instead, by the repetition of a Sapphic rhythm compelling her to leave the time and place when Sappho called upon her, to leave the past and move into the future, the present moment of Swinburne's poem. She approaches, in the cumulative effect of the opening stanzas:

> All the night sleep came not upon my eyelids,
> Shed not dew, nor shook nor unclosed a feather,
> Yet with lips shut close and with eyes of iron
>   Stood and beheld me.
>
> Then to me so lying awake a vision
> Came without sleep over the seas and touched me,
> Softly touched mine eyelids and lips; and I too,
>   Full of the vision,
>
> Saw the white implacable Aphrodite,
> Saw the hair unbound and the feet unsandalled
> Shine as fire of sunset on western waters;
>   Saw the reluctant

Feet, the straining plumes of the doves that drew her.
Looking always, looking with necks reverted,
Back to Lesbos, back to the hills whereunder
    Shone Mytilene;

Heard the flying feet of the Loves behind her
Make a sudden thunder upon the waters,
As the thunder flung from the strong unclosing
    Wings of a great wind.

So the goddess fled from her place, with awful
    Sound of feet and thunder of wings around her;
While behind a clamour of singing women
    Severed the twilight.

(1–24)

Aphrodite enters the poem as a gradual vision, accompanied by sounds that are gradually amplified into song. At first the vision "touched me, softly" but then it is heard as "sudden thunder upon the waters" and in the "wings of a great wind," to reveal an awe-inspiring "awful sound" and "clamour of singing." This amplification may be heard, as well, in the sound effects of Swinburne's verse, his characteristic use of alliteration and assonance, the echoing repetitions of words and phrases, and the pacing of the language. Moreover, as the poem gathers momentum, its rhythm is figured in Swinburne's favorite pun on feet. Aphrodite's "feet unsandaled" are shaped to fit into the metrical feet of his poem, moving slowly in the early stanzas (as we see in the stanzaic enjambment of "reluctant / Feet"), but followed in stanza 5 by "the flying feet of the Loves behind her" and then surrounded in stanza 6 by "sound of feet and thunder of wings around her." Along with its rhetorical amplification, "Sapphics" therefore simultaneously enacts and allegorizes a rhythmic acceleration.

The arrival of the goddess is "reluctant," however, as the poem struggles to set itself into motion. In Sappho's poem, Aphrodite glides effortlessly into view in a golden chariot, drawn by "beautiful swift sparrows whirring their wings" (*ōkees strouthoi . . . pukna dinnentes*), but in Swinburne's poem we hear the double entendre in "the straining plumes of the doves that drew her." Swinburne is straining to recreate the melody of Sappho in Sapphic stanzas, a vehicle of transport not quite so automatic as Aphrodite's chariot. The birds in his poem, while carrying the goddess forward in time, are "looking always, looking with necks reverted, / Back to Lesbos." Their reversion to the past defines "Sapphics" as a recursive structure or self-mirroring vision, as McGann points out: "It is as if Swinburne's poem were Sappho's Ode composed and read 'before a mirror'" (1972: 115). While Sappho calls upon Aphrodite in her ode, in the continuation of Swinburne's poem it is the goddess who calls upon Sappho: "Yea, by her name too / Called her, saying, 'Turn to me, O my Sappho.'" This reversal—Aphrodite returns, asking Sappho to return— demonstrates the degree to which Sappho is the proper name for a song already turning inward as its own inversion, reverting back to itself as a reversible reiteration. The song of Sappho is a tautology: "such a song was that song," we read in line 39, and again in line 66, a mirrored phrase that suggests the difficulty of defining "such a song" except by pointing to "that song." Therefore the recreation of Sapphic song leaves "all reluctant" (67), silent again in the wake of Sappho; all have "fled from before her" (68) and "all withdrew long since" (69).

Nevertheless Swinburne's poem tries to envision what Sappho saw and thus to recreate her Sapphic vision. Surpassing the nine Muses, Sappho is "the tenth," who "sang wonderful things they knew not" (29), and she even turns away from Aphrodite because her music surpasses that of the goddess. She sees her own Lesbian melodies reincarnated in the women of Lesbos:

> Saw the Lesbians kissing across their smitten
> Lutes with lips more sweet than the sound of lute-strings,
> Mouth to mouth and hand upon hand, her chosen,
>   Fairer than all men;
>
> Only saw the beautiful lips and fingers
> Full of songs and kisses and little whispers,
> Full of music; only beheld among them
>   Soar, as a bird soars
>
> Newly fledged, her visible song, a marvel,
> Made of perfect sound and exceeding passion,
> Sweetly shapen, terrible, full of thunders,
>   Clothed with the wind's wings.
>
>   (49–60)

Here "the Lesbians" are the instruments for (and of) Sappho's song. Like Anactoria transformed into "a lyre of many faultless agonies," their bodies are "lutes with lips more sweet than the sound of lute-strings," and when they kiss "across their smitten / lutes," an apt enjambment divides the limbs of the verse in order to compose their limbs into Sappho's melody. Lesbian body parts are doubled "mouth to mouth and hand upon hand" and multiplied into many "beautiful lips and fingers," forming a composite body "full of songs" and "full of music"—a song of the body that is also the body of Sapphic song.

Published along with "Anactoria," "Sapphics" is therefore its companion piece; both poems use lesbian eroticism as a trope for Lesbian melody (and vice versa) and resuscitate the Sapphic corpus as a living body of song. While Anactoria embodies that song, or rather, serves as the figure for its embodiment, in "Sapphics" it is Sappho herself who emerges as the embodiment of her own poetic form. The vision of Lesbians leads to a revelation of "her visible song, a marvel," taking shape in the contours of the Sapphic stanza, "sweetly shapen" to reveal its own form: the rhythms of Sappho incarnated in Sapphic meter, and reincarnated in the "body" of Swinburne's poem.

But just as the Sapphic body disintegrates at the end of "Anactoria" without reintegration into an organically unified form, "Sapphics" simultaneously provokes and revokes an organic reading of poetic form.[17] Sappho's melody may be figured as embodied song, but it is reconstituted in writing and thus anticipates Swinburne's vision of Sappho as a form of material inscription in "On the Cliffs." While there is an emphasis on sound throughout "Sapphics," culminating in the marvel of a "visible song" that is "made of perfect sound," the Sapphic stanzas of Swinburne are based on a meter more readily seen than heard: a metrical experiment that follows the quantitative model of Classical Greek verse. To scan Swinburne's lines on this model, we would mark the long and short syllables that comprise Sappho's meter in Greek, although strictly speaking such quantities are not audible in English. Swinburne therefore creates a stress-analogue pattern that allows the long syllables in Greek to coincide, more or less, with stressed syllables in English. For example:

Newly fledged, her visible song, a marvel,

Made of perfect sound and exceeding passion,

Sweetly shapen, terrible, full of thunders,

Clothed with the wind's wings.

(49–60)

In Greek the Sapphic stanza uses a so-called choriamb (long-short-short-long) as its basic unit: three lines (each composed of two trochees, a choriamb, and a bacchiac) are followed by a truncated fourth line (built on another choriamb). However, within an English accentual/syllabic tradition the Sapphic meter may also be understood more simply as three five-stress lines with a fourth half-line at the end of the stanza. The phrase

---

[17] An example of such organic reading would be Rosanna Warren, who describes Sappho as a myth of form, a "metrical essence" that allows for the regeneration and rebirth of poetry; she considers Swinburne a "reincarnation" of Sappho because his poetry expresses her influence "genetically" in meter and stanza form (1989: 211–12).

"newly fledged, her visible song," for example, could be read according
to traditional foot-scansion as two trochees and a choriamb, but we also
hear it as a steady alternation of stressed and unstressed syllables according to the conventions of English prosody.

Despite Swinburne's virtuosity (itself a "marvel") in creating an English
analogy to long and short quantities in Greek, what we hear is their inaudibility. Likewise, in our brief scansion exercise, what we see is a mark
of their absence. If Sappho's "newly fledged" song is recreated in Swinburne's Sapphic imitation, taking wing in the rhythm of his own fledgling verse, we may hear it (as we heard "the far fall of its fire-fledged
rhyme" in "On the Cliffs") as a question about what it is we are supposed
to hear: a falling cadence or a fall into silence? Indeed, the closer Swinburne comes to perfecting the Sapphic stanza, the less audible it becomes, for Sappho's song can only be made "visible" by the conversion of
rhythm into a metrical pattern: a visual representation of meter that
seems to be "made of perfect sound," because it is now without sound.
This visualization of Sappho's song turns her rhythm into an abstract metrical pattern. In English verse, as John Hollander points out, the Sapphic
stanza is a formal scheme that functions as a written code: "We must conclude that the quantitative experiment is somewhat like a written code—
one needs to count and measure letters in order to determine the system,
while the ear will infer that all sorts of accentual patterns it hears are indeed intended to be systematic. Indeed, one mistakes the rhythm of the
lines for their schematic meter, which latter is hidden in an arbitrary and
arcane system" (1985: 66). On this view the meter of the Sapphic stanza
is a graphic phenomenon, a pattern graphically marked for scansion and
schematized diagrammatically, as follows:

```
-------------------------------
-------------------------------
-------------------------------
        --------------
```

By graphing the meter, we visualize the song of Sappho and allow it to
materialize, in the lines on the page, as a written form that appeals to the
eye instead of the ear, an inscription rather than an utterance.

All that remains of Sapphic rhythm, then, is a metrical grid: a ghostly
form, or "haunting shape" as Rosanna Warren calls it (205), haunting all
poets who follow Sappho. These are the "ghosts of outcast women" that
Swinburne describes at the end of his poem:

> By the grey sea-side, unassuaged, unheard of,
> Unbeloved, unseen in the ebb of twilight,
> Ghosts of outcast women return lamenting,
>   Purged not in Lethe.

> Clothed about with flame and with tears, and singing
> Songs that move the heart of the shaken heaven,
> Songs that break the heart of the earth with pity,
>   Hearing, to hear them.

(73–80)

The women who "return lamenting" nevertheless return another version of Sapphic song to the world; they are now the "Sapphics" to which Swinburne refers in his title, singing songs that echo everywhere. Their singing moves heaven and earth into a shaken, broken rhythm, an echoic repetition of Sappho; the final line of the poem, "hearing, to hear them" is itself a repetition, to suggest the infinite repeatability of this Sapphic rhythm. These women do not reincarnate Sappho, however, nor do they fully remember her melodies. Unassuaged, unheard of, unbeloved, unseen, they are ghostly figures for the Sapphic song that cannot be re-embodied. "Purged not in Lethe," they do not forget; but instead of remembering Sappho, they repeat the memory of her loss. The song of Sappho therefore survives as a song about Sappho, proclaiming the loss of song rather than reclaiming it. The followers of Sappho, women "unheard of," can be read (as the title "Sapphics" encourages us to do) like the Sapphic meter of Swinburne's poem: less a reincarnation of that form than its spectral emanation, in stanzas that follow in the wake of Sappho and are also unheard, even as we read "hearing, to hear them."

    Swinburne's interest in the Sapphic stanza, and his complex use of it as the simultaneous form and content of "Sapphics," can be understood within the context of Victorian metrical theory. A general revival of interest in classical meters influenced the emergence of "the new prosody" in mid-nineteenth-century England; not since Elizabethan experiments in "quantitative" verse had there been such extensive discussion about the possibilities of combining a classical model of meter based on quantity (long and short vowels) with an accentual/syllabic tradition of English poetry based on accent (stressed and unstressed syllables). The systematic elaboration of a quantitative model for English verse extends well beyond the claims of Renaissance prosody, however, and should be historicized as a particularly Victorian phenomenon. A Classical approach to meter reflects a philological turn within nineteenth-century British Classical scholarship and is part of the broader cultural discourse that advocates the return to Classical origins, as Derek Attridge points out: "Only with the new interest in Greece and Rome in the nineteenth century did foot-scansion come into its own as a mode of analysis, accompanied by another round of experiments in English classical meters" (1982: 5).[18]

---

[18] Attridge offers an introduction to "the classical approach" with the proviso that "it is important to see this approach to metre in its historical context" (1982: 5). While much has

By the time Saintsbury published his *History of English Prosody* in 1910, he could therefore look back on the previous century as a progression toward a new metrical science predicated on the foot. Saintsbury argues with vehemence against the "extravagant accentualism" of Edwin Guests's *History of English Rhythms,* an influential ninteenth-century treatise (published in 1838, and again in 1882) that is criticized by Saintsbury for its "apodism" (276) or "unfaith in feet" (277). Guest's *History* is the last gasp of an old English tradition, according to Saintsbury, while his own *History* traces a different historical tradition that culminates in foot-scansion on a classical model; indeed, he hails Swinburne's poetry as "the triumph of the foot-system" (348). The recurring puns on "feet" that I have been tracing in "Anactoria" and "Sapphics" demonstrate how the foot has become the fetish of Victorian metrical theory. In the context of an argument about figuration in Swinburne's poetry, Armstrong observes how "the fetishising concentration on feet/foot . . . creates a metonymic universe of parts" (1993: 413); we may extend this observation into an argument about meter as well, for to the degree that "literal and figural are, as it were, on equal 'footing'" when we read Swinburne, his metonymic universe of parts also materializes metrically, in the foot.

What Saintsbury assumes to be self-evident—the foot as unit of versification—begins as a debate about the merits of classical scansion, earlier in the nineteenth century. Saintsbury himself acknowledges that Swinburne's metrical triumph "could not have come without the man; but it also could not have come without the hour. That hour was the result of two generations" (337). A classical approach to meter is developed in various treatises over several decades, ranging from *The Ancient Rhythmical Art Recovered* by William O'Brien (1843) to *On the Use of Classical Metres in English* by William Johnson Stone (1899). A new edition of Hephaestion's *Handbook of Meters* (to which we owe a metrical reading of Sappho, as I have already suggested) also came into circulation in 1843, edited by Thomas Foster Barham. This edition includes prolegomena on the application of rhythm to ancient meters, as well as imitations of Classical meter in English quantitative verse, in an attempt to bring together two different metrical traditions.[19]

Barham further develops his ideas about Classical prosody in a paper

---

been written on Classical meters in the Renaissance (e.g., Attridge 1974, Woods 1984), no comprehensive study historicizes this aspect of Victorian metrical theory in a way that moves beyond a sweeping historical survey or merely formal description. Studies of particular poets do sometimes lead into a broader discussion of Victorian prosody, such as Taylor 1988 on the meters of Hardy.

[19] For further examples of classical approaches to meter in the nineteenth century, see Appendix A, "Of Books and Articles Dealing with Quantitative Verse and Pseudo-Classical Poems," in Omond 1968.

"On Metrical Time, or, the Rhythm of Verse, Ancient and Modern," delivered in 1860 to the Philological Society. Here Barham expresses regret that "all is left to the untutored ear" in the reading of poetry, both ancient and modern, and attempts a more scholarly exploration of "the principles of rhythm" manifested in various metrical forms. Barham singles out the Sapphic stanza in particular ("the first shall be that beautiful and well-known system named the Sapphic," he writes), and proposes a rhythmic reading that would group the stanza into three lines instead of four.[20] Citing the first stanza of Fragment 31 as example, he concludes, "With this rhythm, the effect of the metre is certainly different from our ordinary mode of reading, but, as it seems to me, it is preferable" (1860: 61). The certainty of his reading is qualified, however, by the phrase "as it seems to me," a perhaps unwitting translation of the words just quoted from Sappho's fragment (*phainetai moi*), and suggesting how much is rendered uncertain by the reading of rhythm through foot scansion: can we really hear the rhythm Barham discerns in the Sapphic stanza, even with a well-tutored ear? Or does it only *seem* audible? The dilemma anticipates Swinburne's representation of that which is inaudible in "Sapphics," as if to revive the lost form much admired by Barham and his contemporaries. Such critics urge the revival of classical meters, despite the difficulty of reconstructing their rhythm; indeed, Classical versification is considered a productive model for English poetry precisely because it departs "from our ordinary mode of reading."

These are questions hovering in the air, during the decades of the nineteenth century when Swinburne was being tutored in prosody, and in his own verse he responds to the new theories of meter. I would argue, in fact, that Swinburne's early metrical experiments are a response to Coventry Patmore's "Essay on English Metrical Law" in particular. First published

---

[20] Barham argues that while the Sapphic system is "technically termed epichoriambic," the verses are formed "essentially of dactyls and trochays [sic]; and as originally written by the poetess, would seem to have been intended for three lines only, the two former trimeters, and the last a tetrameter." The example he offers looks like this (with alternating marks for "arsis" and "thesis"):

Φαίνεταί μοι κῆνος ἴσος θεοῖσιν
: l : l : l
Εμμεν ωνὴρ ὅστις εναντίος τοι
: l : l : l
Ισδάνει, καὶ πλασίον ἀδὺ φωνείσας ὑπακούει.
: l : l : l : l

Needless to say, Barham's metrical notation is idiosyncratic and not further developed in either his century or our own, although now classical scholars do share his skepticism about a "choriambic" base for the Sapphic stanza and agree that the third and fourth lines might be joined more plausibly into one longer line; see Halporn, Ostwald, and Rosenmeyer 1980: 29ff.

in 1857 as a review of various English metrical critics (including Guest on the history of English rhythms, and O'Brien on the recovery of ancient rhythms), this essay was known and avidly read within the circle of Oxford poets, at the time when Swinburne was also a student there.[21] In the essay Patmore develops the Classical approach to meter according to a new prosody that would mediate between the "metrical" or "temporal" model of Latin and Greek verse, and the "rhythmical" or "accentual" model of English verse. While he concedes that "a real change did occur in the transition from the 'metrum' of the ancients to the 'rhythmus' of the moderns" and further admits that "in modern verse, those collocations of accented and unaccented syllables which we call 'feet,' are not true measures" (19–20), nevertheless he devises a scheme that retains the foot as the measurement of "isochronous intervals." Thus he recuperates the possibility for measurement without insisting on the actual or hypothetical quantity of what is measured: "Time measured implies something that measures, *and is therefore itself unmeasured,*" he concludes emphatically, in italics (15).

Patmore's paradigm for prosodic analysis (perhaps less original than he claims it to be) depends on a basic "ictus" that divides verse into a series of regular intervals. The division of time is here figured in spatial terms: "The fact of that division shall be made manifest by an 'ictus' or 'beat,' actual or mental, which like a post in a chain railing, shall mark the end of one space, and the commencement of another. This 'ictus' is an acknowledged condition of all possible metre" (15). On this account all meter, both ancient and modern, is a function of marking. The ictus marks intervals "like a post in a chain railing," simultaneously marking the end of one space and the beginning of another, but without itself taking up time or space. We perceive the spaces between, rather than the mark itself. While the ictus allows meter to materialize, "*it has no material and external existence at all,*" Patmore insists, again in italics (15); it is the process of marking rather than the mark itself. What appears to be a practical lesson in prosody therefore leads Patmore into the more startling insight that meter might be a form of material inscription.

---

[21] Sister Mary Roth's critical edition presents the original text of Patmore's essay (originally entitled "English Metrical Critics" and published in the *North British Review* in August of 1857) along with later revisions (titled "Prefatory Study on English Metrical Law" in 1878 and retitled "Essay on English Metrical Law" for Patmore's collected *Poems* of 1879, and subsequent editions). I refer to the 1857 version, as it circulated in Oxford during Swinburne's student years at Balliol (1856–60). Stobie discusses the early reception of Patmore's essay within "the Oxford set" (1949: 65), which surely would have included Swinburne, although she does not mention him by name. See also Roth's commentary on Patmore for further discussion of his influence on contemporary poets and critics interested in "the new prosody."

This insight is framed, however, by an equally insistent emphasis on an organic theory of prosody, derived in part from Hegel in the opening pages of Patmore's essay. Paraphrasing Hegel's *Aesthetics* on the increasing "spiritualisation" of language,[22] Patmore defines meter as the necessary "corporeal element" within language: "Art must have a body as well as a soul, and the higher and purer the spiritual, the more powerful and unmistakable should be the corporeal element;—in other words the more vigorous and various the life, the more stringent and elaborate must be the law by obedience to which life expresses itself" (7). Meter manifests the corporeality of language in order to counterbalance its tendency toward "the spiritual," but it can do so only by means of an increasingly "stringent and elaborate" law. The imposition of this metrical law is another form of inscription, allowing the "body" of language to materialize through the marking of meter. Thus Patmore's philosophical justification for meter produces the figure of a body and makes possible an organic reading of poetic form, even while his detailed analysis of meter points in the opposite direction, to a "more stringent" formalism.

Throughout the essay Patmore describes a perpetual conflict "between the law of the verse and the freedom of the language" (9) in rather disciplinarian terms that conflate submission to the laws of meter with an almost painful disciplining of the body. The bonds of verse are the necessary "shackles of artistic form," and "the language should always seem to *feel*, though not to *suffer from* the bonds of verse," he writes (8). Moreover, poets themselves should also be made to feel these bonds; at a time when most poets "know nothing and feel nothing of the laws of meter" (50), Patmore insists on the difficult discipline of Classical meters, a formal regimen to which all poets should submit. A slip from "should" to "must" resonates through the essay, as it preaches obedience to the metrical law that it elaborates over many pages, and concludes with a stern warning: even when poetry appears to be "unconscious of the rules," it requires "years of intensely 'conscious' discipline," and young poets in particular "must have the addition of hard discipline" to their inspiration (49).

Swinburne seems to follow Patmore's advice more literally than intended, as he is quick to turn the bonds of verse into a bondage that he would only too willingly suffer. He associates the hard discipline of meter with the even harder discipline of corporal punishment, as we have already seen in the Sapphic scene of instruction, and throughout his private correspondence his early instruction in classical meters is associated with scenes of flogging. In one letter Swinburne describes himself

---

[22] Roth identifies Patmore's source in Hegel's *Aesthetics* and traces Patmore's various readings in Hegel (56–57).

flogged for attempting to write in Galliambics, a "*hard*" meter that led to a hard beating from his tutor; remembering this painful episode, he writes that nothing can "heal the cuts or close the scars which had imprinted on the mind and body . . . a just horror of strange metres" (*Letters* I: 110). And yet in the compulsive counting and recounting of his boyhood floggings, these cuts and scars also account for Swinburne's metrical virtuosity. Swinburne remembers the flogging as a form of rigorous inscription: what has been "imprinted on the mind and body" by flagellation is the experience of meter itself as a painful pleasure, playing out the "ictus" (perfect participle of the Latin *icio,* "to strike") on the body, and leaving its marks there. The rhythmic beating of his body becomes Swinburne's preferred figure for "the function of marking" that Patmore attributes to English meter. The marks left on his body allow it to materialize as a function of meter and make it legible as the body of a poet who has learned his lesson in prosody: a perverse performance of English metrical law that makes the language seem both to *feel* and to *suffer* from the bonds of verse.

Thus in another letter, Swinburne claims to surpass even Tennyson because of his education in the "rule of rhythm" at Eton: "As to my quantities and metre and rule of rhythm and rhyme, I defy castigation. The head master has sent me up for good on that score. Mr. Tennyson tells me in a note that he "envies me" my gift that way. After this approval I will not submit myself to the birch on that account" (*Letters* I: 121). Although Swinburne claims he "will not submit to the birch" again, it is precisely by submitting to its rule that he has a "gift" for verse—not freely given, but strictly imposed by the headmaster at school. His memories of Eton (more hyperbolical than historical, one suspects) take the form of numerous flagellation fantasies, focusing in particular on the body of the boy being birched. From his friend George Powell, for example, he requests "a little dialogue (imaginary) between schoolmaster and boy— from the first summons . . . to the last *cut*" with a special plea to "describe also the effect of each stripe on the boy's flesh—its appearance between cuts" (*Letters* I: 123). The boy is disciplined by an imaginary beating, in a violent inscription that far exceeds Patmore's account of meter yet repeats its logic: just as the "ictus" marks the end of one interval and the beginning of the next, allowing us to perceive the spaces in between, so also Swinburne emphasizes the marking function of the "beat," not only in terms of the marks it leaves behind (the cuts and stripes) but also "its appearance between cuts," its metrical pattern.

Flagellation proves a necessary initiation rite for poets, as we see not only in Swinburne's private correspondence but also in his flagellant verse, and perhaps most strikingly in *The Flogging Block,* a series of twelve unpublished "eclogues" in a mock-pastoral Etonian setting.[23] In the Prologue to this "Heroic" poem, Swinburne invokes "the Muse who presides over the Ceremony of Flagellation" to teach the budding young poet a lesson in rhythm:

> Chief the Stripling Songster's Breech invites
> The full Performance of thy frequent Rites,
> Most the Nurslings of the Muse require
> The Lash that sets their lyric Blood on Fire,
> The Lash that ever when they cry keeps Time,
> When Stroke to Stroke responds in glowing Rhyme.
> And still the humbled Bottom hails the Rod sublime,
> Till Heart & Head the rhythmic Lesson learn
> From Wounds that redden & from Stripes that burn,
> As Twig by Twig imprints the Crimson sign in turn.

The "rhythmic lesson" is enforced by each lash, teaching the "Stripling Songster" to cry in time and respond "stroke by stroke . . . in glowing Rhyme." This rhythmic response is incorporated into the body, and imprinted on the bottom as a "Crimson sign," making the body legible through the marking of meter. The passage resonates, of course, with "Anactoria," where the body of Anactoria is rhythmicized by Sappho, who strikes "pang from pang as note is struck from note" in order to turn her into the very embodiment of Sapphic meter. Swinburne's whipping muse is therefore invoked as another version of Sappho: a mistress of perverse metrical discipline, wielding "the Rod sublime" in order to teach the fine art of suffering meter.

Swinburne's (per)version of Sappho reflects ironically on an image created by nineteenth-century Classical scholars of Sappho as chaste schoolmistress and leads directly into the underworld of Victorian pornography, where flagellating governesses taught young gentlemen a good lesson.[24] Swinburne's poetry did, in fact, circulate in such circles. John Camden Hotten, the rather shady publisher who took over the distribution of *Poems and Ballads*, also offered a special line of books devoted to flagellation, with tempting titles like *The Sublime of Flagellation, Exhibition of Female Flagellants, Lady Bumtickler's Revels,* and *Madame Birchini's Dance.*[25] The last

[23] *The Flogging Block: An Heroic Poem in a Prologue and Twelve Eclogues* by Algernon Charles Swinburne, with illustrations by Simeon Solomon. The original holograph manuscript, written at intervals between 1862 and 1881, is at the British Museum (Ashley Ms. 5256).

[24] The nineteenth-century emergence of "Sappho schoolmistress" is traced by Parker 1993; for discussion of "the English vice," see Gibson 1978.

[25] These titles are included in the "Library Illustrative of Social Progress," attributed to "Henry Thomas Buckle" and dated "London, 1777," but printed in 1872 by Hotten. See Ashbee 1962: 239.

of these features an anonymous parody of Sappho, attributed to a board-ing-school girl who has "just been corrected by her Governess." In the opening stanza, the sublime of flagellation is not so far removed from Swinburne's Sapphic sublime:

> Curst as the meanest wretch is she
> Th'unlucky girl just whipt by thee,
> Who sees and feels thy stinging rage,
> Which nought but time can e'er assuage.[26]

The beating of the birch is repeated in the beat of the poem, and its "stinging rage" has the same impact on the unlucky girl as Sappho (whose verses, we recall, "strike and sting") on Swinburne. Swinburne's Sapphic sublime does not work on this level of parody, however; when we place it within the broader discourse of Victorian "flagellomania," we see how closely his "aesthetic" and "pornographic" writings are linked to the for-mal question of meter.

There is an obvious correspondence between the sublime sado-masochism of "Anactoria" and Swinburne's flagellant verse, but the more abstract formalization of meter in "Sapphics" also corresponds to pas-sages in *The Flogging Block*. In the eclogue entitled "Algernon's Flogging," we see how a body materializes through meter, like the "visible song" of Sappho. The rigorous disciplining of Algernon strikes his body into mu-sical response, and he cries out his pain in perfect lyric meters while a chorus of schoolboys traces the mark of the birch on his back. "Oh, isn't his bottom a pattern when stripped?" one observes with relish, to which another replies, "You can see the rod's marks all down Algernon's back." Disciplined by rhythm and marked by meter, Algernon becomes legible in the stripes and lines left by the flogging on his body. Indeed, these lines are written into Swinburne's manuscript. Three parallel lines that mark the end of the eclogue, at the bottom of the page, also appear to re-mark the lines on Algernon's bottom (figure 8):

> ---------------------
> -----------------
> ----------

---

[26] The poem appears as *"Parody of Sappho's Celebrated Ode"* in *Madame Birchini's Dance: A Modern Tale with Considerable Additions and Original Anecdotes,* in Hotten's "Library Illus-trative of Social Progress," vol. 5: 51–52 [see above, n. 24]. Of course the attribution of the poem to "a child eight years of age, but remarkable quick" is spurious; the author is un-known. It is worth noting here that Hotten did solicit anonymous flagellant verse from Swin-burne in the late sixties and early seventies, for publication in his "special" series; indeed in his preface to Swinburne's *Letters* (I: xlviii), Lang notes that Swinburne was blackmailed by Hotten into collaborating on books like *The Romance of Chastisement* and *Flagellation and the Flagellants,* both published by Hotten in 1870 (*Letters* II: 1–2, 227–28).

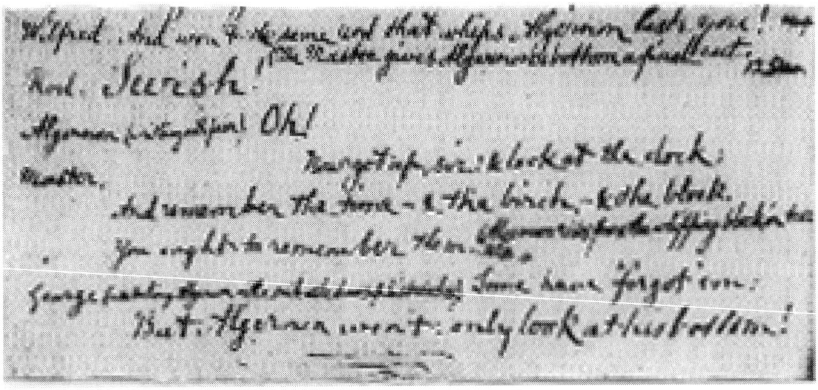

FIGURE 8: Excerpt from "Algernon's Flogging" in *The Flogging Block,*
Algernon Swinburne (1862–1881). By permission of the British Library.
Ashley MS 5256.

The inscription of these lines (in blood on skin, or ink on paper) is the imposition of a metrical pattern, a series of marks not unlike the graphic representation of meter in "Sapphics," allowing a body of song to be visualized graphically on the page. In this way Swinburne's flagellant verse enacts a subjection to English metrical law that produces his entire poetic corpus: the imprinting of a "Crimson sign" on Algernon is Swinburne's ironic lyric signature, outlined on the posteriors and presented to posterity for perverse reading.[27]

Clearly, Swinburne is not among the poets who "know nothing and feel nothing of the laws of meter," according to Patmore's assessment. To the contrary, Swinburne's poetry is made not only to *feel* but to *suffer from* the bonds of verse, in a hyperbolic performance of suffering that puts "the corporeal element" of language on display, playing out the bodily figure produced by Patmore's essay while also undoing that figure. Thus, as we have seen, poems like "Anactoria" and "Sapphics" are simultaneously a form of suffering and a form *for* suffering. Here Swinburne makes explicit a masochistic relation to language that is implicit within British Romanticism. In the Preface to *Lyrical Ballads,* for example, Wordsworth looks to meter for the regulation of feelings when they have "an undue proportion of pain connected with them" or when "there is some danger that the excitement may be carried beyond its proper bounds"; yet, as Adela Pinch has persuasively argued, Wordsworth's poetry also figures meter itself as another source of pain and pleasure, demonstrating a connection

---

[27] This backward logic of lyric reading is further discussed in my forthcoming essay, "On *The Flogging Block:* Algernon Swinburne"; see also "A Poem Is Being Written" (Sedgwick 1993: 177–214).

between meter and masochism that Pinch further traces in a broader nineteenth-century discourse on corporal punishment and aesthetic education.[28] What distinguishes Swinburne from his Romantic precursors is his insistence on that masochistic relation, pushing excitement beyond its proper bounds—beyond a Wordsworthian reading of meter—into an undue proportion of pain.

Suffering meter is part of the "poetics of passion" in all of Swinburne's poetry, as Anthony Harrison reminds us: "Swinburne never forgot the etymological origins of the word 'passion' from the Greek *pathos* and the Latin *passio*, meaning suffering," and Swinburne's interest in "passionate experience" must therefore be understood in terms of self-loss rather than self-assertion, as the expression of suffering (1982: 696–97). I would go one step further, to suggest that what we read as passionate expression in Swinburne is the passion of meter itself: a pathos not inherent in the utterance of a lyric subject, but in subjection to a formal principle. Subjected to metrical law, Swinburne relinquishes control and surrenders to compulsory form, allowing it to speak for him or through him, as if possessed. His passion of meter is an even more extreme example of the "lyric possession" that Susan Stewart discovers in other poets who "employ redundant rhyme and meter as a means of representing the transport or waylaying of subjective intention," for "they demonstrate that we cannot necessarily conclude that strict form signifies authorial mastery or control; it as readily can signify the submersion of will within convention" (1995: 40). This form of lyric possession is a dispossession of the lyric subject, although Stewart is reluctant to give up a claim to the lyric subject altogether: by reading the "symptoms of meter," she describes various displacements of reference (the waylaying of subjective intention, the surrendering of will, the haunting of lyric voice), but with reference to a model of the unconscious that still assumes an individual consciousness.

But suppose, as is the case with Swinburne, that meter is not to be read symptomatically, as if it were the return of the repressed, but as the manifestation of a highly self-conscious nineteenth-century discourse on meter? By suffering meter, Swinburne "consciously" performs a formal structure that does not operate according to an intentional logic: in his poetry, rhythm is an automatic mechanism, a repetition compulsion that

[28] On meter and masochism in Wordsworth, see Pinch 1996; her argument is further elaborated in "Learning What Hurts: 'The School-Mistress,' the Rod, and the Poem" (1999), placing Shenstone's poem "The School-Mistress" within the context of early-nineteenth-century debates on corporal punishment and flagellant literature. Swinburne's flagellant verse demonstrates how these discourses are increasingly formalized and aestheticized toward the end of the century; thus a question about the "healthy" instruction of meter embodied in Shenstone's schoolmistress anticipates the teachings of the "Scholastic Dame" who is invoked as an even more perverse metrical muse by Swinburne at the beginning of "The Flogging Block."

takes control and makes authorial mastery redundant. Edward Thomas recognizes how Swinburne's "confessed experiments in sapphics" disclaim agency: "He does not, like another poet, have to think in his meter; his mastery compels the metre to think for him" (1912: 87–88). Likewise, in an 1889 review of "Mr. Swinburne," Oscar Wilde is interested in "the masterly experiments" of Swinburne's poetry precisely because he seems to have relinquished mastery: "It has been said of him, and with truth, that he is a master of language, but with still greater truth it may be said that Language is his master. Words seem to dominate him" (146). Swinburne appears to be a master of language because language has mastered him. Indeed, by capitalizing "Language" Wilde cannily displaces the proper name of Mr. Swinburne, who is no longer the proper subject of his own poetry; Swinburne's claim to lyricism can only be the surrendering of that lyric persona. "He is the first lyric poet who has tried to make an absolute surrender of his own personality, and he has succeeded," Wilde writes, not without ambivalence; "We hear the song, but we never know the singer. We never even get near him" (148).

Of course that is also how Swinburne describes his relation to Sappho, as we recall: "It is as near as I can come; and no man can come close to her," he writes in "Notes on Poems and Reviews," not only to defend his imitations of Sappho, but to imply that he might at least approximate her very condition of unapproachability: no longer a singer but a song, or rather, its reiteration. The reception of his own poetry is therefore a repetition of Swinburne's Sapphic sublime. Mastered by Sappho and subjected to a Sapphic rhythm, Swinburne is nevertheless admired for his mastery of meter. Saintsbury calls him "the one living master of English prosody" (1910: 334) and upon his death in 1909, Swinburne is eulogized in the obituaries as "an unrivaled master of meter" (Hyder 1970: 242). By the time his *Posthumous Poems* appeared in 1917, the reviews proclaim that he "the great singer was indeed singing for our age" (ibid.: 252), but only in the past tense: a posthumous recuperation of Swinburne, as if he might have been, after all, the Victorian reincarnation of Sappho, whose song also outlived the age of her singing. Thus Swinburne's poetic corpus is constituted, by analogy to the mutilated fragments of Sappho, as a body of writing initially abused by critics but increasingly read as the very embodiment of lyric poetry: a sublime metrical body, suffering meter.

Recollections of Swinburne

Swinburne's perverse reincorporation of "the mutilated fragments" of Sappho leaves us with a question about how to read Swinburne "himself." In the course of his reception, he is increasingly identified with Sappho, according to a logic that repeats Swinburne's Sapphic sublime. In an early review, one of the few to defend *Poems and Ballads,* W. M. Rossetti reinstates the sublime as an aesthetic category for reading Swinburne: "There is a word which was once familiar to the critic of poetry—the word Sublime; now seldom produced, and still seldomer aright producible," he writes. Without "attempting a definition of that word Sublime," Rossetti nevertheless insists that Swinburne deserves the epithet. His praise of Swinburne is fulsome, in a prolonged sentence gradually building up to "that word":

> We find in him an impulse, a majesty, a spontaneity, a superiority to common standards of conception, perception, and treatment, an absoluteness (so to speak) of poetic incitement and subject-matter (rendering him perhaps not likely to be ever very widely admired, but certain to be as intimately and as enthusiastically admired at the latest date to which his works may reach as at the present or any intermediate time), and withal a power and splendour in all the media of poetic expression, a wizardry over the auroral brightness and the "sunless and sonorous gulfs" of song, such as we apprehend to be consistent if not co-extensive with any reasonable definition of the poetic sublime. (Hyder 1970: 89–90)

Superior to "common standards of conception, perception, and treatment," achieving an "absoluteness" that recalls the "literal and absolute words" of Sappho, flying high over the "gulfs of song," Swinburne is elevated—in the cadences of Rossetti's own high Victorian prose—to the status of sublime poet, in the present and in future time.

But if Swinburne appears "consistent if not co-extensive with any reasonable definition of the poetic sublime," the reason is that he extends the sublime beyond its reasonable limits. Throughout his review Rossetti describes Swinburne in distinctly Longinian terms, with a giddy sense of the poetry veering out of control: "a mighty intoxication of poetic diction mounts to his head, and pours in an unruly torrent through his lips, and he forgets the often still nobler office of self-mastery and reticence" (64). The unruly torrent of Swinburne, intoxicated by language that "mounts to his head," makes him sublime; yet this sublimating movement also makes him lose "self-mastery," as he is transported by a force that carries him upward and, at times, too high. "The author's defects," Rossetti concedes, "will be perceived to be ascribable to over-high, not to deficient pitch, and as such to be rightly classed under the terms perversion and excess rather than blunder and bathos" (89). Rossetti therefore introduces a Longinian account of the sublime ("now seldom produced, and still seldomer aright producible") in order to demonstrate how Swinburne might produce the sublime, but only by reproducing it in extreme form, not "aright" but "rightly classed under the terms perversion and excess." This perversion, according to Rossetti, is not moral but rhetorical; it is especially evident in Swinburne's "over-doing" (81), the "continual iteration of certain words, phrases, or images" and "his great love of alliteration" (83), a verbal mechanism that propels his rhythm and rhyme to such a degree that "it must be confessed that his use of it runs into abuse" (84).

More than a mere trick of style, Swinburne's "abuse" of language points to a catachresis that is played out in all of his poetry and especially, as I have suggested, in his Sapphic imitations: Swinburne's Sappho is an embodiment of that catachresis, a figure for the figure of abuse. The rhetoric of abuse is further transferred to Swinburne himself, famously abused by critics for writing poems like "Anactoria." Their attack on Swinburne does not take the form of merely enumerating, as Rossetti does, the "defects" in his style; to critics less partisan than Rossetti, it appears that Swinburne's "over-doing" is also his undoing, allowing the defects of his poetry to be projected onto a deficient and depraved body. Swinburne appears as an increasingly mutilated, emasculated figure in Victorian criticism. In his polemic against Swinburne's "improper feminine muse," for example, Alfred Austin complains of "those falsetto notes which appear to compose most of Mr. Swinburne's emasculated poetical voice" (Hyder 1970: 109), and he questions "his Anactorias" and "his Sapphos" in particular: "But are they masculine? That is the question" (96). A question about Swinburne's poetry becomes "the question" about Swinburne himself, who seems not only feminized by his improper use of language but emasculated by the falsehood of his "falsetto tones." Buchanan's review of *Poems and Ballads* also turns Swinburne into a castrato figure, a "sexless maniac" (Hyder 1970: 30) and "quite the Absalom of modern bards,— long-ringleted, flippant-lipped, down-cheeked, amorous-lidded" (31); Buchanan's ad hominem attack (if we may still call it that) continues in his infamous essay, "The Fleshly School of Poetry," where Swinburne is reduced to "an intellectual hermaphrodite," not unlike the "the *reductio ad horribilem* of . . . intellectual sensualism" in Baudelaire's poetry. The "unwholesome fleshliness" of such poetry reduces the body to separate parts: no longer whole, no longer an aesthetic unity, but a set of self-disarticulating contradictions.

The Victorian critical establishment therefore interprets Swinburne's transgressive language as a transgression of gender, within a rhetorical tradition that assumes "the immoral man will always abuse his body, the body of others, the body or 'figures' of language, and ultimately the 'body politic,'" as Thaïs Morgan points out (1988: 17). The peculiar threat posed by Swinburne is less the immorality of the man than his abuse of language, which may or may not lead to various forms of bodily abuse but also, more fundamentally, calls into question the figure of the body itself.

Swinburne's flagrant disarticulation of the body makes him the most controversial, and perhaps most influential, poet of the eighteen sixties. Every attack on Swinburne only serves to perpetuate that abuse, and even Swinburne's self-defense in "Notes on Poems and Reviews" is a provocation to further abuse. "I have never lusted after the praise of reviewers; I have never feared their abuse," he writes in response to the scathing reviews of "Anactoria" (19), but as a concession to his critics he adds, "I am ready for once to play the anatomist." Swinburne then proceeds to anatomize "Anactoria" as a poem that cannot reproduce the Sapphic body, and throughout the essay he ironically dissects his poetic corpus to show how it "embodies" ideas that refuse organic reading. The disintegrating and unnatural bodies of *Poems and Reviews,* he argues perversely, are repulsive only to readers who insist on their embodiment.

Nevertheless Swinburne depends on such readers not only because their outrage contributes to his visibility as poet (*Poems and Ballads* became a best-seller), but because the violence of their attacks turns him into another body *for* abuse: a body of writing that is read as "sin burning on the paper," the mark of a man whose name has gone into circulation as "Swine-born," a poet whose lyric signature is the abuse of the body (*Letters* I: xxi-xxii). Of course Swinburne, "more be-written and belied than any man since Byron," or so he claims in a letter (*Letters* III: 12), finds a painful pleasure in proclaiming how abused he is by the critics. Not surprisingly, he turns their critical castigation into a series of flagellation fantasies. In a letter of 1867, after the relentless whipping that *Poems and Ballads* received in the press, Swinburne writes that he is "mentally in the same condition as the skin of a public schoolboy after the twentieth or thirtieth application of the birch—too well used to it for any cut of a master's rod to make the tough hide wince" (*Letters* I: 217). And in an earlier letter to Lord Houghton, signed "your much flogged pupil," there is reference to the flogging Swinburne has received from colleagues and critics: "Tennyson and Jowett, the *Athenaeum* and the *Spectator,* have each had their innings. Twice I have been swished in private and twice in public before the whole school—for 'irreverence.' My skin has the marks of the birch still on it" (*Letters* I: 121–22). Both letters point to the imprinting of a lyric sign on the body, as we also saw in Swinburne's flagellant verse, but the marking function is now attributed to the critics who abuse Swinburne: his skin is only "too well used" to their cuts and "has the marks of the birch still on it." Thus Swinburne predicts how he will be read by posterity: the more he is castigated by the critics, the more marks they leave behind, and the more he materializes as a poetic corpus.

Because the lyric figure of Swinburne appears through this process of disfiguration, he is easily caricatured. Rikky Rooksby surveys a century of Swinburne criticism, ranging from Ruskin's description of Swinburne as "demoniac youth" to the "tadpole scholar" that Church describes "leaping on and off chairs 'like a wild creature,' 'a syllable-addict, a word-drunkard,'" and continuing in more recent descriptions of Swinburne as "a small red-headed, bird-voiced eccentric of aristocratic lineage," a "besotted logophile" and a "strident red-headed imp" (Rooksby and Shrimpton 1993: 8–9). To this exaggerated portrait Rooksby wishes to restore "historical significance and human content" (9). But what makes Swinburne significant is precisely the history of his transmission, the distortion of his characteristic features into a poetic body that is no longer human, not only by those who abuse Swinburne but even more by those who admire him as lyric poet par excellence. The parts of Swinburne's body repeatedly singled out by critics—"his aureole of flaming red hair, his feverishly dancing limbs and perpetually fluttering hands" (Quennell, quoted by Rooksby 8)—are decomposed and recomposed on a Longinian model without producing an organically unified form.

The peculiar pathos, or bathos, of this sublime logic is comically illustrated by Max Beerbohm in various cartoons of Swinburne, and especially in "The Small Hours in the 'Sixties at 16, Cheyne Walk—Algernon reading 'Anactoria' to Gabriel and William" (figure 9).[29] Algernon sits by candlelight in the small hours of the night, looking small himself and strangely out of sync with the company to whom he is reciting his poem. In contrast to the looming beard of William Rossetti and the reclining corpulence of Dante Gabriel Rossetti, he is a tiny upright body with foreshortened arms, spindly legs and extended feet, an oversized head on a swan-like neck: in short, a lyricized figure who seems to reincarnate the loose limbs of Sappho in the act of performing his own Sapphic song.

In another portrait, this time in words, Beerbohm also represents Swinburne as an oddly disproportionate body. He recalls visits to the elderly poet in "No. 2, The Pines," with an elaborate description of his physical appearance. "Here, suddenly visible in the flesh, was the legendary being and divine singer," he reminisces, but this vision of Swinburne in the flesh is quickly transfigured into "a strange small figure in grey . . . being of an aspect so unrelated as it was to any species of human kind" (Hyder 1970: 237). There is indeed something unhuman about Swinburne, who cuts a strange figure in Beerbohm's description: "In figure, at first glance, he seemed almost fat; but this was merely because of the way he carried himself, with his long neck strained so tightly back that he

[29] Beerbohm includes this caricature of Swinburne (as well as "Algernon Swinburne taking his Great New Friend Gosse to see Gabriel Rossetti," in which Swinburne is a diminutive figure alongside the towering Gosse) in *Rossetti and His Circle* (London: Heinemann, 1922) and reprinted in 1987 by N. John Hall. In an introductory note, Beerbohm warns his readers "not to regard as perfectly authentic any of the portraits that I here present to you."

FIGURE 9: "Algernon Reading 'Anactoria' to Gabriel and William,"
Max Beerbohm (1922). Courtesy of the Tate Gallery, London. Copyright
the Estate of Max Beerbohm, reproduced by permission
of London Management.

all receded from the waist upwards. . . . I became aware, too, that when
he bowed he did not unbend his back, but only his neck—the length of
the neck accounting for the depth of the bow. His hands were tiny, even
for his size, and they fluttered helplessly, touchingly, unceasingly"
(237–38). As in Beerbohm's cartoon, we see the legendary Swinburne
dissolving into "the divine singer," a body losing all natural proportions,
with his long neck "strained" back so that he is "all receded from the waist
upwards," leaving us with the image of hands that never stop fluttering,
more like a bird than a human being. His body seems possessed, taken
over by a voice not his own, as he "threw back his head, uttering a sound
that was like the cooing of a dove, and forthwith, rapidly, ever so musically, he spoke to us" (239). The "helplessly, touchingly, unceasingly" fluttering hands prepare us for Swinburne's utterance, delivered "rapidly"
and "musically" as if to transpose the movement of his limbs into pure
melody, for Beerbohm hastens to add, "And rather than that he spoke
would I say that he cooingly and flutingly *sang* . . . in a flow of words as
spontaneous as the wordless notes of a bird in song." This portrait of Swinburne as a body spontaneously given over to song, the very embodiment
of lyric, was written at the request of Edmund Gosse, for inclusion in his

biography. In an apologetic note, Beerbohm admits he took refuge in "a reminiscential essay," because "I failed in the attempt to make of my subject a snapshot that was not a grotesque." But any attempt Beerbohm makes to portray Swinburne—in caricature, vignette, or memoir—seems to border on the grotesque, as if remembering Swinburne inevitably involves a dismembering, the deformation of his body.

Probably Beerbohm was influenced by Edmund Gosse, whose *Life of Swinburne* (1917) also portrays the poet as an idealized lyric figure, although not without mockery. There is more than a hint of the grotesque, in fact, in Gosse's supplementary "notes" to the biography.[30] In this notorious essay, entitled "Swinburne's Agitation," Gosse describes Swinburne as a poet who

> under the agitation of his own thoughts became like a man possessed, with quivering hands, eyes thrown up, and voice hollowed to a kind of echoing chant. This strange possession was entirely unconscious. . . . His eyes would be fixed on nothingness, his lips alone would be moving without a sound: until occasional tremors through his limbs would presently announce that he was waking up to speech. Then he would begin in a very low voice, still not looking at me, with some such sentence as "Down all the vista of literary history it is impossible to see a figure, etc. etc." almost as though he were reading out of a book; and then he would turn to recite with an almost excruciating ardour some lines of Aeschylus or Marlowe, or a French lyric. (*Letters* VI: 233–34)

Again the quivering hands, the trembling limbs, the echoing voice turn Swinburne into "a man possessed," no longer himself but taken over by rhythm. His agitation is played out on the body like the rhythms of *eros lusimelēs*, first with "occasional tremors through his limbs," then "waking up to speech" and gradually elevating a "very low voice" to a high pitch of "almost excruciating ardour," to express his lyric passion. During "this strange possession" Swinburne seems to embody the very idea of the lyric poet; the figures "impossible to see" down the vista of literary history may be heard again in his own echoing chant, as he recites other poets "as though he were reading out of a book," except that he has memorized their words and now incorporated them into his own body. The agitation of Swinburne, who seems to reincarnate the rhythms of lyric poetry, may therefore be understood as a form of sublime transport.

---

[30] Gosse drafted his supplementary notes on Swinburne in 1917 after the appearance of his biography, but without publishing the essay. Nevertheless, it circulated enough to become a source of controversy. Lang alludes to "all the huggermugger with which this essay has been surrounded and all the hullabaloo with which it has been heralded" (*Letters* I. xlviii–xlix) and prints the essay for the first time as an appendix to his edition of the Swinburne correspondence (*Letters* VI. 233–48).

At the same time, Gosse reveals another side of Swinburne's agitation, the physical "irregularities" that he feels called upon to describe as "a duty to posterity." "I have therefore decided to write down, with closest attention to the truth as I recall it, or have been able to collect it, the physical characteristics of this extraordinary man," Gosse writes, going on at length to describe how Swinburne abused his body, in sensational details left out of the official biography: his "bouts of abandonment to drink," and "delirium tremens" (242), the "ecstatic pleasure in letting his mind rest on flagellation" and his "mania for suffering pain" (244), and various incidents demonstrating "the excessive tension of Swinburne's nerves" (247). By "collecting" these pieces of information, and thus recollecting a body that is conspicuously falling apart, Gosse repeats the pattern of Swinburne's Sapphic sublime: the loosening of limbs (whether by "occasional tremors," "delirium tremens," or any other version of *eros lusimelēs*) allows Gosse to remember Swinburne as a lyric poet and to reintegrate his poetry into a posthumous poetic corpus. Gosse becomes the first in a long line of Swinburne "collectors": in addition to collecting memories and memorabilia for his *Life of Swinburne,* he collected unpublished materials for Swinburne's *Posthumous Poems* (1917) and *Letters* (1918), and together with Wise he published the collected works of Swinburne in the twenty-volume Bonchurch edition (1925–27). But in reassembling the poetic corpus so successfully, Gosse also succeeds in making the poet look less and less complete; the *Complete Works* are anything but, as Rooskby points out (1993: 2), and the Bonchurch edition leaves so much to be desired that it stimulates a desire for ever more of Swinburne.

The desire to turn Swinburne into a body of writing therefore both assumes and resumes a process of fragmentation; not unlike Sappho, it would seem that Swinburne can only be recollected in scattered parts. Even Mrs. Disney Leith, Swinburne's first cousin who, according to Gosse, "constituted herself the protector of his memory," and contributed to "a sort of conspiracy that Algernon should be presented to posterity as a guileless and featureless model of respectability" (236–37), recollects Swinburne in bits and pieces. Her recollections of the poet (published in 1917 as *The Boyhood of Algernon Charles Swinburne: Personal Recollections by his Cousin, Mrs. Disney Leith, With Extracts from Some of his Private Letters*) are presented in the form of excerpted letters and extracts from diaries, partial narratives that circulate as apocryphal fictions in subsequent biographies of Swinburne. One event in particular ("I cannot call it a reminiscence," she writes, "for I do not remember hearing of it at the time, or, indeed for long after," 13) demonstrates how Swinburne's afterlife is like the fragmentary legacy of Sappho; this story, not quite a memory, serves as parable for the remembering of Swinburne through an increasingly violent dismemberment.

Immediately after describing his most striking physical features, his habit of "shaking his arms and hands when animated" and his "wiry and very agile . . . figure" (which she insists is "quite in proportion," while conceding that his head gave "perhaps the appearance of being large for his small stature," 12–13), Mrs. Leith recounts how Swinburne once endangered himself as a boy by climbing Culver Cliff. To describe his heroic climb of that "great white chalk promontory . . . unassailable to ordinary mortals," she quotes at length from a letter, in his own words:

> I found myself at the foot of Culver Clif; and then all at once it came upon me that it was all very well to fancy or dream of "deadly danger" . . . but that here was a chance of testing my nerve in face of death which could not be surpassed. So I climbed a rock under the highest point, and stripped, and climbed down again, and just took a souse into the sea to steady and strengthen my nerve, which I knew the sharp chill would, and climbed up again. . . . But as I got near the top I remember thinking I should not like to have to climb down again. In a minute or two more I found that I must, as the top part (or top story) of the precipice came jutting out aslant above me. Even a real sea-gull could not have worked its way up without using or spreading its wings. So of course I felt I must not stop to think for one second, and began climbing down, hand under hand, as fast and as steadily as I could, till I reached the bottom, and (equally of course) began to look out for another possible point of ascent at the same height. As I began again I must own I felt like setting my teeth and swearing I would not come down again alive—if I did return to the foot of the cliff again it should be in a fragmentary condition, and there would not be much of me to pick up. (14–15)

Swinburne's ascent to the top part of the precipice is clearly a sublime narrative (or "top story"), dramatizing his aspiration to Longinian heights, and allowing the fledgling poet (like the sea-gull with whom he identifies) to spread his wings. The deadly danger would seem to be the vision of himself shattered at the foot of the cliff, "in a fragmentary condition" without "much of me to pick up," the conversion of "I" into "it," a dismembered body, a fragment.

Yet as the letter continues, this is the fate that Swinburne envisions. When he finally reaches the top of the cliff, the height of his ascent can be measured only by imagining a fall down into the depths: "I lay on my right side helpless, and just had time to think what a sell (and what an inevitable one) it would be if I were to roll back over the edge after all, when I became unconscious—as suddenly and utterly and painlessly as I did many years afterward when I was "picked up at sea" by a Norman fishing boat upwards of three miles (they told me) off the coast of Etretat and could just clutch hold of the oar they held out; "but that is not in this story"—which I only hope is not too long for the reader" (16). Told in retrospect, the story of climbing the cliff anticipates a later story of near-drowning, and through this temporal manipulation the letter begins to sound less autobiographical and more like another version of Swinburne's Sapphic sublime.[31] The episode on Culver Cliff repeats Sappho's leap from the Leucadian Cliff, following a sublime trajectory that seems "inevitable" to Swinburne: ascending to sublime heights in order to dash himself on the rocks, plummeting into the sea and dissolving into unconsciousness. This fantasy of self-fragmentation identifies Swinburne with the figure of Sappho, and the legacy of her leap becomes his own, as Mrs. Leith writes effusively about "the halo of association that will surround Culver Cliff for ever, at least as long as Swinburne's name is remembered!" (17). Swinburne's name, in other words, can be remembered because his body is absorbed into the larger body of the sea, allowing Swinburne to be read (much as we read Swinburne's Sappho) as a figure that appears and disappears in the rhythms of its own scattering.

Such is the "halo of association" that allows Arthur Symons to rediscover the rhythms of the sea in Swinburne's poetry. In *Figures of Several Centuries* (1916), he singles out Swinburne as the most exemplary lyric figure of the previous century, for "to no poet has it been given to create music with words in so literal an analogy with the inflexible and vital rhythmical science of the sea" (1916: 158). The analogy between Swinburne's metrical virtuosity and the "rhythmical science of the sea" serves to naturalize the rhythm of his poetry; Swinburne now seems to dissolve into a larger force of nature, just as Sappho dissolves into a Sapphic rhythm that is repeated throughout the world at the end of "Anactoria" and penetrates all time at the end of "On the Cliffs." Symons literalizes the topos of Swinburne's Sapphic sublime by locating the scene of reading at the seaside: "Reading the earlier and the later Swinburne on a high rock around which the sea is washing, one is struck by the way in which these cadences, in their unending, ever-varying flow, seem to harmonize with the rhythm of the sea. Here one finds, at least, and it is a great thing to find, a rhythm inherent in nature" (161). The "high rock around which

---

[31] The near-drowning to which Swinburne refers is recalled by Guy de Maupassant, who witnessed the rescue of a swimmer swept away in a tidal undercurrent near the Norman coast. He writes that "the reckless bather" was "an English poet, Mr. Algernon Charles Swinburne," who appeared "thin and startling at first glance—a sort of fantastic apparition," reminding him of Edgar Allen Poe. In the description that follows, Swinburne is again deformed (a "very high forehead," joined to a neck that "seemed to have no end," a "torso without shoulders," and "the top of his chest seeming hardly wider than his forehead") in order to create a rhythmicized lyric figure: "This virtually supernatural character was shaken all over by nervous spasms," Maupassant concludes (Hyder 1970: 185–86). Maupassant's recollection (used in the introduction to Gabriel Mourey's French translation of *Poems and Ballads* in 1891) is yet another repetition of Swinburne's Sapphic sublime, as it shapes his reception not only in England but also in France.

the sea is washing" may refer to the Leucadian Cliff where Sappho took the plunge, or to Culver Cliff where Swinburne imagines a similar fate, but it is also where Symons as reader finds himself, literally or figuratively, when he reads the verses of Swinburne. By listening to their ebb and flow, the cadences that "seem to harmonize with the rhythm of the sea," Symons himself repeats the sublime fall into that sea. Transported by Swinburne's rhythm, Symons thus presents himself as prototype for every reader, as if we too will read the poetry of Swinburne to discover "a rhythm inherent in nature."

To turn the cadence of Swinburne's poetry into a natural force, Symons draws on a nineteenth-century assumption that the word *rhythm* is connected to the regular movement of the waves of the sea. The etymology of *rhythm*, derived from the Greek noun *rhuthmos* and the Greek verb *rheo*, "to flow," would seem to confirm the idea that poets learn their rhythms from the sea. However, when submitted to closer linguisic analysis, as demonstrated by Emile Benveniste, the word *rhuthmos* "in its most ancient uses never refers to flowing water, and it does not even mean 'rhythm'" (1971: 282). Benveniste reconstructs another history for the word, as it moves from an early meaning of "form" (in ancient Ionian philosophy, it refers to the disposition and arrangement of parts in a whole, including the form of the letters of the alphabet: a spatial configuration) to a later, more specialized application to "form of movement" (in Plato, dance is a corporal *rhuthmos* determined by measure and numerically regulated: a temporal configuration). Benveniste therefore argues against a tendency to naturalize rhythm, especially with reference to its Greek origins:

> We are far indeed from the simplistic picture that a superficial etymology used to suggest, and it was not in contemplating the play of waves on the shore that the primitive Hellene discovered "rhythm"; it is, on the contrary, we who are making metaphors today when we speak of the rhythm of the waves. It required a long consideration of the structure of things, then a theory of measure applied to the figures of dance and to the modulations of song, in order for the principle of cadenced movement to be recognized and given a name. Nothing is less "natural" than this slow working out. (287)

We may read Benveniste's essay not only as a critique of nineteenth-century philology—interrogating the assumptions shaping an etymology that "was taught more than a century ago, at the beginnings of comparative grammar, and . . . is still being repeated" (281)—but as an implicit response to a tradition of aesthetic idealism that would unify humans and nature under time, by projecting rhythm into nature.

This is the same aesthetic tradition that produces an idealist reading of Swinburne around the turn of the century, as exemplified in the rhapsodies of Symons. If the "principle of cadenced movement" is recognized and given a name in nineteenth-century theories of rhythm, Swinburne is read as the very embodiment of that principle, and perhaps even as the proper name for it. In *Poets and Poetry of the Century* (Miles 1898) Symons again rhapsodizes about the "mastery over poetical form" that enables Swinburne to sing "so naturally that he has sometimes given us only the notes of the music." His naturalized song becomes nature itself, as Symons concludes: "Nature . . . created him in a fit of extravagance" (1910: 284). Yet Swinburne's approach to rhythm is anything but natural, as we have seen; his imitations of Sappho self-consciously reflect on a Sapphic cadence, by turning it into a decadent form, a formal repetition that requires formalist reading. Swinburne is not the primitive Hellene who discovered "rhythm" in the sea (nor did the Hellene, if we follow Benveniste's argument). The revelation of rhythm in his Sapphic sublime returns us, rather, to the formalism of an earlier set of associations de-scribed by Benveniste: the *rhuthmos* associated with *metron*, or meter, which mediates between the spatial and temporal configuration of forms that do not in themselves have organic consistency. By remembering Swinburne as a body dissolving into the sea, we make a metaphor of his Sapphic rhythm, not unlike the "metaphors of me" that Sappho projects into the future at the end of "Anactoria." Just as Benveniste concludes that "it is, on the contrary, we who are making metaphors today when we speak of the rhythm of the waves," it is we who are making metaphors of Swinburne, when we discover the rhythms of the sea in his poetry.

Nevertheless Swinburne's afterlife depends on a metaphorical reading of rhythm, as we see in Thomas Hardy's elegy written upon the death of Swinburne in 1909. In "A Singer Asleep," Swinburne seems to dissolve like Sappho into his own metaphor: his rhythms are repeated in the "un-slumbering sea," where "from cove to promontory" he is "pillowed eter-nally"—a scenario immediately reminiscent of Swinburne's Sapphic sub-lime. Swinburne's corpse is hidden from view, like Sappho's corpus, but in the cadence of Hardy's poem his decomposing limbs are recomposed into the melody of Sapphic song, making him a member of "all the tribe that feel in melodies":

> His singing-mistress verily was no other
> Than she the Lesbian, the music-mother
> Of all the tribe that feel in melodies;
> Who leapt, love-anguished, from the Leucadian steep
> Into the rambling world-encircling deep
>   Which hides her where none sees.
>
> And one can hold in thought that nightly here
> His phantom may draw down to the water's brim,
> And hers come up to meet it, as a dim

Lone shine upon the heaving hydrosphere,
And mariners wonder as they traverse near,
　　Unknowing of her and him.

One dreams him sighing to her spectral form:
"O teacher, where lies hid thy burning line;
Where are those songs, O poetess divine
Whose very orts are love incarnadine?"
And her smile back: "Disciple true and warm,
　　Sufficient now are thine." . . .

(Stanzas VI–VIII)

These stanzas refigure familiar poems of Swinburne—most notably "Ave atque Vale" (the elegy for Baudelaire where the sea sobs around the Lesbian promontories, looking for the Leucadian grave of Sappho) and "Satia te Sanguine" (where the lost limbs of Lesbian Sappho swim loose for the streams to lift)—in order to imagine that Swinburne has finally found Sappho: "his phantom . . . and hers" meet where the waves heave on and on forever, in an eternal rhythm.

And yet, Hardy emphasizes that they meet only in, through, and as a metaphor. The sublime transport of Swinburne and Sappho contrasts with the more ordinary transportation of mariners, who traverse the same sea "unknowing of her and him," unable to feel the melodies of dissolving limbs, unable to hear the rhythm that Hardy projects into the movement of the waves. His vision of Swinburne is a speculation (something that "one can hold in thought"), and presented in the subjunctive ("his phantom may draw down . . . and hers come up") as a mere hypothesis ("One dreams him sighing to her spectral form"). Hardy also represents Swinburne's Sappho as a specular image, a reflection of a reflection, as her form comes up to meet his and his down to hers, each haunting the other like disembodied ghosts. "Where are those songs?" Swinburne sighs to Sappho—a rhetorical question, since her song is lost and cannot be answered except in the echo of his own words. "Sufficient now are thine . . ." is Sappho's response, but the ellipses after "thine" point to the disappearance of Swinburne's song along with hers. If Swinburne once was a "disciple true and warm," reincarnating Sappho, "whose very orts are love incarnadine," now he is also a disintegrating poetic corpus, a cold corpse.

The more we reread Hardy's elegy, the more it resists elegiac reconstitution. The final stanza, where "the waves peal their everlasting strains," echoes the declining cadence of a singer forever falling into silence. There is only a diminishing echo, in the rhyme of the last lines in the poem: "I leave him, while the daylight gleam declines / Upon the capes and chines." These lines do not reintegrate the body of Swinburne, but leave him scattered at sea, as Peter Sacks points out, "*Capes* sugests heads, and *chines* spinal ridges—prominences that are durable yet somehow severed" (1985: 234). While Sacks emphasizes the continuity of a Swinburnean legacy as a possible form of consolation, Hardy's elegy does not perform the usual work of mourning; what remains is "somehow severed," parts of Swinburne that are not quite recollected, scattered limbs, lost songs. The final stanza, in fact, serves to render dead the "I" who should be remembering Swinburne: rather than saying, "he has left me," Hardy says, "I leave him," as if he is the one who is dying. Hardy's elegy observes a logic of melancholia that structures all of his poetry, as Marjorie Levinson argues: a peculiar negativity that may be understood in psychoanalytic terms as the inability to mourn, the repetition of a loss without knowing what is lost, an emptying out of content in writing that claims only a posthumous existence.[32]

The elegist in "A Singer Asleep" is indeed a melancholy figure, one who does not wish to remember Swinburne except by rote repetition of his metaphors and rhythms. The impulse to remember is thus displaced by a compulsion to repeat. Here, in addition to the Freudian conceptualization of melancholia as failed mourning, we can refer back to Freud's 1914 essay, "Recollection, Repetition and Working Through." To define repetition compulsion, Freud describes the patient who remembers nothing of what is forgotten: "He reproduces it not in his memory but in his behavior, he repeats it, without of course knowing that he is repeating it" (369). Furthermore, the greater the resistance to the memory, "the more extensively will expression in action (repetition) be substituted for recollecting" (370). Insofar as the analyst must learn to recognize the rhythms of this repetition, psychoanalysis would seem to be analogous to the metrical analysis of a poem: the measuring of intervals, the marking of a form.[33] But while the purpose of psychoanalysis (terminable or interminable) would be to curb the compulsion to repeat and turn it into a motive for remembering, the purpose of our reading is not to reconstruct Hardy's memory of Swinburne, or indeed to reconstitute Hardy as a subject with a memory. Rather, by staying inside the repetition compulsion, by insisting on the rhythm without the recollection, we see how

[32] In "Object Bondage and Object Loss: Economies of Representation in Hardy's Poetry" (part of a forthcoming book on modernism), Marjorie Levinson connects the logic of melancholia to late-nineteenth-century commodity fetishism, in order to account for a poetry that is highly objectified yet emptied of content, resistant to reading.

[33] For further reflections on the relationship between psychoanalysis and rhythmic reading, and the possibility of a "Freudian" theory of lyric, see Rowlinson 1994; through the poetry of Tennyson, he develops an account of formalist reading that is also relevant to later Victorian poets like Swinburne and Hardy, insofar as "the materiality of language—manifested most notably in its rhythmic articulations and in its iterability—haunts this poetry" (ibid.: vii).

Hardy's elegy enacts another way to read Swinburne, by memorization.

Hardy presents a scene of reading in stanza 3 of his elegy, the poet's first encounter with the words of Swinburne: "I walked and read with a quick glad surprise / New words, in classic guise." Sacks calls this stanza an "elegiac fixing of a highly particularized and intense moment in the past," and finds a pun in "quick" to demonstrate how Hardy is enlivened by "absorption of the dead man's power . . . so crucial to the work of mourning and inheritance" (1985: 231). According to Sacks, Hardy identifies with Swinburne through the double reference of "new words, in classic guise," referring not only to Swinburne's poetry but also to the present poem. But this identification also works to consign Hardy's poem to the past, for by repeating "new words, in classic guise" Hardy's own words might turn out be merely old words, in new disguise: the reiteration and evacuation of Swinburne's words, now a dead poetic corpus. From this perspective, the "elegiac fixing" that Sacks describes is more like a melancholy fixation on a moment in the past, without moving forward into mourning; the elegy is caught in a repetition, where an obsession with meter becomes a symptom of the inability to remember what those words might have meant.

The scene of reading is therefore inserted into Hardy's elegy as a memory of memorization, not unlike the moment in "On the Cliffs" where Swinburne describes his first encounter with Sappho, when "thy first Lesbian word / Flamed on me." The revelation of a Sapphic rhythm, as we saw in that poem, was mediated by a material inscription or "notation," the conversion of "tones" into "notes" that would allow for the performance of Sappho's song in written form. These are the "notes" that Hardy discovers in the pages of Swinburne's poetry, as well:

> The passionate pages of his earlier years,
> Fraught with hot sighs, sad laughters, kisses, tears;
> Fresh-fluted notes, yet from a minstrel who
> Blew them not naively, but as one who knew
> Full well why thus he blew.
>
> (Stanza 4)

The stanza emphasizes that Swinburne's "fresh-fluted notes" were not "naively" performed as melodies, but self-consciously mediated by writing, and stanza 2 likewises places its emphasis on the self-conscious artifice of Swinburne's poetry, as it dropped "In fulth of numbers freaked with musical closes, / Upon Victoria's formal middle time / His leaves of rhythm and rhyme." While Swinburne is identified as a "singer" in the title of Hardy's elegy, what he leaves behind circulates in written form, in "leaves" and "pages" (not unlike the rhythm and rhyme that are left on Hardy's page, when he ends the elegy with "I leave him"). The metaphor of a natural rhythm, projected onto the sea in the first and last stanzas of Hardy's elegy in an attempt to remember Swinburne, is therefore interrupted in the middle stanzas by the recounting of more mechanical, metrical effects that Hardy has memorized: if Swinburne's pages appear "passionate" and "fraught," the reason is their "numbers freaked with musical closes," a music measured in intervals according to the rules of prosody in mid-century England, "Victoria's formal middle time." This mechanical account of meter, as a written notation that achieves "musical closes" by the regulation of form, stands in contrast to an organic reading that would associate the poetry of Swinburne with the rhythms of nature and the natural embodiment of song.

Hardy's elegy refers us in particular to Swinburne's early metrical experiments, in the book that Hardy as a young man carried in his breast-pocket, according to Housman: "It was Moxon's first edition of *Poems and Ballads*, worn where it should be worn, just over the heart" (277). The book carried "just over the heart" is what Hardy learned by heart, memorizing the various meters of Swinburne and apparently incorporating them into his body as if they were second nature to him, much as Swinburne learns to incorporate the rhythms of Sappho in the Sapphic scene of instruction. As Dennis Taylor amply demonstrates in his book on *Hardy's Metres and Victorian Prosody,* "Hardy more or less began his poetic career by imitating classical verse," and these early imitations are mediated by Swinburne's classical verse, especially the Sapphic stanza; thus *Wessex Poems* begins with a poem in Sapphic meter ("The Temporary the All") and Hardy's experiments with the Sapphic stanza (both strict and loose) throughout his work can be traced back to the metrical marks in his personal copy of Swinburne's *Poems and Ballads,* where Hardy scanned two lines of Swinburne's "Sapphics" (Taylor 1988: 258). These marks demonstrate how meter must be recorded, in writing, before it can be memorized. Hardy "incorporates" this Sapphic rhythm into his own poetic corpus, not by internalizing what was dictated to him, but by repeating the process of its externalization. Meter proves to be a form of automatic writing, a mechanism for remembering something that was never forgotten because it was never "inside" Hardy to begin with, nor indeed "in" Swinburne either.

Hardy's elegy is a keen response to Swinburne's formalism, as its fixation on melancholy repetition defines lyric reading in terms of memorization rather than remembering. Swinburne is dead, and his corpus scattered; neither the poet nor his poetry is recollected in organic form; there is only the "phantom" of a "spectral form," the ghost of meter. Furthermore, the death of Swinburne allows Hardy to assume a posthumous relation to his own poetic corpus, as well. Even when Swinburne was still alive, he seemed to live as if already dead; in conversation apparently the two poets "laughed and condoled with each other on having been the two most abused of living writers" (Murfin 1978: 82). Even in this personal "recollection," instead of remembering Swinburne, Hardy emphasizes the disfiguring of the lyric poet as a figure; the peculiar use of the past tense projects the fragmentary condition of Swinburne into the future as the necessary condition for his afterlife. It is as if both poets, "having been the most abused of living writers," are pronouncing themselves already dead. In this way they repeat the fate of Sappho, whose transmission in "mutilated fragments" becomes the determining pattern for their own reception: Hardy, like Swinburne, like Sappho, will be remembered only by the compulsive repetition of that dismemberment.

Hardy is not the only one to identify Swinburne's posthumous existence as the necessary condition for his lyricism. Housman begins an essay on Swinburne by describing the poet as if he had already been dead a long time: "When Mr. Swinburne died, April 1909, at the age of 72, he might as well have been dead for a quarter of a century" (277), and again, "Swinburne died last year, thirty years later than he would have died if the gods had loved him" (295). Despite his reputation as "our only great living poet," Swinburne's poetry appears to be a long-dead corpus on which Housman performs a relentless post mortem. The earlier poetry, he concedes, created new meters and recreated old; Swinburne successfully "resuscitated the heroic couplet" and "upon these dry bones Swinburne brought up new flesh and breathed into them a new spirit" (284–85). But to exhume and resuscitate the dead is not the same as giving them life; it makes them undead, and in this respect the early verse only serves to anticipate the later poetry which, according to Housman, is truly dead. Monotonous, mannered, perfunctory, repetitious, bookish, and stillborn, the late poems of Swinburne are "mechanically" assembled rather than organically unified. "In fact," Housman concludes, "he came to write like an automaton, without so much as knowing the meaning of what he said" (293). But the automatism of Swinburne's writing can be understood as another version of rhythmic transport, the conversion of "natural" rhythms into a metrical sublime that was implicit, all along, in his Sapphic imitations.

Critics after Housman have often repeated his judgment of Swinburne, without realizing that the very terms of this assessment are embedded, still, in Swinburne's Sapphic sublime. While Swinburne was read at the turn of the century as the Victorian reincarnation of Sappho, Modernist readers several decades later were no longer interested in remembering Swinburne as a metrical body, be it living or dead. Their repudiation of Swinburne was also a rejection of Victorian prosody, because its regulation of rhythm felt like an unnatural and mechanical imposition of meter: increasingly difficult to read, and write, and memorize. Writing in 1937,

Douglas Bush therefore finds Swinburne an altogether unmemorable poet: "Diffuse and undisciplined vagueness of emotion and expression make almost everything of Swinburne's pleasurable and forgettable; one remembers neither parts nor wholes" (355). More recently, over the past three decades, there has been renewed critical effort to reconstruct Swinburne's literary corpus and to reconstitute his reputation as lyric poet. In the collection of essays edited by Rooskby entitled *The Whole Music of Passion,* for example, the emphasis is very much on making Swinburne's "whole" again, while Jerome McGann develops another approach to the reconstruction of Swinburne in *Swinburne: An Experiment in Criticism:* he impersonates different voices in dialogue to develop partial, self-interrupting interpretations of the poetry without integrating them into a unified portrait of the poet.

If Rooksby's collection responds to Bush's complaint by remembering wholes, McGann's experiment therefore responds by recollecting Swinburne only in parts. For when we return to Swinburne, we should not forget how Hardy last left him: not a poet to be remembered, but one who is memorized. Swinburne's poetry is easy to memorize and many generations have done so, as McGann points out: "When *Poems and Ballads* was published the undergraduates at Oxford quickly memorized long passages from that truly memorable book . The accounts of Swinburne's contemporaries reinforce the evidence of dictionaries of quotations, that Swinburne is an exceedingly memorable poet" (286). Indeed, it is so easy to memorize Swinburne that "phrases and passages come randomly to mind" and McGann goes on to enumerate, at random, the passages and quotations that he himself has memorized. Reading Swinburne is, inevitably, a repetition compulsion: instead of recollecting the entire poetic corpus, McGann collects the parts of Swinburne that come to mind, in a rhythm that is automatic, a self-starting mechanism beyond intention and conscious control. But in order to conclude his experiment in criticism, McGann finally moves from the parts to the whole, from passages that are "quickly memorized" to his admiration of "that truly memorable book" to the celebration of "an exceedingly memorable poet," as if Swinburne himself has been reclaimed by rote repetition of his words. "For this, if for nothing else, he too is unforgotten," McGann writes, in his very last sentence. But is Swinburne remembered by being "unforgotten"? What if Bush is right, not in his negative valuation of Swinburne's poetry, but in the recognition that "one remembers neither parts nor wholes"? If, as I have suggested, Swinburne disappears and reappears like Sappho in self-scattering rhythm, then we need not recollect the poet nor remember the poetic corpus in order to read Swinburne's poetry: his limbs can be loosened, again.

P.S. SAPPHO

Writing as Postscript

SO FAR, I have been declining the name of Sappho in each chapter by embedding my reading of a Sapphic fragment within an argument about Victorian poetics. Fragment 31 was the crux of chapter 1, where I demonstrated how the recurring break in Sappho's broken tongue calls into question the assumption of lyric voice. In the second chapter, fragment 2 was my point of departure for reading a "lesbian" topography in the lyrics of Michael Field. And in chapter 3, I suggested an allegorical reading of rhythm in fragment 130 that gives form to Swinburne's Sapphic sublime. Expanding the scope of my argument in the present chapter, I want to show how a theory of lyric reading in which Sappho is continually declined also delineates a logic played out in literary history. Alongside the improper significations of the name, Sappho circulated as proper name for the "Poetess" in Victorian women's verse. Popular poetesses throughout England and America were identified with a Sapphic persona that seemed to personify poetry written for the "personal" expression of "feminine" sentiment. Despite the publication of sentimental lyric in a nineteenth-century literary marketplace that capitalized on women writers, and despite the popular appeal of their verse to a wide range of readers, it was represented as merely private utterance unmediated by the publicity of print. "The poetry of women (unlike the novels written by women) has, from Sappho downwards, been almost entirely subjective and personal," announces an 1868 essay entitled "Poetesses," reiterating the popular opinion that women poets write spontaneously to express themselves, but in a style too sentimental, too conventionally feminine, to be memorable: "We presume, women, in writing poetry, draw their style from other women, and thus miss that largeness and universality which alone compels attention, and preserves a work through all changes of sentiment and opinion" (*Saturday Review* 25:679). Women poets seem to descend from Sappho, but they decline the name only by falling—"from Sappho downwards" and "through all changes of sentiment"—into namelessness.

The decline of Sappho defines a succession of nineteenth-century women poets who are indeed mostly forgotten in the twentieth century, although in recent years critics have begun a gradual reclamation of the "Poetess" as an important figure within literary history. Feminist criticism in particular has been interested in reclaiming a literary tradition of "lost" women poets, whose names are now being (re)introduced into the canon of nineteenth-century poetry through a wide range of anthologies and reprinted editions.[1] Revisionary readings of the canon by feminist critics often assume a rhetoric of loss, in fact, as if it is only by losing women poets that we can read them anew. The publication of new collections depends on this recuperative gesture, as in the advertisement for *Victorian Women Poets: An Anthology* (Leighton and Reynolds 1995), which "aims to recover the lost map of Victorian women's poetry"; or *British Women Poets of the 19th Century* (Higonnet 1996), which "restores the voices and reputations of these 'lost' artists"; or *Nineteenth-Century Women Poets* (Armstrong, Bristow and Sharrock 1996), which "rediscovers rich and diverse female traditions"; or *Nineteenth-Century American Women Poets: An Anthology* (Bennett 1997), which reclaims "previously neglected" poetry. While the process of rediscovering and rereading Victorian women's verse has been facilitated by these timely collections, it is worth noting that they are marketed according to a logic not unlike the broad circulation of popular poetesses in nineteenth-century collections, such as *The Female Poets of Great Britain* (Rowton 1848), *The British Female Poets* (Bethune 1848), *The Female Poets of America* (Griswold 1848), and *The American Female Poets* (May 1848), all published around the same time as well. To discover these women poets, again, in recent (re)collections is to repeat a prior act of recovery.

If the recovery of such a tradition is predicated on the forgetting of women poets, the reason is not that their poetry is forgettable (as "we presume" in the essay on "Poetesses") nor that they have been forgotten (as feminist reclamations of "the Poetess" tend to assume), but rather that literary history is produced by the repetition of this effacement. Indeed, the loss of the "Poetess" is already predicted in the verse of nineteenth-century poetesses as the very means of its literary transmission. Rather than reconstructing a Sapphic tradition of women poets, or constructing a model of female authorship that identifies the woman poet with Sappho, I demonstrate in this chapter how various women poets turn to Sappho as a trope for performing the infinitely repeatable loss of the "Poetess." The versing of Sappho in nineteenth-century women's

---

[1] The recent boom in publishing collections of Romantic and Victorian women poets has produced useful companion collections of critical essays as well, e.g., Feldman and Kelley 1995, Leighton 1996, Amstrong and Blain 1998. On anthologizing Victorian women poets, see also Blain 1997.

verse proves to be a complex rhetorical performance of historical consequence, precisely because the groundless figure of Sappho—forever falling—foregrounds the problem of reading this occasion as a singular historical event. Instead of transmitting a certain history, the repetition of the trope points to the entry of the Poetess into history as an always uncertain event.

My reading therefore interrogates the progressive politics of feminist criticism, insofar as it has created a genealogy of women poets whose progress toward authorial voice and female authorship is understood to be a continuous line of historical development and gradual self-empowerment. The literary history I propose will proceed more recursively, simultaneously reading forward through various Sapphic imitations from the early to the late nineteenth century, and reading backward to demonstrate the foresight of poetesses we now read with hindsight. Because the figure of Sappho—often hovering in the *chiaroscuro* between visual and verbal representation—appears in their poetry by the same recursive logic, it will be increasingly difficult to distinguish foreground and background in the course of this chapter. Out of an infinite series of Victorian Sapphos, how shall I bring even a few into focus? How to trace the shadowy outlines of a vanishing figure? How to set the scene for this disappearance?

In the visual arts, Sappho is conventionally portrayed just before her fatal leap from the Leucadian Cliff, singing her last song of love for the young Phaon before plunging down to the waves.[2] In this moment of suspended animation, poised between life and death, she is always about to fall into a future already past. This vision of Sappho is mediated by Ovid, who presents her as a posthumous figure in "Sappho to Phaon." The elegiac epistle, included in Ovid's *Heroides,* is a suicide letter in which the grief-stricken Sappho, abandoned by Phaon, also seems to have abandoned her own lyric persona. The opening lines of her lament emphasize the displacement of Greek song by the Latin letter(s):

> When you saw these letters from my eager hand
> could your eye recognize the sender
> or did you fail to recognize their author
> until you could read my name, "Sappho"?
> Since I am famous for the lyric do you
> wonder why my lines vary in length?
> But I weep and tears fit well the elegy—
> a lyre cannot bear the weight of tears.[3]

---

[2] For a survey of representations of Sappho in the visual arts, see Tomory 1989 and Judith Stein's 1981 Ph.D dissertation, "The Iconography of Sappho, 1775–1875."

[3] Here and throughout, I quote the English translation of Ovid's *Heroides* by Harold Is-

Sappho declares herself to be author of elegiac measures written as "a letter from my diligent hand" (*studiosae littera dextrae*) and signed "in the author's name Sappho" (*auctoris nomina Sapphus*). This Sapphic signature is a postscript to the Sapphic songs she once sang, a P.S. placed at the beginning of the letter and prescribing the end of Sappho as lyric poet. "I do not make songs now for a well-tuned string," she announces early in the poem,[4] and again later on: "The gift of song I enjoyed will not answer / my call; lyre and plectrum are silent."[5] Throughout the poem, she is lamenting not only the loss of Phaon but the loss of lyric voice as well, and toward the end she even writes her own epitaph, as she imagines her lyre dedicated to Phoebus with a verse inscribed below in the name of Sappho: "Phoebus, the grateful poetess Sappho to you brings a lyre."[6] Written in the third person, as if she is already dead, this self-inscription predicts the death of Sapphic voice in the very act of writing her suicidal epistle: even before leaping from the cliff, Sappho has fallen as silent as her lyre.

Of course Sappho's silence is belied by the 220 lines of this literary "female complaint," demonstrating how eloquent she still is. This eloquence no longer depends on the figure of voice, however, but on a figure of writing that converts Greek lyric into Latin elegy, and Sapphic eros into elegiac pathos. Not only is the elegiac epistle written in the name of Sappho in the opening lines of the poem, but in the final lines it is identified as a letter to be sent *after* her name:

> But if you wish to flee far from Sappho of Pelasgos—
> —though you can find no reason for such a flight—
> at least you must permit a letter

---

bell (1990: 131–45), and the Latin text from Palmer's edition (1908: 91–100), lines 1–8:

> Ecquid, ut aspecta est studiosae littera dextrae,
> Protinus est oculis cognita nostra tuis?
> An, nisi legisses auctoris nomina Sapphus,
> Hoc breve nescires unde veniret opus?
> Forsitan et quare mea sint alterna requiras
> Carmina, cum lyricis sim magis apta modis.
> Flendus amor meus est: elegiae flebile carmen;
> Non facit ad lacrimas barbitos ulla meas.

[4] Line 13: Nec mihi, dispositis quae iungam carmina nervis.
[5] Lines 198–99: Non mihi respondent veteres in carmina vires:
  Plectra dolore tacent, muta dolore lyra est.
[6] Line 183: Grata lyram posui tibi, Phoebe, poetria Sappho.

cruel though it must surely be to tell me this woe,
And I will find my fate in Leucadia's waves![7]

Thus Sappho signs off on the *epistula*, before leaping into the waves. But if she is scripted to die in these fateful words, the fate of her epistle is to survive in written form: it is a postscript that will be delivered to a reader after her death, a dead letter that nevertheless lives on in our reading of it. Sappho's address to Phaon therefore serves as an address to anyone who will read the epistle; Phaon, the ferryman who remains so mysteriously unidentified, is a metaphor for the reader who transports Sappho into the future by anticipating a death that has already happened. This preposterous scenario is repeated every time we read Ovid's poem: Sappho leaps into her afterlife by metalepsis, enacting a temporal transposition that forces us to read simultaneously forward and backward in time.

The history of Sappho's reception is determined—indeed, predetermined—by this Ovidian narrative, as has been amply demonstrated by Joan DeJean in *Fictions of Sappho* and Lawrence Lipking in *Abandoned Women and Poetic Tradition*. Translations and imitations of "Sappho to Phaon" proliferate from the Renaissance onward and well into the nineteenth century, identifying Sappho with the fictional persona created by Ovid, and leading DeJean to the conclusion that Ovid was less concerned with Sappho's afterlife than his own claim to fame: "*Heroides* 15 recounts Ovid's accession to literary primacy, his 'invention,' *through* Sappho, of a form that was to guarantee his immortality" (1989: 74). Sappho is the medium for the transmission of his poem: her dead persona survives in the new epistolary genre invented by Ovid and entitles him to literary survival as well. DeJean reads the Ovidian epistle as "Ovid's signature piece," focusing in particular on the Sapphic signature in the opening lines, where Sappho's name takes the form of a masculine adjective: "*Auctoris nomina Sapphus* is Ovid's signature in the feminine, the author's name he devised to take possession of his prototype for the literature of a new age." (74) According to this argument, Ovid signs his own name "in the feminine" by using *Sapphus* in the masculine, appropriating the proper name of Sappho and establishing a precedent for the "brutal usurpation of female literary authority" among his successors, so that "the female voice finally exists only in its male recreation, and the female signature stands for male literary authority. 'Sappho, c'est moi'" (77).

---

[7] Lines 217–20:   Sive iuvat longe fugisse Pelasgida Sapphon,
                  —Nec tamen invenies, cur ego digna fugi—
                  Hoc saltem miserae crudelis, epistula dicat,
                  Ut mihi Leucadiae fata petantur aquae!

The assumption of this lyric "I" is exactly what Ovid's epistle calls into question, however. To claim authorship on the model of Sappho is to pre-dict one's own death, the impossibility of writing in the first person: to say "it is I" (or "c'est moi") is already a displacement of the first-person ut-terance, a postscript. DeJean's authoritative reading of "Sappho to Phaon" presumes Sappho and Ovid to be authorial figures to whom she can attribute "female literary authority" and "male literary authority." But just as Sappho's authorship is open to question, Ovid's authority is equally questionable; there is even question as to whether Ovid is the au-thor of this Sapphic epistle. Without pursuing further debate about the authenticity of the poem, its internal logic already points to the possibil-ity of a poetic tradition that does not claim original authorship.[8] It is a tradition of posthumous writing, presenting each Sapphic signature as yet another postscript to the postscript: P.S. Sappho, P.P.S. Sappho, P.P.P.S.Sappho, and so on *ad infinitum*. Where, in this seemingly endless series of Sapphic signatures, is the original author? Rather than taking possession of Sappho or usurping a literary authority that was never pos-sessed by Sappho, the Ovidian epistle defines Sapphic authorship in terms of authorial dispossession: Sappho is a nonoriginary figure, falling into an infinitely repeatable death.

Writing in the wake of Ovid's Sappho, nineteenth-century women poets repeatedly return to this scenario. They adopt the Ovidian model of writing as postscript, in order to reflect on the rhetorical predicament of the Victorian Poetess who is expected to write *as* a woman. A woman writing as a woman, Peggy Kamuf has observed, is a proposition that re-peats itself: "One can find only arbitrary beginnings for the series, and no term which is not already a repetition: '. . . a woman writing as a woman writing as a . . . '" (1980: 298). Because there is no "original" woman to stop this recursive logic, the poetess is identified with the always already dead lyric persona of Sappho. This Sapphic (non) persona appears in sentimental lyric, not as a form of self-identification (as if saying "Sappho, c'est moi" could ever reclaim female authorial identity) but as an infinite series of substitutions. The self-replicating performance of Sappho's sui-cide in Victorian women's verse is a gesture of de-personification, demon-strating how "woman" is personified to produce a pathos that is curiously impersonal, or "sentimental" precisely because it poses a question about how to read such personifications. What is performed in sentimental lyric is the rhetorical and historical overdetermination of an indeterminacy in

---

[8] Although DeJean notes the authenticity debate (1989: 61, 333; see also Tarrant 1981), she assumes Ovid's authorship and strategically subsumes questions about identifying Ovid as author into a question about Ovid's authorial identification. "The debate about the au-thenticity of *Heroides* 15 is perhaps the most appropriate response to Ovid's conflicted de-sire for Sappho," she concludes (76), thus reinstating the authorial status of Ovid.

personification, which, as Barbara Johnson writes, is "a trope available for occupancy by either subjects or linguistic entities, the difference between them being ultimately indeterminable" (1987: 45). Sappho is such a trope, "available for occupancy" yet also advertising its vacancy.

The rhetorical question posed by personifications of Sappho—vacillating between the re-animation and de-animation of a dead poetic figure—is especially relevant within the broad historical perspective outlined by Catherine Gallagher in *Nobody's Story: The Vanishing Acts of Women Writers in the Marketplace, 1670–1820*. According to Gallagher, women writers appear through a series of displacements and disappearances— or "vanishing acts"—within an English literary marketplace that is increasingly "feminized" by the early nineteenth century. While eighteenth-century copyright law established proprietary rights for authors, it also served to define female authorship in terms of economic dispossession and authorial disembodiment. The woman writer (like the fictional characters in her novels) was common property for the purpose of sympathetic appropriation: a "Nobody," not quite anonymous or nameless but nevertheless a freely appropriable proper name, within a circuit of literary and economic exchange that capitalized on women writers for profit and made them into popular figures for sentimental identification. This form of identification—allowing "everybody" to identify with "Nobody's story," and the woman writer to be identified with "Nobody"—is presented by Gallagher on a narrative model in order to account for a rhetoric of dispossession in eighteenth-century female authorship, but it can be extended beyond the novel into an account of nineteenth-century women's verse. Here a narrative structure of identification is transposed into a question of personification that structures lyric as a genre and enables women writers to reflect further on the problem of personifying the Poetess. Thus "Nobody's story" becomes the story of Sappho, a name that lends itself to endless appropriations by the Poetess, whose name also belongs to nobody and to everybody.

My own story about Victorian Poetesses refers back to several Romantic precursors, beginning with Mary Robinson, who circulated in the name of Sappho at the turn of the nineteenth century. In 1796 she published *Sappho and Phaon: A Series of Legitimate Sonnets* as her postscript to Ovid's postscript to Sappho, and two years later *The Morning Post* conferred on her "the dignified title of *the English Sappho*" (20 January 1798: 2). But her entitlement to this proper name must be read, alongside various other names adopted by Robinson in the course of her poetic career, as the making of a name without fixed authorial identity. *The Morning Post* contributed to the commodification of Mary Robinson as a "newspaper poet," whose poems were distributed daily to a wide range of readers. She wrote for a column of "original poetry" in which "original" authors were often pseudonymous or anonymous, as Judith Pascoe has argued in further detail: "for Mary Robinson, the 'self' that claims authorship of the poems is a curious array of free-floating and non-totalized personae" (Pascoe 1995: 262). Likewise, rather than legitimating Robinson's claim to authorship, the "legitimate sonnets" in *Sappho and Phaon* present Sappho as another free-floating persona, a first-person lyric "I" who is perpetually displaced.

In the "Sonnet Introductory, " the first in the series, Robinson announces her Sapphic theme as a series of variations, to "sweep the Muse's lyre / In varying cadence." This "cadence" is a dying fall that will be repeated in the sonnets to follow, as Sappho dies again and again. The fourth sonnet, for example, begins in the first person singular ("Why, when I gaze on Phaon's beautiful eyes") but is curiously estranged from its own utterance as the "I" is lost in the "eyes" of Phaon, until finally "—Sappho dies!" Substituting for "I dies," this exclamation is an impossible grammatical construction that Robinson's sonnet nevertheless contemplates as the condition of its own utterance: a preposterous proposition, like Ovid's epistle. Robinson's Sappho repeats the metaleptic leap of Ovid's Sappho, as the sonnet sequence vacillates between various tenses, seemingly out of sequence, introducing past events in the present tense or future events in the past tense. Sonnet 41 demonstrates this temporal loop most dramatically, as it begins by asking (in the present) if Sappho having leaped (in the past) will be remembered (in the future):

> Oh! can'st thou bear to see this faded frame,
>> Deform'd and mangled by the rocky deep?
>> Wilt thou remember, and forbear to weep,
> My fatal fondness, and my peerless fame?
> Soon o'er this heart, now warm with passion's flame,
>> The howling winds and foamy waves shall sweep;
>> Those eyes be ever clos'd in death's cold sleep,
> And all of Sappho perish but her name!

The memory of Sappho (literally, the re-membering of a body "deform'd and mangled by the rocky deep") is created by confounding the future with the present and the present with the past. The rhetorical question "can'st thou bear to see" is in the present tense yet refers to what will happen in the future, while the rhetorical question "wilt thou remember" is in the future tense yet refers to what will have happened in the past. Sappho is thus suspended in what is about to happen: "soon" the waves "shall sweep" over her and "those eyes be ever clos'd in death's cold sleep." The omission of a future auxiliary verb in this line adds to the ambiguity, suggesting not only that "those eyes [shall] be ever clos'd" but that those eyes might already be, and have always been, "ever closed"—a death that has already happened, like the destiny prescribed for the "I" in this series of sonnets. Sappho is forever identified with the loss of the first person singular, a name that survives because it cannot be attached to an "I": "And all of Sappho perish but her name!"

Nevertheless the name might be reclaimed for posterity, as we see in the volta from octave to sestet:

> Yet, if the Fates suspend their barb'rous ire,
> If days less mournful, Heav'n designs for me!
> If rocks grow kind, and winds and waves conspire,
> To bear me softly on the swelling sea;
> To Phoebus only will I tune my lyre,
> "What suits with Sappho, Phoebus, suits with thee!"

Because Sappho's fate is defined by temporal suspension, even the Fates themselves might "suspend their barb'rous ire" long enough for a reversal of death into life. The sestet reverses the terms introduced by the octave: the death one cannot "bear to see" in the opening line might "bear me softly on the swelling sea" toward new life, and the "faded frame" of Sappho's body be revived in the form of "my lyre," dedicated to Phoebus rather than Phaon. The winds and waves that drown Sappho thus "conspire" to create new inspiration, projected beyond Sappho into a Sapphic tradition mediated by future poets who will re-frame the lyric "I" in their own poetry. This mediation is made explicit in the final line of the sonnet where Robinson quotes Pope's translation of Ovid's imitation of Sappho, augmented by a footnote that cites Ovid's words, in Latin: Robinson thus re-frames the "I" and attributes it to "Sappho," but only as a name in quotation marks, cited by a long tradition of poets that now also includes herself.

Rather than claiming a Sapphic signature, Robinson defers it by projecting Sappho from the distant past into an equally distant future. In the Preface to her sonnets, Robinson defines poetry as the inspiration of a "MUSE," who allows the poet to muse on "remote futurity" and "seizes events as yet unknown to man."[9] It would seem that Sappho is another version of that "MUSE," as Robinson later proclaims "Sappho . . . knew that she was writing for future ages,"[10] and anticipates a tradition of women poets "as yet unknown" but who will be known—like Sappho—in future ages as well. She predicts their emergence at the end of her Pref-

---

[9] From Robinson's "Preface" to *Sappho and Phaon* (1796: 11). The muse's meditation on "remote futurity," from a poem by William Cowper, is strategically cited by Mary Robinson to insert a feminine difference, "as yet unknown to man," in the very act of reciting words already known to man. McGann also notices "a shrewd use of the feminine pronoun" in Robinson's quotation of Cowper, turning his thought into "her thought" (1996: 105). On Robinson's use of Sappho to create a feminine myth of authorship, see Peterson 1994a.

[10] From Robinson's "Account of Sappho," also prefaced to *Sappho and Phaon* (1796: 26).

ace, where she pays tribute to "my illustrious country-women" who "ennoble themselves by the unperishable lustre of MENTAL PRE-EMINENCE" (1796: 16). Such women are pre-eminent in the literal sense of the Latin (*prae-eminere*): they move forward and rise above, writing for the moment when they will be remembered as "illustrious." However, just as sonnet 42 concludes that "all of Sappho perish but her name," their "unperishable lustre" is only visible through the reflection of an "I" that has already perished. In his reading of Robinson, Jerome McGann therefore concludes that Robinson's Sappho is a "prophetic instrument" for women poets, as they are called forth from the past and recalled from the future, without actually existing in the present (1996:109). This prophecy is an important turning point in the history of "the poetry of sensibility" as it is told by McGann, who interprets the Preface to *Sappho and Phaon* as a "manifesto to establish feeling and emotion as intellectual and philosophical grounds for poetry," (97) and reads Robinson's sonnets as fertile ground for the growth of nineteenth-century sentimental lyric.[11]

But if the Preface to *Sappho and Phaon* raises the possibility of finding new "grounds" for poetry—a tradition of Victorian women's verse, prophetically announced through the figure of Sappho—it falls to the sonnets to perform this foundational claim as itself an act of falling, or continually losing ground. In *Thoughts on the Condition of Women* (1799), Robinson confidently asserts that "poetry has unquestionably risen high in British literature from the production of female pens," yet in turning to Sappho her own poetry demonstrates that women poets rise to authorship only by falling: they survive by repeating the death of Sappho. This downward trajectory differs from the poets ascending toward "high" Romanticism in the early nineteenth century. In "The I Altered," Stuart Curran argues that women poets at the turn of the century offer an alternative perspective on the construction of a (male) Romantic subject: Mary Robinson's generation exemplifies the alienation and alteration of lyric subjectivity, as their "self-reflexive dialectic continually verges on a version of Romantic irony" and reflects "a profound awareness among these poets of being themselves dispossessed" (Curran 1988: 198, 205). I would contend, however, that the effect of this self-reflexiveness is not to constitute a female subject as an ironically alienated other, but to make

---

[11] While McGann turns to Mary Robinson to establish feeling as "philosophical grounds for poetry," Adela Pinch further interrogates such a claim in *Strange Fits of Passion: Epistemologies of Emotion, Hume to Austen*. She turns to the poetry of Charlotte Smith, who was Robinson's contemporary, in order to define sentimentality as "the affective dimension of an epistemological conflict over the origins of feelings" (70). The dispossession of Sappho in nineteenth-century women's verse is a further elaboration of this logic, beautifully elucidated by Pinch: "If sentimental verse was inevitably a woman's genre in the late eighteenth century, it was so only by making the feelings expressed not her own" (8).

it disappear altogether: there is no "I" to speak of. Even the suggestion that poetesses are profoundly aware "of being themselves dispossessed" implies they possess an awareness "of themselves" as "selves" to be identified, when their poetry calls into question the very possibility of such an identification. The depths into which they fall are profound indeed, but not as the revelation of a deep interiority or internalized irony; it is the abyss of female authorship, where the Poetess proves to be the personification of an empty figure.

Thus in the course of the nineteenth century, the Poetess and Sappho become increasingly interchangeable names for another generic category, namely "Woman." The first entry in Mary Cowden Clarke's popular *World-Noted Women, or, Types of Womanly Attributes of All Lands and Ages* (1857) is dedicated to Sappho: "The name of Sappho is almost identical in the mind with the word Poetess. Hundreds of women have written verse; but of the very few women who have attained the renown of living to posterity as worthy to bear the honoured title of poetess, Sappho ranks preeminent." (1857: 2) Although Sappho lived before "hundreds of women" who have written verse, in "living to posterity" she outlives them all. Her posthumous fame makes her "pre-eminent," like the "MENTAL PRE-EMINENCE" that Robinson attributed to her countrywomen as well. Clarke seems to identify Sappho with the British poetess in particular, as she turns "the word Poetess" into "the honoured title of poetess," converting the name into a noun in order to confer that title on Sappho's English successors. More than a "world-noted woman" and a "womanly type," Sappho is the very prototype of that type, the primary example of the exemplary woman. "Sappho is a shining exemplar of glowing womanhood, and high passion moulded into that 'bright particular star' of humanity— a Poetess," Mary Cowden Clarke concludes (21), ending her essay as she began, by affirming Sappho to be the truly *proper* name for the Poetess.

Celebrated as a feminine ideal in nineteenth-century encyclopedias of exemplary women, female biographies, and other treatises on the "genius" of woman, Sappho becomes the emblem of Victorian womanhood. The canonization of the Poetess depends on a conflation of poet worship and woman worship, constructing a generic idea of woman that shapes the reception of many Victorian women poets. But as Tricia Lootens has demonstrated so eloquently in *Lost Saints,* this construction proves to be an empty monument, "more like pâpier-maché than marble," insofar as "the metaphoric figures of such canonized nineteenth-century women poets were shaped around vacancy" (1996: 10). Sappho is the perfect model for the pâpier-maché monument, a hollow construction plastered with poetic fragments like shreds of paper, easily torn apart to reveal an absent core: disintegrating on the outside and empty on the inside, an evacuated figure. The association of Sappho with women poets throughout the nineteenth century demonstrates to what degree the evacuation of the figure is a necessary condition of female canon formation, as Lootens concludes: "At their most glorious, then, nineteenth-century women writers are canonized by a process that almost inevitably guarantees their downfall: from a long-term literary historical point of view, they are made secular saints and lost at the same time" (74).

In a portrait of Sappho included in *World-Noted Women,* we can see how Sappho's elevation into "a shining exemplar of glowing womanhood" by Mary Cowden Clarke guarantees the downfall of the Poetess (figure 10).[12] To illustrate the "womanly attributes" of Sappho, this feminine figure embodies Clarke's idealized description of the Poetess, pouring out her passionate song, accompanied by a lyre. The contours of the lyre that she cradles close to her heart are like the soft curves of her rounded arms and shoulders, forming part of her body or perhaps transforming the entire body into a lyrical instrument. With her delicate fingers plucking the lyre, she seems to play on her own heartstrings in a moment of heavenly inspiration. The wind sweeping through her loose hair and free-flowing robes animates the figure of Sappho, like a breeze playing melodies on an Aeolian harp, or a breath of inspiration: she is the perfect embodiment of a lyric figure. But this inspired moment is also the moment of expiration, as we know that Sappho is breathing her last words before plunging down to her death. Because Clarke is reluctant to present Sappho as a fallen woman, she rejects Sappho's leap as a myth: "They who relate this story of her fail to state whether Sappho lost her life, or survived, after precipitating herself from the rock," she writes in her essay (12). In the portrait featured alongside the essay, however, Sappho is about to fall: she hovers in midair with her eyes raised upward, precariously suspended between heaven and earth, the sky above and the sea far below. The suspense heightens the pathos of the figure, even as she falls. "Whether Sappho lost her life, or survived" therefore turns out to be a moot question, since she enters the afterlife in the very act of falling. Rather than "living to posterity," as Clarke's essay declares, in the nineteenth century Sappho is forever dying for posterity.

Sappho's Leap

In "A Vision of Poets" (1844), Elizabeth Barrett Browning apostrophizes Sappho: "O poet-woman! None foregoes / The leap, attaining the re-

---

[12] The portrait of Sappho appears as the frontispiece for *World-Noted Women* and is identified on the title page as the first of "seventeen engravings on steel, from original designs by Charles Staal," alongside a motto from Shakespeare: "The world's large tongue proclaims you." The engraver is Francis Holl.

FIGURE 10: Frontispiece from *World-Noted Women*, Mary Cowden Clarke (1857). Courtesy of Library of Congress, Washington, D.C.

SAPPHO

FIGURE 11: Etching of Sappho by Queen Victoria (1841). Reproduced
in "Queen Victoria as Etcher" (Brinton 1900).

pose." What "none foregoes" is a foregone conclusion not only for Sappho, who attains "repose" by leaping to her death, but for a long line of women poets who "re-pose" as Sappho: by repeating a metaleptic leap into posterity, they too attain the Sapphic pose. Even Queen Victoria repeats the pose, in an etching dated 1841 and signed in her name (figure 11).[13] Here the poetess appears yet again, according to pictorial convention, on the edge of a cliff. Casting a long shadow on the rock behind her, she gazes ahead into the distance, where the sun sinks ominously below the horizon, as if to foreshadow Sappho's fatal plunge into the waves. Poised between life and death, she is suspended in the metalepsis of "before" and "after," contemplating her afterlife. The profile looks as though it might be the young queen herself, not long after ascending to the throne yet already descending into her afterlife, when she will be im-

[13] The etching is reproduced in Brinton 1900: 510. I am grateful to Mary Loeffelholz for calling "this *very* Victorian Sappho" to my attention.

mortalized as the ideal of Victorian womanhood, and monumentalized as the ruler of an empire on which the sun never sets: a very Victorian Sappho, indeed.

Of course such a prospect seems inevitable only in retrospect, at the end of Victoria's long reign, when a reversal of historical perspective (simultaneously prospective and retrospective) allows the queen's picture of Sappho to be identified as a depiction of the queen herself. Published the year before her death, the article in which her etching appears is written as if the queen had already faced her dying moment, like Sappho, long ago. "It would be hard to refine upon the poetic beauty and dramatic intensity of Sappho as etched by Her Majesty the Queen," the article gushes: "Behold an Aspasia from across the sea, the Tenth Muse, the sad singer pausing an instant in a final appeal before flinging herself over that 'far projected rock of woe.' Her Majesty's *mise-en-scène* is economy personified. Sappho kneels on a high promontory overlooking the sea; her hands are clasped, her hair clings loosely about her neck and shoulders; across burnished waters a prickly sun sinks below the horizon. It is simple and impassioned" (Brinton 1900: 509–10). The picture may seem "simple and impassioned," but its effects are complex. If the queen seems to project herself into the fate of the sad singer, "before flinging herself over that 'far projected rock of woe,'" this is also our projection of the queen's projection of Sappho's projection: a series of projections presented as a single scene, a "*mise-en-scène*" that is "economy personified" not only because it is simply drawn but because it condenses many scenes into one; the Queen might even be seen as the very personification of a Victorian economy that sends this picture of womanhood into historical circulation.[14] "Her Majesty's *mise-en-scène*" is more like a *mise-en-abîme*, the occasion for—or literally, another fall into—an infinite regress of past and future representations of Sappho, whose fatal leap is never a single event, but the repetition of a moment that exceeds its own occasion.

For Victorian women poets, to follow Sappho is therefore to leap into an abyss of visual and verbal representation. Margaret Reynolds surveys a century of increasingly "self-reflexive songs about the tradition of the woman poet who sings Sappho's song" (1996: 300), a tradition that evolves from early Romantic imitations that "could only rehearse the destructive cycle of posing and singing, leaping and silencing" (300) to later versions that finally "succeeded in breaking out of the Victorian pattern of destructive repetition of the Sappho myth" (302). To impose a historical progression on what she considers to be the "destructive repetition" of this "destructive cycle," Reynolds draws on a model of literary history

---

[14] Of course, the queen is the personification of Victorian economy in every sense, as Munich notes: the Queen's Head circulating on the first penny postage stamp served to personify domestic economy in Victorian England (Munich 1996: 132–33).

that assumes a developing poetic tradition, and a feminist critical paradigm that affirms the development of a women's tradition in particular. She argues that women poets gradually move away from Sappho's dying fictions, in order to claim a living voice: "For most of the nineteenth century the main body of daughter-texts by women poets descend not from the authentic writings of the real Sappho," Reynolds asserts (280), emphasizing that it is only toward the end of the century, "when an authentic text for Sappho was being rediscovered" that women poets were able to create "a new kind of Sappho song" (302).[15]

This emphasis on the authentication and self-authorization of women's voices extends the feminist perspective outlined by Angela Leighton in *Victorian Women Poets: Writing against the Heart*. Leighton also describes Sappho's leap as a recurring theme in Victorian women's verse, a legacy of "self-silencing" that is increasingly "a bid for self-expression," creating "a tradition of 'last songs' which are also, paradoxically, some of the first that women poets sing" (1992: 36). If such a tradition seems to originate in the loss of voice, Leighton emphasizes the gradual assumption of authorial voice by women poets as they define "a poetry of their own" that can be "written and read as part of a self-consciously female tradition" (1). For Leighton as well as Reynolds, the development of Victorian women's verse depends on a reclamation and revival of Sapphic voice, and this version of feminist literary history also informs the selection and organization of poems in the anthology of Victorian women poets co-edited by Leighton and Reynolds; their collection begins, in fact, with "The Last Song of Sappho" by Felicia Hemans.

Yet the precarious Sapphic pose also re-poses a problem for feminist critics who would reclaim the woman from the postscript. In a tradition of nonoriginal writing defined by perpetual self-postponement, how can we refer to the original "voice" of the woman writer or the poetry she writes as her "own"? How do we even refer to the woman poet "herself"? The problem of biographical reading is a central concern for Leighton, whose chapters on Victorian women poets are divided between literary biography and poetic analysis: a division into two parts, reflecting a split between "woman and poet, life and works" and demonstrating that "the self who lives is not the same as the self who writes," although Leighton is quick "not to say that the first is simply irrelevant and 'dead'" (1992: 4–5). Pointing out that "the very energy of feminist criticism derives from

---

[15] In nineteenth-century England there is indeed a shift in Sappho's reception, initially mediated by Ovid's imitation of Sappho, but increasingly informed by the scholarly reconstruction of Greek fragments attributed to Sappho. However, I would not conclude—as Reynolds does—that "an authentic text for Sappho was being re-discovered" at the end of the century (1996: 302); as I have argued in Chapter 1, the desire to construct an "authentic text" for Sappho is itelf a Victorian legacy.

this inner tension" between reading poetry as "outwardly referential" and "inwardly self-referring" (5–6), Leighton proceeds to tell the "life story" of Victorian women poets alongside the "death story" that is often told in their poetry, and concludes that a self-referential reading of such poems is done "at the expense of historicism, contextualisation or even reference itself" (6). However, she also notices that a recurring "condition of suspended reference" in their poetry cannot be separated from "the reality of the woman poet's life and history" (7). Might the "life story" not be another version of the "death story," then, another repetition of Sappho's leap? How do we reconstruct the "life and history" of the woman poet, if not by metalepsis? Like "the self who writes," the "self who lives" is relevant to our reading precisely because she is already "dead," in quotation marks. The suspension of Sappho at the moment of leaping demonstrates not only the difficulty of distinguishing between what is "outwardly referential" and "inwardly self-referring" in Victorian women's verse but allows the question of "historicism, contextualisation, or even reference itself" to be posed as a fall: a fall through history, which is another story of falling.

The story of a fall is told by Paul de Man as well, within the context of a theoretical argument that tries to account for the referential force of texts. As Cathy Caruth explains in "The Claims of Reference," the recurring figure of a falling body in de Man's writing enacts the reassertion of a referential moment that is felt in falling. "The impact of reference is felt, not in the search for an external referent, but in the necessity and failure of theory," she observes; "What theory does, de Man tells us repeatedly, is fall; and in falling, it refers" (1995: 103).[16] The fatal fall of theory is played out not only in de Man's reading of philosophical texts, but enacted in his rhetorical readings of nineteenth-century lyric, and especially Wordsworth, whose "relentless fall into death" is another story de Man tells us repeatedly (1993: 82). In various interpretations of Wordsworth's Boy of Winander, for example, de Man considers the representation of a past death (the dead boy, a third person "he") in anticipation of a future death (Wordsworth himself, a first person "I") to be an impossible substitution, because one cannot refer to one's own death as an empirical event; the Wordsworthian prolepsis, according to de Man, "is in fact metalepsis, a leap outside thematic reality into the rhetorical fiction of the sign" (1993: 201–2).[17] While "this leap cannot be repre-

---

[16] Alongside Caruth's discussion of the falling body within a philosophical context, see also the psychoanalytic reading proposed by Hertz, who traces the hanging body as one of the recurring "lurid figures" in de Man's writing (Hertz 1989, 1990).

[17] This interpretation of the Boy of Winander appears in an interpolation added by de Man to his Gauss lecture (1993: 201–2). For an analysis of this passage in Wordsworth and a detailed comparison of de Man's various readings of it, see Bahti 1995.

sented, nor can it be reflected upon within the inwardness of a subject,"
it is precisely by leaping into a rhetorical fiction that it becomes possible
to reflect on death as a nonempirical event, no longer experienced
"within the inwardness of a subject" and impossible to refer back to a first-
person "I" (201).

If "death is a displaced name for a linguistic predicament," as de Man
infamously concludes in a subsequent essay on Wordsworth (1984: 81),
Sappho is another name for that displacement in nineteenth-century sentimental lyric. Indeed, the linguistic predicament described by de Man is
so overdetermined in Sapphic poems by Victorian poetesses, it would
seem that the end point of de Man's theory is their very point of departure, the place from which they leap. Again and again they turn to Sappho's leap to present a moment (death, namely) that cannot be reflected
upon within the inwardness of a subject. The metalepsis of all these leaping women demonstrates how "a leap outside thematic reality into the
rhetorical fiction of the sign" (in de Man's terms) might reassert a force
that is neither "outwardly referential" nor "inwardly self-referring" (in
Leighton's terms). For if the impact of reference is to be felt in falling,
the figure of Sappho dramatizes the pathos implicit in such an account
of reference, a pathos that exceeds the occasion of its own fall yet nevertheless performs the effect of falling. What befalls Sappho in Victorian
women's verse gives us another perspective on the complexity of sentimental lyric: it foregounds the instability of referential ground and by the
force of this rhetorical effect produces excessive affect, or "sentiment."
By reading the leap rhetorically rather than thematically—as the iterability of an effect rather than the statement of a theme, a productive reiteration rather than a "destructive repetition"—we can rethink the
rhetoric of women's sentimental verse as the forceful performance of its
own iteration: indeed, if we recognize sentimental lyric by the troping on
its own sentimental performance, Sappho's leap is the occasion for performing sentimentality *as* a trope.

The poetic career of Letitia Elizabeth Landon, most famous and most
infamous of the early Victorian poetesses, can be understood as a recursive reiteration of this trope. To Victorian readers, it seemed that her mysterious death in 1838 was predicted by the Sapphic imitations she published in the two preceding decades, and even when Landon was alive,
her poetry was already read from the perspective of its afterlife. In the
1820s she began publishing verses under the initials L. E. L. in *The Literary Gazette* and—like Mary Robinson in the previous generation—quickly
became a commodity in the booming market for women's sentimental
verse. And like so many women poets, Landon (re)turns to Sappho in
order to reflect on her conversion into yet another popular poetess. An
early poem by Landon, entitled "Sappho" and printed in the *Gazette* as a

"poetic sketch" in 1822, performs a claim to posthumous fame for "L. E. L." through the dead persona of Sappho.[18] In the opening lines, Sappho is sketched as a figure for "thousands" to look upon and worship:

> She leant upon her harp, and thousands looked
> On her in love and wonder—thousands knelt
> And worshipp'd in her presence—burning tears,
> And words that died in utterance, and a pause
> Of breathless, agitated eagerness,
> First gave the full heart's homage: then came forth
> A shout that rose to heaven; and the hills,
> The distant valleys, all rang with the name
> Of the Aeolian SAPPHO—every heart
> Found in itself some echo to her song.
>
> (1–10)

Landon's "sketch," although unillustrated, draws on pictorial convention and the popular genre of the picture poem to present Sappho as we would expect to see her, just before the leap, poised in "a pause / Of breathless, agitated eagerness." Leaning down on her harp, Sappho seems to deliver "words that died in utterance," but these words are immediately revived and volleyed back in a resounding echo through hills and distant valleys: as Sappho falls, the world responds with "a shout that rose to heaven." She is heard only by means of such echoes, as "the name / Of the Aeolian SAPPHO" is deferred until line 9, suspended in the pause of yet another enjambment and mediated by the response of "every heart" that finds "in itself some echo to her song." Indeed, it is not clear in line 5 whether "breathless, agitated eagerness" describes her song or their response, nor is it even identified as "song" until line 10, after its echoing. The opening lines—a long and involuted sentence, interrupted by dashes, colons, and semicolons—therefore introduce Sappho's song as a form of repetition rather than origination.

Not only is Landon's Sappho a meditation on how a lyric figure is mediated by the recurring moment of its reception, but we also see here how the popular reception of "L. E. L." might follow a similar logic. Her "Sketch" of Sappho renarrates the Ovidian story in curiously overlapping tenses, slipping between past and present verbs, to emphasize that Sappho has been forgotten by Phaon but is now remembered by posterity. While "PHAON / Soon forgot the fondness of his Lesbian maid," his forgetting is contrasted with the memory of Sappho, "echoed" and "remembered" long after her death, as the poem concludes:

[18] "Sappho" was first published in the *The Literary Gazette* (May 4, 1822: 282) and later reprinted in *The Vow of the Peacock* (1835: 115–20); it is included, with small variations, under "Additional Poems" in Landon 1990: 566–68.

- - - - There is a dark rock looks on the blue sea;
'Twas there love's last song echoed—there She sleeps,
Whose lyre was crown'd with laurel, and whose name
Will be remember'd long as Love or Song
Are sacred—the devoted SAPPHO!   L. E. L.

Conflating present ("There is"), past ("'Twas there"), and future ("Will be"), the final lines of this "Poetic Sketch" create a picture of Sappho devoted to "Love or Song" in the abstract, an effect detached from its cause; Phaon is no longer in the picture, and what survives is a name: "—the devoted SAPPHO!" The Sapphic signature is separated from the rest of the poem by a dash, a clear demarcation of the name as a postscript, and its juxtaposition with the initials "L. E. L." adds yet another signature to be read in the name of Sappho: a postscript to what is already postscript.

The Improvisatrice, published two years later in 1824, reflects even more self-reflexively on the identification of L. E. L. with Sappho. The eponymous heroine of this long and intricate dramatic monologue is an anonymous "improvisatrice," skilled in many arts. Early in the poem she describes a portrait that she has painted of Sappho, poised at the moment of death, and also transcribes the dying words of Sappho that she has composed into a song; thus Sappho is made into a speaking picture, albeit a persona that can only speak because it is already dead. Just as the earlier "Sketch" of Sappho began with "words that died in utterance," the Sapphic song now performed by the improvisatrice is presented as another dying utterance:

Sappho's Song.

FAREWELL, my lute! —and would that I
    Had never waked thy burning chords!
Poison has been upon thy sigh,
    And fever has breathed in thy words.

Yet wherefore, wherefore should I blame
    Thy power, thy spell, my gentlest lute?
I should have been the wretch I am,
    Had every chord of thine been mute.

It was my evil star above,
    Not my sweet lute, that wrought me wrong:
It was not song that taught me love,
    But it was love that taught me song.

If song be past, and hope undone,
    And pulse, and head, and heart are flame;

It is thy work, thou faithless one!
But, no!—I will not name thy name!

Sun-god! lute, wreath are vowed to thee!
Long be their light upon my grave—
My glorious grave—yon deep blue sea:
I shall sleep calm beneath its wave!

(4)

The inspiration of this lyric is in its expiration: the "I" expires in a "sigh" in stanza one, the "lute" falls "mute" in stanza two, and the "song" is relegated to the past in stanzas three and four. In the final stanza Sappho dedicates herself to death, the "glorious grave" of the sea where she shall "sleep calm beneath its wave," falling into silence as the song ends.

Yet "Sappho's Song" is inflected by grammatical and rhetorical nuances—the manipulation of conditional verbs, conjunctions, anaphoras, and apostrophes—that suggest the prolongation of her song even, and especially, past death. When Sappho laments, "Would that I / Had never waked thy burning chords," it is a contrary to fact condition, as she is striking up new chords in her own rhyming words. She prolongs the song itself by repeating words ("wherefore, wherefore," and "my grave—my glorious grave") and phrases ("It was my evil star. . . . It was not song . . . But it was love") and conjunctions ("And pulse, and head, and heart"). Thus, when she asks the rhetorical question, "Should I blame / Thy power, thy spell, my gentlest lute," it is clear that she cannot help but fall under its musical spell again; although she wonders "if song be past," it continues in the present performance. Her lute is brought to life in the opening apostrophe, and just before ending the song Sappho predicts the afterlife of her lute and wreath: "long be their light upon my grave." The song survives, detached from Phaon ("But no!—I will not name thy name!") so that it may circulate freely in Sappho's name.

The refusal to "name thy name" is necessary for the survival of "Sappho's Song," which could be read in the name of Sappho (who sings the song) but might also be read in the name of the anonymous improvisatrice (who recites the song as part of her monologue), or in the name of L. E. L. (who writes the song as part of her poem): the transmission of the song through the text now before us depends on the continual postponement of the name. The very moment of parting with the lute turns out to be the prolongation of its "power" and "spell," giving it the power to spell out other names, including the echoing letters of "L. E. L." The dying words of Sappho ("FAREWELL, my lute") are echoed in the dying words of the improvisatrice at the end of her monologue ("be this kiss a spell! / My first! my last! FAREWELL! — FAREWELL!" [32]), and this doubled "FAREWELL" is redoubled in the spelling of the name L. E. L., who is thus identified with the improvisatrice much as the improvisatrice is identified with Sappho. However, such identifications are made only by proclaiming the end of Sapphic song, turning them into a series of reflections without an identifiable original, a resounding echo without origin.

In a further amplication of this echo effect, *The Improvisatrice* ends by echoing the beginning of L. E. L.'s earlier "Poetic Sketch," where (we will recall) Sappho was sketched as "she leant upon her harp," already a figure for infinitely echoing song. So also the improvisatrice is painted in a pose of infinite decline, leaning on her harp and falling yet again, in a Sapphic self-portrait described in the epilogue to *The Improvisatrice:*

> She leant upon a harp:—one hand
>   Wandered, like snow, amid the chords;
> The lips were opening with such life,
>   You almost heard the silvery words.
> She looked a form of light and life,
>   All soul, all passion, and all fire;
> A priestess of Apollo's, when
>   The morning beams fall on her lyre;
> A Sappho, or ere love had turned
> The heart to stone where once it burned.

> (33)

Not only has the improvisatrice anticipated her own death in this self-portrait, but it illustrates that she was dead all along: from the retrospective perspective of the epilogue, the dramatic monologue turns out to have been delivered by an already-dead persona. What "looked a form of light and life," its lips "opening with such life" and a voice "almost heard," was an artful illusion, the creation of yet another Sappho whose death is repeated in order to create the appearance of life. While we may not be astonished to learn that "love had turned / The heart to stone"—the prescribed epitaph for "a Sappho" whose fate was entirely predictable—what is astonishing in these final lines is their insistence on de-animating the figure of Sappho. In death the improvisatrice can finally be named "Sappho," but only by turning the proper into a common name, "a Sappho," a depersonified non-persona. As in her earlier "Sketch" of Sappho, L. E. L signs off on *The Improvisatrice* with a generic Sapphic signature: a further postscript to the previous postscript, a "P. S. Sappho" where the name of Sappho survives only in the repetition of the P. S., in a long series of Sapphic signatures that includes L. E. L. but neither begins nor ends there.

We see the poetess literally declining into the abyss of the name, in a later edition of *The Poetical Works of Letitia Elizabeth Landon, "L. E. L."* (1873). Here an engraving is presented alongside "Sappho's Song," a fem-

SAPPHO.

FIGURE 12: Illustration in *The Poetical Works of L.E.L.*, William Bell Scott (1873).

inine figure falling over the edge of a cliff with the sea below (figure 12).[19] She has dropped her lyre and lost her footing, as she seems about to sink down to the bottom of the sea, and lower, down to the name below the picture: "Sappho." But even here, at the bottom edge of the frame, the name cannot properly ground the falling figure of Sappho. Is it a repre-

[19] The illustration is by the poet and artist William Bell Scott, in an 1873 edition of Landon's *Poetical Works*. The edition is reproduced by Sypher, who observes that the engraver's name also "seems to read downwards among the rocks on the left side" (1990: 21).

sentation of Sappho, or a representation of the improvisatrice representing Sappho, or a representation of L. E. L. representing the improvisatrice representing Sappho, or a representation of Letitia Elizabeth
Landon representing L. E. L. representing the improvisatrice representing Sappho? The figure keeps falling through every representational
frame, so that readers eager to find "a Sappho" in Letitia Elizabeth Landon discover instead an infinite regress of Sapphos.

Nevertheless it is through the perpetual repetition of this falling figure
that L. E. L. was made into a name as a popular poetess. *The Literary Gazette*
acclaimed *The Improvisatrice* as a poetic performance that "would, alone,
entitle the fair author to the name of the English Sappho," and throughout her poetic career she was known as a "Song-Born Sappho of Our Age"
and a poetess of "sighs / Attuned to Sappho's shell" (McGann and Riess
1997: 362, 369), as well as (in Disraeli's less flattering description) the
"snub-nosed Brompton Sappho." The association of "L. E. L." with Sappho allowed Landon's poetry to circulate in a literary market that thrived
on poetesses and turned "L. E. L." into a product for literary consump-
tion, as Glennis Stephenson argues in *Letitia Landon: The Woman Behind
L. E. L:* "Landon's poetic self is, therefore, in part imposed upon her—
the product of a variety of social, cultural, and even economic conditions,
the product of the demands and responses of her readers, her critics, and
her publishers, and later, even of the gossip that was circulated and the
numerous memoirs that were written about her. But it is also, in part, a
calculated case of self-projection" (1995: 3–4). However, I would question Stephenson's distinction between the poetic persona and the historical person, since the "self-projection" she describes can only be projected as a leap into the rhetorical fiction of Sappho; every reading of
L. E. L. (including Stephenson's own, as she acknowledges) "grows out
of a desire to interpret the woman in a way that confirms certain predetermined notions about the woman as poet" (8). How then can we "distinguish the woman behind L. E. L." when the poetry performs the overdetermination of that very question? The construction of a Sapphic (non)
persona points to the problem of trying to reconstruct a historical person as well.

The desire to discover a woman behind, and even *in*, the letters of the
name is spelled out in the popular Victorian biography by Laman Blanchard, who published *The Life and Literary Remains of L. E. L.* in 1841, in
the wake of her sensational and mysterious death. Just as Landon specialized in poetical sketches of dead women, Blanchard presents his
book to the reading public as a "sketch of the literary and personal life
of L. E. L." in order to create a portrait of the dead poetess as a woman
of letters (1841: v). Indeed, all that remains of the life is letters, in every
sense. In addition to compiling posthumous verse attributed to L. E. L.

and selected letters drawn from her personal correspondence, Blanchard includes a memoir of the life, from a happy childhood to the tragic death. This seemingly personal record of the poetess, beginning with "anecdotes of her infancy," continually emphasizes the conversion of L. E. L. into a figure for reading and being read. "L. E. L. was a reader almost in her cradle," Blanchard claims, recounting that "she was taught to read by an invalid friend and neighbour, who amused herself by scattering the letters of the alphabet over the carpet, and making her little pupil pick them up as they were named" (5–6). The anecdote foreshadows how the infant poetess will grow up to be named by scattered letters of the alphabet, "L. E. L.," and be remembered in the scattering of her literary works as a woman of letters: a proper name. "The three letters very speedily became a signature of magical interest and curiosity," according to Blanchard, and soon "the initials became *a name*" (30). The appeal of L. E. L. was in fact the namelessness of the name, as Blanchard speculates: "Perhaps the L.E. L. itself, the compromise between the anonymous and the full announcement, the partial revelation, the namelessness of the name, had the effect of stimulating curiosity" (31). Her name was made by stimulating readers to imagine its letters—"the L. E. L. itself"—as a revelation of the poetess herself.

This, at least, is how Blanchard imagines her in his own poem, "On First Seeing the Portrait of L. E. L.," reprinted in *The Life and Literary Remains of L. E. L.*[20] Blanchard's poem recalls the initial revelation that those three magical letters spelled out the name of Letitia Elizabeth Landon, when she was first revealed to the curious public as a young poetess. Rather than addressing her in the second person, Blanchard introduces the letters of her name as if they had already acquired a life of their own in his imagination. "Ye thrice fair letters, can ye be / A lady, after all?" he asks, in an elaborate apostrophe to "Ye alphabetic Graces!" and gives life to the initials by imagining many possible acronyms: "Logic, Ethics, Lays"; "Lives, Episodes, and Lyrics"; "Love, Eden, and the Lyre"; "Light, Elegance, and Laughter"; and "The Lily, Eglantine, / And then another Lily"; the last of which shows the name to be a palindrome, allowing L. E. L. to be read the same way forward and backward. This progression (or infinite regression) of associations is brought to a stop upon seeing L. E. L. personified in a portrait, the very personification of the poetess: "Now fancy is dead, no thought can strike," writes Blanchard in a brief moment of regret, "And L. E. L. is—simply like / This dainty little picture." By the end of his poem, however, he is only too willing to exchange the allegorical personification of letters for the fiction of a biographical persona, al-

---

[20] "On First Seeing the Portrait of L. E. L." is anonymously reprinted in Blanchard 1841: 145–46, and attributed to Blanchard himself by McGann and Riess, who note that its first date of publication is uncertain (1997: 367).

lowing L. E. L. to be read as if she were "simply like" the picture. Because the anonymous figure has finally been given a face and a name, Blanchard concludes: "These three initials—nameless name— / Shall never be *dead letters!*"

Of course the animation of dead letters—like the echoing "spell" of the lute in "Sappho's Song"—is predicated on the death of the poetess, suggesting that the course of L. E. L.'s poetic career is predetermined by the dying words of Sappho. Thus, in the posthumous reconstruction of her "life and literary remains," Blanchard not only collects the remnants of L. E. L. like Sapphic fragments but also recollects her death like the demise of Sappho, narrating in detail how the poetess was found dead (an accident? a murder? a suicide?) at Cape Coast Castle, and how "the remains of L. E. L. were, on the following day, consigned to a grave dug near the Castle" (255). With both the literal corpse and the literary corpus of L. E. L. now "consigned" to the grave, the name circulates more than ever as a Sapphic signature. All the poems seem to be written in anticipation of the death: "The verses even of her gay and eager youth abound in distrusting views of life, in melancholy forebodings," Blanchard writes (33), and throughout his book he quotes lines published by L. E. L. as if they were predictions of her own fate: "How completely were her own lines verified, 'I seem to stand beside a grave, / And stand by it alone'" (257). Like the words attributed to Sappho in Ovid's epistle, the words of L. E. L. survive as postscript to a death that has already happened. The entire life of L.E.L. is thus to be read as a repetition of Sappho's fate: a poetess whose rise to fame is inevitably a fall, a name that "shall never be dead letters" because it has fallen into its afterlife.

Blanchard is not the only one to read L. E. L. by metalepsis, which turns out to be the most popular trope for her reception in mid-Victorian England. In an 1840 essay paying tribute to the poetess, for example, William Howitt contemplates the tragedy of L. E. L. by looking back on her earlier poetry.[21] To illustrate how "the very words of her first heroine might have literally been uttered as her own," he quotes a stanza from *The Improvisatrice* (McGann and Riess 1997: 348):

> Sad were my shades; methinks they had
> > Almost a tone of prophecy—
> I ever had, from earlier youth,
> > A feeling what my fate would be.

In order to project the fate of L. E. L. simultaneously into and out of her poem, Howitt reads the words as if they were "literally . . . her own," and

---

[21] Howitt's tribute to L. E. L. was published in *Fisher's Drawing Room Scrap Book for 1840* and is reprinted in McGann and Riess 1997: 346–51.

indeed he insists on a completely "literal" reading of all her poems: the "one singular peculiarity of the poetry of L. E. L.," according to Howitt, is that "it is entirely her own" (348). Yet the fate predicted for the improvisatrice (as we have seen) is that she will be disowned by the very words that are attributed to her: they are not her own, after all, but a Sapphic utterance without origin. Every attempt to read L. E. L. "literally" therefore turns out to be mediated by quotation, as in an obituary also published in 1840, by William Maginn.[22] Like Howitt, Maginn quotes from the poetry of L. E. L. to describe the fate "she had herself predicted, though speaking the character of another" (McGann and Riess 1997: 344):

> Mine shall be a lonelier ending,
> Mine shall be a wilder grave,
> Where the shout and shriek are blending,
> Where the tempest meets the wave.

Here again, the ending that would seem to be "mine"—belonging to L. E. L. as "literally . . . her own"—does not properly belong to anyone; it is a Sapphic scenario that makes her fate not only predictable but infinitely repeatable. The same words are cited at the end of Blanchard's biography (1841: 295) and recited in a final elegiac sentence that resonates with her poem: "She sleeps in the barren sands of Africa, and the mournful music of the billows, to which she listened in her solitary sea-girt dwelling, is now the dirge that resounds over her distant grave." (301) Like Sappho, L. E. L. is lost in the sounds of the sea, a figure for resounding echoes.

Does this mean that the poetry of L. E. L. "could only repeat the same story over and over," as Anne Mellor concludes? According to Mellor, Landon embodied rather than critiqued her society's definition of the ideal woman and thus, "having taken her culture's limited construction of gender as ontological 'truth,' Landon could only map a terrain whose roads all converged on the same centre, the same dead end" (1993: 114). But if we read Landon's poetry rhetorically, as I have suggested, we begin to see how the same dead-end story may be repeated not to posit the "ontological truth" of gender but to pose a question about the ontology and epistemology of woman: what, indeed, can be known about "the woman" that feminist criticism would like to discover "behind L. E. L."? To read dead letters as the embodiment of a (once) living woman would be to re-enter the fantasy of literal reading in Blanchard's poem, "On First Seeing the Portrait of L. E. L." The letters are seen to embody a woman by reading a woman back into the letters, turning her into a figure that is read

---

[22] Maginn's obituary notice for L. E. L. was published in *Fraser's Magazine* in January of 1840; it is excerpted in Blanchard 1841: 295–98 and reprinted in McGann and Riess 1997: 341–45.

the same way forward and backward, like the palindrome of the name. "Don't be quite so much your own nominative," L. E. L writes in her correspondence, mocking herself for writing too much in the first person singular: "Truly, they ought to have placed *I* instead of *A* at the beginning of the alphabet" (quoted by Blanchard 1841: 86–87). Even here in a seemingly "personal" letter, the subject that appears in the nominative is not prior to writing (the fantasy of an "I" placed "at the beginning of the alphabet") but already written; it first appears as "I" after the transposition of letters.

The repetition of the dead end also troubles Germaine Greer in "The Sad Tale of L. E. L.," a chapter that looks for "the real face of a woman" in the various tales of the poetess, only to find the woman gone (1995: 261). Greer concludes her chapter with the by now predictable elegiac gesture of quoting a verse, to illustrate how "L. E. L. wrote her own epitaph" (358):

> The future never renders to the past
>   The young beliefs entrusted to its keeping.
> Inscribe one sentence—life's first truth and last
>   On the pale marble where our dust is sleeping—
>   We might have been.

In Greer's feminist reading, L. E. L. falls short of being the woman she "might have been"; her poetry demonstrates the failure of a poetess, whose "future never renders to the past" an earlier promise of fame. But if we are to read her verse as epitaph, it is ironic not only because it refuses to monumentalize the poetess but because posterity remembers her precisely because of this fall into namelessness: the lines are not her own epitaph, but prescribed for a long line of readers who remember L. E. L. by forgetting what she might have been. The verse quoted by Greer is already quoted in the nineteenth-century biography by Blanchard (1841: 296), who quotes it in turn from Maginn's 1840 obituary, and in each version of the sad tale of L. E. L. the woman is simultaneously projected out of and into the poetry in order to proclaim her death, as we see in Maginn's rhetorical question: "Who wrote those lines? Miss Landon! What *she* might have been, is now idle to conjecture." (McGann and Riess 1997: 345) Yet only through conjecture can "*she*" be projected into the poem as the one who "wrote those lines." For just as "the future never renders to the past" what "might have been," the poem will not render an authorial name; at the moment where composition and reception seem to merge, L. E. L. is already a postscript.

While reading from a twentieth-century feminist perspective, Greer therefore replays the same metaleptic logic that shapes the Victorian reception of L. E. L. Greer's book, *Slip-Shod Sibyls: Recognition, Rejection*

and the Woman Poet, sets out to explore what happens "when an un-
schooled, almost unlettered female begins to express in herself in verse"
(i), and in a running polemic against "the excesses of poetesshood" (xv),
the chapter on L. E. L. serves as a primary exhibit: a poetess made into a
marketable commodity, created and then destroyed by the London literary establishment, demonstrating "in a concise and appalling way the
complex of causes that have excluded women from a full participation in
literary culture" (259). But to read L. E. L. as an "almost unlettered female"—as if female authorship is not mediated by letters of every kind,
and therefore fully participating in nineteenth-century literary culture—
is to perpetuate the conventions of reading that assume sentimental lyric
to be a purely private and unmediated form of self-expression, without
critical reflection. Greer's suspicion of the Poetess as a viable cultural category leads her to dismiss Victorian poetesses as failed precursors to modern women poets; "seldom aware that the distinguishing characteristic of
poetry is ambiguity," the slip-shod poetess is (in Greer's view) to be distinguished from the true woman poet, who does not emerge until after
1900 (xvi, xxiii).

Only Christina Rossetti escapes this rather damning assessment of
nineteenth-century poetesses, although even in her case Greer insists "it
is important to distinguish Rossetti's sham utterances from her real poetry, the poetess from the woman poet" (xix). The early verse of Rossetti
is too much mediated by L. E. L., according to Greer, who illustrates her
point by quoting "A Pause of Thought," composed by the young Christina
in 1848:

> I looked for that which is not, nor can be
> And hope deferred made my heart sick in truth:
> But years must pass before a hope of youth
> Is resigned utterly.

This would seem to be one of "Rossetti's sham utterances," as Greer comments that "the despairing mood of this kind of writing can be considered a mere literary convention, by Byron out of L. E. L." (378). Rossetti's
lines do indeed echo L. E. L.'s so-called "epitaph," as if they are pausing
in thought on the inscription "we might have been" in order to inscribe
an even greater sense of doom: "that which is not, nor can be." The
"young beliefs" entrusted to the future but lost in the past by L. E. L. are
refigured by Rossetti not only as "hope deferred" in the past but "a hope
of youth" that is "resigned utterly" in the future. The lines of resignation
attributed to L. E. L. are thus re-signed in the name of Christina Rossetti,
but only as a more extreme form of resignation: a signature that utterly
empties out the "I" that we might assume to be the source of the utterance. When we read "I looked for that which is not, nor can be," we also

reflect on the very act of looking for that which is not, nor can be, an "I."
If we look for an authentic lyric subject in these lines, we would overlook
this canny inscription of literary convention as itself a subject for reflection: a critical oversight that limits Greer's understanding of what is at
stake in sentimental lyric in general and skews her reading of L. E. L.'s
legacy in the next generation of Victorian poetesses, including Rossetti.

A more promising approach to reading "the gush of the feminine" in
nineteenth-century women's poetry, as Isobel Armstrong proposes, is to
notice how L. E. L. "throws the whole weight of speculation on the status
of action and perception, making an interpretative problem of events"
(1995: 29–30). The force of such weight is thrown into Sappho's leap, as
we have seen, in a recurring rhetorical performance that makes a "problem of events" by enacting a temporal disjunction. Armstrong observes
that an ambiguous doubling of verbs in the poems of L. E. L. is "enough
to create a gap between events and the perception of them as events, a
dislocation or hiatus between perception and the representation of perception"; in addition to creating "an afterimage or the sense of 'fleeting'
copy," this "fractional gap opening up in the doubled verb creates a space
for interpretative maneuever," where "the flickering verb allows a moment of interrogation" (30). This hiatus is inhabited by Christina Rossetti
as well, I would argue, as she discovers in L. E. L. an afterimage of Sappho—a "fleeting copy" produced by "the flickering verb"—that opens a
space for two early Sapphic imitations by Rossetti, as yet another moment
for interpretation and interrogation. In 1846 Rossetti composed a short
lyric, entitled "Sappho," that reflects on the dying words of Sappho, and
in 1848 she meditates further on Sappho's afterlife in a longer poem,
"What Sappho Would Have Said Had Her Leap Cured Instead of Killing
Her."[23] In both poems the utterance is a "sham," an empty form that self-
consciously situates itself within a long legacy of past and future invoca-
tions of Sappho. By taking the poetic function of the sham utterance
more seriously, we can see how the reworking of L. E. L.'s Sappho in Rossetti's early verse is crucial for defining her poetics, and also call into question Greer's distinction between the poetess and the woman poet who
writes "real poetry."

No doubt Rossetti's interest in Sappho derives from many previous
translations and imitations,[24] but since Sappho was especially associated

---

[23] "Sappho" was privately printed by Christina Rossetti in *Verses Dedicated to Her Mother*
(1847); it also appears in Rossetti's notebook manuscript in her sister's handwriting and is
reprinted in Crump's variorum edition (Rossetti 1990: 81–82, 392). "What Sappho Would
Have Said" was not published during Rossetti's lifetime but appears in the variorum edition
(Rossetti 1990: 166–69, 423).

[24] In her dissertation chapter, "Lyric's Drama and Sappho's Conversions," Margaret Lin-
ley notes that the young Christina was familiar with translations of Sappho; the 1711 ver-

with L. E. L. throughout the 1840s, the decade following her sensational death, it is not surprising to hear an echo of L. E. L. in "Sappho," written by Rossetti at age sixteen:

> I sigh at day-dawn, and I sigh
> When the dull day is passing by.
> I sigh at evening, and again
> I sigh when night brings sleep to men.
> Oh! it were better far to die
> Than thus for ever mourn and sigh,
> And in death's dreamless sleep to be
> Unconscious that none weep for me;
> Eased from my weight of heaviness,
> Forgetful of forgetfulness,
> Resting from pain and care and sorrow
> Thro' the long night that knows no morrow;
> Living unloved, to die unknown,
> Unwept, untended and alone.

Like L. E. L., Rossetti plays with the rhyme of "I" and "sigh" to suggest the expiration of a first-person lyric subject, and indeed the only appearance of "I" is in the phrase "I sigh," repeated five times at the beginning of the poem as a diminuendo of dissolving sighs. This anaphora differs from the apostrophe in "Sappho's Song," however, where L. E. L. makes the survival of Sapphic song depend upon an address to Sappho's lute, if not Sappho herself; but in Rossetti's "Sappho," the figure of song fades along with the expiring "I," leaving nothing to attribute to the name of "Sappho" except the vocative, "Oh!" As the final sighs of "I" give way to echoes of "O"—pure apostrophe, without origin in the first person singular—Rossetti's poem performs the total evacuation of a lyric subject that loses consciousness and "knows no morrow." Suspending Sappho in the moment where being reverts to non-being, Rossetti uses the infinitives "to be" and "to die" to prolong the hiatus (or "fractional gap") introduced by the doubling of verbs in L. E. L.'s Sappho poems, and through a series of negations at the end of her own poem even the name of Sappho is rendered anonymous: not only "unconscious" and "forgetful of forgetfulness," but something to be forgotten, "unloved," "unknown," "unwept," "untended."

The desire to be "unconscious" can be read, ironically, as a self-conscious reflection on an "I" that never dies; it is situated simultaneously before

---

sion of fragment 31 by Ambrose Philips (discussed in my first chapter) appears twice in the *Commonplace Book of Frances Rossetti*, once as "Translation of a Fragment of Sappho" and again as "Ode by Sappho." I thank Margaret for sharing her research at the University of British Columbia Angeli-Dennis Collection with me.

and after death, without ever being released from the burden of its end-less iteration. To be "eased from my weight of heaviness" is impossible, as Sappho continues falling into the future of being read, a self-perpetuat-ing metalepsis: although she aspires to "forgetfulness," such forgetting is a way to be remembered after all. The poem is therefore called "Sappho," not to recall a forgotten sign that "knows no morrow" and is "unknown," but to make her into a sign for forgetting, precisely because the name is so well-known. This curious coincidence of remembering and forgetting is further played out in Rossetti's later lyric, "Song" (1862). Beginning with the hypothesis of a dead "I" ("When I am dead, my dearest"), the first stanza of this ironic epitaph invents an equally hypothetical "thou" who hovers ambiguously between remembering and forgetting ("And if thou wilt, remember, / And if thou wilt, forget"), while the second stanza con-cludes by making the "I" indifferent to memory ("Haply I may remem-ber, / And haply may forget"). Thus both "thou" and "I" are projected into a future act of memory that is not internalized within a subject and serves only to remember a forgetting. Indeed, by remembering the ear-lier poem in the context of the later poem, we project "Sappho" into a fu-ture "Song" that has forgotten the name of Sappho: the "I" in Rossetti's "Song" is now anonymous. What is the point of such forgetting, leaving Sappho unnamed and ever more forgotten, like the perpetual un-nam-ing of "Monna Innominata"?

Rossetti wrote many poems "where Sappho is not named, but similar themes are reworked," as Margaret Reynolds notes (1996: 282). In her reading the "Song" of Rossetti "takes on quite another significance if it is put into the tradition of the woman poet singing Sappho's 'last song,'" because then "it becomes a poem about that very tradition," addressed "by the woman poet herself" and "to the audience of women poets" who might thus "re-member Sappho" (293). But Reynolds also points out a re-curring problem for the woman poet who tries to remember Sappho; in a subtle reading of "'Reflection,'" she argues that Rossetti reflects on the image of "a woman poet" whose existence is already mediated by the quo-tation marks in the title and further refracted in the poem itself as a se-ries of reflections, to create "a self-conscious looking at the self looking at Sappho who is and is not a self-portrait" (283). But since this image is only recognizable as a reflection and never named, except perhaps as "Reflection," it would seem that the repetition of a Sapphic theme in Ros-setti's verse takes the form of forgetting, rather than remembering Sap-pho. A poetic tradition ironically predicated on not remembering Sap-pho is dramatized by Rossetti in the second of her early Sappho poems: "What Sappho Would Have Said Had Her Leap Cured Instead of Killing Her." This dramatic monologue verges on parody of previous Sapphic odes—including those of L. E. L.—in order to resist the memory of Sappho and to insist, instead, on the reiteration of a Sapphic trope increasingly devoid of content.

Seeming to have survived the leap, Sappho is introduced in the opening stanzas as an exhausted figure, the shadow of a former self that has been emptied out and knows only emptiness: "I seek in vain; a shadow-pain / Lies on my heart; and all in vain" (stanza 2). What Sappho desires more than death is total oblivion, described in stanzas 5 and 6:

> Methinks this is a drowsy place:
>> Disturb me not: I fain would sleep:
>> The very winds and waters keep
> Their voices under; and the race
> Of Time seems to stand still, for here
> Is night or twilight all the year.
>
> A very holy hushedness
>> Broods here for ever: like a dove
>> That, having built its nest above
> A quiet place, feels the excess
> Of calm sufficient, and would fain
> Not wake, but drowse on without pain.

The *vanitas* of Sappho's being—the monotonous repetition of her life and death "in vain . . . all in vain"—turns into a desire for nonbeing: "I fain would sleep" and "fain not wake." This state of suspended nonanimation, where "Time seems to stand still" and a "hushedness broods" in motionless silence, creates "a quiet place" in the middle of the poem, without consciousness of pain. For a moment, then, Sappho forgets her fate (imagining herself "unconscious" and "forgetful of forgetfulness," as in Rossetti's earlier poem "Sappho") and anticipates a future of forgetting and being forgotten (as in Rossetti's later "Song"): " I will lie down; and quite forget / The doubts and fears that haunt me yet," she proclaims in stanza 8.

In stanza 10, however, it becomes clear that Sappho cannot "quite forget," for she is haunted "yet"—not only by the past, but by the future as well. She falls into a future that is a repetition of the past:

> Ah, would that it could reach my heart,
>> And fill the void that is so dry
>> And aches and aches;—but what am I
> To shrink from my self-purchased part?
> It is in vain; is all in vain;
> I must go forth and bear my pain.

The conditional utterance of the poem (what Sappho "would" have said, if it "would" be possible to "fill the void" of her being) here gives way to a rhetorical question, "But what am I?" The rest of this stanza (later added to the poem[25]) returns us to the Sapphic pose where all appears (again) "in vain . . . in vain." Sappho must accept a "self-purchased part" of suffering pain, a "part" that is "purchased" and played out at the expense of herself; there is no "I" apart from this pain. Bearing pain (in every sense of the verb "to bear") is the only way to conceive of Sappho as a lyric "I" that is emptied out in the course of its (re)production. The question "what am I" is answered with "I must go forth," ironically giving birth to a female lyric subject that is produced by bearing the pain of the past and reproduced by bearing this pain into the future. Sappho is not cured, then, but doomed to leap again and again without ever dying; because the leap has not killed her, she must repeat it, endlessly.

The poem therefore concludes with an invocation to pain: "Oh come again, thou pain divine, / Fill me and make me wholly thine" (stanza 11). While Reynolds reads these final lines as the fulfillment of Sappho's being ("this 'cured' and empty Sappho asks to be herself again," 286), I would argue to the contrary that Sappho is further emptied out into a vicarious figure for others to "fill," not herself at all but "wholly thine." The emptying out of this figure makes Rossetti's Sappho not unlike L. E. L. 's nameless improvisatrice, whose Sapphic performance also produces a generic figure for a series of vicarious identifications, as we have seen: the memory of "a Sappho" that is a perpetual deferral, or forgetting, of the proper name. But writing in the wake of L. E. L., whose fate it was to be ironically remembered in the name of Sappho, Rossetti goes one step further into the abyss of the Sapphic pose by turning it into an even more radically reflexive performance of a "self-purchased part."

What Rossetti's Sappho poems put on display, in other words, is the *figurality* of the figure: a rhetorical feat that anticipates a description by her brother of a small statue of Sappho, seen in a London gallery in 1850. In one of his "Notices of Fine Art," Dante Gabriel Rossetti describes this statue, "of exquisite though peculiar character," quite lyrically: "Sappho sits in abject languor, her feet hanging over the rock, her hands left in her lap, where her harp has sunk; its strings have made music assuredly for the last time. The poetry of the figure is like a pang of life in the stone; the sea is in her ears, and that desolate look in her eyes is upon the sea; and her countenance has fallen" (1887: 499). By projecting "abject languor" into this object, Rossetti animates the motionless statue into a feminine figure oscillating between life and death: with "her feet hanging over the rock" and her "desolate look . . . upon the sea," she seems about

---

[25] Rebecca Crump notes that a separate page containing lines 57–66 (the second half of the tenth stanza and the entire eleventh stanza) is inserted at the end of Rossetti's poem (Rossetti 1990: 423). The final stanza leaves behind Phaon in order to make Christ the prototype for Sappho's suffering, as she follows in "His footsteps."

to leap, but because "her harp has sunk" and "her countenance has fallen," it also seems her leap has already happened. And as always, it is in the moment of suspended animation that this Sappho seems to come to life: although her song has been heard "assuredly for the last time," nevertheless Rossetti insists that "the poetry of the figure is like a pang of life in the stone." In this artful phrase Rossetti makes "the poetry of the figure" that he sees in the statue even more visible, not only because he turns Sappho's death pangs into "a pang of life" but because the ambiguously animated figure turns out to be a poetic figure for the process of animation itself: "*like* a pang of life," but not alive at all. The "peculiar character" of Sappho derives from this simultaneous personification and depersonification, as "that desolate look in her eyes" seems lifelike to our eyes precisely because it is devoid of life.

This is also the desolate outlook of Christina Rossetti's early Sappho poems. Like her brother (and he, like her) she reflects on "the poetry of the figure" by presenting Sappho as a lifeless form to be animated by the onlooker, or a reader, but only through the revelation of its lifelessness: the more Sappho is personified, the emptier the persona. Such reflection on the figure *as* figure is a recurring feature of Rossetti's later poetry as well, where she practises a poetics of postponement very much in keeping with a women's tradition of writing as postscript, in order to explore various forms of self-effacement, erasure, renunciation, and negation. It is difficult, then, to distinguish between the "sham utterances" and the "real poetry" of Christina Rossetti, or between the "poetess" and the "woman poet," as Greer would have us do. Rossetti is implicitly aligned with nineteenth-century poetesses who turn to the trope of Sappho, and in further troping on the trope she makes explicit a figural logic that has become a definining feature of women's sentimental lyric by the middle of the nineteenth century. Just as Mary Robinson and L. E. L. became known as English Sapphos earlier in the century, Rossetti therefore came to be called Sappho as well: toward the end of century, Edmund Gosse compared Rossetti to Sappho in order to praise her as "one of the most perfect poets of the age" (1893: 215).

If such praise implies a distinction between imperfect poetess and perfect poet, the reason is not that the latter has perfected strategies of "ambiguity" lacking in the former, but that the self-reflexive figurations of the poetess are read, by convention, as unambiguously transparent. "They write from impulse, and rapidly as they think," writes George Bethune in *The British Female Poets:* "Scarcely any of them seem to have inverted their pen. As the line came first to the brain, so it was written; as it was written, so it was printed" (1848: viii-ix). The figure of Sappho impulsively leaping from the cliff would seem to exemplify the unthinking "impulse" of women's writing. But in the repetition of that metalepsis, as we have seen, Victorian poetesses have already "inverted their pen" in order to perform a reversal that runs contrary to the sequence of Bethune's sentence. The Sapphic script they follow is always a postscript: as it was printed, so it was written, and as it was written, so the line came to the brain, as an inspiration already expired, turning any straightforward reading of Sappho's leap into an event more complex than anyone might have thought.

Personifying the Poetess

In the proliferation of poetesses in Victorian England, we see that "the Poetess" is not a stable term, but a contested category with controversial and often contradictory implications for the public performance of womanhood. It is possible to trace two dominant lines of descent in the genealogy of the nineteenth-century Poetess, as Virginia Blain observes, associating L. E. L. with extravagant pathos and Felicia Hemans with the domestication of sympathy, but as Blain further argues, this genealogy should not obscure other popular poetesses who were also influential figures in the transition from late Romantic to early Victorian poetics (Blain 1995: 32). Caroline Norton, for example, ranks first in a list of "Modern English Poetesses" who are summoned together as "nine muses" by John Lockhart, in an influential 1840 essay for the *Quarterly Review*. Despite differences in their poetry, what these poetesses have in common is an appeal to the sympathy of the reader, as he writes: "When we venture to lift a pen against women, straightway *apparent facies;* the weapon drops pointless on the marked passage; and whilst the mind is bent on praise or censure of the poem, the eye swims too deep in tears and mist over the poetess herself in the frontispiece, to let it see its way to either" (Lockhart 1840: 374–75). On this account, we read in order to discover a picture of the poetess in her poem. The face or figure appears (*apparent facies*) before us, "straightway," no longer mediated by words but producing an unmediated, immediate response of sympathy in the reader. As "the eye swims too deep in tears," we become sentimental readers: we blur the difference between the "I" who reads and the "I" who writes, effacing ourselves in order to identify with the face of "the poetess herself in the frontispiece."

This model of sympathetic identification is a convention of sentimental reading, of course, and it depends on personification. Yet what seems most personal in sentimental lyric proves most abstract, as "the poetess herself" is less a person than a persona that emerges at a time when poetry is increasingly defined in terms of its personifying function.[26] While personification conventionally endows a figure with the agency of a person, what we have seen so far in the Sappho poems of Mary Robinson, L. E. L., and Christina Rossetti is the performance of "woman" as a personified abstraction whose personal agency is suspended. The difficulty of claiming personhood through personification is evident in the public persona of Caroline Norton as well, and further elaborated in both her poetry and her polemical prose. In *The Dream and Other Poems* (1840), the volume so enthusiastically reviewed by Lockhart, Norton published a short lyric entitled "The Picture of Sappho," which I will read as a response to previous versions of Sappho by women poets—especially Felicia Hemans—and in conjunction with Norton's pamphlets on English laws for women.[27] Norton's rhetorical presentation of the Sapphic (non)persona is closely linked to Victorian debates about the Woman Question, and in particular the historical and political questions about representing the claims of womanhood within a legal system that did not recognize married women as persons. Thus we shall see how "The Picture of Sappho" might be, yet is not, a picture of the poetess, just as the picture of "the poetess herself in the frontispiece" might be, yet is not, a picture of Caroline Norton.

The exemplary poetess who moves Lockhart to tears is, in fact, drawn from the example of Caroline Norton. Without explicitly naming her as the poetess in the frontispiece, his description alludes to the sentimental portrait in Norton's book of poetry, *The Dream*, depicting Norton in a dreamy, pensive pose, with her chin resting on one hand and the other hand hovering near her heart (figure 13).[28] It seems she has just placed the book she was reading on the table, face down, in a gesture to be repeated by the sentimental reader of her own book, tearfully musing on the true face of "the poetess herself" rising up from those pages: a face familiar to most readers, since she had become a persona very much in the public eye in the course of the previous decade. She was famous in aristocratic circles as the granddaughter of William Sheridan and the

[26] As Steven Knapp has argued, the confusion of literal and figurative agency that troubles eighteenth-century theories of personification is naturalized in the early nineteenth century, making it possible for readers to identify with personified abstractions as if they were real persons, and eventually to identify with the figure of the poet as personification of "the ideal of literary agency itself" (1985: 141). My argument suggests that the gendering of this ideal demonstrates an ongoing ambivalence toward personification in the nineteenth century as well.

[27] "The Picture of Sappho" is published in *The Dream and Other Poems* (Norton 1840: 202–5) and reprinted in Leighton and Reynolds 1995: 136.

[28] The portrait appears in the frontispiece of *The Dream and Other Poems* (1840). It is an engraving by F. C. Lewis, after a drawing by Edwin Landseer, and the signature "Caroline Eliz[abeth] S[heridan] Norton" is reproduced below the engraving.

FIGURE 13: Frontispiece from *The Dream and Other Poems,* Caroline Norton (1840). Courtesy of The Lilly Library, Indiana University.

friend of Lord Melbourne, and infamous as "The Honorable Mrs. Norton," pilloried in public by her estranged and not so honorable husband, Charles Norton. After marrying the eighteen-year-old Caroline Sheridan in 1827 for her high status and small inheritance, Charles Norton launched a series of attacks on her character for his own political advantage and personal profit, including the 1836 suit for divorce, accusing Lord Melbourne of an adulterous liaison with Norton's wife, and several court cases to settle financial disputes.[29] The name of Caroline Norton had also been associated with controversy during parliamentary debates from 1837 to 1839 on the Infants and Child Custody Bill, when she was engaged in a prolonged custody battle for her own sons. Because the details of her private life were published in the popular press as a source of constant speculation and interest for a literary market thriving on scandal, Lockhart hails her as "the Byron of our modern poetesses" (1840: 376). Like Byron, she was a *cause celèbre,* a celebrated personality whose writings were read as personal expression; "she has very much of that intense personal passion by which Byron's poetry is distinguished," Lockhard writes (ibid.).

The comparison with Byron continues throughout the nineteenth century, as in Eric Robertson's 1883 anthology of *English Poetesses.* Again, Norton is invoked as "the female Byron" and her portrait discovered in her book of poetry: "Macaulay somewhere likens the poetry of Byron to that species of toy-book in which a single face made of india-rubber pierces many pages, and forms the head to a different body on each page. The simile might to a moderate extent be applied to Mrs. Norton's methods of work. In all her poems we are constantly reminded of herself—a very interesting person to be reminded of" (Robertson 1883: 242). Just as Lockhart directs us to discover "the poetess herself" in the poetry, in Robertson's tribute to the poetry of Mrs. Norton we are also "reminded of herself—a very interesting person." The persona seems more lifelike, more like a person, albeit in toy-book form and mediated by a simile: no longer simply a figure in the frontispiece, she is now more intrusively three-dimensional, a "face made of india-rubber" that "pierces many pages." There are two similes embedded in this curious passage, in fact; the first "likens" Byron to a rubber face, and the second likens Norton to Byron, so that she becomes a rubber copy of an already rubbery figure. Not unlike Byron, yet not entirely like him either (after all, the simile is applicable only "to a moderate extent"), she embodies a persona that keeps peeking through the poetry—on each page a different body, yet the same face.

[29] For a biographical account of these and subsequent controversies in the life of Caroline Norton, see Acland 1948 and Forster 1984: 13–52; for critical analysis of Norton's various self-representations in the public presentation of her case, see Poovey 1988: 51–88.

The embodiment of that logic in the pages of Norton's verse differs from the body of Byron's poetry, however. As a *female* Byron, she embodies a persona that is also curiously depersonified. The presumed similarity or resemblance between the two poets introduces a gendered difference that marks Norton as feminine because she lacks a masculine self, as we see in Fredric Rowton's description of her in *The Female Poets of Great Britain* (1853): "Mrs. Norton has a fervour, a tenderness, and a force of expression which greatly resemble Byron's, there cannot be a doubt; but there all similarity ceases. Byron is the personification of passionate selfishness; his range of sympathy is extremely small; Mrs. Norton, on the other hand, has a large and generous heart, essentially unselfish in its feelings, and universal in its sympathies" (Rowton 1853: 409). In contrast to Byron, "the personification of passionate selfishness," Mrs. Norton's poetry conveys "unselfish" feeling and "universal" sympathies that extend beyond the self. The "force of expression" that characterizes Byron's poetry and defines his character is read as an expression of selflessness in Norton's poetry, making her into a character without a self. Selflessly, Norton's poetry lends itself to personification: instead of expressing her own person, she is characterized by the absence of personhood. If, as Andrew Elfenbein has argued, Byron was the model for a new authorial role as "personality" in the nineteenth century, Norton's circulation as a personality suggests a different model for nineteenth-century female authorship: her poetry calls into question our investment in such a persona and demonstrates how the poetess might come to personify the very problem of personification.[30]

This rhetorical problem has political implications, since the "personal" reading of Norton's poetry emerges at a time when women lost their claim to personhood upon entering into a marriage contract. Before the reform of property law in nineteenth-century England, married women could not own property in their own name and had no legal existence apart from their husbands; they occupied a no-man's-land, an impersonal category of nonpersons without entitlement to self-representation. The non-existence of women within a representational system that nevertheless produced the reality of their suffering informed Norton's lifelong campaign for legal reform, which she conducted through pamphlets and

---

[30] Elfenbein argues that "the selling of Byron established an unprecedented closeness between the author's image and his or her audience" (1995: 52), although I would add that a precedent for such identification was already established by the selling of women poets earlier in the century. Elfenbein focuses primarily on Byron as model for female authorship in the course of the century, and Mermin also notes that "in the 1820's and '30s Letitia Landon and Caroline Norton made poetic careers mostly with quasi-Byronic narratives" (1993: 8), although here, too, a reversal of perspective might allow us to see how Byron's poetic career is modeled on female authorship as well.

polemics in the popular press as well as in her novels and poems. "A married woman . . . is non-existent in law," Norton wrote in *English Laws for Women* (1854), presenting herself as an ironically representative case: "I was 'non-existent,' except for the purpose of suffering, as far as the law was concerned" (1978: 166). Dispossessed of property and a proper name, woman exists "for the purpose of suffering"; rather than representing herself, woman *suffers* representation. Norton's interrogation of the Sapphic persona can be understood in this context as well, as she extends the problem of identifying the poetess "herself" into a legal discourse that left married women unidentified: both in lyric and in law, she questions the implications of representing a woman who can only be represented as a nonperson.

Not unlike Christina Rossetti, who reflects on Sappho as an empty persona for the perpetuation of pain, Norton shows how woman is presented "for the purpose of suffering" by reflecting on previous representations of Sappho. But if, as I have suggested, Rossetti's Sappho is closely aligned with L. E. L., the most immediate precursor for Norton's Sappho is Felicia Hemans. The title of Norton's poem, "The Picture of Sappho," refers back to a long tradition of depicting Sappho, and it also responds more specifically to "The Last Song of Sappho," published by Hemans in 1834.[31] In her headnote to the poem, Hemans writes that it was inspired by a picture of Sappho: "Suggested by a beautiful sketch, the design of the younger Westmacott. It represents Sappho sitting on a rock above the sea, with her lyre cast at her feet. There is a desolate grace about the whole figure, which seems penetrated with the feeling of utter abandonment."[32] Hemans's poem was published without the sketch however, and it quickly displaces the claims of pictorial representation even while claiming to be derived from it. In the headnote, the phrase "it represents" slips from visual to verbal representation, as "it" could refer to either the sketch or the poem: what "there is" in the sketch is now only visible in the poem, which turns "the whole figure"—a mute portrait—into a figure for Sapphic voice. Thus "the feeling of utter abandonment" conveyed by the sketch is converted into an abandoned utterance that we may or may not attribute to Sappho, depending on whether we read the title as subjective or objective genitive: the last song "of" Sappho may be her own song, or a song about her, deliberately obscuring the source of the utterance.

---

[31] "The Last Song of Sappho" was first published in *National Lyrics, and Songs for Music* in 1834, the year before the death of Felicia Hemans, and reprinted posthumously in *Poetical Works* of 1839.

[32] The sketch to which Hemans refers is, most likely, a preliminary drawing for a sculpture; I have not been able to locate the sketch. However, since the poem was published without the sketch, it displaces pictorial representation of Sappho even while claiming to be derived from it.

The figure of voice in "The Last Song of Sappho" is created by a direct address to the sea, a lyric apostrophe that is sustained throughout the poem, beginning with its opening lines: "Sound on, thou dark unslumbering sea! / My dirge is in thy moan." Hovering ambiguously between "my dirge" and "thy moan," the sound of Sappho's voice is simultaneously projected into and out of the sea, which resounds in response to her. Through the second person address Sappho looks for release from first person utterance, as she exclaims in stanza 2: "Oh! let your secret caves be stirred, / And say, dark waters! will ye give me *peace?*" Echoed by the sea's secret caves and dark waters, Sappho's "I" would dissolve into the vocative "O," as she proclaims again in stanza 7: "—With a lone heart, a weary frame— / O restless deep! I come to make them thine!" This reciprocal echoing of a song both "mine" and "thine" is exemplified in the shift from "Oh!" to "O!" attempting to mediate between what Barbara Johnson (in her essay on "Apostrophe, Animation and Abortion") calls "the 'O' of the pure vocative, Jakobson's conative function, or the pure presencing of the second person, and the 'oh' of pure subjectivity, Jakobson's emotive function, or the pure presencing of the first person"[33] (Johnson 1987: 187). The apostrophe is structured by this mediation between the second person and the first person, indefinitely prolonging Sappho's last song by dissolving the solitary lyric subject into a more fluid state of being. The subjective "oh" thus appears in the final line of the poem, to express the desire of the lyric "I" for its own dissolution: "—*Alone* I come—oh! give me peace, dark sea!"

The suspension of Sapphic utterance leads Marlon Ross to conclude that "The Last Song of Sappho" is not a "reclaiming of self" but a blurring of the boundaries between selves, in order to create the possibility for sympathetic identification. "Sappho needs to be listened to and responded to," he observes (1989: 298). His reading of the poem makes Sappho into a model for the "affectional poetics" of Felicia Hemans: the second-person address invites a response in the reader, who might reclaim Sappho's song by giving voice to the poem. And yet, this appeal to Sapphic voice is ironically framed by the description of Sappho in the epigraph, "with her lyre cast at her feet," where she has already cast off the lyre and lost her voice. What is "suggested" by the painting and "seems penetrated" with feeling is suggestively animated by the sympathy that the

---

[33] In her essay "Apostrophe, Animation and Abortion," Johnson develops a theoretical argument about the gendering of apostrophe in recent abortion poems that I find useful for understanding the apostrophic structure of poems by nineteenth-century women poets (1987: 184–99). From a historical perspective, I would further suggest that the (de)animating effects of apostrophe and the difficulty of distinguishing between "I" and "you" are problems of personification that contemporary women poets have inherited from nineteenth-century sentimental lyric.

poem provokes; but it is still a dead persona. Rather than bringing Sappho to life, the lyric apostrophe proclaims her death, in a self-consciously abortive gesture that may explain why Byron was quick to dismiss Hemans as a poet "too stiltified and apostrophic" (1982: VII.324). But of course, the "stiltification" of the apostrophe is precisely the point of this poem, since Hemans's Sappho can claim voice only through the rhetorical performance of its dispossession. "The Last Song of Sappho" therefore provokes a response from the reader not unlike the response recorded by Hemans herself, after seeing a statue of Sappho: "Altogether, it seems to speak piercingly and sorrowfully of the nothingness of fame, at least to woman" (Chorley 1836: II.143). Here, too, what "seems to speak" is not a woman but an "it" that is animated by our sympathy, but only to bespeak its own nothingness: since fame (from the Greek verb φημί, "I speak") is derived from the act of speaking and being spoken about, it means nothing to "woman" because "she" does not speak.

Caroline Norton further meditates on "the nothingness of fame, at least to woman" in her own poem, "The Picture of Sappho," published six years after "The Last Song of Sappho." Reynolds suggests that Norton's poem "is probably, like Hemans's, based on Westmacott's picture, but in this case Norton writes herself into the poem as the viewer of the portrait and questions its likeness to life" (1996: 281). By assuming that Norton's poem is also based on Westmacott, however, we miss the opportunity to read it in relation to Hemans—to read Norton's poem, in other words, as a picture of the picture of the picture of Sappho. Sappho is placed within a regressive structure of representation, where "likeness to life" is no longer at issue; even more than Hemans, whose Sappho is suspended in a lyric apostrophe that displaces the picture of Sappho, Norton's poem suggests there is no real picture and no real Sappho. While the conflation of objective and subjective genitive in "The Last Song of Sappho" allows us to speculate how a song *about* Sappho might still belong *to* Sappho, "The Picture of Sappho" can be read as a more skeptical critique of the genitive in its title. What "The Picture of Sappho" picturing? What is it a picture *of*? Norton has been read as a poet "of refined sympathy and eye for the picturesque" (Robertson 1883: 243), but to my eye at least, there is a profoundly antipictorial impulse in Norton's poem; it is picturesque only to the extent that it pictures the problem of sympathetic identification with Sappho.

The affectional poetics of Hemans therefore lead directly into the sentimentalism of Norton, as the latter simultaneously repeats and empties out the former. If the Sappho of Hemans seems to speak in the first person by apostrophizing the sea, the opening stanza of Norton's poem apostrophizes the figure of Sappho itself in an even more "stiltified" apostrophe:

THOU! whose impassion'd face
The Painter loves to trace
Theme of the Sculptor's art and Poet's story—
How many a wand'ring thought
Thy loveliness hath brought,
Warming the heart with its imagined glory!

The act of apostrophizing gives face to the figure of Sappho in order to make it seem "impassion'd," a rhetorical gesture that is further thematized in the transition from "THOU!" to "Theme." As "Theme of Sculptor's art and Poet's story," Sappho becomes the object of representations that make her "imagined glory" sound ambiguous: merely imaginary, perhaps, and whose imagination is it anyway? The ambiguity of syntax in lines 4–5 raises this question, as it makes "thy loveliness" both subject and object of "many a wand'ring thought." Our desire to identify sympathetically with Sappho may be a way of "warming the heart," but it also contributes to "chilling that heart of flame" in stanza 7. We imagine Sappho as a living figure at the beginning of the poem, only to discover her death later on; indeed, our imagination of her presupposes her death.

Jonathan Culler points out that apostrophic poems often draw attention to the problematic structure of second-person address, by introducing a series of withdrawals, questions, or self-parodying gestures (1981: 143–44). The second stanza of Norton's poem accordingly moves from the vocative into an interrogation of "thou":

Yet, was it History's truth,
That tale of wasted youth,
Of endless grief, and Love forsaken pining?
What wert thou, thou whose woe
The old traditions show
With Fame's cold light around thee vainly shining?

These two questions present Sappho as an increasingly impossible personification, precariously poised at the point where the thematic turns rhetorical and the rhetorical turns thematic. The first question uses "of"—like the ironic genitive in the poem's title—to undo any claims to truth "about" Sappho. The second question—"What wert thou?—uses "what" as its grammatical subject in order to suspend claims to Sappho as a person. More questions follow in the next five stanzas, to make Sappho into an increasingly provisional persona: "Didst thou . . . sit?" (stanza 3); "Didst thou . . . yearn?" (stanza 5); "Didst thou . . . wait?" (stanza 6); "Didst thou . . . hide thyself?" (stanza 7). The separation of "didst thou" from the verb that completes has the effect of suspending personal agency in the poem; indeed, most of its action depends on participles that leave their subject in suspension, such as "thy heart was breaking," or "unwilling to believe thyself forsaken," or "thou wert in peace reposing!"

But in stanza 8, the poem breaks out of the interrogative mode and abandons the conditional verbs of the preceding stanzas: beginning with the exclamation "Yea," it seems to affirm the accumulation of conventional associations in order to make Sappho into the object of sympathy. Yet the euphemism for Sappho's death—answering the question "what wert thou" with the seemingly simple response "thou wert in peace"—cannot simply describe her as dead: as she was never alive to begin with, she doesn't die. She is doomed to be undead, or forever dying, recalling perhaps the title of Norton's earlier volume of poems, *The Undying One.* Sappho is suspended in the eternal repetition of "the tale they tell" about her, in stanza 9:

> Such is the tale they tell!
> Vain was thy beauty's spell—
> Vain all the praise thy song could still inspire—
> Though many a happy band
> Rung with less skilful hand
> The borrowed love-notes of thy echoing lyre.

The verbs here hover ambiguously between past and future. The line, "Vain all the praise thy song could still inspire," suggests that Sapphic song did indeed inspire praise at one time—however much in vain—and may inspire it again. At the same time, a pun on "still" suggests that Sappho's song—then as well as now—can only speak of its own silence, to inspire a poetic tradition predicated on the loss of voice. By the same logic, if "the borrowed love-notes of thy echoing lyre" have been "rung" in the past, they might be "rung" again in the future, but only "with less skilful hand" to acknowledge its own echoing and borrowing, rather than making a claim to Sapphic voice. Norton's poem therefore perpetuates a Sapphic tradition, to which it belongs, even while critiquing it.

It is possible, if we read the poem thematically, to interpret the final stanza as an attempt to distinguish between Sappho as literary persona and Sappho as woman, between "Poet's story" and "History's truth." But if we read the poem rhetorically, the final stanza also points to the problem of presenting woman except as yet another personification:

> FAME, to thy breaking heart
> No comfort could impart,
> In vain thy brow the laurel wreath was wearing;
> One grief and one alone
> Could bow thy bright head down—
> Thou wert a WOMAN, and wert left despairing!

What defines Sappho *as* a woman is less the love of Phaon (who is, by now, out of the picture) than the simple assertion that she *is* a woman. This circular logic assumes the being of woman by identifying her as a woman, and finds expression in the curious redoubling of the phrase "one grief and one alone"; likewise the doubled syntax of "thou wert . . . and wert" in the final line makes "woman" synonymous with "despairing," a participle that leaves her suspended, ready to fall again into a deadly repetition of the representation—any representation—which is the fate from which "The Picture of Sappho" cannot save her.

Unable to distinguish between "History" and "Poet's story," then, the final stanza registers the deeper irony of the question posed in stanza 2: "Was it History's Truth?" If initially we are tempted to ask the truth "about" Sappho, from the perspective of the final stanza we must ask again, what would be the truth "of" history? What truth, in other words, could history tell of Sappho except that "it"—her experience "as" a woman—cannot be represented within the inwardness of a subject? Because these are rhetorical questions to which history can make no answer, WOMAN is invoked at the end of the poem, in capital letters, as the very embodiment of this dilemma—or rather, its disembodied allegorical personification, and therefore not a person at all. Instead of picturing Sappho, Norton's poem therefore puts on display its own rhetorical performance, beginning with the emphatic invocation to "THOU!" and ending just as emphatically with the exclamation "WOMAN . . . !" In this performance of rhetorical pathos, "The Picture of Sappho" becomes an exemplary sentimental lyric: it questions the personification produced by its own apostrophe, evacuating the figure of Sappho even while asking us to identify with that vacuous figure.

I do not wish to argue, however, that the pathos of the poem—its *affect*—is merely rhetorical effect; the question it poses about "History's Truth" points to the persistence of certain historical effects. How different is "the tale they tell" about Sappho from the sad story of Norton's life? How might the emptiness of Sappho's fame reflect the defamation of Norton's character? Separated from a violent husband, robbed of her reputation, denied custody of her children, dispossessed of her property, slandered by the press, Norton herself also seems to personify suffering womanhood. It is a reading encouraged by biographies such as *The Life of Mrs. Norton, With Portraits* by Jane Perkins (1910), introducing Norton as "a personage whose reputation as a poetess and a writer stood much higher among our grandmothers than it does today . . . less as an author than as a beautiful, unfortunate woman, the target of a great deal of cruel scandal, ill remembered, but never quite forgotten" (xiii). Although the poetry is forgotten, being "too intimate a part of herself . . . to be expected to survive her," the poetic persona of Norton will survive, according to Perkins: "The lyric touch, too often wanting in her verses, is never lacking in her life; her own story, told in her own dramatic words, is her real contribution to the literature of her century" (xiii). However, the popular reception of Norton makes it difficult to distinguish between the lyric persona and the real woman; she proves a perfect poetess to the extent that her poems can be read as "her own story," and indeed, with every sensational twist and turn in the plot of that life story, Norton's poetry became more appealing to her contemporaries. "The last three or four years have made Mrs. Norton a greater writer than she was; she is deeper, plainer, truer," Lockhart comments in *The Quarterly Review* (1840: 376), and another reviewer in *A New Spirit of the Age* also praises her poems of 1840 as verses written "from the dictates of a human heart in all the eloquence of beauty and individuality" (Norton 1978: xv).

But what seems dictated from the heart turns out to be dictated by the law, as Norton's poetry is written from legal dictates that denied "the eloquence . . . of individuality" to Norton and to every married woman in English. In *English Laws for Women in the Nineteenth Century* (1854), Norton narrates all she has suffered under the law in the course of her marriage: "A mock-trial, in which I do not 'exist' for defence; a gross libel, in which I do not 'exist' for prosecution; a disposition of property, in which I do not 'exist' for my own rights or those of my children; a power of benefiting myself by literary labour, in which I do not 'exist' for the claim in my own copyrights. *That,* is the negative and neutralizing law, for married women in England" (Norton 1854: 167). The law is exercised negatively for women after the marriage contract, neutralizing their claim to any kind of ownership: legal rights, property rights, maternal rights, authorial rights, even the right to assert one's own existence. Norton can only assert her non-existence in prose that negates the "I," implicitly placing the first person in quotation marks as well: if I do not "exists" is it not also true that "I" does not exist? The "I" is not an original self entitled to self-possession but appears as a negated subject, already dispossessed of what it cannot properly own. The ironic assertion of the first person singular in this political treatise points to a similar rhetorical problem as the second person address to Sappho in Norton's poem, presenting an empty persona rather than representing a person. "The Picture of Sappho" therefore circulates in the context of other writing by Norton to demonstrate the dispossession of woman, and according to a logic that made Norton into a public persona as well, as she increasingly personified the plight of married women as nonpersons.

During the years immediately preceding the publication of "The Picture of Sappho," Norton started to write in support of reforming marriage laws. In the midst of her bitter custody battle, she found herself without proprietary rights and proper representation, as she laments in a letter to Mary Shelley from 1837: "The rights of property are the only rights really and efficiently protected; and the consideration of property the only one which weighs with the decision made in a court of justice."[34] Her response to this legal predicament was to send herself into circulation by publishing verse, semi-autobiographical fiction and polemical pamphlets that would appeal to popular sentiment, making Norton into a persona for sympathetic identification, if not a properly identifiable person. She describes to Mary Shelley a pamphlet written to intervene in parliamentary debates about maternal custody: "I finished my 'Observations on the Natural Claims of the Mother' last week, and it is now printing at Ridgway's. . . . I have ordered them to print now 500 copies as for *private* (!) circulation."[35] The ironies of circulating a "*private* (!)" self in public are not lost on Norton, especially if that self is said not to exist legally and has no legal say in the causes that most concern her. Nevertheless the pamphlet had real political effect in promoting the Bill for Infant Custody, introduced in 1837 but not passed until 1839. In the course of long debates, it was called "Mrs. Norton's Bill" by her opponents, who attacked the bill by attacking her character: an *ad hominem* attack that was ironically *ad feminam*, turning Norton into the very personification of the bill without recognizing her as a person to be represented by the bill.

Norton responded to such personal attacks with another pamphlet, "A Plain Letter to the Lord Chancellor on the Infant Custody Bill," published in 1839 under the pseudonym of Pearce Stevenson. Here Norton represents herself in the third person, calling attention to the fact that a woman is unable to defend herself in the first person: "She can make no defence, although *hers* is the character at issue" (Norton 1978: 9). Only by assuming a male pseudonym can Norton reconstruct her character and claim authority to narrate "the real History" of the bill, in order to refute innuendos and accusations about its "secret History" in her own personal story. The pamphlet is thus presented as a "Plain Letter," a seemingly impersonal, objective account that is written to dispel "the ridiculous doubt whether Mrs. Norton used her woman's tears and woman's arguments" to influence parliament and public opinion (90). But the pamphlet still makes a "feminine" appeal to sentiment, as it emphasizes the precarious position of women in nineteenth-century England: even

---

[34] The letter to Mary Shelley is dated January 5, 1837, and excerpted in Perkins 1910: 133–36. Norton's grievance about maternal custody is immediately followed by a meditation on the memoir of Felicia Hemans (published in the previous year by Chorley). "I also was much struck and affected by the simple story conveyed in all Mrs. Hemans's letters," Norton writes (134), whose identification with the "true mother's spirit" of Hemans and her troubled marriage suggests another reason for aligning the two poetesses.

[35] Quoted in Perkins 1910: 133. Norton's pamphlet was published in 1837, but under a different title: *The Separation of Mother and Child by the Law of Custody of Infants Considered.*

the most proper woman, whose propriety is not in question, lacks a proper name. Not only does she lose her name in marriage, but the word *woman* itself is but an inflected variant of man: we are asked to "consider the position of the *woman*" in relation to the man (90), to reflect on "*woman's nature*" as distinct from man (97), to question what man will "inflict on a *woman*" (93) and to wonder why "the word *woman* signifies a *bad woman*" (95). Italics are used to draw attention to the word *woman,* like the emphatic capital letters of "WOMAN" left despairing at the end of "The Picture of Sappho." Composed around the same time, both the pamphlet and the poem turn *woman* into a personified abstraction, the former to construct a polemical argument about the namelessness of women and the latter to perform that polemical claim in rhetorical form, by interrogating the name of Sappho.

By presenting herself simultaneously as female victim (Mrs. Norton) and male defender (Pearce Stevenson) in "A Plain Letter," Norton anticipates the complex rhetorical maneuvers in *English Laws for Women in the Ninteeenth Century,* published fifteen years later. Norton's various strategies in the public presentation of her case have been analyzed by Mary Poovey, who points out that Norton draws on a generic melodramatic script with a familiar cast of characters including victimized woman, villain, and avenger. "When Caroline Norton dramatized her history in the form of a melodrama, she capitalized on the greater latitude granted literature to explore these mattters and she sought to enlist her reader's sympathies," Poovey observes (1988: 83). In this appeal to sympathy, however, Norton's rhetoric depends as much on the conventions of nineteenth-century sentimental lyric as on Victorian melodrama. In *English Laws* she narrates her story in the first person, to bear witness to her suffering: "My history *is real,*" she insists, adding disingenuously: "I know there is not poetry in it to attract you" (1978: 173). Nevertheless her rhetorical performance, designed to attract the sentimental reader, takes the form of a carefully contrived anaphora that elevates her story into poetry: "I *really* wept and suffered in my early youth . . . . I *really* suffered the extremity . . . I *really* lost my young children . . . I *really* have gone through much, that if it were invented would move you" (173). The refusal of literary "invention" is a sentimental convention, creating the illusion of immediate sympathetic identification that would leave readers weeping, like the reader moved to tears by the poetess in the frontispiece.

In her insistence on what she *really* suffered, Norton returns us to the question posed by "The Picture of Sappho," where Sappho's suspension between "Poet's story" and "History's truth" leaves us unable to distinguish between the two: either way, in the performance of her suffering, the woman loses ground. In addition to re-posing the question of Sappho's leap, Norton even concludes *English Laws* in a distinctly Sapphic pose: "Or, do not think at all about me; forget by whose story this appeal was illustrated . . . and let *my* part in this, be only as a voice borne by the wind—as a cry coming over the waves from a shipwreck, to where you stand safe on the shore—and which you turn and listen to, not for the sake of those who call,—you do not know them,—but because it is a cry for HELP" (175). The heightened rhetoric of her treatise leads, in the last sentence, to a lyric cry detached from its source: no longer Norton's story narrated by herself, but "a voice borne by the wind" and "coming over the waves" to provoke a sympathetic response in the listener standing safely on shore. Meanwhile the figure of Norton seems to dissolve like Sappho into the sea, losing ground in a final "cry for HELP." This is a self-conscious performance of the female complaint, a literary genre derived from Ovid's *Heroides* and defined by Lauren Berlant as "an aesthetic 'witnessing' of injury" that becomes an influential paradigm for a female public discourse (Berlant 1988: 243).[36] Ending with this performative plea, the treatise turns Norton into a poetic persona with a political vocation, calling out for all the married women who remain voiceless, nameless, and helpless before the injustices of the law.

According to Poovey, "Norton was able to identify these injustices because she had personally endured them, but being able to voice them in such explicitly political terms required transforming herself from the private sufferer of private wrongs into an articulate spokesperson in the public sphere" (1988: 64). While Poovey develops a narrative model for "Norton's self-authorization" (65) alongside the model of melodrama, I would argue that Norton's circulation in the public sphere depends even more on a lyric model, precisely because sentimental lyric is the genre for personifying the poetess as "private sufferer of private wrongs." Without presenting herself in "explicitly political terms," the poetess has the implicitly political function of representing public concerns as if they were private, demonstrating the ideological work of lyric as well as the ideological work of gender in mid-Victorian England. To become "an articulate spokesperson in the public sphere," Norton is transformed not *from* but *into* "the private sufferer," a lyric persona that complicates the politics of voice in Poovey's account. The political intervention made by Norton is to "voice" injustices through the performance of voice itself as a figure, the "cry for HELP" that seems personal but is detached from the

---

[36] In Berlant's argument, the female complaint is a genre of contested discourse situated "in the space between a sexual politics that threatens structures of patriarchal authority and a sentimentality that confirms the inevitability of the speaker's powerlessness" (Berlant 1990: 244). Although Berlant tends to emphasize the limitations of this form of female public discourse as "an oppositional utterance that declares its limits in its very saying" (244), she adds in a note that "the witnessing and even documentary value of the female complaint depends entirely on the context of its inception and the context of its utterance" (257).

expression of any particular person. Indeed, if this lyric outcry served to provoke legislative reform, it was not by speaking for women as such but, as Poovey herself has argued, to advance the cause of reformers concerned with eliminating structural contradictions in England's legal system.

Thus Norton's "voice" was readily borrowed by others when parliament debated a bill on the reform of marriage and divorce laws, first proposed by Lord Chancellor Cranworth in 1854 and finally approved in the 1857 Matrimonial Causes Act. In the interval, Norton published "A Letter to the Queen on Lord Chancellor Cranworth's Marriage and Divorce Bill" (1855), a seemingly personal plea that circulated for the purposes of being read in public. Lord Lyndhurst quoted passages from Norton in his speech to parliament and Lord Brougham considered the letter "as clever a thing as ever was written" (Perkins 1910: 248–49). By addressing the queen directly in the second person, Norton cleverly constructs a voice in the first person singular that testifies to its own non-existence and draws attention to the irony that "married women shall be 'non-existent' in a country governed by a female Sovereign" (1855: 3–4). While the Queen embodies the possibility of sovereign womanhood, she does so only symbolically, and indeed the very existence of the "Queen" (an abstract category that exists apart from the woman who is queen) reinforces the fact that all other married women are non-existent. Thus, at the beginning of the letter, Norton identifies herself "as one who has grievously suffered, and is still suffering, under the present imperfect state of the law" (2), whereas the Queen, by contrast, is identified at the end of the letter as "the one woman in England who *cannot* suffer wrong" (154). Although both are women, the difference between them is that one can claim a proper name and a proprietary self, while the other cannot.

Norton's appeal to the queen therefore concerns the legal status of the signature: while this letter is signed in her own name—no longer with a pseudonym, unlike the earlier letter of "Pearce Stevenson"—Norton demonstrates that she can never "own" her signature. The contract she signed with her estranged husband to settle debts is invalid; her family inheritance is in his name; the copyright to her works belongs to him. Everything she writes, in other words, can be reappropriated by her husband as his own personal property, just as her name ultimately still belongs to him. The only way to constitute herself as a writer, then, is not by claiming her rights but by proclaiming "the fact of having suffered wrong": "I combine, with the fact of having suffered wrong, the power to comment on and explain the cause of that wrong; which few women are able to do. For *this*, I believe, God gave me the power of writing. . . . If I were to die tomorrow, it would still be a satisfaction to me that I had so striven. Meanwhile, my husband has a legal lien (as he has publicly proved), on the copyright of my works. Let him claim the copyright of

THIS" (153). The pathos of "*this*"—the power of writing, to bear testimony to how women suffer—is that Norton's claim to female authorship ultimately produces THIS—a document that cannot belong to her because she does not own the copyright. To mediate between these two positions—the claim to *this* and the disowning of THIS—Norton strikes another Sapphic pose, midway through the passage: "If I were to die tomorrow. . . . " Here she anticipates a death that might validate her writing after all, for although she admits that her letter to the Queen is "Only A Women's Pamphlet" (154), it ends with a signature that turns Norton's non-existence into a form of literary survival. At a historical moment when women's signatures have no historical effect, in "a free nation, where, with a Queen on the throne, all other married women are legally NON-EXISTENT," as she writes at the end of the letter, she must sign in the name of her husband: "I remain . . . CAROLINE ELIZABETH SARAH NOR-TON" (155). By underscoring the signature itself, Norton leaves written evidence of being NON-EXISTENT: like Sappho she is left a WOMAN and despairing, a name that remains, but whose historical effects can only be traced—yet again—in the postscript.

Woman's Cause

"The Honorable Mrs. Norton" became a famous name on both sides of the Atlantic, even and especially if that signature was not properly speaking her own, since it might then be reappropriated in the name of women in general. She was considered one of the primary poetesses in the generation after Hemans and L. E. L., so popular that poems were reprinted in her name in America, without her authorization and sometimes even without her authorship.[37] Thus in 1841, one year after Lockhart's influential essay on "Modern English Poetesses," Edgar Allan Poe published a review in an American periodical proclaiming Norton to be "unquestionably,—since the death of Mrs. Hemans, the queen of English song" (1841: 93). In Norton's verse, Poe discerns a poetic style that he actively

---

[37] In response to unauthorized reprints of her poetry in the American market, Norton comments wrily: "A compliment has been late paid me on the other side of the Atlantic, which I confess I have received very unwillingly. I allude to the printing of my published poem ["The Dream"] in an American paper, a huge mammoth, a very boa-constrictor of a paper, which has contrived to swallow it all. Now anxious as I naturally am to become acquainted with, and popular among, my friends in 'the Far West,' yet, if it so pleased them, I could wish to be more formally introduced." Norton further notes that poems not her own have been circulating in her name as well: "Of a still more equivocal nature is the compliment (if compliment it can be called) of printing and publishing poems as mine which are not from my pen, and of whose authorship I know nothing" (Perkins 1910: 177).

patronizes (in every sense) among American poetesses as well.[38] "Mrs. Norton," he writes, "possesses one quality which distinguishes her above all other writers, in this or in any tongue—we mean in giving utterance to, what is emphatically, *the poetry of woman*" (94). Whether this phrase is to be read as subjective or objective genitive remains unclear, however, as Poe continues, "Every line betrays the woman—each verse breathes the tender, the melting, the peculiar eloquence of the sex. Scarcely a page, moreover, occurs . . . which does not bear testimony to woman's suffering and worth" (94). Is woman the subject or the object of "*the poetry of woman*"? She is made synonymous with the experience and the expression of suffering, which she must bear in order to "bear testimony" to her worth; this is "the peculiar eloquence of the sex," the ability to turn pain into poetry. It would seem that "every line betrays the woman," not only because Norton's poetry portrays Norton in particular or woman in general, but because the woman is also betrayed by her own eloquence: every line she writes prolongs the pain that defines her womanhood. If by definition "the woman" must suffer, then "emphatically, *the poetry of woman*" is both the performance and the perpetuation of that suffering.

Of course, this rhetoric of suffering womanhood is only too familiar in mid-nineteenth-century America. Extending her discussion of the female complaint into American cultural history, Berlant argues that a popular nineteenth-century discourse of feminized sentimentality evolved and revolved around a generic figure, "the female woman," whose testimony of pain was commodified for various kinds of sympathetic identification. As "a mode of abstraction that has no a priori political implications for the power of women," (Berlant 1992: 270) the female complaint was nevertheless deployed for various political purposes, ranging from conservative to radical strategies for the domestication, reformation, or emancipation of "woman." In the writing of Fanny Fern, Berlant discerns another strategic response to this sentimental abstraction, "not by rendering women's experience generic, but by expressing the frustration of *being* generic" (278). According to Berlant, Fern creates the possibility of a "punctuated identification," allowing the reader to identify with disconnected and contradictory points in her prose, rather than looking for narrative exemplification. Virginia Jackson further argues that this formal structure of identification is precisely the point of women's sentimental lyric, a genre rather strikingly omitted from Berlant's account of female sentimentalism, given the popularity of the genre for performing the female complaint.[39] Indeed, what Poe calls "*the poetry of woman*" would seem

---

[38] On Poe's construction of "The Poetess," see Richards 1999, part of her book in progress on Poe's circle of poetesses and the cultural forms of American poetry.

[39] To clarify the idea of "punctuated identification," Berlant argues that Fern's manipulation of the female complaint "installs woman's writing as a part of an ongoing pedagogy

to be the performance of that formal structure, the very form of "the form of sentiment."

There are important points of convergence, then, between the Victorian Poetess and the nineteenth-century American Poetess, and surely no reading of "Victorian Sappho" could proceed without acknowledging that the Sapphic (non)persona circulated widely in America as well as England. A long line of American Sapphos has been traced by Emily Stipes Watts (1977: 76–86), and Cheryl Walker also observes that "after Hemans's poetry began to be published in this country in the early nineteenth century, American women poets started seeing their work in terms of a line of women writers going all the way back to Sappho" (1982: 27). Of course the exchange between British and American poetesses is not a single line of influence but a continual crossing and transformation of the conventions associated with nineteenth-century sentimental lyric, as women on both sides of the Atlantic turn to Sappho to perform the pathos of "woman" as an empty figure. Notwithstanding its vacuity, that figure is increasingly invoked in woman's cause toward the end of the century, as feminist movements in both England and America discovered in Sappho a progressive ideal of womanhood that could be projected into futurity. In the concluding pages of this chapter, I suggest how this narrative of progress—a legacy with us, still, in twentieth-century Anglo-American feminist readings of nineteenth-century Anglo-American women poets—is also an infinite regress, a falling back through history toward a moment in the (future) past, when Sappho is yet again lost.

Out of many American Sapphos, I would like to consider the example of Elizabeth Oakes Smith, born Elizabeth Prince in 1806 and married to the American writer Seba Smith in 1823, at the age of sixteen and "unfit for the occasion," as she later wrote in her autobiography (Wyman 1924: 44). She had aspired to become a teacher of girls, a career that would elevate not only her pupils but herself to a higher womanly ideal through

---

about how to negotiate the contested life of femininity. Most important, her witnessing of bourgeois feminine sensibility is here raised to a hermeneutic at the level of the *punctum:* it is the point to which the author and reader of the female sentimental text will return" (Berlant 1992: 278). By posing the question of identification as a "hermeneutic," Berlant comes close to articulating the formal questions that define sentimental lyric as a genre, but her emphasis is on prose rather than poetry. The question of genre is central in Jackson's formulation of "the literature of misery," as she questions the exclusion of sentimental lyric from Berlant's discussion of "the female complaint" and (more generally) from recent debates about sentimentalism and gender in antebellum culture. In *Dickinson's Misery,* Jackson makes a strong argument for lyric as "the most visible stage for midnineteenth-century sentimental exchange" and demonstrates how gender and genre are implicated in the rhetorical performance of sentiment to produce a "rhetorical pathos." On the cultural work performed by the American poetess in the realm of domestic literary sentiment, see also Loeffelholz 1997.

education. Instead she fell into an unhappy marriage, an "occasion" that determined the course of her lifelong activism as a feminist and a writer, as she wrote in a wide range of literary genres—poetry, fiction, journalism, criticism—to support her family, and continued lecturing in support of women's higher education as well. Like Caroline Norton, she published polemics against the doctrine of marital coverture in the American legal system, which also merged the legal existence of the wife with the husband and prevented married women from keeping property in their own name. As an eloquent spokeswoman for women's rights in America, she became a pre-eminent woman in her own right: "Seldom has a woman in any age acquired such ascendancy by the mere force of a powerful intellect," the statesman Henry Clay said in her behalf (Wyman 1924: 9).[40]

But the ascendancy of Oakes Smith should also be understood in terms of a historical descent or decline, framed in her own writing according to the conventions of sentimental texts, which—if we follow Berlant's argument about the female woman—"tended to see the relation between the historical particular and the transcendental woman as a relation of fallen to fulfilled sign" (269). By subscribing to the idea of a transcendental woman as a "fulfilled sign" that would transcend history, Oakes Smith repeatedly inscribes the particular woman in history (including the story she writes of her own life) as an already "fallen sign," inevitably falling from the ideal. In *Woman and Her Needs,* a series of feminist lectures published in 1851, Oakes Smith names *Woman* with a capital *W* as the ideal word, to which the world must aspire: "The world needs the admixture of Woman thought in its affairs; a deep, free, woman-souled utterance is *needed*" (1974:19). The world "needs" Woman because history finds its fulfillment in that word, and "woman-souled utterance" (such as her own, perhaps) is "*needed*" because it would give form to "Woman thought."

Again, it is not clear whether such utterance (like "giving utterance to, what is emphatically, *the poetry of woman,*" in Poe's phrase) would define "Woman" as subject or object, or whether "thought" is the act of thinking or being thought about, or whether it is even possible to think "Woman thought" in the present tense. While *Woman and Her Needs* proclaims the need (the many needs or purposes) for Woman in the world, it is also a plea for the needs of women in a world where Woman does not yet exist. Indeed, women have fallen from the ideal of Woman: "The majority of women in society are suffering in the absence of wholesome,

---

[40] I have learned much from recent work on Elizabeth Oakes Smith by Virginia Jackson and Eliza Richards; it is because of their archival expertise and critical insights that I realized the relevance of this very famous yet "forgotten" American poetess to my argument about Victorian poetesses.

earnest, invigorating subjects of thought," Oakes Smith believes (17), and because they are prevented from thinking, "Woman has stooped from her high place" (19) and "occupies a false position" (49). Only by taking measure of the distance between the particular historical woman and the transcendental Woman can women ascend to a higher position: such women, she writes, are "the worthy to be called Woman" (13). Their occupation is the amelioration of womanhood, a vocation or calling that will allow them "to be called" Woman, but only as a projection into the future, by means of an infinitive.

The rise and fall of Woman is embodied (predictably enough) in the figure of Sappho. In 1858 Oakes Smith begins an essay—a review of *Sappho, a Tragedy in Five Acts, After the German of Grillparzer, Translated by Edda Middleton*[41]—with a meditation on Sappho as one of the great names in history, and "the most wonderful woman of any time or place":

> Hazlett [sic], in speaking of the great names which have come down the steeps of time, says, "Those must have been great men whose shadows extend so far." The remark applies as well to a woman, and most especially to one whose shadow covers more than two thousand years of time and space. Sappho was, without doubt the most wonderful woman of any time or place—beautiful, impassioned, and inspired. Tradition makes her unfortunate also. We do not believe in this, because we do not believe that poets who sing mournfully are necessarily sad at heart. Weighed by their genius they must be; but their wailing cadences of love unrequited, do but show the depths of their passionateness, which no human ministry can ever reach; they rejoice with superhuman joy, and their sorrow in like manner is unearthly in kind. (1858: 141)

The descent of Sappho—as she "comes down the steeps of time" and sings in "wailing cadences" to show "the depth" of passion—is also the means of her transcendence: her song can be sublimated into "superhuman joy" because her "unearthly" sorrow never touches ground, as if in falling ever downward she is also falling upward. The sublime Sappho therefore has a destiny quite apart from Phaon, who is but an earthly being. "Whether Sappho ever loved a youth named Phaon or not is of little moment," Oakes Smith writes, because the genius of Sappho transcends her own historical moment: "Full up to her own time was she in thought, and infinitely beyond hers and ours also in inspiration" (141).

Oakes Smith draws her inspired vision of Sappho from an English translation of the German play by Franz Grillparzer, who rewrote the

---

[41] I am grateful to Eliza Richards for sharing with me the clipping of the review essay on Sappho, published anonymously by Oakes Smith in *Emerson's Magazine and Putnam's Monthly* (August 1858: 141–45); I thank Jean Borger and Lee Behlman for their persistence in tracking down the citation.

Ovidian narrative as a Romantic tragedy.[42] Oakes Smith admires this idealized drama because it shows that women "weighed by their genius" can be raised to new heights. From her perspective, the betrayal of Sappho by Phaon ("for whose dear sake she had proposed to live a simple life, and strike the lyre henceforth to 'Single praise of still domestic joy,'" 142) ultimately saves Sappho from betraying her own genius. Sappho gives up the songs of domesticated womanhood ("she is no longer the suffering woman," 142) in order to endure more heroic agonies and, ultimately, to die a sublime death in Grillparzer's tragedy:

> Sappho, when she ceases to complain; when she submits to her fate, is grand and heroic; she sweeps across the page, as we see her cross the horizon of the ages, a beautiful phantom, a hint of the greatness of which the sex may be capable; she is divested of all that is unpoetic—all that weighs her to earth, and approaches the gods. She . . . who would for love's dear sake forget the song of the nightingale and the flight of the eagle, and sit like a household deity in the shadow of the hearthstone, finds herself suddenly compelled to her own sphere—forced up the hights [sic] of renown; compelled to strike her golden lyre to the sharp cadences, the penetrating numbers of the unattained. (143)

As Oakes Smith envisions her sweeping "across the page" and "cross the horizon," Sappho is the dramatic embodiment of a chiasmus, the crossing of two contrary movements, simultaneously upward and downward. Sappho rises above "all that weighs her to earth" and soars beyond the domestic sphere "to her own sphere," the pure air of poetry. Yet it is only by bowing down ("when she submits to her fate") that she can be "forced up" to those heights, where she is "compelled" to perform the "sharp cadences" of a never-ending fall, sending her higher and higher yet forever falling short of "the unattained." Thus Sappho is fated to rise by falling, according to a paradox not unlike Oakes Smith's invocation of "the worthy to be called Woman" in *Woman and Her Needs*. What Woman is "to be called" in the future is recalled through Sappho, the prophetic projection of "a beautiful phantom" that gives "a hint of the greatness of which the sex may be capable."

By reading Grillparzer's attempt to give dramatic form to the lyric persona of Sappho, Oakes Smith dramatizes her own reading of the true

---

[42] Grillparzer's *Sappho,* which first appeared in German in 1818, inspired various English translations and imitations by nineteenth-century women poets. In addition to the translation published by Edda Middleton in 1858, Ellen Frothingham published a translation in 1876, and Estelle Lewis (known as "Stella" and associated with Poe, until she left America to live in London) wrote a popular play entitled *Sappho: A Tragedy in Five Acts* (first edition in 1875, sixth edition in 1881). Stuart Curran has also drawn my attention to Catherine Grace Garnett's *Sappho,* a Romantic closet drama published in 1824 and now available electronically through the Brown Women Writer's Project.

woman poet. Although this phantom of Woman thought is only a shadow of the past and a hint of what yet to come, in Grillparzer's drama Oakes Smith discovers "touches of rare thought and beautiful insights, making the Sappho of Grillparzer our Sappho for the time being" (141). To make her into "our Sappho" means that she is no longer "the Sappho of Grillparzer," however, but a Sappho who belongs to everyone "for the time being," in a long historical succession of Sapphos. Oakes Smith emphasizes the temporal mediation of the figure, since it is through her version of Middleton's version of Grillparzer's version of previous versions that the story of Sappho can be read "as if" it has just happened: "The drama wears so much the air of verisimilitude that we read the record of passion and sorrow as if it were a tale of yesterday, though twenty-five centuries, have each in turn taken up the sad cadence of the sorrows and the glories of Sappho" (144). Not only is the "verisimilitude" of Grillparzer's drama confirmed by Sappho's decline over twenty-five centuries (a historical declension that makes "the Sappho" into his Sappho, her Sappho, our Sappho, all Sapphos), but the perpetual performance of this decline makes Sappho very similar to women poets in the nineteenth century, having "each in turn taken up the sad cadence" in order to repeat the fall of Sappho.

That "sad cadence" is taken up in turn by Oakes Smith as well, who represents Sappho's drama "as if it were a tale of yesterday" in the cadences of her own prose and concludes her essay with a poem. "In connection with the story of Sappho we subjoin an ode written by ourself, as not inappropriate to the occasion," she writes in her final sentence and then reprints her "Ode to Sappho," written and published a decade earlier.[43] Thus, in a characteristic switch of her argument from prose into poetry, Oakes Smith turns Middleton's translation of Grillparzer's translation of Sappho's story into an occasion for her own lyric performance: another fall. In her ode, Sappho seems to sweep across the page again, falling from line to line and strophe to strophe:

Ode to Sappho

Bright, glowing Sappho! child of love and song!
Adown the blueness of long distant years
Beams forth thy glorious shape, and steals along
Thy melting tones, beguiling us to tears.
Thou priestess of great hearts,
Thrilled with the secret fire
By which a god imparts
The anguish of desire—

---

[43] "Ode to Sappho" by Elizabeth Oakes Smith was published in Griswold 1848: 189, and reprinted in its entirety by Oakes Smith at the end of her 1858 essay on Sappho.

For meaner souls be mean content—
Thine was a higher element.

Over Leucadia's rock thou leanest yet,
   With thy wild song, and all thy locks outspread;
The stars are in thine eyes, the moon hath set—
   The night dew falls upon thy radiant head;
     And thy resounding lyre—
       Ah! not so wildly sway:
     Thy soulful lips inspire
       And steal our hearts away!
   Swanlike and beautiful, thy dirge
   Still moans along the Aegean surge.

No unrequited love filled thy lone heart,
   But thine infinitude did on thee weigh,
And all the wildness of despair impart,
   Stealing the down from hope's own wing away.
     Couldst thou not suffer on,
       Bearing the direful pang,
     While thy melodious tone
       Through wondering cities rang?
   Couldst thou not bear thy godlike grief,
   In godlike utterance find relief?

Devotion, fervor, might upon thee wait:
   But what were these to thine? all cold and chill,
And left thy burning heart but desolate;
   Thy wondrous beauty with despair might fill
     The worshipper who bent
       Entranced at thy feet:
     Too affluent the dower lent
       Where song and beauty meet!
   Consumed by a Promethean fire
   Wert thou, O daughter of the lyre.

Alone, above Leucadia's wave art thou,
   Most beautiful, most gifted, yet alone!
Ah! what to thee the crown from Pindar's brow?
   What the loud plaudit and the garlands thrown
     By the enraptured throng,
       When thou in matchless grace
     Didst move with lyre and song,
       And monarchs gave thee place?
   What hast thou left, proud one? what token?
   Alas! a lyre and heart—both broken!

What was previously narrated by Oakes Smith in her essay as "the despair and the catastrophe of the Leucadian leap" (141) is now lyricized in a long apostrophe, suspending Sappho "over Leucadia's rock" and "above Leucadia's wave." She is an ethereal "glorious shape" that rises up to "a higher element," transcending the world in an upward movement. Yet she is also a figure for lyric descent, invoked as "child *of* song" and "daughter *of* the lyre," descending "adown the blueness of long distant years" and weighed down by her infinitude: "thine infinitude did on thee weigh." This figure descends through history by forever falling forward ("thou leanest yet") and leaving the echoing sounds from "thy resounding lyre" in her wake: "thy dirge / Still moans along the Aegean surge." Of course "still" also refers to the silencing of her song, as Sappho can only be apostrophized in the past tense: "Consumed by a Promethean fire / Wert thou, O daughter of the lyre." If Sappho is the embodiment of "Woman thought"—a female Prometheus, always thinking ahead of her time—she is also doomed to be consumed by a fire that she has stolen from the gods. Like Prometheus, she finds no relief in the "godlike utterance" of her "godlike grief," which is passed along like a torch over the years: Sappho "beams forth" through time, and as her song "steals along" (in stanza 1) each time it will "steal our hearts away" (in stanza 2). Sapphic song, it would seem, does not properly belong to Sappho but is the stealing of something already stolen, perpetuating a loss that leads to the total evacuation of the final stanza, where nothing is left of Sappho but an empty token: "Alas! a lyre and heart—both broken!"

This dispossession of Sappho is contrasted with the "crown from Pindar's brow," bequeathed on the poet celebrating victory within the tradition of the epinician ode. In reviewing Grillparzer's drama, Oakes Smith especially admires the opening scene where Sappho enters as a "Laureat," wearing a laureled crown after winning a poetic victory: "The scene opens with the triumphal return of the poet, (we never use the feminine terminations as applied to mind) crowned as victor from the Olympic festivals," Oakes Smith writes (141). She refuses the term *poetess* to describe Sappho and later insists, again, that "the true woman poet sings irrespective of sex . . . as if she were lavishing the fondness of a man upon some ideal subject" (144). But her own "Ode to Sappho" seems to fall short of this ideal, as it performs the "feminine termination" of Sappho as a poetess, after all. In the final stanza, the plaudits and garlands conferred on her prove meaningless within a Sapphic tradition where song is the transference of loss: not a triumphant act of naming a victor, but the proclamation of a failure, a falling-away from the proper name. Just as Oakes Smith terminates her essay on the word *occasion*, her ode to Sappho terminates in a falling cadence and a feminine rhyme: an anti-epinician gesture that turns the ode into the occasion for a dirge, catastrophically un-naming Sappho in the very act of apostrophizing her.

By concluding her review of Grillparzer with her own poem, Oakes Smith retraces the trajectory of all poetesses falling in Sappho's wake: the repetition produces a generic figure, not for "expressing the frustration of *being* generic" (as Berlant reads the female complaint) but for performing the endless reproduction of the figure itself (as Jackson reads the literature of misery). Oakes Smith emphasizes the reproducibility of the figure at the end of her review of Middleton's book: she makes a point of praising the "splendid" portrait of Sappho, "beautifully engraved on steel" in the frontispiece, which turns out to be a copy of the frontispiece in Mary Cowden Clarke's *World-Noted Women* (figure 10), and she also praises the typography of the book as "a fine specimen of the mechanic arts of the country." While this compliment to American publishing is a conventional gesture, it serves a rhetorical purpose in pointing to Sappho as a nonoriginal figure, a figure that can be mechanically reproduced in engraving or typography, and even anonymously reprinted, as Oakes Smith reprints her own "Ode to Sappho" without a name, as well. "It must be gratifying to an author to be so handsomely presented to the eye of the public," Oakes Smith concludes at the end of her review (144). But who, in this age of mechanical reproduction, is the author? Sappho? Ovid? Grillparzer? Middleton? Oakes Smith? The authorial "I" presented to the public eye circulates as a cipher, "an author" who is not named. To invoke Sappho is therefore to invoke an empty figure; like the "woman-souled utterance" that Oakes Smith anticipates in *Woman and Her Needs,* the prophetic Sapphic utterance that is needed to bring Woman into being also evacuates that being.

Nevertheless the prospect of re-imagining Woman in the name of Sappho is a recurring theme in nineteenth-century Anglo-American feminism: Sappho is made into a woman's cause, simultaneously named *in* the cause of women and *as* the cause of Woman. In her study of feminism and the category of "women" in history (appropriately titled in the interrogative, *Am I That Name?*), Denise Riley argues that feminist movements have always played out the indeterminacy of "women," even while laying claim to this category as foundational: the history of feminism is best understood as "a struggle against over-zealous identifications," since "feminism must negotiate the quicksands of 'women' which will not allow it to settle on either identities or counter-identities, but which condemn it to an incessant striving for a brief foothold" (Riley 1988: 5). If Sappho is repeatedly invoked as a placeholder for "Woman" by American and British feminists, it is because the figure loses its footing: in the "brief foothold" before she falls again, Sappho lends herself to fundamentally different claims about women within nineteenth-century debates on womanhood.

The British feminist Mary Catherine Hume, for example, demonstrates how Sappho becomes an increasingly contested figure within the context of the Victorian Woman Question.[44] In 1862 Hume published a Sappho poem suggested by a statue of Sappho in order to address—even more explicitly than the poems of Felicia Hemans or Caroline Norton, also suggested by pictures of Sappho—the problem of sympathetic identification with the Sapphic figure.[45] The poem is written in Miltonic blank verse, and by justifying the ways of god to woman, it seeks to convert Sappho's despair into the hope that Victorian women will become "happier Christian Sapphos" who "find in the bitterest cup, not death—but life!" But to make this future promise at the end of her poem, Hume begins by meditating on past representations of Sappho, and in particular a marble statue that is apostrophized in the opening lines:

> MARVELLOUS SAPPHO! Triumph of the art
> That wakes a soul in marble! The crushed heart
> Of woman, in her utterest hopelessness
> Looks forth in thee—nay! looks not forth;—we guess,
> We feel it, in this numb collapse of life,
> O'ertaxed by love's last agony. The strife
> Is over now; the very consciousness
> Of anguish, baffled in its own excess,
> Fades from the brow and vacant-closing eye;
> The lip, still quivering with a last-drawn sigh
> Involuntary; the low-drooping head,
> (Not bowed, but drooping) lax, ungarlanded;
> The hand, loose-lying on the slackened knee,
> Yea, but each slight, soft, nerveless curve to see,
> Who could misread thy story? Who mistake
> Exhaustion's apathy?—from which to wake
> Is but despair!—and that last, fatal leap!

The "MARVELLOUS SAPPHO" here addressed is mediated by representation in another medium: not a woman but a name attributed to a statue that is a "triumph" of art, precisely because it displays "the crushed heart / Of woman." Projected into this figure is the dejection of woman, in "utterest

---

[44] Susan Brown offers an excellent account of Victorian feminist poetics through the example of Hume (Brown 1994). On Sappho's association with shifting and contested constructions of the Poetess in the Victorian period, see also Brown's essay, "The Victorian Poetess" in *The Cambridge Companion to Victorian Poetry*, ed. Joseph Bristow (Cambridge: Cambridge University Press, forthcoming).

[45] "Sappho; A Poem, by Mary C. Hume, Reprinted from the Intellectual Repository" is dated January 1861 and was published as a single poem in 1862, with a headnote: "This Poem was suggested by a beautiful Statue, the work of the sculptor Duprèz, at Florence, of the famed Greek poetess, Sappho, who, being deserted by her lover, is said to have committed suicide by leaping from a rock into the sea."

hopelessness" and "numb collapse," whose "very consciousness / Of anguish" has transformed her into a lifeless form,"baffled in its own excess." By exceeding all feeling she seems devoid of feeling now, expiring (with "vacant-closing eye" and "last-drawn sigh") before our very eyes.

But of course the seemingly vacated and exhausted figure of Sappho displayed by the statue is brought to life through the rhetorical display of pathos in the poem. The lip "still quivering" seems on the verge of speech, and "the low-drooping head" almost moves in the reiteration or the participle, "(Not bowed, but drooping)." Sappho's apathetic pose provokes sympathy, as "we" identify with the despair that "looks forth in thee—nay! looks not forth; we guess / We feel it." How the statue looks depends on our act of looking, negating "what "looks forth in thee" in order to assert how "we guess" and "feel." The passivity of the statue ("lax" with "hand, loose-lying" and "slackened knee") encourages an increasingly active vicarious response, and indeed it is only by means of such vicarious identification that "it" can be named "SAPPHO" and personified as a (dying) woman to be addressed as "thee." The apostrophe, simultaneously de-animating and re-animating Sappho, turns reflexively on itself: "Who could misread thy story? Who mistake / Exhaustion's apathy?" Sappho is read here as the figure both *of* and *for* vicarious identification, transferring "the very consciousness of anguish" to the consciousness of viewers (or readers). Our increasingly self-conscious identification with the unconscious statue is also finally "baffled in its own excess," however, as we anticipate "that last, fatal leap!"—a precipitous exclamation that leaves us on the verge of leaping and losing consciousness, as well.

At this moment when pathos is "baffled in its own excess," the poem is interrupted and the lyric apostrophe turns into a dialogue:

> "No!" said one there beside me, as, in deep
> Delight of admiration rapt, I stood;
> "Praise it not! Like it not! It is not good
> To image woman thus."

By introducing an interlocutor who says "No!" Hume places the preceding scenario in quotation marks, framing the identification with Sappho in the opening lines not only as a manipulation of woman's "heart" by man's "art" but also as a convention of women's sentimental lyric. Returning to consciousness, the poem critiques the figure of Sappho as displayed in the statue and replayed in its own lyric apostrophe. The lyric "I" so "rapt" in admiration is admonished not to repeat the dejection of Sappho, but rather to reject both the image and the identification with the image: to "like it not" and also not to be like it. To "image woman thus" is to create sympathetic identifications that leave woman "self-betrayed," we are told:

"But, oh! this loss
Of all true womanhood—this soulless mood
Of hopeless, abject weakness—understood
Aright, what speaks it? Woman, self-betrayed
To coward, slavish passion; disarrayed
Of all her gracious self-rule, chaste as free—
'Tis hateful, terrible!"
                    "But these things be!"
I answered with a sigh.
                    Yet spaks't thou sooth!
It is not good, it is not woman's truth
To her high, heavenly birthright, so to stake
Her all on any cast, for any sake
To gamble with, as thus to be o'erthrown
By any loss! Let then her voice disown,
Henceforth, the slander man-writ on her brow.

Rather than presenting Sappho as an idealized figure for female identification, the statue now seems to represent "the loss / Of all true womanhood," because it prevents women from speaking for themselves.
"What speaks it?" The question is a *double entendre,* emphasizing that the
statue does not speak even while asking what it speaks and by what agency
it is spoken; from the perspective of the speaker who interrupts the lyric
meditation, the statue bespeaks the fall of woman from "gracious self-
rule" and into self-abnegating silence. It is an aesthetic embodiment of
woman's disembodiment, and therefore not to be trusted.

The nearly expired lyric "I" answers only "with a sigh" at first but recovers from its lyric lapse by entering into dialogue with the other
speaker: "Yet spaks't thou sooth!" The poem becomes a mouthpiece for
"woman's truth," as it is seen and spoken from another perspective; by
disowning what is "man-writ" about Sappho, woman comes to own and
claim "her voice," and to proclaim a feminist vocation. The poem suggests a feminist politics predicated on voice, not because it would reclaim
the true voice of Sappho but because it provokes an active response from
the reader: a response prescribed by the poem, first as a fall into sentimental reading and then as a call to action that redeems the fallen reader,
not unlike Milton's fortunate fall. Thus Hume articulates a "politics of poetics" that Susan Brown has analyzed in further detail: placing Hume's
poem within the context of debates about the fallen woman in nineteenth-
century England, and more specifically in relation to the middle-class
feminist campaign in the 1860s to repeal the Contagious Diseases Acts,
Brown argues for "a crucial connection between the poetics of Hume's
poem and the political strategies adopted by feminist repealers: for, just

as Hume's speaker decided that female voices were needed to combat destructive male-authored images of women, the repealers felt that their representation of the fallen woman was necessary to oppose the false representations, by men, of prostitution" (1994: 214). What is at stake is not only false representations but the very question of representation itself, as Brown points out, since Hume begins her poem with a meditation on a statue of Sappho, in order to reflect on the material consequences of representing women.

Hume critiques not only male-authored but also female-authored representations, as her poem simultaneous invokes and revokes Sappho's association with a tradition of women's sentimental lyric that is only too familiar to nineteenth-century readers. Writing several decades after earlier Victorian poetesses such as L. E. L. and Rossetti, or Hemans and Norton, whose Sapphic performances depend increasingly on emptying out the figure of Sappho, the high Victorian feminist poetics of Hume would make Sappho into a figure for the fulfillment of, and by, woman. In her call for political action, Hume coincides with the campaign for the education and productive employment of women launched by Frances Power Cobbe. In "What Shall We Do with Our Old Maids?" (1862), Cobbe calls upon women to exercise their creative powers for the first time in history. "Till of very late years it was, we think, perfectly justifiable to doubt the possibility of women possessing any creative artistic power," she writes; "To originate any work of even second-rate merit was what no woman had done. Sappho was a mere name, and between her and even such a feeble poetess as Mrs. Hemans, there was hardly another to fill up the gap of the whole cycle of history" (Cobbe 1996: 248). For Cobbe as well as Hume, the transmission of Sappho through women's sentimental lyric provokes ambivalence, as if Sappho survives merely as a name to be invoked by feeble poetesses: not the source of original poetry, but second-rate repetitions that leave a "gap" in history rather than filling it. But now, according to Cobbe, is the moment for women to reclaim poetry for their own purposes, transforming what "no woman" has done into a new voice for a new woman, soon to become "The New Woman" and no longer a mere name.

Implicit in the call to women poets is a narrative of historical progress and social amelioration that shapes feminist politics in the final decades of the nineteenth century. Indeed, Susan Brown suggests that Frances Power Cobbe may have served as inspiration for an epic poem entitled *Sappho,* published by Catharine Amy Dawson [Scott].[46] Born in 1865 and

---

[46] Susan Brown makes a persuasive case for reading Frances Power Cobbe as a model for Dawson's Sappho, in "Reforming Sappho: Catharine Amy Dawson Among the Aesthetes," a paper presented at our 1994 MLA panel on "Sapphic Authorship in Nineteenth-Century England." I have benefited much from conversations with Susan Brown, as well as Linda Peterson and Stuart Curran, who also participated in the panel.

a self-proclaimed feminist by the age of twenty, the young Dawson asked in her confession book, "*If not yourself, who would you be?*" and answered for herself: "The Sappho of this age" (Watts 1987: 13). She composed an epic about Sappho as her first book for publication in 1889, although it did not circulate much: most copies were burned in a fire at the publisher's warehouse, an unfortunate incident (or coincidence) that nevertheless enhanced Dawson's identification with the "burning" Sappho. From this point onward "Victorian Amy became known as Sappho to her contemporaries and friends," as her daughter recounts in *Mrs. Sappho: The Life of C. A. Dawson Scott, Mother of International P. E. N.* (Watts 1987: 16). In the 1890s Dawson was active in Women's Suffrage and Women Writer's Dinners in London, and in the following decades a literary circle developed around "Mrs. Sappho" as if she really had become the Sappho of her age, if not as a famous writer herself then as an inspiration for other, more famous writers.[47] But despite the obscurity of Dawson's early epic poem, it is quite an extraordinary performance, written on the model of *Aurora Leigh* to announce the beginning of a new era for women writers. In reclaiming Sappho for a feminist cause, Dawson anticipates the claims of later feminist critics who construct a literary genealogy for women poets by placing them on a historical continuum.

In *Sappho* the lyric impulse of women's sentimental verse is framed within a longer verse narrative that projects a feminist vision of history into the future. Before the epic begins, a sonnet of dedication invokes "those women of a parted hour/ Whose sorrows urged my song." While poetesses from the past may be Dawson's point of departure, she is "urged" forward in time to a new song that will depart from their "sorrows" and introduce another theme: the story of Sappho's growth as a woman poet and as the founder of a school for young women, who will continue to grow with time, even after Sappho's death. Book I introduces a sorrowful Sappho in a familiar melancholy mood, but when she strikes her lyre a new chord is heard:

> My soul awakes
> To stir of aspiration, to the flush
> Of floating dreams exalted into sound,
> And once again before the silence falls

---

[47] The literary ambitions of Catharine Amy Dawson Scott took various forms, including various novels, poems, and articles that she published between 1889 and 1933, and the organization of clubs to support other writers as well: in 1917 she founded the To-Morrow Club for young would-be authors, and in 1921 she founded P. E. N. International for poets, essayists, and novelists. Her early poetry received mixed praise from Robert Browning, who found it full of "aspiration" but wanting in "originality" (Watts 1987: 9); the work awaits a more thorough critical reassessment.

> Would loose its heavy burden and arise
> On wings of melody. What will my lyre?
>
> (4)

No longer the expiring "I" of sentimental lyric, Dawson's Sappho awakens to renewed inspiration and ambition, a "stir of aspiration" that is the beginning of her epic autobiography. Although she is now at the end of her life, Sappho calls upon her lyre ("what will my lyre?") as an instrument for narrating how she came to be a poet. Educated by her brother Cleon, who left her "boy-like in bearing" and "unversed in household ways, unmeet to rule a home" (24), the young Sappho refused the domesticated lives of married women and discovered her lyric vocation in a prophetic dream:

> Arise! thou child of music, and lament
> Till grief be but a roll of rhythmic song!
> So shall thy soul be comforted, and turn
> To nobler issues.
>
> (93–94)

This call to action depends on the conversion of lament into pure song; by performing grief to the point of exhaustion, Sappho will finally "turn to nobler issues" and fill her song with new content. An epic Sappho thus emerges from a long line of lyric Sapphos, although it is only after the tradition of emptying out Sapphic song that Dawson is able to imagine other possibilities issuing forth from Sappho.

Having narrated the development of Sappho from maidenhood into "full woman" in Books I and II, Dawson makes her into a feminist prophet in Book III. Just as Sappho is herself awakened "to stir of aspiration" by her lyre, she uses the lyre to stir and inspire a crowd of women with her message:

> Behold, and take my message: "Stir yourselves,
> Ye sleepers in the highways of the world,
> And live for God and Good and Liberty!
> Fling off the bonds of custom, dare to think
> And to be true!" O woman! you have set
> A fence, a fence, and everywhere a fence
> About your steps, until you only know
> To turn in the same paths your mothers trod.
>
> (110)

Is the invocation "O woman" a lament or a turn to nobler issues? The apostrophe transforms the multitude of women being addressed into a generic category that is both fallen and ideal. On the one hand, "woman" is too much tied down by the past ("the bonds of custom") and too grounded in the present (forever taking the same steps and treading the same paths); on the other hand, "woman" might be fulfilled in the future if she would only "dare to think / And to be true!" The projection of this womanly ideal into the future would also be the reclamation of a long-lost ideal, as Sappho proclaims: "We, ashamed of the unworthy Past, / Shall in the future find our Golden Age" (113). The women in the audience respond to this inspirational rhetoric by offering their daughters for education in Sappho's school, to uplift them into "a wise maidenhood . . . walking free of the old customs" (127). The "maiden-school" thrives, much to the chagrin of the priests, who incite a mob to burn it to the ground and forbid Sappho to teach in Book IV.

Instead of lamenting the school's collapse, however, Sappho turns it into another prophetic occasion:

> Though to-day
> Has cast our labour to the winds of heaven,
> Its sparks shall, scattering, light a wrath and rage
> In every noble household, till from loss
> Shall spring the beacons of a mightier work,—
> In every city, woman-colleges—
> In every city, a free womanhood—
> In every city, justice, purity,—
> And all such holiness as women-souls
> Have shed around them since the birth of time.
>
> (198–99)

Refiguring the revolutionary rhetoric of Shelley's "Ode to the West Wind," Dawson's epic scatters ashes and sparks from a more domestic hearth—the womanly sphere—into a world awakened by the trumpet of Sappho's feminist prophecy: a vision of what will come to be "in every city," repeated three times in the incantation of this verse. But if Sappho is one of the unacknowledged legislators of the world, her prophecy is necessarily predicated on her failure, since it is only "from loss" that the "beacons of a mightier work" become visible in the future. What is spoken through Sappho is not her own words, but a poem as of yet unwritten for readers as of yet unborn. Sappho's death at the end of the poem is therefore to be read as a sacrifice for posterity, which will forget the words that have made the future possible:

> Lo! I have spoken, and my words are nought;
> More idle than a little wave that curls
> Its foamy crest upon the ocean's back,
> Murmurs a little, sinks upon the shore,
> And is forgotten. Yet I am content
> To leave the revelation of the truth

To riper ages and a nobler race—
Content to leave it in God's hands, and trust.
The seeds are scattered, and His kindling grace
May strengthen them to overspread the earth,
In centuries to come. It well may be
That I have wasted dew on arid soil
That bears no grain. It may be that my songs,
May be mis-sung by babes, whose infant lips
Have scarcely learnt to frame the notes of speech.
But be thou Judge, O Giver! and if thought
Of the world-evil but to reprobate,
Or sensuous image hath defiled my verse,
Blot me from history, —my name, my deeds
Hurried into oblivion, as the corpse
Of the dead leper at the city-gate.
Thou gavest song unto a woman's lips,
And she restores it, pure as mother-thoughts
Woven above the sleepers on their breasts.

(209)

The words of Sappho are "nought," like the evanescent swelling of a wave, which rises and falls and is forgotten; her words will be scattered by the wind and her songs misremembered by "infant lips" that cannot speak; she will be blotted from history, and her name "hurried into oblivion."

And yet this forgetting is part of the historical process that allows Sappho to live on, past death. The Sapphic corpus, like "the corpse of the dead leper," must be cast out before it can be reincorporated and transfigured. Here again, the echoes from Shelley's ode—where waves are lifted by the revolutionary winds of history, and seeds are planted in the earth like corpses waiting for rebirth—give greater resonance to Dawson's vision of Sappho, as well as giving a different resonance to the Shelleyan prophecy: his prophetic song has been given "unto a woman's lips," and her "mother-thoughts" will nurture future readers with a vision of history, reconceived from a maternal perspective. Dawson thus imagines a matrilineal line of women poets descending from Sappho, and just before Sappho herself descends into "the bosom of the waves" (209), she invokes her female descendants: "Oh, noble hearts / That beat with mine upon our common cause . . . This is no farewell" (210). Sappho's cause becomes a common cause, carried on in the name of all women, even when the name of Sappho is forgotten.

The epic ambition of Dawson's epic poem, it would seem, is to create a continuous historical narrative out of the reiteration of Sappho's leap: to project Sappho into (future) history by reading repetition as progress.

In this respect the poem is part of a larger discourse of social transformation that informed late-nineteenth-century women's movements, which (despite various differences in their internal politics) all depended on the formulation of a new social sphere where it would be possible to contemplate the education, enfranchisement, and emancipation of women. The politics of nineteenth-century "sociological feminism," as Riley describes it, is predicated on an idea of progress that would allow the idea of the "social" and of "women" to come into being: "Both this 'social' and 'women' lean forward, as concepts, into a future which is believed to sustain them. It is as if 'women,'" who have been erroneously or ignorantly represented, might yet, reconstructed, come into their own. In many later-nineteenth- and indeed early-twentieth-century addresses on the Woman Question, they are caught up not in being, where they are massively midunderstood, but in becoming. If 'women' can be credited with having a tense, then it is a future tense" (1988: 47). So also Dawson's poem ends in the future tense: it imagines Sappho as a persona (if not quite a historical person) that leans forward, falling into the process of becoming that will eventually call woman into being.

But if the visionary feminism of Dawson's *Sappho* is a transfiguration of Shelley's prophetic ode, we might ask (as Paul Fry does of Shelley) whether such a vision of the future "can decisively affirm any continuous, unified myth of history," or indeed whether prophecy can ever be anything other than "an intimation of the need for further intimation" (Fry 1980: 213). Fry points to a failing implicit in the poet's calling, making the ode into a vehicle for "ontological and vocational doubt" (2) that leaves the poet in crisis about the historical efficacy of lyric. So also, the feminist vocation of poets like Oakes Smith, Hume, and Dawson raises doubts about Sappho as embodiment of woman's cause. Is it possible to call woman into being through Sappho, when that name is but an intimation of the need for further intimation? How can the discontinuous repetition of Sappho's fall affirm the continuity of history? As I have argued in the course of this chapter, the versing of Sappho by nineteenth-century women poets is a continual reversal that cannot be read as forward progress but is better understood as a metalepsis. Sappho's association with "the women's movement" shows how history keeps falling backward and lapsing into forgetfulness, according to the recursive logic of sentimental lyric: rather than narrating history, each version of Sappho allows history to be re-versed.

This forgetting is repeated in the twentieth century, for example by Amy Lowell in "The Sisters," a poem that meditates on female literary genealogy by ironically invoking Sappho as something forgotten: "There's Sapho, now I wonder what was Sapho?" (1955: 235). The problem of personifying Sappho—turning "what" into someone who can be addressed in the second person—leads Lowell to exclaim, "Ah me! I wish I could have talked to Sapho," and finally to conclude that Sappho is not a woman at all: "And she is Sapho—Sapho—not Miss or Mrs., / A leaping fire we call so for convenience." Lowell thus alludes to the legacy of Sappho's leap in Victorian women's verse and seems to align herself with that tradition, as she remembers Mrs. Browning, "speculating, as I must suppose, / In just this way on Sapho." But Lowell concludes by projecting Victorian poetesses into the past in order to project herself into the future of women's poetry, bidding her precursors "Good-bye" and "Good night." As a modernist postscript to Victorian postscripts to Sappho, Lowell's poem consigns them to the past in order to claim a Sapphic signature that also turns out to be posthumous: first published posthumously in *What's O'Clock* (1925), "The Sisters" defines female authorship as a temporal reversal rather than a linear genealogy.

The metalepsis is further played out in twentieth-century feminist criticism: when feminist literary critics recuperate a history of women poets through the figure of Sappho, they repeat the loss that such poetry anticipates. In "Sapphistries," for example, Susan Gubar attempts to construct a female genealogy by aligning various women modernists with Sappho, but this reclamation of a long-lost Sapphic lyricism is yet another repetition of nineteenth-century reclamations of Sappho, always already lost and recovered and lost again (1984: 43–62). Or, in another attempt to rethink women's literary history, Betsy Erkkila reads Lowell's "The Sisters" as a poem that exemplifies an ambivalence about female genealogies, but without calling into question why the poem places Sappho "at the origins of a specifically female lyric tradition" to begin with (1992: 9).[48] Feminist classical scholars have likewise returned to Sapphic origins, without interrogating the historical mediations that make the reconstruction of Sappho suddenly seem so urgent and so long overdue. Is this the dead end of feminist criticism, or is there another way to loop through the instant replay of Sappho's leap?

I have offered an overview of nineteenth-century poetesses—a view from the cliff, as it were—not only in order to demonstrate that the leap can be historically played out to different ends, but also in order to redefine the ends of literary history. By reading "forgotten" Sappho poems by Victorian women poets in succession, we can see how they predict their own forgetting; indeed, the success of Victorian women's verse depends

---

[48] In response to "earlier feminists [who] tended to treat women's literary history as something that was *there* to be recuperated and reclaimed by literary critics," Erkkila proposes "a model of women's literary history that engages the central paradox of feminism: it does its work even as it recognizes the instability and potential impossibility of its subject" (1992: 4). Yet her reading of "The Sisters" does not recognize the invocation of Sappho as both cause and effect of that paradox.

on the repetition of a loss or failure that is the very means of its literary transmission. How else can we read the impossible "I" in Mary Robinson's Sappho sonnets, or the identification of L. E. L. with the posthumous persona of Sappho, or Christina Rossetti's self-negating response to that Sapphic legacy, or the utter abandonment of Sappho in the poetic sketch by Felicia Hemans, or the picture of Sappho (de)personified by Caroline Norton, or Elizabeth Oakes Smith's performance of the catastrophic fall of woman through Sappho, or the Miltonic redemption of that fallen figure in the feminist poetics of Mary Catherine Hume, or the epic failure of Catharine Amy Dawson's Sappho? If all such poems are doomed to fail, then nothing succeeds like failure.

 CONCLUSION

EPITAPH

THE CHAPTERS of *Victorian Sappho* could be read in reverse, to suggest a chronology for the evolution of Victorian lyric through the figure of Sappho. I might have started with the final chapter, tracing the emergence of Sappho as proper name for the Poetess within sentimental women's verse of the early Victorian period, setting the stage for Algernon Swinburne's sensational reappropriation of this lyric figure for high Victorian poetics, and continuing with the conversion of Sappho of Lesbos into a lesbian Sappho by Michael Field toward the end of the century. And I might have ended with my first chapter, demonstrating how Wharton's late Victorian edition of the Sapphic fragments exemplifies a rhetoric of fragmentation that persists in twentieth-century ideas about lyric as well. Reading backward through the preceding chapters, we would then be reading forward in time in order to discover a chronological narrative about Sappho's reception in nineteenth-century England: while earlier versions of Sappho are primarily mediated by Ovid, the translation of this posthumous Sapphic persona from Latin into English poetry gradually gives way to a Sapphic corpus reconstructed from Greek fragments and translated into a vision of Sappho as a fragmentary form, the very embodiment of lyric. The continual dismembering and remembering of this feminine figure is a Victorian legacy that haunts us even now, in contemporary lyric theory and in current Sappho studies, as I suggested in my introduction.

However, it is only in retrospect that the outlines of such a narrative can be discerned. If *Victorian Sappho* offers a retrospective chronology, it is to be understood as another instance of the metaleptic logic that I have been tracing in the name of Sappho. This logic suggests an alternate model for literary history and reception studies, in as much as it complicates the assumption of historical progress and calls into question the seemingly fixed vantage point of the reader in the present. The moment when a "history of reception" becomes visible can itself be historicized as a recursive structure, and it requires more complex reading than straightforwardly sequential analysis: there is no *a priori* Sappho and no linear progression in the long history of reading Sappho, no single line of descent in declining the name. The study of Sappho's reception must proceed by analyzing our own moment of reading as another displacement, a specular repetition rather than an originary scene. In *Victorian Sappho* a reception history and a theory of literary transmission therefore merge with the question of lyric reading, variously posed in the foregoing chapters to show that my point of departure as a reader of the Sapphic fragments is another vanishing point. Suspended in the metalepsis of reading, projecting the past into the future and the future into the past, I will find myself in the same non-place as the spectral "I" of Sappho; I am preoccupied by a lyric moment, the "here" and "now" of lyric reading, that is neither here nor there.

Fragment 55 foreshadows how "I" vanishes in the moment of reading. Written in the future anterior, it is an ironic epitaph predicting the death of the woman to whom it is addressed:

κατθάνοισα δὲ κείση οὐδέ ποτα μναμοσύνα σέθεν
ἔσσετ᾽ οὐδὲ πόθα εἰς ὕστερον· οὐ γὰρ πεδέχης βρόδων
τῶν ἐκ Πιερίας, ἀλλ᾽ ἀφάνης κἀν Ἀίδα δόμῳ
φοιτάσης πεδ᾽ ἀμαύρων νεκύων ἐκπεποταμένα.

Dead you will lie there and no memory of you
Shall there be and no desire for you in time to come; for you have no share
In the roses of Pieria, but unseen even in the house of Hades
You shall flit among the fading corpses, flown away.

According to ancient sources, these are the words of Sappho to a woman who does not read poetry.[1] This unmusical woman has "no share in the roses of Pieria," the flowers bestowed by the muses. She is not to be found among the muses in Pieria, their place of birth, but is doomed to die and haunt the house of Hades as a nameless shadow, more fleeting than the shades of the dead. Invisible, she has already "flown away" beyond reach, beyond desire, beyond memory.

Fragment 55 substitutes forgetting for remembering: instead of recording a past memory, it records a forgotten future; instead of making an inscription, it marks an erasure; instead of bringing the dead to life, it finds the living dead. The irony of the epitaph is implicit in the very structure of address, as the poem is directed in the second person singular to a "you" whose death is the necessary condition for the utterance. Here apostrophe, usually understood as the animation of an absent or dead being through second-person address, is reversed to point to the de-animation of "you." What will happen to the woman "in time to come" (*eis hysteron*) has already happened, by dint of a rhetorical *hysteron proteron* that proclaims her dead before having been alive; her nonbeing is framed

---

[1] Stobaeus cites fragment 55 as the words "of Sappho to an uneducated woman" (Σαπφοῦς πρός ἀπαίδευτον γυναῖκα); according to Plutarch, the lines were written by Sappho either "to a wealthy woman" (πρός τινα πλουσίαν) or "to an uncultured, ignorant woman" (πρός τινα τῶν ἀμούσων καὶ ἀμαθῶν γυναικῶν) (Campbell 98–99).

by the past participles "dead" (*katthanoisa*) and "flown away" (*ekpepota-mena*), the first and last words of the poem. "You" can exist only in the impossible future perfect, as someone who will have been dead. Letter by letter, fragment 55 thus spells out the erasure of the unlettered woman. Indeed, since she is either unliterary or illiterate, how will she decipher the letters in the poem addressed to her? If she is remembered only by being forgotten, who will do the forgetting? Who, in other words, will be the reader of fragment 55?

Paradoxically, the fate of the woman who will not read the poem is also the fate of anyone who does read it; every reader is, inevitably, implicated in this *hysteron proteron*. Anne Carson considers the address to "you" in fragment 55 a direct address to the reader: "The second person singular verbs of the poem locate us within some woman by calling her 'you.' You transact your own invisibility by living in the present as if you were already dead—which, by the time you realize it, you are" (Prins and Shreiber 1997: 224). By revealing the reversibility of the living and the dead, fragment 55 predetermines the death of the reader as well. But if the poem is literally unreadable to the unlettered woman that it seeks to obliterate, the literate reader is obliterated in the very act of trying to read it literally, as Carson suggests:

> Your trap is the small Greek word *kai,* a conjunction meaning "and," which appears in verse 3 abbreviated to a single *k* and conjoined by crasis to the preposition *en* following it: *kan.* Now crasis is a metrical license permitting the compression of two open vowels into one long syllable for time-saving purposes. Crasis quickens the connective action of the conjunction *kai* and syncopates your posthumous nonentity upon its counterpart in present life. By the time you realize the retroactive force of this conjunction, you have already floated forward to verse 4 and to your darkening future, leaving behind you, lodged in a single kappa, the whole implication of your life without roses. (224)

In this cannily literal reading, Carson discovers the obliteration of the reader in a single letter. The joining of *kai* and *en* in the phrase "even in the House of Hades" (*kan Aida dōmoi*) marks not only the loss of two vowels but the loss of an entire life span, contracted into a kappa: it marks the disappearance of the lyric moment that the reader tries to inhabit. According to Carson's wry definition of crasis ("Now crasis is . . . "), the poem is defined by the hastening of this "now," a compression of the past and the future that results in the elision of the present and turns it into a postscript. To read fragment 55 is to be trapped in this temporal loop, for "by the time you realize" (a phrase Carson repeats, emphasizing the repeatability of the trap) the "you" will already be gone, no longer real. The reader thus becomes a "posthumous nonentity," another nameless shadow to be forgotten.

Lest it seem I am lost in someone else's reading of the fragment—as indeed I am—my fate is not without precedent. As I try to translate this deadly text back to the future, I am not the only one to be consigned to oblivion; my signature is but one in a long series of translators. Here are four Victorian versions of fragment 55 from Wharton's edition of Sappho (113–17), to be placed alongside the previous translation implicitly signed in my name:

> Woman dead, lie there;
> No record of thee
> Shall there ever be,
> Since thou dost not share
> Roses in Pieria grown.
> In the deathful cave,
> With the feeble troop
> Of the folk that droop,
> Lurk and flit and crave,
> Woman severed and far-flown.
>
> WILLIAM CORY, 1858.

> Thou liest dead, and there will be no memory left behind
> Of thee or thine in all the earth, for never didst thou bind
> The roses of Pierian streams upon thy brow; thy doom
> Is writ to flit with unknown ghosts in cold and nameless gloom.
>
> EDWIN ARNOLD, 1869.

> Yea, thou shalt die,
> And lie
> Dumb in the silent tomb;
> Nor of thy name
> Shall there be any fame
>> In ages yet to be or years to come:
> For of the flowering Rose,
> Which on Pieria blows,
>> Thou hast no share:
> But in sad Hades' house,
> Unknown, inglorious,
>> 'Mid the dim shades that wander there
>> Shalt thou flit forth and haunt the filmy air.
>
> J. A. SYMONDS, 1883.

> When thou fallest in death, dead shalt thou lie, nor shall thy memory
> Henceforth ever again be heard then or in days to be,

Since no flowers upon earth ever were thine, plucked from Pieria's spring,
Unknown also 'mid hell's shadowy throng thou shalt go wandering.

ANON., Love in Idlenesss, 1883.

The date of each translation is recorded as if it might be an epitaph: the name, followed by the year when the translator discovered "you" to be dead again. Proclaiming the death of an anonymous woman, every version of fragment 55 ironically anticipates the future of the translator who has already disappeared in signing his name below: from William Cory to Edwin Arnold to J. A. Symonds to "Anonymous," his name disappears in her namelessness.

Of course, each translator has left a different trace of this disappearance; each time, the trap is sprung in another way. In Cory's version, the sequence from past participle into future verb shades into the imperative ("Woman dead, lie there"), followed by a future that is contrary to fact ("No record of thee / Shall there ever be"): after all, there is a record in the very letters that mark her absence. Indeed, because the woman "severed and far-flown" is disconnected from the second-person address at the end of the translation, she has more mobility in death than in life: once she is "far-flown," she will never simply "lie there." Or rather her death "lies," in a double entendre made even more explicit in Arnold's translation: "Thou liest dead." Does the woman lie dead, or is the death a lie? Arnold begins with the address to "Thou," deferring the death until the third word, so that the reversal of the apostrophe in the epitaph becomes its central question. He translates the final lines as an epitaphic gesture ("thy doom / is writ to flit with unknown ghosts") that marks the inscription of the woman's doom in writing yet leaves her free to "flit" beyond the words that fix her "there" in the poem; she will haunt the future. This future haunting is affirmed by Symonds, characteristically with "yea" in the opening line of his translation: "Yea, thou shalt die, / And lie / Dumb in the silent tomb." Here too, the silence of the woman who will "lie / dumb" is belied by the writing that records her namelessness for posterity: "Nor of thy name / Shall there be any fame / In ages yet to be or years to come," is the epitaph that remains, ironically, in her name. The irony redoubles when the anonymous woman is translated by the translator who is named "Anonymous." Even "when thou fallest in death," we see in this translation how the shadow of the name rises up, again and again.

Fragment 55 therefore serves as my long-postponed epitaph, or postscript, for the lyric subject we call Sappho. Despite the attribution of the fragment to Sappho and a long tradition of reading it in her name, there is no "I" to speak of here: like "you," the "I" is un-named, removed from the poem in order to change the proper name into anonymous multi-

plicity. As in the forgetting of proper names, the afterlife of Sappho is defined by this perpetual displacement: the name has no proper place of
return, and what appears in its place is the ability to disappear in the
name of Sappho. Back and forth it flits invisibly in the house of Hades, a
fleeting phantom always moving between life and death, the future and
the past, hovering before us, still.

WORKS CITED

Acland, Alice. 1948. *Caroline Norton.* London: Constable.

Addison, Joseph. 1711. *The Spectator.* Nos. 223, 229, 233.

Anderson, Peter. 1993. "The Sterile Star of Venus: Swinburne's Dream of Flight." *The Victorian Newsletter* 84: 18–24.

Armstrong, Isobel. 1995. "The Gush of the Feminine." In Feldman and Kelley 1995: 13–32.

———. 1993. *Victorian Poetry: Poetry, Poetics and Politics.* London: Routledge.

Armstrong, Isobel, and Virginia Blain, eds. 1998. *Women's Poetry Late Romantic to Late Victorian: Gender and Genre.* Hampshire: Macmillan.

Armstrong, Isobel, Joseph Bristow, and Cath Sharrock, eds. 1996. *Nineteenth-Century Women Poets.* Oxford: Clarendon Press.

Ashbee, Henry Spencer (pseud. Pisanus Fraxi). [1877] 1962. *Bibliography of Prohibited Books.* Vols. 1–3. Rpt., New York: G. Legman.

The Athenaeum. 1889. Review of *Long Ago,* Michael Field. No. 3220 (July 13): 56–57.

Attridge, Derek. 1982. *The Rhythms of English Poetry.* New York: Longman.

———. 1974. *Well-Weighed Syllables: Elizabethan Verse in Classical Meters.* Cambridge: Cambridge University Press.

Aviram, Amitai. 1994. *Telling Rhythm: Body and Meaning in Poetry.* Ann Arbor: University of Michigan Press.

Bahti, Timothy. 1996. *Ends of the Lyric: Direction and Consequence in Western Poetry.* Baltimore: The Johns Hopkins University Press.

———. 1995. "The Unimaginable Touch of Tropes." *Diacritics* 25.4: 39–58.

Balmer, Josephine. Tr. 1988. *Sappho: Poems and Fragments.* Secaucus: Meadowland Books.

Barham, Thomas Foster. 1860. "On Metrical Time, or, the Rhythm of Verse, Ancient and Modern." *Transactions of the Philological Society* I: 45–62.

Barnard, Mary. 1958. *Sappho: A New Translation.* Berkeley: University of California Press.

Barnstone, Willis. 1993. *The Poetics of Translation: History, Theory, Practice.* New Haven: Yale University Press.

———, tr. 1988. *Sappho and the Greek Lyric Poets.* New York: Schocken Books.

Beerbohm, Max. [1922] 1987. *Rossetti and His Circle.* Ed. N. John Hall. Reprint, London: Heinemann.

Benjamin, Walter. 1982. *Illuminations.* Tr. Harry Zohn. Glasgow: Fontana/Collins.

Bennett, Paula, ed. 1997. *Nineteenth-Century American Women Poets: An Anthology.* Oxford: Blackwell.

Benveniste, Emile. 1971. *Problems in General Linguistics.* Tr. Mary Elizabeth Meek. Miami: University of Miami Press.

Bergk, Theodor. 1882. *Poetae Lyrici Graeci.* Vol 3. Leipzig: Teubner.

Berlant, Lauren. 1992. "The Female Woman: Fanny Fern and the Form of Sentiment." In Samuels 1992: 265–340.

————. 1990. "The Female Complaint." *Social Text* 19/20 (Fall 1988): 237–59.

Besant, Walter. 1892. "On Literary Collaboration." *The New Review* 6 (1892): 200–209.

Bethune, George. [1848] 1860. *The British Female Poets: With Biographical and Critical Notices.* New York: Hurst.

Bing, Peter. 1988. *The Well-Read Muse: Present and Past in Callimachus and the Hellenistic Poets.* Gottingen: Vandenhoeck and Ruprecht.

Blain, Virginia. 1997. "Anthologizing Women Poets." *Journal of Victorian Culture* 2.2: 291- 301.

————. 1996. "'Michael Field, the Two-headed Nightingale': Lesbian Text as Palimpsest." *Women's History Review* 5.2: 239–57.

————. 1995. "Letitia Elizabeth Landon, Eliza Mary Hamilton, and the Genealogy of the Victorian Poetess." *Victorian Poetry* 33.1 (Spring): 31–51.

Blanchard, Laman. 1841. *The Life and Literary Remains of L.E.L.* 2 vols. London: Henry Colburn.

Brinton, Christian. 1900. "Queen Victoria as an Etcher." *The Critic* (June): 501–10.

Brisman, Leslie. 1977. "Swinburne's Semiotics." *Georgia Review* 31: 578–97.

————. 1984. "Of Lips Divine and Calm: Swinburne and the Language of Shelleyan Love." In *Romanticism & Language,* ed. Arden Reed. Ithaca: Cornell University Press, 247–62.

Bronfen, Elisabeth. 1992. *Over Her Dead Body: Death, Femininity, and the Aesthetic.* New York: Routledge.

Broomfield, Andrea, and Sally Mitchell, eds. 1996. *Prose by Victorian Women: An Anthology.* New York: Garland.

Brown, Susan. 1994. "A Victorian Sappho: Agency, Identity, and the Politics of Poetics." *English Studies in Canada* 20.2 (June): 205–25.

————. (Forthcoming). "The Victorian Poetess." In *The Cambridge Companion to Victorian Poetry,* ed. J. Bristow. Cambridge: Cambridge University Press.

Buckler, William E. 1980. *The Victorian Imagination: Essays in Aesthetic Exploration.* New York: New York University Press.

Burnett, Anne Pippin. 1983. *Three Archaic Poets: Archilochus, Alcaeus, Sappho.* Cambridge: Harvard University Press, 1983.

Burnett, Timothy A. J. 1993. "Swinburne at Work: The First Page of 'Anactoria.'" In Rooksby and Shrimpton, 1993: 148–58.

Bush, Douglas. 1963. *Mythology and the Romantic Tradition in English Poetry.* New York.

Butler, Judith. 1991. "Imitation and Gender Insubordination." In *Inside/Out: Lesbian Theories, Gay Theories,* ed. Diana Fuss. New York: Routledge, 13–31.

Byron, George Gordon Noel. 1982. *Letters and Journals.* Ed. Leslie Marchand. 12 vols. Cambridge: Harvard University Press.

Calame, Claude. 1997. *Choruses of Young Women in Ancient Greece: Their Morphology, Religious Role, and Social Functions.* Tr. Derek Collins and Jane Orion. Lanham: Rowman and Littlefield.

Campbell, D. A. 1982. *Greek Lyric, Volume I: Sappho and Alcaeus.* Cambridge: Harvard University Press.

Carson, Anne. 1990. "'Just for the Thrill' : Sycophantizing Aristotle's *Poetics.*" *Arion* 1.1: 142- 54.

———. 1986. *Eros the Bittersweet.* Princeton: Princeton University Press.

Caruth, Cathy. 1995. "The Claims of Reference." In *Critical Encounters: Reference and Responsibility in Deconstructive Writing,* ed. Cathy Caruth and Deborah Esch. New Brunswick: Rutgers University Press, 92–105.

Chase, Cynthia, ed. 1993. *Romanticism.* London: Longman.

———. 1986. *Decomposing Figures: Rhetorical Readings in the Romantic Tradition.* Baltimore: The Johns Hopkins University Press.

Chorley, Henry F. 1836. *Memorials of Mrs. Hemans with Illustrations of Her Literary Character from Her Private Correspondence.* 2 vols. London: Saunders and Otley.

Clarke, Mary Cowden. 1857. *World-Noted Women; or, Types of Womanly Attributes of All Lands and Ages.* New York: D. Appleton.

Cobbe, Frances Power. [1862] 1996. "What Shall We Do with Our Old Maids?" In *Prose by Victorian Women: An Anthology,* ed. Andrea Broomfield and Sally Mitchell. New York: Garland, 235–61.

Cook, David A. 1971. "The Content and Meaning of Swinburne's 'Anactoria.'" *Victorian Poetry* 9.1–2:77–93.

Culler, Jonathan. 1988. "The Modern Lyric: Generic Continuity and Critical Practice." In *The Comparative Perspective on Literature: Approaches to Theory and Practice,* ed. Clayton Koelb and Susan Noakes. Ithaca: Cornell University Press, 284–99.

———. 1985a. "Reading Lyric." In *Yale French Studies* 69: 98–106.

———. 1985b. "Changes in the Study of the Lyric." In Hosek and Parker 1985: 38–54.

———. 1981. *The Pursuit of Signs: Semiotics, Literature, Deconstruction.* Ithaca: Cornell University Press.

Curran, Stuart. 1988. "Romantic Poetry: The I Altered." In Mellor 1988: 185–207.

Dana, Charles A. 1857. *The Household Book of Poetry.* New York: D. Appleton.

Dawson [Scott], Catharine Amy. 1889. *Sappho.* London: Kegan Paul.

DeJean, Joan. 1989. *Fictions of Sappho, 1546–1937.* Chicago: University of Chicago Press.

Dellamora, Richard. 1994. *Apocalyptic Overtures: Sexual Politics and the Sense of an Ending.* New Brunswick: Rutgers University Press.

———. 1990. *Masculine Desire: The Sexual Politics of Victorian Aestheticism.* Chapel Hill: University of North Carolina Press.

de Man, Paul. 1996. *Aesthetic Ideology.* Ed. Andrzej Warminksi. Minneapolis: University of Minnesota Press.

———. 1993. *Romanticism and Contemporary Criticism: The Gauss Seminar and Other Papers.* Ed. E. S. Burt, Kevin Newmark, and Andrzej Warminski. Baltimore: Johns Hopkins University Press.

———. 1985. "Lyrical Voice in Contemporary Theory." In Hosek and Parker 1985: 55–72.

———. 1984. *The Rhetoric of Romanticism.* New York: Columbia University Press.

Derrida, Jacques. 1977. "Signature Event Context." *Glyph* 1:172–97.

Dickson, Jay. 1996. "Surviving Victoria." In *High and Low Moderns: Literature and*

Culture, 1889–1939, ed. Maria DiBattista and Lucy McDiarmid, 23–46. Oxford: Oxford University Press.

Dowling, Linda. 1994. *Hellenism and Homosexuality in Victorian Oxford.* Ithaca: Cornell University Press.

———. 1986. *Language and Decadence in the Victorian Fin de Siècle.* Princeton: Princeton University Press.

du Bois, Page. 1995. *Sappho Is Burning.* Chicago: University of Chicago Press.

Edelman, Lee. 1994. *Homographesis: Essays in Gay Literary and Cultural Theory.* New York: Routledge.

Elfenbein, Andrew. 1995. *Byron and the Victorians.* Cambridge: Cambridge University Press.

Erkkila, Betsy. 1992. *The Wicked Sisters: Women Poets, Literary History, and Discord.* New York and Oxford: Oxford University Press.

Faderman, Lillian. 1981. *Surpassing the Love of Men: Romantic Friendship and Love between Women from the Renaissance to the Present.* New York: William Morrow.

Feldman, Paula, and Theresa M. Kelley, eds. 1995. *Romantic Women Writers: Voices and Countervoices.* Hanover: University Press of New England.

Ferguson, Frances. 1992. *Solitude and the Sublime: Romanticism and the Aesthetics of Individuation.* New York: Routledge.

Field, Michael. 1933. *Works and Days: From the Journal of Michael Field.* Ed. T. and D. C. Sturge Moore. London: John Murray.

———. 1893. *Underneath the Bough: A Book of Verses.* London: Bell.

———. 1889. *Long Ago.* London: Bell.

Fineman, Joel. 1986. *Shakespeare's Perjured Eye: The Invention of Poetic Subjectivity in the Sonnets.* Berkeley: University of California Press.

Fletcher, Pauline. 1986. "The Sublime Recovered." In *Pre-Raphaelite Poets: Modern Critical Views,* ed. Harold Bloom. New York: Chelsea House, 185–203.

Fornaro, Sotera. 1991. "Immagini di Sappho." In *Rose di Pieria,* ed. Francesco de Martino. Bari: Levante, 137–61.

Forster, Margaret. 1984. *Significant Sisters: The Grassroots of Active Feminism.* New York: Oxford University Press.

Foss, Chris. 1996. "'Birds of a Feather': On Swinburne's Nightingale and Shelley's Skylark." *The Victorian Newsletter* 89:17–23.

Freeman, Barbara. 1995. *The Feminine Sublime: Gender and Excess in Women's Fiction.* Berkeley: University of California Press.

Freud, Sigmund. [1914] 1958. "Remembering, Repetition and Working Through." In *The Standard Edition of the Complete Psychological Works of Sigmund Freud,* ed. James Strachey. London: The Hogarth Press and the Institute of Psychoanalysis, vol. 12: 145–56.

Frothingham, Ellen. 1876. *Sappho: A Tragedy in Five Acts: A Translation from the German Play by Franz Grillparzer.* Boston: Roberts Brothers.

Fry, Paul. 1983. "Longinus at Colonus: The Grounding of Sublimity." *The Reach of Criticism: Method and Perception in Literary Theory.* New Haven: Yale University Press, 47–86.

———. 1980. *The Poet's Calling in the English Ode.* New Haven: Yale University Press.

Fuss, Diana. 1989. *Essentially Speaking: Feminism, Nature, and Difference.* New York: Routledge.

Fyfe, W. Hamilton, and W. Rhys Roberts, trs. and eds. 1991. *Artistotle, Longinus, Demetrius.* Cambridge: Harvard University Press.

Gallagher, Catherine. 1994. *Nobody's Story: The Vanishing Acts of Women Writers in the Marketplace 1670–1820.* Oxford: Oxford University Press.

Gans, Eric. 1981. "Naissance du moi lyrique: Du Féminin au masculin." *Poétique* 46: 129–39.

Gentili, Bruno. 1988. *Poetry and Its Public in Ancient Greece: From Homer to the Fifth Century.* Tr. A. Thomas Cole. Baltimore: Johns Hopkins University Press.

Gibson, Ian. 1978. *The English Vice.* London: Duckworth.

Gilbert, Sandra, and Gubar, Susan. 1979. *Shakespeare's Sisters: Feminist Essays on Women Poets.* Bloomington: Indiana University Press.

Goldhill, Simon. 1991. *The Poet's Voice: Essays on Poetics and Greek Literature.* Cambridge: Cambridge University Press.

Gosse, Edmund. 1893. "Christina Rossetti." *The Century Magazine* 24: 211–17.

———. [1912] 1917. *The Life of Swinburne.* London: Macmillan.

———. 1919. "The First Draft of Swinburne's 'Anactoria.'" *Modern Language Review* 14: 271–77.

Grafton, Anthony. 1983. "Polyhistor into Philolog: Notes on the Transformation of German Classical Scholarship, 1780–1850." *History of Universities* 3:159–92.

Grahn, Judy. 1985. *The Highest Apple: Sappho and the Lesbian Poetic Tradition.* San Francisco: Spinsters, Ink.

Gray, J. M. 1889. Review of *Long Ago* by Michael Field. *The Academy* No. 892 (June 8): 388–89.

Greenberg, Robert A. 1991. "'Erotion,' 'Anactoria,' and the Sapphic Passion." *Victorian Poetry* 29.1: 79–87.

———. 1976. "Swinburne and the Redefinition of Classical Myth." *Victorian Poetry* 14.3: 175–95.

Greene, Ellen, ed. 1997a. *Reading Sappho: Contemporary Approaches.* Berkeley: University of California Press.

———. 1997b. *Re-Reading Sappho: Reception and Transmission.* Berkeley: University of California Press.

———. 1994. "Apostrophe and Women's Erotics in the Poetry of Sappho." *Transactions of the American Philological Association* 124: 41–56.

Greer, Germaine. 1995. *Slip-Shod Sibyls: Recognition, Rejection and the Woman Poet.* London: Viking.

———. 1982. "The Tulsa Center for the Study of Women's Literature: What We Are Doing and Why We Are Doing It." *Tulsa Studies in Women's Literature* 1.1: 5–26.

Gregory, Eileen. 1997. *H. D. and Hellenism: Classic Lines.* New York: Cambridge University Press.

Grenfell, B. P., and A. S. Hunt, eds. 1914. *The Oxyrhynchus Papyri,* Part X. London: Egypt Exploration Fund.

Griswold, Rufus Wilmot. 1848. *The Female Poets of America.* Philadelphia: Moss.

Gubar, Susan. 1984. "Sapphistries." *Signs* 10: 43–62.

Guerlac, Suzanne. 1985. "Longinus and the Subject of the Sublime." *New Literary History* 16.2: 275–89.

———. 1990. *The Impersonal Sublime: Hugo, Baudelaire, Lautréamont.* Stanford: Stanford University Press.

Guest, Edwin. 1838. *History of English Rhythms.* London: William Pickering.

H.D. (Hilda Doolittle). 1979. *End to Torment.* New York: New Directions.

Haefner, Joel, and Carol Shiner Wilson, eds. 1994. *Re-Visioning Romanticism: British Women Writers, 1776–1873.* Philadelphia: University of Pennsylvania Press.

Hall, John. 1652. *"Peri Hypsous" or Dionysius Longinus "Of the Height of Eloquence" Rendered Out of the Original.* London.

Hallett, Judith P. 1979. "Sappho and Her Social Context: Sense and Sensuality." *Signs* 4: 447–64.

Halporn, James W., Martin Ostwald, and Thomas G. Rosenmeyer. 1980. *The Meters of Greek and Latin Poetry.* Norman: University of Oklahoma Press.

Hardy, Thomas. 1930. *The Collected Poems of Thomas Hardy.* 4th ed. London: Macmillan.

Harrison, Antony H. 1982. "Swinburne's Losses: The Poetics of Passion." *English Literary History* 49: 689–706.

Heitsch, Ernst. 1962. "Sappho 2, 8, und 31, 9L-P." *Rheinisches Museum* 105: 284–85.

Hemans, Felicia. 1839. *Poetical Works, with a Memoir of Her Life, by Her Sister, C. Harriet Hughes.* 7 vols. Edinburgh: William Blackwood.

Hertz, Neil. 1990. "More Lurid Figures." *Diacritics* 20.3: 2–49.

———. 1989. "Lurid Figures." In *Reading de Man Reading,* ed. Lindsay Waters and Wlad Godzich. Minneapolis: University of Minnesota Press, 82–105.

———. 1985. *The End of the Line: Essays on Psychoanalysis and the Sublime.* New York: Columbia University Press.

Hewitt, Mary E. 1854. *Poems: Sacred, Passionate, and Legendary.* New York: Lamport, Blakeman and Law.

———. 1845. "Translation of an Ode of Sappho." *The Broadway Journal* 1.24 (June 14): 379.

Higonnet, Margaret, ed. 1996. *British Women Poets of the 19th Century.* New York: Meridian.

Hollander, John. 1985. *Vision and Resonance: Two Senses of Poetic Form.* 2nd ed. New Haven: Yale University Press.

Homans, Margaret. 1998. *Royal Representations: Queen Victoria and British Culture, 1837–1876.* Chicago: University of Chicago Press.

Homans, Margaret, and Adrienne Munich, eds. 1997. *Remaking Queen Victoria.* Cambridge: Cambridge University Press.

Hosek, Chaviva, and Patricia Parker. 1985. *Lyric Poetry: Beyond New Criticism.* Ithaca: Cornell University Press.

Housman, A. E. 1969. "Swinburne." *The Cornhill Magazine* 1061 (Autumn): 380–400.

Howitt, William. [1840] 1997. "L. E. L." Rpt. in McGann and Riess 1997, 346–51.

Huddleston, Joan, ed. 1982. *Caroline Norton's Defense: English Laws for Women in the Nineteenth Century.* Chicago: Academy Chicago.

Hume, Mary Catherine. 1862. "Sappho: A Poem." London: F. Pitman.

Hyder, Clyde Kenneth. 1972. *Swinburne as Critic.* London: Routledge.

———, ed. 1970. *Swinburne: The Critical Heritage.* New York: Barnes and Noble.

————, ed. 1966. *Swinburne Replies: Notes on Poems and Reviews, Under the Microcope, Dedicatory Epistle*. Syracuse: Syracuse University Press.

————. 1933. *Swinburne's Literary Career and Fame*. Durham: University of North Carolina Press.

Irigaray, Luce. 1985. *This Sex Which Is Not One*. Tr. Catherine Porter. Ithaca: Cornell University Press.

Jacobs, Carol. 1975. "The Monstrosity of Translation." *Modern Language Notes* 90: 755–66.

Jacobson, Howard. 1974. *Ovid's Heroides*. Princeton: Princeton University Press.

Jackson, Virginia. (forthcoming). *Dickinson's Misery*. Stanford: Stanford University Press.

————. 1997. "'Faith in Anatomy': Reading Emily Dickinson." In Prins and Shreiber 1997, 85–108.

————. 1996. "Dickinson's Figure of Address." In *Dickinson and Audience*, ed. Martin Orzeck and Robert Weisbuch. Ann Arbor: University of Michigan Press, 77–103.

Jay, Peter, and Caroline Lewis. 1996. *Sappho through English Poetry*. London: Anvil Press Poetry.

Jenkyns, Richard. 1982. "The Poetry of Sappho and Its Reputation." In *Three Classical Poets: Sappho, Catullus, and Juvenal*. London: Duckworth, 1–84.

————. 1980. *The Victorians and Ancient Greece*. Cambridge: Harvard University Press.

Johnson, Barbara. 1994. *The Wake of Deconstruction*. Oxford: Blackwell.

————. 1987. *A World of Difference*. Baltimore: The Johns Hopkins University Press.

Johnson, W. R. 1982. *The Idea of Lyric: Lyric Modes in Ancient and Modern Poetry*. Berkeley: University of California Press.

Johnston, William R. 1982. *The Nineteenth Century Paintings in the Walters Art Gallery*. Baltimore: Walters Art Gallery.

Kamuf, Peggy. 1988. *Signature Pieces: On the Institution of Authorship*. Ithaca: Cornell University Press.

————. 1980. "Writing Like a Woman." In *Women and Language in Literature and Society*, ed. S. McConnell-Ginet et al. New York: Praeger, 284–99.

Kenner, Hugh. 1971. *The Pound Era*. Berkeley: University of California Press.

Knapp, Steven. 1985. *Personification and the Sublime: Milton to Coleridge*. Cambridge: Harvard University Press.

Koestenbaum, Wayne. 1989. *Double Talk: The Erotics of Male Literary Collaboration*. London: Routledge.

Koniaris, George L. 1968. "On Sappho Fr. 31 (L.-P.)." *Philologus* 112: 173–86.

Laird, Holly. 1995. "Contradictory Legacies: Michael Field and Feminist Restoration." *Victorian Poetry* 33.1: 111–28.

Lamb, Jonathan. 1993. "Longinus, the Dialectic, and the Practice of Mastery." *English Literary History* 60: 545–67.

Landon, Letitia Elizabeth. (L.E.L.). [1873] 1990. *Poetical Works of Letitia Elizabeth Landon, "L. E. L."*, ed. F. J. Sypher. Rpt. New York: Scholars' Facsimiles.

————. 1824. *The Improvisatrice; and Other Poems*. London: Hurst, Robinson.

————. 1822. "Sappho." *The Literary Gazette*, 4 May: 282.

Lang, Cecil Y. 1968. *The Pre-Raphaelites and Their Circle*. Chicago: University of Chicago Press.

Lardinois, Andre. 1997. "Who Sang Sappho's Songs?" In Greene 1997a: 150–72.

————. 1994. "Subject and Circumstance in Sappho's Poetry." *Transactions of the American Philological Assocation* 124: 57–84.

————. 1991. "Lesbian Sappho and Sappho of Lesbos." In *From Sappho to de Sade: Moments in the History of Sexuality,* ed. J. N. Bremmer. New York: Routledge, 15–35.

Leighton, Angela, ed. 1996. *Victorian Women Poets: A Critical Reader.* Oxford: Blackwell.

————. 1992. *Victorian Women Poets: Writing against the Heart.* Charlottesville: University of Virginia Press.

Leighton, Angela, and Margaret Reynolds, eds. 1995. *Victorian Women Poets: An Anthology.* Oxford: Blackwell.

Leith, Mrs. Disney (Mary Gordon). 1917. *The Boyhood of Algernon Charles Swinburne: Personal Recollections by His Cousin Mrs. Disney Leith with Extracts from Some of his Private Letters.* London: Chatto and Windus.

Levinson, Marjorie. 1986. *The Romantic Fragment Poem.* Chapel Hill: University of North Carolina Press.

Lewis, Estelle Anna (Stella). [1875]. 1881. *Sappho: A Tragedy in Five Acts.* Rpt., London: Trubner.

Lewis, Philip E. 1985. "The Measure of Translation Effects." In *Difference in Translation,* ed. Joseph Graham. Ithaca: Cornell University Press, 31–62.

Lidov, Joel B. 1993. "The Second Stanza of Sappho 31: Another Look." *American Journal of Philology* 114: 503–35.

Lipking, Lawrence. 1988. *Abandoned Women and Poetic Tradition.* Chicago: Chicago University Press.

Lobel, Edgar, and Denys Page, eds. 1955. *Poetarum Lesbiorum Fragmenta.* Oxford: Oxford University Press.

Locard, Henri. 1979. "Works and Days: The Journals of 'Michael Field.'" *Journal of the Eighteen Nineties Society* 10: 1–9.

Lockhart, John G. 1840. "Modern English Poetesses." *Quarterly Review* 66 (June): 374–418.

Loeffelholz, Mary. 1997. "Who Killed Lucretia Davidson? or, Poetry in the Domestic-Tutelary Complex." *The Yale Journal of Criticism* 10.2 (Spring): 271–93.

————. 1996. "One of the Boys?" *The Women's Review of Books* 13.7 (April): 15–16.

————. 1991. *Dickinson and the Boundaries of Feminist Theory.* Urbana: University of Illinois Press.

Lootens, Tricia. 1996. *Lost Saints: Silence, Gender, and Victorian Literary Canonization.* Charlottesville: University Press of Virginia.

Lowell, Amy. 1955. *The Complete Poetical Works.* Boston: Houghton Mifflin.

Maginn, William. [1840] 1997. "Preface to Our Second Decade." In McGann and Riess 1997, 431–45.

May, Caroline. [1848] 1853. *The American Female Poets.* Rpt., Philadelphia: Lindsay & Blakiston.

McEvilley, Thomas. 1978. "Sappho, Fragment 31: The Face behind the Mask." *Phoenix* 32: 1–18.

McGann, Jerome. 1996. *The Poetics of Sensibility: A Revolution in Literary Style.* Oxford: Oxford University Press.

————. 1972. *Swinburne: An Experiment in Criticism*. Chicago: University of Chicago Press.

McGann, Jerome, and Daniel Riess, eds. 1997. *Letitia Elizabeth Landon: Selected Writings*. Peterborough, Ontario: Broadview Press.

Meese, Elizabeth. 1990. "Theorizing Lesbian: Writing—A Love Letter." In *Lesbian Texts and Contexts: Radical Revisions*, ed. Karla Jay and Joanne Glasgow. New York: New York University Press, 70–87.

Mellor, Anne K., ed. 1988. *Romanticism and Feminism*. Bloomington: Indiana University Press.

————. 1993. *Romanticism and Gender*. New York: Routledge.

Mermin, Dorothy. 1993. *Godiva's Ride: Women of Letters in England, 1830–1880*. Bloomington: Indiana University Press.

Middleton, Edda. 1858. *Sappho: A Tragedy in Five Acts, After the German of Franz Grillparzer*. New York: D. Appleton.

Miles, Alfred H., ed. 1898. *The Poets and Poetry of the Century*. Vol. VI. London: Hutchinson.

Mill, John Stuart. 1976. *Essays on Poetry*. Ed. F. Parvin Sharpless. Columbia: University of South Carolina Press.

Miller, Marion Mills, tr., and David More Robinson, ed. 1925. *The Songs of Sappho: Including the Recent Egyptian Discoveries*. New York: Frank-Maurice.

Miller, Paul Allen. 1994. *Lyric Text and Lyric Consciousness*. New York: Routledge.

Mills-Courts, Karen. 1990. *Poetry as Epitaph: Representation and Poetic Language*. Baton Rouge: Louisiana State University Press.

Moers, Ellen. 1976. *Literary Women*. New York: Doubleday.

Moore, Lisa. 1992. "'Something More Tender Still Than Friendship': Romantic Friendship in Early-Nineteenth-Century England." *Feminist Studies* 18.3: 499–520.

Morgan, Thaïs E. 1992a. "Violence, Creativity, and the Feminine: Poetics and Gender Politics in Swinburne and Hopkins." In *Gender and Discourse in Victorian Literature and Art*, ed. Antony H. Harrison and Beverly Taylor. DeKalb: Northern Illinois University Press, 84–107.

————. 1992b. "Male Lesbian Bodies: The Construction of Alternative Masculinities in Courbet, Baudelaire, and Swinburne." *Genders* 15: 37–57.

————. 1988. "Mixed Metaphor, Mixed Gender: Swinburne and the Victorian Critics." *Victorian Newsletter* 73: 16–19.

————. 1984. "Swinburne's Dramatic Monologues: Sex and Ideology." *Victorian Poetry* 22.2: 175–95.

Moriarty, David J. 1986. "'Michael Field' (Edith Cooper and Katherine Bradley) and Their Male Critics." In *Nineteenth-Century Women Writers of the English-Speaking World*. New York: Greenwood Press, 121–42.

Most, Glenn. 1982. "Greek Lyric Poets." In *Ancient Writers: Greece and Rome*, ed. T. J. Luce. New York: Charles Scribner, 76–84.

Munich, Adrienne. 1996. *Queen Victoria's Secrets*. New York: Columbia University Press.

Murfin, Ross C. 1978. *Swinburne, Hardy, Lawrence, and the Burden of Belief*. Chicago: University of Chicago Press.

Nagy, Gregory. 1996. *Poetry as Performance: Homer and Beyond*. Cambridge: Cambridge University Press.

————. 1992. "Homeric Questions." *Transactions of the American Philological Association.* 122: 17–60.

————. 1974. *Comparative Studies in Greek and Indic Meter.* Cambridge: Harvard University Press.

Norsa, Medea. 1937. "Versi di Saffo in un Ostrakon del IIa.C." *Annali della Scuola Normale Superiore di Pisa* 2.6: 8–15.

Norton, Caroline. 1978. *Selected Writings: Facsimile Reproductions with an Introduction and Notes.* Ed. James O. Hoge and Jane Marcus. New York: Scholars' Facsimiles.

————. 1855. *A Letter to the Queen on Lord Chancellor Cranworth's Marriage and Divorce Bill.* London: Longman.

————. 1854. *English Laws for Women in the Nineteenth Century.* London.

————. 1840. *The Dream, and Other Poems.* London: Henry Colburn.

————. 1839. *A Plain Letter to the Lord Chancellor on the Infant Custody Bill.* London: James Ridgway.

————. 1830. *The Undying One and Other Poems.* London: Henry Colburn and Richard Bentley.

Oakes Smith, Elizabeth. [1851] 1974. *Woman and Her Needs.* New York: Fowlers and Wells. In *Liberating the Home,* ed. Leon Stein and Annette K. Baxter. New York: Arno Press, 1–120.

————. 1858. "Sappho." *Emerson's Magazine and Putnam's Monthly* 7.41 (August): 141–45.

————. 1846. *The Poetical Writings of Elizabeth Oakes Smith.* New York: J. S. Redfield, Clinton Hall.

O'Brien, William. 1843. *The Ancient Rhythmical Art Recovered.* Dublin.

O'Higgins, Dolores. 1990. "Sappho's Splintered Tongue: Silence in Sappho 31 and Catullus 51." *American Journal of Philology* 111: 156–67.

Omond, T. S. 1968. *English Metrists.* New York: Phaeton Press.

Ovidius, P. Naso. 1990. *Heroides.* Tr. Harold Isbell. New York: Penguin Classics.

————. 1908. *Heroides.* Ed. Arthur Palmer. Oxford: Clarendon Press.

Page, Denys. 1955. *Sappho and Alcaeus: An Introduction to the Study of Ancient Lesbian Poetry.* Oxford: Oxford University Press.

Paglia, Camille A. 1990. *Sexual Personae: Art and Decadence from Nefertiti to Emily Dickinson.* New Haven: Yale University Press.

Parker, Holt. 1993. "Sappho Schoolmistress." *Transactions of the American Philological Association* 123: 309–51.

Parry, Milman. 1971. "The Traces of the Digamma in Ionic and Lesbian Greek." In *The Making of Homeric Verse.* Oxford: Oxford University Press, 391–403.

Pascoe, Judith. 1995. "Mary Robinson and the Literary Marketplace." In Feldman and Kelley 1995: 252–68.

Patmore, Coventry. 1857. *Essay on English Metrical Law.* Ed. Sister Mary Roth. Washington, D.C.: The Catholic University of America Press.

Patrick, Mary Mills. 1912. *Sappho and the Island of Lesbos.* Boston: Houghton Mifflin.

Perkins, Jane Gray. 1910. *The Life of Mrs. Norton.* London: John Murray.

Peterson, Linda. 1994a. "Becoming an Author: Mary Robinson's *Memoirs* and the

Origins of the Woman Artist's Autobiography." In Haefner and Wilson 1994: 36–50.

———. 1994b. "Sappho and the Making of Tennysonian Lyric." *English Literary History:* 121–37.

Philips, Ambrose. 1715. *The Works of Anacreon and Sappho: Done from the Greek, by Several Hands.* London, 61–75.

Pinch, Adela. 1999. "Learning What Hurts: 'The Schoolmistress,' the Rod and the Poem." In *The Lessons of Romanticism,* ed. Thomas Pfau and Robert Gleckner. Durham: Duke University Press.

———. 1996. *Strange Fits of Passion: Epistemologies of Emotion from Hume to Austen.* Stanford: Stanford University Press.

Poe, Edgar Allan. 1965. *The Complete Works.* Ed. James A. Harrison. New York: AMS Press.

———. 1845. "The Premature Burial." *The Broadway Journal* 1.24 (June 14): 369–73.

———. 1841. Review of *The Dream and Other Poems* by the Hon. Mrs. Norton. *Graham's Magazine* 18.2 (February): 93–95.

Poovey, Mary. 1988. *Uneven Developments: The Ideological Work of Gender in Mid-Victorian England.* Chicago: University of Chicago Press.

Powell, Jim. 1993. *Sappho: A Garland.* New York: Farrar, Straus, Giroux.

Prins, Yopie. 1998. "Personifying the Poetess: Caroline Norton, 'The Picture of Sappho.'" In Armstrong and Blain 1998: 50–67.

———. 1997. "Sappho's Afterlife in Translation." In Greene 1997b, 35–67.

———. 1995a. "Sappho Doubled: Michael Field." *The Yale Journal of Criticism* 8.1 (Spring 1995):165–86.

———. 1995b. "A Metaphorical Field: Katherine Bradley and Edith Cooper." *Victorian Poetry 33.1* (Spring 1995):129–48.

Prins, Yopie, and Maeera Shreiber, eds. 1997. *Dwelling in Possibility: Women Poets and Critics on Poetry.* Ithaca: Cornell University Press.

Privitera, G. A. 1969. "Ambiguità antitesi analogia nel fr. 31 L.P. di Saffo." *Quaderni Urbinati di Cultura Classica* 8: 37–80.

Psomiades, Kathy Alexis. 1997. *Beauty's Body.* Stanford: Stanford University Press.

Raymond, Meredith. 1971. *Swinburne's Poetics: Theory and Practice.* The Hague: Mouton.

Rayor, Diane, tr. 1991. *Sappho's Lyre: Archaic Lyric and Woman Poets of Ancient Greece.* Berkeley: University of California Press.

Reynolds, Margaret. 1996. "'I Lived for Art, I Lived for Love' : The Woman Poet Sings Sappho's Last Song." In Leighton 1996: 277–306.

Richards, Eliza. (forthcoming). "'The Poetess' and Poe's Performance of the Feminine." *Arizona Quarterly.*

Ridenour, George M. 1978. "Time and Eternity in Swinburne: Minute Particulars in Five Poems." *English Literary History* 45.1: 107–29.

Riede, David. 1986. "Bard and Lady Novelist: Swinburne and the Novel of (Mrs.) Manners." *The Victorian Newsletter* 69: 4–7.

———. 1978. *Swinburne: A Study of Romantic Mythmaking.* Charlottesville: University Press of Virginia.

Riley, Denise. 1988. *"Am I That Name?" Feminism and the Category of 'Women' in History*. Minneapolis: University of Minnesota.

Robbins, Emmett. 1980. "'Whenever I Look at You . . .': Sappho Fragment Thirty-One." *Transactions of the American Philological Association* 110: 255–61.

Robertson, Eric. 1883. *English Poetesses: A Series of Critical Biographies, with Illustrative Extracts*. London: Cassell.

Robinson, David M. [1923] 1963. *Sappho and Her Influence*. Rpt., New York: Cooper Square Publishers.

Robinson, Mary. [Pseud. Anne Frances Randall]. 1799. *Thoughts on the Condition of Woman, and on the Injustice of Mental Subordination*. London: Longman.

———. 1796. *Sappho and Phaon: In a Series of Legitimate Sonnets, With Thoughts on Poetical Subjects and Anecdotes of the Grecian Poetess*. London: S. Gosnell.

Roche, Paul. Tr. 1991. *The Love Songs of Sappho*. New York: Signet Classic.

Rooksby, Rikky. 1995. "Swinburne's Internal Centre: Reply to an Article." *The Victorian Newsletter* 87: 25–29.

Rooksby, Rikky, and Nicholas Shrimpton, eds. 1993. *The Whole Music of Passion: New Essays on Swinburne*. Hants, England: Scolar Press.

Ross, Marlon. 1989. *The Contours of Masculine Desire: Romanticism and the Rise of Women's Poetry*. Oxford: Oxford University Press.

Rossetti, Christina. 1990. *The Complete Poems of Christina Rossetti: A Variorum Edition*. Vol. 3. Ed. R. W. Crump. Baton Rouge: Louisiana State University Press.

———. 1847. *Verses: Dedicated to Her Mother*. London: G. Polidori.

Rossetti, Dante Gabriel. 1887. "Marochetti (1850)." In *The Collected Works of Dante Gabriel Rossetti*, ed. William M. Rossetti. Boston: Roberts Brothers, vol. 2: 499.

Rowlinson, Matthew. 1994. *Tennyson's Fixations: Psychoanalysis and the Topics of the Early Poetry*. Charlottesville: University Press of Virginia.

Rowton, Frederic. [1848] 1853. *The Female Poets of Great Britain*. Rpt., Philadelphia: Henry C. Baird.

Rudiger, H. 1933. *Sappho, Ihr Ruf und Ruhm bei der Nachwelt*. Leipzig: Dieterich, 1933.

Saake, Helmut. 1972. *Sapphostudien: Forschungsgeschichte, biografische und literärische Untersuchungen*. Munich: Schoningh.

Sacks, Peter M. 1985. *The English Elegy: Studies in the Genre from Spenser to Yeats*. Baltimore: The Johns Hopkins University Press.

Saintsbury, George. 1910. *A History of English Prosody*. Vol. III, *From Blake to Mr. Swinburne*. London: Macmillan.

Samuels, Shirley, ed. 1992. *The Culture of Sentiment: Race, Gender, and Sentimentality in Nineteenth-Century America*. New York: Oxford University Press.

Sedgwick, Eve Kosofksy. 1993. *Tendencies*. Durham: Duke University Press.

Segal, Charles. 1974. "Eros and Incantation: Sappho and Oral Poetry." *Arethusa* 7.2: 139–60.

Sieburth, Richard. 1984. "Poetry and Obscenity: Baudelaire and Swinburne." *Comparative Literature* 36.4 (Fall): 343–53.

Skinner, Marilyn. 1993. "Woman and Language in Archaic Greece, or, Why Is Sappho a Woman?" In *Feminist Theory and the Classics*, ed. Nancy Sorkin Rabinowitz and Amy Richlin. New York: Routledge, 125–44.

Smith, William. 1739. *Dionysius Longinus on the Sublime, Translated from the Greek, with Notes and Observations and Some Account of the Life, Writings, and Character of the Author.* London: J. Watts.

Smith, William. 1840. *Dictionary of Greek and Roman Biography and Mythology.* 3 vols. London: John Murray.

Snell, Bruno. 1953. *The Discovery of the Mind: The Greek Origins of European Thought.* Tr. T. G. Rosenmeyer. Cambridge: Harvard University Press.

———. 1931. "Sappho's Gedicht φαίνεταί μοι κεῖνος." *Hermes* 66: 71–90.

Snyder, Jane McIntosh. 1997. *Lesbian Desire in the Lyrics of Sappho.* New York: Columbia University Press.

———. 1991. "Public Occasion and Private Passion in the Lyrics of Sappho of Lesbos." In *Women's History and Ancient History,* ed. Sarah B. Pomeroy. Chapel Hill: University of North Carolina Press, 1–19.

———. 1989. *The Woman and the Lyre: Women Writers in Classical Greece and Rome.* Carbondale: Southern Illinois University Press.

Sprawson, Charles. 1993. *Haunts of the Black Masseur: The Swimmer as Hero.* New York: Pantheon.

Stanton, Domna, ed. 1984. *The Female Autograph.* New York: New York Literary Forum.

Stehle, Eva. 1997. *Performance and Gender in Ancient Greece: Nondramatic Poetry in Its Setting.* Princeton: Princeton University Press.

Stephenson, Glennis. 1995. *Letitia Landon: The Woman behind L.E.L.* Manchester: Manchester University Press.

———. 1992. "Letitia Landon and the Victorian Improvisatrice: The Construction of L.E.L." *Victorian Poetry* 30.1: 1–17.

Stewart, Susan. 1995. "Lyric Possession." *Critical Inquiry* 22.1: 34–63.

Stobie, Margaret R. 1949. "Patmore's Theory and Hopkins' Practice." *University of Toronto Quarterly* 19: 64–80.

Stodart, Mary. 1842. *Female Writers: Thoughts on Their Proper Sphere and on Their Powers of Usefulness.* London: Seeley and Burnside.

Stone, William Johnson. 1899. *On the Use of Classical Metres in English.* Oxford.

Sturge Moore, T., and D. C. Sturge Moore, eds. 1933. *Works and Days: From the Journal of Michael Field.* London: John Murray.

Sturgeon, Mary. 1922. *Michael Field.* New York: Macmillan.

Svenbro, Jesper. 1993. *Phrasikleia: An Anthropology of Reading in Ancient Greece.* Tr. Janet Lloyd. Ithaca: Cornell University Press.

Swinburne, Algernon Charles. 1966. *Swinburne Replies,* ed. Clyde K. Hyder. Syracuse: Syracuse University Press.

———. 1959. *The Swinburne Letters,* ed. Cecil Lang. 6 vols. New Haven: Yale University Press.

———. 1952. *Lesbia Brandon.* Ed. Randolph Hughes. London: The Falcon Press.

———. 1925. *The Complete Works of Algernon Charles Swinburne.* Ed. Sir Edmund Gosse and Thomas James Wise. Bonchurch Edition, 20 vols. London: Heinemann.

Symonds, John Addington. 1873. *Studies of the Greek Poets.* Vol. 1. London: Smith, Elder.

Symons, Arthur. 1916. *Figures of Several Centuries.* London: Constable.

Sypher, F. J. 1990. *Poetical Works of Letitia Elizabeth Landon, "L.E.L.": A Facsimile Re-*

production of the 1873 Edition. Delmar, New York: Scholars' Facsimiles and Reprints.

Tarrant, R. J. 1981. "The Authenticity of the Letter of Sappho to Phaon (*Heroides XV*)." *Harvard Studies in Classical Philology* 85: 133–53.

Taylor, Dennis. 1988. *Hardy's Metres and Victorian Prosody.* Oxford: Oxford University Press.

Thomas, Edward. 1912. *Algernon Charles Swinburne: A Critical Study.* London: Martin Secker.

Thompson, John. 1961. *The Founding of English Metre.* New York: Columbia University Press.

Tomory, Peter. 1989. "The Fortunes of Sappho: 1770–1850." In *Rediscovering Hellenism: The Hellenic Inheritance and the English Imagination,* ed. G. W. Clarke. Cambridge: Cambridge University Press, 121–35.

Tucker, Herbert. 1995. "Review Essay: *Victorian Poetry: Poetry, Poetics, and Politics* by Isobel Armstrong." *Victorian Poetry* 33.1 (Spring 1995): 174–87.

Turner, Frank M. 1981. *The Greek Heritage in Victorian Britain.* New Haven: Yale University Press.

Turyn, A. 1942. "The Sapphic Ostrakon," *Transactions of the American Philological Association* 73: 308–18.

Vanita, Ruth. 1996. *Sappho and the Virgin Mary: Same-Sex Love and the English Literary Imagination.* New York: Columbia University Press.

Verducci, Florence. 1985. *Ovid's Toyshop of the Heart: "Epistulae Heroidum."* Princeton: Princeton University Press.

Vicinus, Martha. 1994a. "The Adolescent Boy: Fin de Siècle Femme Fatale?" *Journal of the History of Sexuality* 5.1 (July): 90–114.

———. 1994b. "Lesbian History: All Theory and No Facts or All Facts and No Theory?" *Radical History Review* 60: 57–75.

Vickers, Nancy. 1980. "Diana Described: Scattered Woman and Scattered Rhyme." In *Writing and Sexual Difference,* ed. Elizabeth Abel. Chicago: University of Chicago Press, 95–109.

Vincent, John. 1997. "Flogging Is Fundamental: Applications of Birch in Swinburn's *Lesbia Brandon.*" In *Novel Gazing: Queer Readings in Fiction,* ed. Eve Kosofsky Sedgwick, Durham: Duke University Press, 269–95.

Wagner-Lawlor, Jennifer. 1996. "Metaphorical 'Indiscretion' and Literary Survival in Swinburne's 'Anactoria.'" *Studies in English Literature* 36: 917–34.

Walker, Cheryl. 1982. *The Nightingale's Burden: Women Poets and American Culture Before 1900.* Bloomington: Indiana University Press.

Warren, Rosanna. 1989. "Sappho: Translation as Elegy." In *The Art of Translation: Voices from the Field,* ed. R. Warren. Boston: Northeastern University Press, 199–216.

Watts, Emily Stipes. 1977. *The Poetry of American Women from 1632 to 1945.* Austin: University of Texas Press.

Watts, Marjorie. 1987. *Mrs. Sappho: The Life of C. A. Dawson Scott, Mother of International P. E. N.* London: Duckworth.

Welcker, Friedrich Gottlieb. 1816. *Sappho von Einem Herrschenden Vorurtheil Befreyt.* Göttingen: Vandenhoek and Ruprecht.

West, M. L. 1970. "Burning Sappho." *Maia* 22: 307–30.

Wharton, Henry Thornton. [1898] 1974. *Sappho. Memoir, Text, Selected Renderings, and a Literal Translation.* 4th ed. Rpt., Amsterdam: Liberac.

White, Chris. 1996. "The Tiresian Poet: Michael Field." In Leighton 1996, 148–61.

———. 1992. "'Poets and Lovers Evermore' : The Poetry and Journals of Michael Field." In *Sexual Sameness: Textual Differences in Lesbian and Gay Writing,* ed. Joseph Bristow. London: Routledge, 26–43.

Whitford, Margaret. 1989. "Rereading Irigaray." In *Between Feminism and Psychoanalysis,* ed. Teresa Brennan. New York: Routledge, 106–26.

Wilde, Oscar. [1889] 1968. "Mr. Swinburne's Last Volume." Rpt. in *The Artist as Critic: Critical Writings of Oscar Wilde,* ed. Richard Ellman. New York: Random House, 146–49.

Will, Fredric. 1966. "Sappho and Poetic Motion." *Classical Journal* 61: 259–62.

Williamson, Margaret. 1995. *Sappho's Immortal Daughters.* Cambridge: Harvard University Press.

Wills, Gary. 1967. "Sappho 31 and Catullus 51." *Greek, Roman and Byzantine Studies* 8:167-97.

Wilson, Lyn Hatherly. 1996. *Sappho's Sweetbitter Songs: Configurations of Female and Male in Ancient Greek Lyric.* New York: Routledge.

Winkler, John. 1990. *The Constraints of Desire: The Anthropology of Sex and Gender in Ancient Greece.* New York: Columbia University Press.

Woods, Susanne. 1984. *Natural Emphasis: English Versification from Chaucer to Dryden.* San Marino: The Huntington Library.

Wyman, Mary Alice, ed. 1924. *Selections from the Autobiography of Elizabeth Oakes Smith.* New York: Columbia University Press.

Zeiger, Melissa. 1986. "'A Muse Funereal': The Critique of Elegy in Swinburne's 'Ave atque Vale.'" *Victorian Poetry* 24.2: 173–88.

Zonana, Joyce. 1990. "Swinburne's Sappho: The Muse as Sister-Goddess." *Victorian Poetry* 28: 39–50.

Zuntz, Guenther. 1951. "On the Etymology of the Name Sappho." *Museum Helveticum* 8: 12–35.

INDEX OF SAPPHIC FRAGMENTS

AND TESTIMONIA

GENERAL INDEX

Addison, Joseph, 44, 46, 52

Aeolians, 61, 62, 99

Aeschylus, 140n, 162

afterlife (*Nachleben*) of Sappho, 13, 15, 23, 28, 40, 51, 116, 178, 246–47, 251; of Queen Victoria, 15n, 187; of Swinburne, 163, 167, 172–73; in translation, 28, 40–41, 51. *See also* reception, of Sappho

Alcaeus, 56, 59

Alma-Tadema, Sir Laurence, 56; "Sappho and Alcaeus," 56n, 57 (fig. 1)

Anacreon, 5n

Anactoria, 128, 130n, 131, 141, 143, 144, 152. *See also* Swinburne, Algernon Charles, "Anactoria"

Andromeda, 9

Anonymous, "*Parody* of Sappho's Celebrated *Ode*," 153n

anthropomorphism, 19, 20. *See also* personification

Antiphanes, *Sappho*, 25. *See also* Sapphic Riddle

Aphrodite, 10, 11, 12, 85, 96, 97, 98, 99, 103, 108, 138, 139, 141, 142, 143

apostrophe, 32, 90, 106, 120, 127, 134–35, 185, 194, 204, 215–17, 233, 235, 236, 247, 250. *See also* vocative "O"; invocation

Archilochus fr. 67a, 131n

Aristaenetus, 24

Armstrong, Isobel, 7, 117, 135n, 175 and n, 203; *Nineteenth-Century Women Poets* (coauthored with J. Bristow and C. Sharrock), 175

Atthis, 85, 139

Attridge, Derek, 146 and n

Aurora Leigh, 239

Austin, Alfred, 158

authorship, Byronic model of, 213 and n; dual, 82–83, 84; female, 15, 104, 175–76, 180, 182n, 184, 202, 213, 225, 244; multiple, 74; of Norton, Caroline, 225n; of Ovid, 179 and n; of Sappho, 12, 179. *See also* collaboration

Aviram, Amitai, 128 and n

ballad, 123n

Balmer, Josephine, 6

Barham, Thomas Foster, 147, 148 and n

Barnard, Mary, *Sappho: A New Translation*, 5 and n

Barnstone, Willis, 6n, 41n

Baudelaire, 150, 168

Beerbohm, Max, 160; *Rossetti and His Circle*, 160n, 162

Benjamin, Walter, "The Task of the Translator," 40, 41 and n

Bennett, Paula, *Nineteenth Century American Women Poets: An Anthology*, 175

Benveniste, Emile, 166, 167

Bergk, Theodor, 53, 54, 59n, 64, 71, 72, 100n

Berlant, Lauren, 223 and n, 226 and n, 234

Berlant, Lauren, 223 and n, 226 and n, 234

Bethune, George, *The British Female Poets*, 175, 208, 209

biography: of C. A. Dawson Scott, 239; of Caroline Norton, 212n, 219–20; of L. E. L., 197–98; as problem in feminist criticism, 104, 189; of Sappho, 58; of Swinburne, 162–63

bisexuality, 93–94

Blain, Virginia, 79n, 175n, 209

Blanchard, Laman, 197–201; *The Life and Literary Remains of L. E. L.*, 197–98; "On First Seeing the Portrait of L. E. L.," 198–201

body: of book, 56; disfigured or abused, 6, 17, 44, 113–17, 126, 151–54, 181; dying or dead, 29, 37, 39, 45, 46, 48, 51, 125, 185, 197; falling, 190 and n; female, 27, 40, 98, 100, 101, 106, 143, 185; giving birth, 25, 40; "male lesbian," 112–13; of language, 120, 150, 158; of poem, 37, 114, 144; rhythmicized, 17, 112–14, 120, 125, 128 and n, 137, 152, 162; of Swinburne, 121, 140, 153, 156, 158–60, 161 (fig. 9), 168–69. *See also* dismemberment; Sapphic corpus

Bourget, Paul, definition of "decadence," 68

ABOUT THE AUTHOR

Yopie Prins is Associate Professor of English and Comparative Literature at the University of Michigan.